Documents in Western Civilization

Volume I:
To 1740

PEARSON

Prentice
Hall

UPPER SADDLE RIVER, NEW JERSEY 07458

© 2004 by PEARSON EDUCATION, INC.
Upper Saddle River, New Jersey 07458

ISBN 0-13-182860-6
Printed in the United States of America

\

CONTENTS

Contents

The Early Modern World (1500–1800)

PART 1
The Ancient Near East

1.1 New Theories about Human Development

Since the 1950s, theories about life among early humans have centered on "traditional" male and female roles, with men responsible for hunting and women for domestic duties and child rearing. In the following excerpt, Barbara Ehrenreich reviews new developments in the theories about the origins of human evolution that challenge these traditional views.

Source: Barbara Ehrenreich, "The Real Truth about the Female," *Time* (March 8, 1999, vol. 153, no. 9).

There were always plenty of prima facie reasons to doubt the Mr. and Mrs. Man-the-Hunter version of our collective biography, such as the little matter of size, or, in science-speak, "sexual dimorphism." If men and women evolved so differently, then why aren't men a whole lot bigger than they are? In fact, humans display a smaller size disparity between the sexes than do many of our ape cousins—suggesting (though not proving) that early men and women sometimes had overlapping job descriptions, like having to drive off the leopards. And speaking of Paleolithic predators, wouldn't it be at least unwise for the guys to go off hunting, leaving the supposedly weak and dependent women and children to fend for themselves at base camp? Odd too, that Paleolithic culture should look so much like the culture of Levittown circa 1955, with the gals waiting at home for the guys to come back with the bacon. In what other carnivorous species is only one sex an actual predator?

Beginning in the '70s, women began to elbow their way into the field and develop serious alternatives to the old, male-centered theory of human evolution. It shouldn't matter, of course, what sex the scientist is, but women had their own reasons for being suspicious of the dominant paradigm. The first revisionist blow came in the mid-'70s, when anthropologists Adrienne Zihlman and Nancy Tanner pointed out that among surviving "hunting" peoples, most of the community's calories—up to 70%—come from plant food patiently gathered by women, not meat heroically captured by men. The evidence for Stone Age consumption of plant foods has mounted since then. In 1994 paleobotanist Sarah Mason concluded that a variety of plant material discovered at the Paleolithic site of Dolni Vestonice in the Czech Republic was in fact edible roots and seeds. At the very least, it seems, the Paleolithic dinner was potluck, and it was probably the women who provided most of the starches, salad and raspberry-mousse desserts. The mother-of-us-all was beginning to look a little peppier and more self-reliant.

Not that even the most efficient gatherer gal doesn't need a little help now and then, especially when she's lactating. Nursing a baby may look pretty effortless, but it can burn up 500 calories a day—the equivalent of running about five miles. Where was the help coming from? Was the female completely dependent on her male significant other, as the prevailing theory has always implied? An alternative possibility lay buried in the mystery of menopause. Nature is no friend of the infertile, and in most primates, the end of childbearing coincides with the end of life, so it was always hard to see why human females get to live for years, even decades, after their ovaries go into retirement. Hence the "grandma hypothesis": maybe the evolutionary "purpose" of the postmenopausal woman was to keep her grandchildren provided with berries and tubers and nuts, especially while Mom was preoccupied with a new baby. If Grandma were still bearing and nursing her own babies, she'd be too busy to baby-sit, so natural selection may have selected for a prolonged healthy and mature, but infertile, stage of the female life cycle.

To test this possibility, anthropologist Kristen Hawkes made quite a nuisance of herself among the hunting-gathering Hadza people of Tanzania, charting the hour-by-hour activities of 90 individuals, male and female, and weighing the children at regular intervals. The results, published in late 1997 and reported by Angier in detail, established that children did better if Grandma was on the case—and, if not her, then a great-aunt or similar grandma figure. This doesn't prove the grandma hypothesis for all times and all peoples, but it does strongly suggest that in the Stone Age family, Dad-the-hunter was not the only provider. The occasional antelope haunch might be a tasty treat, but as Hawkes and her co-workers conclude about the Hadza, "it is women's foraging, not men's hunting, that differentially affects their own families' nutritional welfare." If the grandma hypothesis holds up, we may have to conclude that the male-female pair bond was not quite so central to human survival as the evolutionary psychologists assume. The British anthropologist Chris Knight—who is, incidentally, male—suggests that alliances among females may have been more important in shaping the political economy of Paleolithic peoples.

The thinking that led to man-the-hunter was largely inferential: if you bring the women along on the hunt, the children will have to come too, and all that squalling and chattering would surely scare off the game. This inference was based on a particular style of hunting, familiar from Hemingway novels and common to the New England woods in October, in which a small band of men trek off into the wild and patiently stalk their prey, a deer or two at a time. But there is another way to get the job done known as "communal hunting," in which the entire group—women, men and children—drive the animals over a cliff or into a net or cul-de-sac. The Blackfoot and other Indians hunted bison this way before they acquired the horse—hence all those "buffalo jumps" in the Canadian and American West—and net hunting is the most productive hunting method employed by the Mbuti people of the Congo today. When driving animals into a place where they can be slaughtered, noise is a positive help, whether it's the clashing of men's spears or the squeals of massed toddlers.

But there was only indirect evidence of communal hunting in Paleolithic times until archaeologist Olga Soffer came across the kind of clue that, a gender traditionalist might say, it took a womanly eye to notice. While sifting through clay fragments from the Paleolithic site of Pavlov in what is now the Czech Republic, she found a series of parallel lines impressed on some of the clay surfaces—evidence of woven fibers from about 25,000 years ago. Intrigued to find signs of weaving from this early date, Soffer and her colleagues examined 8,400 more clay fragments from the same and nearby sites, eventually coming across the traces of a likely tool of the communal hunt—a mesh net. The entire theory of man-the-hunter had been based on "durable media," Soffer explains, meaning items like the sharpened stones that can serve as spearheads, rather than softer, biodegradable goods like baskets, fabrics and nets. But in archaeologically well-preserved prehistoric sites, such as those found underwater or in dry caves, the soft goods predominate over the durable by a ratio of about 20 to 1. If the hard stuff was the work of men, then "we've been missing the children, the women, the old people," she asserts. Thanks to Soffer's sharp eye, Paleolithic net hunting is no longer invisible, and in net hunting, Soffer says, "everybody participates."

Furthermore, as Mary Zeiss Stange points out in her 1997 book *Woman the Hunter*, there's no reason to rule out women's hunting with hard-edged weapons too, perhaps even of their own making. Among the Tiwi Aborigines of Australia, hunting is considered women's work, and until the introduction of steel implements, it was done with handmade stone axes the women fashioned for themselves. By putting women's work back into the record, the new female evolutionary scientists may have helped rewrite the biography of the human race. At least we should prepare to welcome our bold and resourceful new ancestor, Xena the hunter princess.

The news of Soffer's discovery... will disconcert many feminists as well as sociobiologists. After all, the gratifying thing about man-the-hunter was that he helped locate all the violence and related mischief on the men's side of the campfire: no blood on our hands! But there are other reasons to doubt the eternal equation of masculinity with aggression and violence, femininity with gentleness and a taste for green salads. In ancient Greece and Sumer the deities of the hunt, Artemis and Ninhursag, were female—extremely female, if you will, since these were also the goddesses who presided over childbirth. Even more striking is the association of ancient goddesses with nature's original hunters, the predatory animals. In Anatolia, the predator goddess was Kybele, known as the commander of lions. In Egypt she was Sekhmet, portrayed as a lioness whose "mane smoked with fire [and whose] countenance glowed like the sun."

Images of goddesses tell us nothing about the role of actual women, but they do suggest that about 3,000 years ago, at the dawn of human civilization, the idea of the fearsome huntress, the woman predator, generated no snickers among the pious.

Questions:
1. What are the new theories being suggested?
2. Why are earlier theories being questioned?
3. What kinds of evidence are being used to support the new theories?

1.2 An Egyptian Hymn to the Nile

"Hymn to the Nile" is thought to have been composed for a festival in Thebes celebrating the annual flooding of the Nile River. Its date is unknown.

Source: Adoph Erman, The Literature of the Ancient Egyptians, trans. A.M. Blackman (London: Methuen & Co., Ltd., 1927), pp. 146-49, reprinted in John L. Beatty and Oliver A. Johnson, eds., Heritage of Western Civilization, volume 1, 7th edition (Englewood Cliffs, NJ: Prentice Hall, 1991), pp. 19-20).

Praise to thee, O Nile, that issueth from the earth, and cometh to nourish Egypt. Of hidden nature, a darkness in the daytime....

That watereth the meadows, he that R-e[1] hath created to nourish all cattle. That giveth drink to the desert places, which are far from water; it is his dew that falleth from heaven.

Beloved of K-eb,[2] director of the corn-god; that maketh to flourish every workshop of Ptah.[3]

Lord of fish, that maketh the water-fowl to go upstream....

That maketh barley and createth wheat, so that he may cause the temples to keep festivals.

If he be sluggish,[4] the nostrils are stopped up,[5] and all men are impoverished; the victuals of the gods are diminished, and millions of men perish.

If he be niggardly the whole land is in terror and great and small lament.... Khnum[6] hath fashioned him. When he riseth, the land is in exultation and every body is in joy. All jaws begin to laugh and every tooth is revealed.

He that bringeth victuals and is rich in food, that createth all that is good. The revered, sweet-smelling.... That createth herbage for the cattle, and giveth sacrifice to every god, be he in the underworld, in heaven, or upon earth.... That filleth the storehouses, and maketh wide the granaries, that giveth things to the poor.

He that maketh trees to grow according to every wish, and men have no lack thereof; the ship is built by his power, for there is no joinery with stones....

... thy young folk and thy children shout for joy over thee, and men hail thee as king. Unchanging of laws, when he cometh forth in the presence of Upper and Lower Egypt. Men drink the water....

He that was in sorrow is become glad, and every heart is joyful. Sobk,[7] the child of Neith, laugheth, and the divine Ennead, that is in thee, is glorious.

Thou that vomitest forth, giving the fields to drink and making strong the people. He that maketh the one rich and loveth the other. He maketh no distinctions, and boundaries are not made for him.

Thou light, that cometh from the darkness! Thou fat for his cattle. He is a strong one, that createth....

... one beholdeth the wealthy as him that is full of care, one beholdeth each one with his implements.... None that (otherwise) goeth clad, is clad,[8] and the children of notables are unadorned....

He that establisheth right, whom men love.... It would be but lies to compare thee with the sea, that bringeth no corn.... no bird descendeth in the desert....

Men begin to play to thee on the harp, and men sing to thee with the hand.[9] Thy young folk and thy children shout for joy over thee, and deputations to thee are appointed.

He that cometh with splendid things and adorneth the earth! That causeth the ship to prosper before men; that quickeneth the hearts in them that are with child; that would fain have there be a multitude of all kinds of cattle.

When thou art risen in the city of the sovereign, then men are satisfied with a goodly list.[10] "I would like lotus flowers," saith the little one, "and all manner of things," saith the... commander, "and all manner of herbs," say the children. Eating bringeth forgetfulness of him.[11] Good things are scattered over the dwelling....

When the Nile floodeth, offering is made to thee, cattle are slaughtered for thee, a great oblation is made for thee. Birds are fattened for thee, antelopes are hunted for thee in the desert. Good is recompensed unto thee.

Offering is also made to every other god, even as is done for the Nile, with incense, oxen, cattle, and birds (upon) the flame. The Nile hath made him his cave in Thebes, and his name shall be known no more in the underworld....

All ye men, extol the Nine Gods, and stand in awe of the might which his son, the Lord of All, hath displayed, even he that maketh green the Two River-banks. Thou art verdant, O Nile, thou art verdant. He that maketh man to live on his cattle, and his cattle on the meadow! Thou art verdant, thou art verdant: O Nile, thou art verdant.

Questions:
1. What values or elements of civilization does this document highlight?
2. Can you link these elements with what you have learned about this civilization?

---

[1] The sun-god.
[2] The earth-god.
[3] Ptah, the craftsman, who fashions everything, could effect nothing without the Nile.
[4] On the occasion of a deficient inundation.
[5] Men no longer breathe and live.
[6] The ram-headed god, who fashions all that is.
[7] Sobk has the form of a crocodile and will originally have been a water-god, who rejoices in the inundation.
[8] For hard work, clothes are taken off.
[9] It is an old custom to beat time with the hand while singing.
[10] I.e., a multitude of good things.
[11] The Nile.

1.3 The Epic of Gilgamesh

First written down around 2000 B.C.E., The Epic of Gilgamesh is one of the oldest surviving works of world literature. Based on a real historical figure, King Gilgamesh of Uruk (r. c. 2700 B.C.E.), it tells the story of Gilgamesh's travels, adventures, and search for immortality. In the process, it provides evidence of ancient ideas about death, humanity, and kingship.

> **Source:** *The Epic of Gilgamesh*, introduction and translation by N.K. Sandars (New York: Penguin Books, 1972), pp. 61–65, 67–69, 85–86, 89, 108–111, 116–17. Copyright © N.K. Sandars, 1960, 1964, 1970. Reproduced by permission of Penguin Books Ltd.

Their first adventure is to secure timber from the distant Cedar Forest, which is guarded by the ogre Humbaba, whom they must kill. Upon their return to Uruk, the fierce Ishtar, goddess of love, tries to entice Gilgamesh into marriage; however, because Gilgamesh and Enkidu spurn Ishtar, she sends down the Bull of Heaven to punish them. Gilgamesh and Enkidu kill this creature, thereby angering the powerful Enlil, king of the gods, who takes his revenge by killing Enkidu. King Gilgamesh is devastated by his friend's death and laments humanity's fate.

The second half of the epic is devoted to Gilgamesh's quest for his secret of life. He descends into the Netherworld in search of Utnapishtim, to whom the gods had granted immortality and from whom he hopes to learn the key to life. When the two meet, Utnapishtim introduces Gilgamesh to the story of the Great Flood, which had killed all life save for Utnapishtim, his family, and the animals he had placed in his great ship. At the end of the Flood tale, Utnapishtim tells Gilgamesh of a certain Plant of Life that can give immortality. Gilgamesh is able to retrieve this plant and bring it back to the living; yet his hopes are dashed when it is eaten by a snake. At the end of the poem, Gilgamesh can only lament the human fate, old age and death.

I will proclaim to the world the deeds of Gilgamesh. This was the man to whom all things were known; this was the king who knew the countries of the world. He was wise, he saw mysteries and knew secret things, he brought us a tale of the days before the flood. He went on a long journey, was weary, wornout with labour, returning he rested, he engraved on a stone the whole story.

When the gods created Gilgamesh they gave him a perfect body. Shamash the glorious sun endowed him with beauty. Adad the god of the storm endowed him with courage, the great gods made his beauty perfect, surpassing all others, terrifying like a great wild bull. Two thirds they made him god and one third man.

In Uruk he built walls, a great rampart, and the temple of blessed Eanna for the god of the firmament Anu, and for Ishtar the goddess of love. . . .

THE COMING OF ENKIDU

Gilgamesh went abroad in the world, but he met with none who could withstand his arms till he came to Uruk. But the men of Uruk muttered in their houses, "Gilgamesh sounds the tocsin for his amusement, his arrogance has no bounds by day or night. No son is left with his father, for Gilgamesh takes them all, even the children; yet the king should be a shepherd to his people. His lust leaves no virgin to her lover, neither the warrior's daughter nor the wife of the noble; yet this is the shepherd of the city, wise, comely, and resolute."

The gods heard their lament, the gods of heaven cried to the Lord of Uruk, to Anu the god of Uruk. . . . When Anu had heard their lamentation the gods cried to Aruru, the goddess of creation, "You made him, O Aruru, now create his equal; let it be as like him as his own reflection, his second self, stormy heart for stormy heart. Let them contend together and leave Uruk in quiet."

So the goddess conceived an image in her mind, and it was of the stuff of Anu of the firmament. She dipped her hands in water and pinched off clay, she let it fall in the wilderness, and noble Enkidu was created. There was a virtue in him of the god of war, of Ninurta himself. His body was rough, he had long hair like a woman's; it waved like the hair of Nisaba, the goddess of corn. His body was covered with matted hair like Samuqan's, the god of cattle. He was innocent of mankind; he knew nothing of the cultivated land.

Enkidu ate grass in the hills with the gazelle and lurked with wild beasts at the water-holes; he had joy of the water with the herds of wild game. But there was a trapper who met him one day face to face at the drinking-hole, for the wild game had entered his territory. On three days he met him face to face, and the trapper was frozen with fear. He went back to his house with the game that he had caught, and he was dumb, benumbed with terror. His face was altered like that of one who has made a long journey. . . .

So the trapper set out on his journey to Uruk and addressed himself to Gilgamesh saying, "A man unlike any other is roaming now in the pastures; he is as strong as a star from heaven and I am afraid to approach him. He helps the wild game to escape; he fills in my pits and pulls up my traps." Gilgamesh said, "Trapper, go back, take with you a harlot, a child of pleasure. At the drinking-hole she will strip, and when he sees her beckoning he will embrace her and the game of the wilderness will surely reject him."

Now the trapper returned, taking the harlot with him. After a three days' journey they came to the drinking-hole, and there they sat down; the harlot and the trapper sat facing one another and waited for the game to come. For the first day and for the second day the two sat waiting, but on the third day the herds came; they came down to drink and Enkidu was with them. The small wild creatures of the plains were glad of the water, and Enkidu with them, who ate grass with the gazelle and was born in the hills; and she saw him, the savage man, come from far-off in the hills. The trapper spoke to her: "There he is. Now, woman, make your breasts bare, have no shame, do not delay but welcome his love. Let him see you naked, let him possess your body. When he comes near uncover yourself and lie with him; teach him, the savage man, your woman's art, for when he murmurs loves to you the wild beats that shared his life in the hills will reject him."

She was not ashamed to take him, she made herself naked and welcomed his eagerness; as he lay on her murmuring love she taught him the woman's art. For six days and seven nights they lay together, for Enkidu had forgotten his home in the hills; but when he was satisfied he went back to the wild beasts. Then, when the gazelle saw him, they bolted away; when the wild creatures saw him they fled. Enkidu would have followed, but his body was bound as though with a cord, his knees gave way when he started to run, his swiftness was gone. And now the wild creatures had all fled away; Enkidu was grown weak, for wisdom was in him, and the thoughts of a man were in his heart. So he returned and sat down at the woman's feet, and listened intently to what she said, "You are wise, Enkidu, and now you have become like a god. Why do you want to run wild with the beasts in the hills? Come with me. I will take you to strong-walled Uruk, to the blessed temple of Ishtar and of Anu, of love and heaven; there Gilgamesh lives, who is very strong, and like a wild bull he lords it over men." . . .

And now she said to Enkidu, "When I look at you you have become like a god. Why do you yearn to run wild again with the beasts in the hills? Get up from the ground, the bed of a shepherd." He listened to her words with care. It was good advice that she gave. She divided her clothing in two and with the other half she clothed him and with the other herself; and holding his had she led him like a child to the sheepfolds, into the shepherds' tents. There all the shepherds crowded round to see him, they put down bread in front of him, but Enkidu could only suck the milk of wild animals. He fumbled and gaped, at a loss what to do or how he should eat the bread and drink the strong wine. Then the woman said, "Enkidu, eat bread, it is the staff of life; drink the wine, it is the custom of the land." So he ate till he was full and drank strong wine, seven goblets. He became merry, his heart exulted and his face shone. He rubbed down the matted hair of his body and anointed himself with oil. Enkidu had become a man; but when he had put on man's clothing he appeared like a bridegroom.

Now Enkidu strode in front and the woman followed behind. He entered Uruk, that great market, and all the folk thronged round him where he stood in the street in strong-walled Uruk. The people jostled; speaking of him they said, "He is the spit of Gilgamesh." "He is shorter." "He is bigger of bone." "This is the one who was reared on the milk of wild beasts. His is the greatest strength." The men rejoiced: "Now Gilgamesh has met his match. This great one, this hero whose beauty is like a god, he is a match even for Gilgamesh."

In Uruk the bridal bed was made, fit for the goddess of love. The bride waited for the bridegroom, but in the night Gilgamesh got up and came to the house. Then Enkidu stepped out and stood in the street and blocked the way. Mighty Gilgamesh came on and Enkidu met him at the gate. He put out his foot and prevented Gilgamesh from entering the house, so they grappled, holding each other like bulls. They broke the doorposts and the walls shook. Gilgamesh bent his knee with his foot planted on the ground and with a turn Enkidu was thrown. Then immediately his fury died. When Enkidu was thrown he said to Gilgamesh, "There is not another like you in the world. Ninsun, who is as strong as a wild ox in the byre, she was the mother who bore you, and now you are raised above all men, and Enlil have given you the kingship, for your strength surpasses the strength of men." So Enkidu and Gilgamesh embraced and their friendship was sealed. . . .

[After they had become good friends, Gilgamesh and Enkidu set out for the Cedar Forest (possible southern Turkey or Phoenicia) in order to secure wood for the city. Before they got to the wood, however, they had to kill a fire-breathing ogre called Humbaba. Succeeding in this mission, they returned to Uruk, where Gilgamesh was offered marriage by the goddess of love, Ishtar (or Inanna).]

Gilgamesh opened his mouth and answered glorious Ishtar, "If I take you in marriage, what gifts can I give in return? What ointments and clothing for your body? I would gladly give you bread and all sorts of food fit for a god. I would give you wine to drink fit for a queen. I would pour out barley to stuff your granary; but as for making you my wife—that I will not. How would it go with me? Your lovers have found you like a brazier which smolders in the cold, a back-door which keeps out neither squall of wind nor storm, a castle which crushes the garrison, pitcher that blackens the bearer, a water-skin that chafes the carrier, a stone which falls from the parapet, a battering-ram turned back from the enemy, a sandal that trips the wearer. Which of your lovers did you ever love for ever? What shepherd of yours has pleased you for all time?" . . .

[Gravely insulted by the king's words, Ishtar asked her father, Anu, to punish Gilgamesh by sending the Bull of Heaven to ravage the land. Gilgamesh and Enkidu managed to kill the bull, whose hind leg Enkidu tore off and flung at the goddess. Such a serious offense against the gods demanded immediate punishment; thus did Enkidu fall ill and die.]

So Enkidu lay stretched out before Gilgamesh; his tears ran down in streams and he said to Gilgamesh, "O my brother, so dear as you are to me, brother, yet they will take me from you." Again he said, "I must sit down on the threshold of the dead and never again will I see my dear brother with my eyes." . . .

[Gilgamesh was unreconciled to the death of his beloved friend Enkidu. He decided to make a long and difficult journey to the Netherworld in order to search for the secret of immortality. There he encountered the Sumerian Akkadian Noah called Utnapishtim (or Ziusudra). Utnapishtim tells Gilgamesh of a Flood that had been sent by the gods to destroy all life except for Utnapishtim and his family.]

"In those days the world teemed, the people multiplied, the world bellowed like a wild bull, and the great god was aroused by the clamour. Enlil heard the clamour and he said to the gods in council, 'The uproar of mankind is intolerable and sleep is no longer possible by reason of the babel.' So the gods agreed to exterminate mankind. Enlil did this, but Ea because of his oath warned me in a dream. He whispered their words to my house of reeds, 'Reed-house, reed-house! Wall, O wall, hearken reed-house, wall reflect; O man of Shurrupak, son of Ubara-Tuttu; tear down your house and build a boat, abandon possessions and look for life, despise worldly goods and save your soul alive. Tear down your house, I say, and build a boat. These are the measurements of the barque as you shall build her: let her beam equal her length, let her deck be roofed like the vault that covers the abyss; then take up into the boat the seed of all living creatures.'

"In the first light of dawn all my household gathered round me, the children brought pitch and the men whatever was necessary. On the fifth day I laid the keel and the ribs, then I made fast the planking. The ground-space was one acre, each side of the deck measured one hundred and twenty cubits, making a square. I built six decks below, seven in all. I divided them into nine sections with bulkheads between. I drove wedges where needed, I saw to the punt-poles, and laid in supplies. The carriers brought oil in baskets, I poured pitch into the furnace and asphalt and oil; more oil was consumed in caulking, and more again the master of the boat took into his stores. I slaughtered bullocks for the people and every day I killed sheep. I gave the shipwrights wine to drink as though it were river water, raw wine and red wine and oil and white wine. There was feasting then as there is at the time of the New Year's festival; I myself anointed my head. On the seventh day the boat was complete.

"Then was the launching full of difficulty; there was shifting of ballast above and below till two thirds was submerged. I loaded into her all that I had of gold and of living things, my family, my kin, the beast of the field both wild and tame, and all the craftsmen. I sent them on board, for the time that Shamash had ordained was already fulfilled when he said, 'In the evening, when the rider of the storm sends down the destroying rain, enter the boat and batten her down.' The time was fulfilled, the evening came, the rider of the storm sent down the rain. I looked out at the weather and it was terrible, so I too boarded the boat and battened her down. All was now complete, the battening and the caulking; so I handed the tiller to Puzur-Amurri the steersman, with the navigation and the care of the whole boat. . . .

"For six days and six nights the winds blew, torrent and tempest and flood overwhelmed the world, tempest and flood raged together like warring hosts. When the seventh day dawned the storm from the south subsided, the sea grew calm, the flood was stilled; I looked at the face of the world and there was silence, all mankind was turned to clay. The surface of the sea stretched as flat as a roof-top; I opened a hatch and the light fell on my face. Then I bowed low, I sat down and I wept, the tears streamed down my face, for on every side was the waste of water. I looked for land in vain, but fourteen leagues distant there appeared a mountain, and there the boat grounded; on the mountain of Nisir the boat held fast, she held fast and did not budge. One day she held, and a second day on the mountain of Nisir she held fast and did not budge. A third day, and a fourth day she held fast on the mountain and did not budge; a fifth day and a sixth day she held fast on the mountain. When the seventh day dawned I loosed a dove and let her go. She flew away, but finding no resting-place she returned. Then I loosed a swallow, and she flew away but finding no resting-place she returned. I loosed a raven, she saw that the waters had retreated, she ate, she flew around, she cawed, and she did not come back. Then I threw everything open to the four winds, I made a sacrifice and poured out a libation on the mountain top. Seven and again seven cauldrons I set up on their stands, I heaped up wood and cane and cedar and myrtle. When the gods smelled the sweet savour, they gathered like flies over the sacrifice."

[Utnapishtim then revealed to Gilgamesh the secret of immortality. With the aid of his ferryman, Urshanabi, King Gilgamesh secured this mysterious prickly plant, but his hopes for future rejuvenation were not to be.]

"Gilgamesh, I shall reveal a secret thing, it is a mystery of the gods that I am telling you. There is a plant that grows under the water, it has a prickle like a thorn, like a rose; it will wound your hands, but it you succeed in taking it, then your hands will hold that which restores his lost youth to a man."

When Gilgamesh heard this he opened the sluices so that a sweet-water current might carry him out to the deepest channel; he tied heavy stones to his feet and they dragged him down to the water-bed. There he saw the plant growing; although it pricked him he took it in his hands; then he cut the heavy stones from his feet, and the sea carried him and threw him on to the shore. Gilgamesh said to Urshanabi the ferryman, "Come here, and see this marvellous plant. By its virtue a man may win back all his former strength. I will take it to Uruk of the strong walls; there I will give it to the old men to eat. Its name shall be 'The Old Men Are Young Again'; and at last I shall eat it myself and have back all my lost youth." So Gilgamesh returned by the gate through which he had come, Gilgamesh and Urshanabi went together. They travelled their twenty leagues and then they broke their fast; after thirty leagues they stopped for the night.

Gilgamesh saw a well of cool water and he went down and bathed; but deep in the pool there was lying a serpent, and the serpent sensed the sweetness of the flower. It rose out of the water and snatched it away, and immediately it sloughed its skin and returned to the well. Then Gilgamesh sat down and wept, the tears ran down his face, and he took the hand of Urshanabi: "O Urshanabi, was it for this that I toiled with my hands, is it for this I have wrung out my heart's blood? For myself I have gained nothing; not I, but the beast of the earth has joy of it now. Already the stream has carried it twenty leagues back to the channels where I found it. I found a sign and now I have lost it. Let us leave the boat on the bank and go."

After twenty leagues they broke their fast, after thirty leagues they stopped for the night; in three days they had walked as much as a journey of a month and fifteen days. When the journey was accomplished they arrived at Uruk, the strong-walled city. Gilgamesh spoke to him, to Urshanabi the ferryman, "Urshanabi, climb up on to the wall of Uruk, inspect its foundation terrace, and examine well the brickwork; see if it is not of burnt bricks; and did not the seven wise men lay these foundations? One third of the whole is city, one third is garden, and one third is field, with the precinct of the goddess Ishtar. These parts and the precinct are all Uruk."

This too was the work of Gilgamesh, the king, who knew the countries of the world. He was wise, he saw mysteries and knew secret things, he brought us a tale of the days before the flood. He went on a long journey, was weary, worn out with labour, and returning engraved on a stone the whole story.

Questions:
1. What elements of this epic do you also find in Homer's Odyssey?
2. Why was Enkidu created and how was he changed?
3. In the second half of the epic, what is Gilgamesh seeking? Does he succeed in this quest?
4. What part of the epic is the most familiar to you?

1.4   Hittite Laws

The Hittites emerged as a major power around 1520 B.C.E when King Telipinus seized the throne and unified his people. In time, Hittite power grew to rival that of Egypt. The Hittite laws included here express the society's values, structure, and priorities.

> **Source:** "The Hittite Laws," trans. Albrecht Goetze, in *Ancient Near Eastern Texts Relating to the Old Testament,* 3rd ed. with supplement, ed. James B. Pritchard. Copyright © renewed 1969 by Princeton University Press. Reprinted with permission of Princeton University Press.

1. If anyone kills a man or a woman in a quarrel, he shall be declared liable for him/her. He shall give four persons, man or woman, and pledge his estate as security.
2. If anyone kills a male or female slave in a quarrel, he shall be declared liable for him/her. He shall give two persons, man or woman, and pledge his estate as security.
3. If anyone strikes a free man or woman and he/she dies, (only) his hand doing wrong, he shall be declared liable for him/her. He shall give two persons and pledge his estate as security.
4. If anyone strikes a male or a female slave and he/she dies, (only) his hand doing wrong, he shall be liable for him/her. He shall give one person and pledge his estate as security.
7. If anyone blinds a free man or knocks out his teeth, they would formerly give one mina of silver; now he shall give twenty shekels of silver and pledge his estate as security.

8. If anyone blinds a male or female slave or knocks out his/her teeth, he shall give ten shekels of silver and pledge his estate as security.

9. If anyone batters a man's head, they would formerly give six shekels of silver; he who was battered would receive three shekels of silver, and they would receive three shekels of silver for the palace. Now the king has abolished the (share) of the palace and only he who was battered received three shekels of silver.

10. If anyone batters a man so that he falls ill, he shall take care of him. He shall give a man in his stead who can look after his house until he recovers. When he recovers, he shall give him six shekels of silver, and he shall also pay the physician's fee. Later version of 10: If anyone injures a free man's head, he shall take care of him. He shall give a man in his stead who can look after his house until he recovers. When he recovers, he shall give him ten shekels of silver, and he shall also pay the physician's fee. If it is a slave, he shall pay two shekels of silver.

11. If anyone breaks a free man's hand or foot, he shall give him twenty shekels of silver and pledge his estate as security.

12. If anyone breaks the hand or foot of a male or a female slave, he shall give ten shekels of silver and pledge his estate as security. Later version of 11 and 12: If anyone breaks a free man's hand or foot, in case he is permanently crippled, he shall give him twenty shekels of silver. But in case he is not permanently crippled, he shall give him ten shekels of silver. If anyone breaks a slave's hand or foot, in case he is permanently crippled, he shall give him ten shekels of silver. But in case he is not permanently crippled, he shall give him five shekels of silver.

13. If anyone bites off a free man's nose, he shall give thirty shekels of silver and pledge his estate as security.

14. If anyone bites off the nose of a male or female slave, he shall give thirty shekels of silver and pledge his estate as security.

17. If anyone causes a free woman to miscarry—if (it is the ninth or) the tenth month, he shall give ten shekels of silver, if (it is) fifth month, he shall give five shekels of silver and pledge his estate as security.
Later version of 17: If anyone causes a free woman to miscarry, he shall give twenty shekels of silver.

18. If anyone causes a slave-woman to miscarry, if (it is) the tenth month, he shall give five shekels of silver.

22. If a slave runs away and anyone brings him back—if he seizes him in the vicinity, he shall give him shoes; if on this side of the river, he shall give him two shekels of silver; if on the other side of the river, he shall give him three shekels of silver.

23. If a slave runs away and goes to the country of Luwiya, he shall give to him who brings him back six shekels of silver. If a slave runs away and goes to an enemy country, whoever brings him nevertheless back, shall receive him (the slave) himself.

24. If a male or female slave runs away, the man at whose hearth his master finds him/her, shall give a man's wages for one year, (namely) x shekels of silver, or a woman's wages for one year, namely x shekels of silver.

27. If a man takes a wife and carries her to his house, he takes her dowry with her. If the woman dies, they turn her property into (property) of the man, and the man also receives her dowry. But if she dies in the house of her father, and there are children, the man will not receive her dowry.

29. If a girl is betrothed to a man and he has given the bride-price for her, but the parents subsequently abrogate the contract and withhold her from the man, they shall make double compensation.

32. If a slave takes a free woman, the provision of the law is the same for them.

33. If a slave takes a slave-girl, the provision of the law is the same for them.

57. If anyone steals a bull—if it is a weanling, it is not a bull; if it is a yearling, it is not a bull; if it is a two-year-old, that is a bull—they would formerly give thirty (head of) cattle. Now he shall give fifteen (head of) cattle, (specifically) five two-year-olds, five yearlings (and) five weanlings and he shall pledge his estate as security.

60. If anyone finds a bull and removes the brand, (if) its owner traces it out, he shall give seven (head of) cattle; he shall give (specifically) two two-year-olds, three yearlings, and two weanlings and he shall pledge his estate as security.

61. If anyone finds a stallion and removes the brand, (if) its owner traces it out, he shall give seven horses; he shall give (specifically) two two-year-olds, three yearlings, and two weanlings and he shall pledge his estate as security.

94. If a free man steals a house, he shall give (back) the respective goods; they would formerly give for the theft one mina of silver, but now he shall give twelve shekels of silver. If he has stolen much, they shall impose a heavy fine upon him; if he has stolen little, they shall impose a small fine upon him and pledge his estate as security.

98. If a free man sets a house on fire, he shall rebuild the house. Whatever was lost in the house, whether it is man, cattle or sheep, he shall replace as a matter of course.

99. If a slave sets a house on fire, his master shall make compensation in his stead. They shall cut off the slave's nose (and) ears and shall give him back to his master. But if he does not make compensation, he will lose that (slave).

172. If a man saves a free man's life in a year of famine, he shall give (a person) like himself. If he is a slave, he shall give ten shekels of silver.

173. If anyone rejects the judgment of the king, his house shall be made a shambles. If anyone rejects the judgment of a dignitary, they shall cut off his head. If a slave rises against his master, he shall go into the pit.

188. If a man does evil with a sheep, it is a capital crime and he shall be killed. They bring him to the king's court. Whether the king orders him killed or whether the king spares his life, he must not appeal to the king.

189. If a man violates his own mother, it is a capital crime. If a man violates his daughter, it is a capital crime. If a man violates his son, it is a capital crime.

192. If a man's wife dies (and) he marries his wife's sister, the shall be no punishment.

193. If a man has a wife and then the man dies, his brother shall take his wife, then his father shall take her. If in turn also his father dies, one of the brother's sons shall take the wife whom he had. There shall be no punishment.

197. If a man seizes a woman in the mountains, it is the man's crime and he will be killed. But if he seizes her in (her) house, it is the woman's crime and the woman shall be killed. If the husband finds them, he may kill them: there shall be no punishment for him.

198. If he brings them to the gate of the palace and declares: "My wife shall not be killed" and thereby spares his wife's life, he shall also spare the life of the adulterer and shall mark his head. If he says, "Let them die, both of them!" . . . The king may order them killed, the king may spare their lives.

199. If anyone does evil with a pig, (or) a dog, he shall die. They will bring him to the gate of the palace and the king may order them killed, the king may spare their lives; but he must not appeal to the king. If an ox leaps at a man, the ox shall die, but the man shall not die. A sheep may be proffered in the man's stead and they shall kill that. If a pig leaps at a man, there shall be no punishment.

Questions:
1. Was there legal equality among the Hittites?
2. Why would we say that the Hittite code closely approximates that of the Visigoths?

1.5 Hammurabi's Law Code

In the twenty-second year of his reign, the Amorite King Hammurabi (d. 1750 B.C.E.), who had made Babylon his capital and conquered Mesopotamia, issued a comprehensive code of laws. He caused them to be inscribed on stones that were erected at crossroads and in marketplaces throughout his kingdom so that all his subjects would know them. A selection of these laws follows.

Source: gopher://gopher.vt.edu: 10010/11/, translated by Leonard W. King
[Accessed through http:// eawc.evansville.edu/anthology/hammurabi.htm]

When Anu the Sublime, King of the Anunaki, and Bel, the lord of Heaven and earth, who decreed the fate of the land, assigned to Marduk, the over-ruling son of Ea, God of righteousness, dominion over earthly man, and made him great...; then Anu and Bel called by name me, Hammurabi, the exalted prince, who feared God, to bring about the rule of righteousness in the land, to destroy the wicked and the evil-doers; so that the strong should not harm the weak; so that I should rule over the black-headed people like Shamash, and enlighten the land, to further the well-being of mankind....

When Marduk sent me to rule over men, to give the protection of right to the land, I did right and righteousness in..., and brought about the well-being of the oppressed.

THE CODE OF LAWS

[to ensure good justice]

3. If any one bring an accusation of any crime before the elders, and does not prove what he has charged, he shall, if it be a capital offense charged, be put to death.

5. If a judge try a case, reach a decision, and present his judgment in writing; if later error shall appear in his decision, and it be through his own fault, then he shall pay twelve times the fine set by him in the case, and he shall be publicly removed from the judge's bench, and never again shall he sit there to render judgement.

[criminal law of property]

8. If any one steal cattle or sheep, or an ass, or a pig or a goat, if it belong to a god or to the court, the thief shall pay thirtyfold therefore; if they belonged to a freed man of the king he shall pay tenfold; if the thief has nothing with which

to pay he shall be put to death.

21. If any one break a hole into a house (break in to steal), he shall be put to death before that hole and be buried.

22. If any one is committing a robbery and is caught, then he shall be put to death.

23. If the robber is not caught, then shall he who was robbed claim under oath the amount of his loss; then shall the community, and... on whose ground and territory and in whose domain it was compensate him for the goods stolen.

[property laws concerning agriculture and irrigation]

42. If any one take over a field to till it, and obtain no harvest therefrom, it must be proved that he did no work on the field, and he must deliver grain, just as his neighbor raised, to the owner of the field.

45. If a man rent his field for tillage for a fixed rental, and receive the rent of his field, but bad weather come and destroy the harvest, the injury falls upon the tiller of the soil.

46. If he do not receive a fixed rental for his field, but lets it on half or third shares of the harvest, the grain on the field shall be divided proportionately between the tiller and the owner.

48. If any one owe a debt for a loan, and a storm prostrates the grain, or the harvest fail, or the grain does not grow for lack of water; in that year he need not give his creditor any grain, he washes his debt-tablet in water and pays no rent for this year.

53. If any one be too lazy to keep his dam in proper condition, and does not so keep it; if then the dam break and all the fields be flooded, then shall he in whose dam the break occurred be sold for money, and the money shall replace the corn which he has caused to be ruined.

55. If any one open his ditches to water his crop, but is careless, and the water flood the field of his neighbor, then he shall pay his neighbor corn for his loss.

[laws governing debts and obligations]

108. If a tavern-keeper (feminine form) does not accept corn according to gross weight in payment of drink, but takes money, and the price of the drink is less than that of the corn, she shall be convicted and thrown into the water.

117. If any one fail to meet a claim for debt, and sell himself, his wife, his son, and daughter for money or give them away to forced labor: they shall work for three years in the house of the man who bought them, or the proprietor, and in the fourth year they shall be set free.

121. If any one store corn in another man's house he shall pay him storage at the rate of one gur1 for every five ka2 of corn per year.

122. If any one give another silver, gold, or anything else to keep, he shall show everything to some witness, draw up a contract, and then hand it over for safe keeping.

123. If he turn it over for safe keeping without witness or contract, and if he to whom it was given deny it, then he has no legitimate claim.

[laws concerning marriage, family, and inheritance]

128. If a man take a woman to wife, but have no intercourse with her, this woman is no wife to him.

129. If a man's wife be surprised [in a sexually compromising situation] with another man, both shall be tied and thrown into the water, but the husband may pardon his wife and the king his [subjects].

130. If a man violate the wife (betrothed or child-wife) of another man, who has never known a man, and still lives in her father's house, and sleep with her and be surprised, this man shall be put to death, but the wife is blameless.

131. If a man bring a charge against one's wife, but she is not surprised with another man, she must take an oath and then may return to her house.

133. If a man is taken prisoner in war, and there is a sustenance in his house, but his wife leave house and court, and go to another house: because this wife did not keep her court, and went to another house, she shall be judicially condemned and thrown into the water.

134. If any one be captured in war and there is not sustenance in his house, if then his wife go to another house this woman shall be held blameless.

136. If any one leave his house, run away, and then his wife go to another house, if then he return, and wishes to take his wife back: because he fled from his home and ran away, the wife of this runaway shall not return to her husband.

137. If a man wish to separate from a woman who has borne him children, or from his wife who has borne him children: then he shall give that wife her dowry, and a part of the usufruct of field, garden, and property, so that she can rear her children. When she has brought up her children, a portion of all that is given to the children, equal as that of one son, shall be given to her. She may then marry the man of her heart.

138. If a man wishes to separate from his wife who has borne him no children, he shall give her the amount of her purchase money and the dowry which she brought from her father's house, and let her go.

142. If a woman quarrel with her husband, and say: "You are not congenial to me," the reasons for her prejudice must be presented. If she is guiltless, and there is no fault on her part, but he leaves and neglects her, then no guilt attaches to this woman, she shall take her dowry and go back to her father's house.

143. If she is not innocent, but leaves her husband, and ruins her house, neglecting her husband, this woman shall be cast into the water.

145. If a man take a wife, and she bear him no children, and he intend to take another wife: if he take this second wife, and bring her into the house, this second wife shall not be allowed equality with his wife.

148. If a man take a wife, and she be seized by disease, if he then desire to take a second wife he shall not put away his wife, who has been attacked by disease, but he shall keep her in the house which he has built and support her so long as she lives.

149. If this woman does not wish to remain in her husband's house, then he shall compensate her for the dowry that she brought with her from her father's house, and she may go.

154. If a man be guilty of incest with his daughter, he shall be driven from the place (exiled).

157. If any one be guilty of incest with his mother after his father, both shall be burned.

158. If any one be surprised after his father with his chief wife, who has borne children, he shall be driven out of his father's house.

159. If any one, who has brought chattels into his father-in-law's house, and has paid the purchase-money, looks for another wife, and says to his father-in-law: "I do not want your daughter," the girl's father may keep all that he had brought.

160. If a man bring chattels into the house of his father-in-law, and pay the "purchase price" (for his wife): if then the father of the girl say: "I will not give you my daughter," he shall give him back all that he brought with him.

163. If a man marry a woman and she bear him no sons; if then this woman die, if the "purchase price" which he had paid into the house of his father-in-law is repaid to him, her husband shall have no claim upon the dowry of this woman; it belongs to her father's house.

168. If a man wish to put his son out of his house, and declare before the judge: "I want to put my son out," then the judge shall examine into his reasons. If the son be guilty of no great fault, for which he can be rightfully put out, the father shall not put him out.

170. If his wife bear sons to a man, or his maid-servant have borne sons, and the father while still living says to the children whom his maid-servant has borne: "My sons," and he count them with the sons of his wife; if then the father die, then the sons of the wife and of the maid-servant shall divide the paternal property in common. The son of the wife is to partition and choose.

180. If a father give a present to his daughter-either marriageable or a prostitute (unmarriageable)-and then die, then she is to receive a portion as a child from the paternal estate, and enjoy its usufruct so long as she lives. Her estate belongs to her brothers.

184. If a man do not give a dowry to his daughter by a concubine, and no husband; if then her father die, her brother shall give her a dowry according to her father's wealth and secure a husband for her.

185. If a man adopt a child and to his name as son, and rear him, this grown son can not be demanded back again.

190. If a man does not maintain a child that he has adopted as a son and reared with his other children, then his adopted son may return to his father's house.

[laws concerning physical harm to persons or animals]

195. If a son strike his father, his hands shall be hewn off.

196. If a man put out the eye of another man, his eye shall be put out.

197. If he break another man's bone, his bone shall be broken.

198. If he put out the eye of a freed man, or break the bone of a freed man, he shall pay one gold mina.

199. If he put out the eye of a man's slave, or break the bone of a man's slave, he shall pay one-half of its value.

200. If a man knock out the teeth of his equal, his teeth shall be knocked out.

201. If he knock out the teeth of a freed man, he shall pay one-third of a gold mina.

202. If any one strike the body of a man higher in rank than he, he shall receive sixty blows with an ox-whip in public.

203. If a free-born man strike the body of another free-born man or equal rank, he shall pay one gold mina.

204. If a freed man strike the body of another freed man, he shall pay ten shekels in money.

205. If the slave of a freed man strike the body of a freed man, his ear shall be cut off.

206. If during a quarrel one man strike another and wound him, then he shall swear, "I did not injure him wit-

tingly," and pay the physicians.

207. If the man die of his wound, he shall swear similarly, and if he (the deceased) was a free-born man, he shall pay half a mina in money.

208. If he was a freed man, he shall pay one-third of a mina.

209. If a man strike a free-born woman so that she lose her unborn child, he shall pay ten shekels for her loss.

210. If the woman die, his daughter shall be put to death.

211. If a woman of the free class lose her child by a blow, he shall pay five shekels....

212. If this woman die, he shall pay half a mina.

213. If he strike the maidservant of a man, and she lose her child, he shall pay two shekels....

214. If this maid-servant die, he shall pay one-third of a mina.

[liability laws and fair prices]

219. If a physician make a large incision in the slave of a freed man, and kill him, he shall replace the slave with another slave.

221. If a physician heal the broken bone or diseased soft part of a man, the patient shall pay the physician five shekels in money.

222. If he were a freed man he shall pay three shekels.

223. If he were a slave his owner shall pay the physician two shekels.

224. If a veterinary surgeon perform a serious operation on an ass or an ox, and cure it, the owner shall pay the surgeon one-sixth of a shekel as a fee.

225. If he perform a serious operation on an ass or ox, and kill it, he shall pay the owner one-fourth of its value.

228. If a builder build a house for some one and complete it, he shall give him a fee of two shekels in money for each sar of surface.

229. If a builder build a house for some one, and does not construct it properly, and the house which he built fall in and kill its owner, then that builder shall be put to death.

230. If it kill the son of the owner the son of that builder shall be put to death.

231. If it kill a slave of the owner, then he shall pay slave for slave to the owner of the house.

232. If it ruin goods, he shall make compensation for all that has been ruined, and inasmuch as he did not construct properly this house which he built and it fell, he shall re-erect the house from his own means.

234. If a shipbuilder build a boat of sixty gur for a man, he shall pay him a fee of two shekels in money.

235. If a shipbuilder build a boat for some one, and do not make it tight, if during that same year that boat is sent away and suffers injury, the shipbuilder shall take the boat apart and put it together tight at his own expense. The tight boat he shall give to the boat owner.

239. If a man hire a sailor, he shall pay him six gur of corn per year.

244. If any one hire an ox or an ass, and a lion kill it in the field, the loss is upon its owner.

245. If any one hire oxen, and kill them by bad treatment or blows, he shall compensate the owner, oxen for oxen.

247. If any one hire an ox, and put out its eye, he shall pay the owner one-half of its value.

249. If any one hire an ox, and God strike it that it die, the man who hired it shall swear by God and be considered guiltless.

251. If an ox be a goring ox, and it shown that he is a gorer, and he do not bind his horns, or fasten the ox up, and the ox gore a free-born man and kill him, the owner shall pay one-half a mina in money.

257. If any one hire a field laborer, he shall pay him eight gur of corn per year.

258. If any one hire an ox-driver, he shall pay him six gur of corn per year.

261. If any one hire a herdsman for cattle or sheep, he shall pay him eight gur of corn per [year].

263. If he kill the cattle or sheep that were given to him, he shall compensate the owner with cattle for cattle and sheep for sheep.

267. If the herdsman overlook something, and an accident happen in the stable, then the herdsman is at fault for the accident which he has caused in the stable, and he must compensate the owner for the cattle or sheep.

282. If a slave say to his master: "You are not my master," if they convict him his master shall cut off his ear.

THE EPILOGUE

Laws of justice which Hammurabi, the wise king, established. A righteous law, and pious statute did he teach the land. Hammurabi, the protecting king am I. I have not withdrawn myself from the men, whom Bel gave to me, the rule over whom Marduk gave to me, I was not negligent, but I made them a peaceful abiding-place.... That the strong might not injure the weak, in order to protect the widows and orphans, I have in Babylon the city where Anu and Bel raise high their head, in E-Sagil, the Temple, whose foundations stand firm as heaven and earth, in order to bespeak justice in the land, to settle all disputes, and heal all injuries, set up these my precious words, written upon my memorial stone, before the image of me, as king of righteousness.

The king who ruleth among the kings of the cities am I. My words are well considered; there is no wisdom like unto mine. By the command of Shamash, the great judge of heaven and earth, let righteousness go forth in the land: by the order of Marduk, my lord, let no destruction befall my monument. In E-Sagil, which I love, let my name be ever repeated; let the oppressed, who has a case at law, come and stand before this my image as king of righteousness; let him read the inscription, and understand my precious words: the inscription will explain his case to him; he will find out what is just, and his heart will be glad, so that he will say:

"Hammurabi is a ruler, who is as a father to his subjects, who holds the words of Marduk in reverence, who has achieved conquest for Marduk over the north and south, who rejoices the heart of Marduk, his lord, who has bestowed benefits for ever and ever on his subjects, and has established order in the land."

... If a succeeding ruler considers my words, which I have written in this my inscription, if he do not annul my law, nor corrupt my words, nor change my monument, then may Shamash lengthen that king's reign, as he has that of me, the king of righteousness, that he may reign in righteousness over his subjects.

If this ruler do not esteem my words, which I have written in my inscription, if he despise my curses, and fear not the curse of God, if he destroy the law which I have given, corrupt my words, change my monument, efface my name, write his name there, or on account of the curses commission another so to do, that man... may the great God (Anu), the Father of the gods, who has ordered my rule, withdraw from him the glory of royalty, break his scepter, curse his destiny. May Bel, the lord, who fixeth destiny, ... order with his potent mouth the destruction of his city, the dispersion of his subjects, the cutting off of his rule, the removal of his name and memory from the land. ... May Bel curse him with the potent curses of his mouth that can not be altered, and may they come upon him forthwith.

Questions:
1. What are the authority and principles on which this law code is based?
2. How are the law codes similiar to the "Laws of the Hebrews" in document 1.6?
3. What do these two law codes reveal about the social structure, family, and the position of women in each society?

1.6 Laws of the Hebrews

The basis of Hebrew law is the code of moral law known as the Ten Commandments that, according to the account in Genesis, their God Yahweh gave them on Mt. Sinai in the thirteenth century B.C.E. The Hebrews also had other laws and customs they followed that applied those broad principles more specifically.

Source: The Bible, New International Version, © 1973, 1978, 1984, International Bible Society. Ex. 20: 1-17, Ex. 21-23, passim.

EXODUS 20: 1-17

The Ten Commandments

1. And God spoke all these words:
2. "I am the LORD your God, who brought you out of Egypt, out of the land of slavery.
3. "You shall have no other gods before [besides] me.
4-6. "You shall not make for yourself an idol in the form of anything in heaven above or on the earth beneath or in the waters below. You shall not bow down to them or worship them; for I, the LORD your God, am a jealous God, punishing the children for the sin of the fathers to the third and fourth generation of those who hate me, but showing love to a thousand [generations] of those who love me and keep my commandments.
7. "You shall not misuse the name of the LORD your God, for the LORD will not hold anyone guiltless who misuses his name.
8-11. "Remember the Sabbath day by keeping it holy. Six days you shall labor and do all your work, but the seventh day is a Sabbath to the LORD your God. On it you shall not do any work, neither you, nor your son or daughter, nor your manservant or maidservant, nor your animals, nor the alien within your gates. For in six days the LORD made the

heavens and the earth, the sea, and all that is in them, but he rested on the seventh day. Therefore the LORD blessed the Sabbath day and made it holy.

12. "Honor your father and your mother, so that you may live long in the land the LORD your God is giving you.

13. "You shall not murder.

14. "You shall not commit adultery.

15. "You shall not steal.

16. "You shall not give false testimony against your neighbor.

17. "You shall not covet your neighbor's house. You shall not covet your neighbor's wife, or his manservant or maidservant, his ox or donkey, or anything that belongs to your neighbor."

EXODUS 21

Regarding Slaves and Servants

1. "These are the laws you are to set before them:

2. "If you buy a Hebrew servant, he is to serve you for six years. But in the seventh year, he shall go free, without paying anything.

3. "If he comes alone, he is to go free alone; but if he has a wife when he comes, she is to go with him.

4. "If his master gives him a wife and she bears him sons or daughters, the woman and her children shall belong to her master, and only the man shall go free.

5-6. "But if the servant declares, 'I love my master and my wife and children and do not want to go free,' then his master must take him before the judges. He shall take him to the door or the doorpost and pierce his ear with an awl. Then he will be his servant for life.

7. "If a man sells his daughter as a servant, she is not to go free as menservants do.

Regarding Crimes of Violence

12. "Anyone who strikes a man and kills him shall surely be put to death.

13. "However, if he does not do it intentionally, but God lets it happen, he is to flee to a place I will designate.

17. "Anyone who curses his father or mother must be put to death.

18-19. "If men quarrel and one hits the other with a stone or with his fist *[or tool]* and he does not die but is confined to bed, the one who struck the blow will not be held responsible if the other gets up and walks around outside with his staff however, he must pay the injured man for the loss of his time and see that he is completely healed.

20-21. "If a man beats his male or female slave with a rod and the slave dies as a direct result, he must be punished, but he is not to be punished if the slave gets up after a day or two, since the slave is his property.

22. "If men who are fighting hit a pregnant woman and she gives birth prematurely *[or she has a miscarriage]* but there is no serious injury, the offender must be fined whatever the woman's husband demands and the court allows.

23-25. "But if there is serious injury, you are to take life for life, eye for eye, tooth for tooth, hand for hand, foot for foot, burn for burn, wound for wound, bruise for bruise.

26. "If a man hits a manservant or maidservant in the eye and destroys it, he must let the servant go free to compensate for the eye.

27. "And if he knocks out the tooth of a manservant or maidservant, he must let the servant go free to compensate for the tooth.

Regarding Liability Regarding Property

28. "If a bull gores a man or a woman to death, the bull must be stoned to death, and its meat must not be eaten. But the owner of the bull will not be held responsible.

29. "If, however, the bull has had the habit of goring and the owner has been warned but has not kept it penned up and it kills a man or woman, the bull must be stoned and the owner also must be put to death.

30. "However, if payment is demanded of him, he may redeem his life by paying whatever is demanded.

31. "This law also applies if the bull gores a son or daughter.

32. "If the bull gores a male or female slave, the owner must pay thirty shekels *[about 12 ounces]* of silver to the master of the slave, and the bull must be stoned.

33-34. "If a man uncovers a pit or digs one and fails to cover it and an ox or a donkey falls into it, the owner of the pit must pay for the loss; he must pay its owner, and the dead animal will be his.

35. "If a man's bull injures the bull of another and it dies, they are to sell the live one and divide both the money and the dead animal equally.

36. "However, if it was known that the bull had the habit of goring, yet the owner did not keep it penned up, the owner must pay, animal for animal, and the dead animal will be his.

EXODUS 22

1. "If a man steals an ox or a sheep and slaughters it or sells it, he must pay back five head of cattle for the ox and four sheep for the sheep.

2-3. "If a thief is caught breaking in and is struck so that he dies, the defender is not guilty of bloodshed; but if it happens after sunrise, he is guilty of bloodshed. A thief must certainly make restitution, but if he has nothing, he must be sold to pay for his theft.

5. "If a man grazes his livestock in a field or vineyard and lets them stray and they graze in another man's field, he must make restitution from the best of his own field or vineyard.

6. "If a fire breaks out and spreads into thornbushes so that it burns shocks of grain or standing grain or the whole field, the one who started the fire must make restitution.

14. "If a man borrows an animal from his neighbor and it is injured or dies while the owner is not present, he must make restitution.

15. "But if the owner is with the animal, the borrower will not have to pay. If the animal was hired, the money paid for the hire covers the loss.

Regarding Relationships and Ethical Behavior

16. "If a man seduces a virgin who is not pledged to be married and sleeps with her, he must pay the bride-price, and she shall be his wife.

17. "If her father absolutely refuses to give her to him, he must still pay the bride-price for virgins.

18. "Do not allow a sorceress to live.

19. "Anyone who has sexual relations with an animal must be put to death.

20. "Whoever sacrifices to any god other than the LORD must be destroyed.

21. "Do not mistreat an alien or oppress him, for you were aliens in Egypt.

22. "Do not take advantage of a widow or an orphan.

23. "If you do and they cry out to me, I will certainly hear their cry.

24. "My anger will be aroused, and I will kill you with the sword; your wives will become widows and your children fatherless.

25. "If you lend money to one of my people among you who is needy, do not be like a moneylender; charge him no interest.

26-27. "If you take your neighbor's cloak as
a pledge, return it to him by sunset, because his cloak is
the only covering he has for his body. What else will he sleep in? When he cries out to me, I will hear, for I am compassionate.

31. "You are to be my holy people....

EXODUS 23

1. "Do not spread false reports. Do not help a wicked man by being a malicious witness.

2-3. "Do not follow the crowd in doing wrong. When you give testimony in a lawsuit, do not pervert justice by siding with the crowd, and do not show favoritism to a poor man in his lawsuit.

4. "If you come across your enemy's ox or donkey wandering off, be sure to take it back to him.

5. "If you see the donkey of someone who hates you fallen down under its load, do not leave it there; be sure you help him with it.

6. "Do not deny justice to your poor people in their lawsuits.

7. "Have nothing to do with a false charge and do not put an innocent or honest person to death, for I will not acquit the guilty.

8. "Do not accept a bribe, for a bribe blinds those who see and twists the words of the righteous.

9. "Do not oppress an alien; you yourselves know how it feels to be aliens, because you were aliens in Egypt.

10. "For six years you are to sow your fields and harvest the crops,

11. "But during the seventh year let the land lie unplowed and unused. Then the poor among your people may get food from it, and the wild animals may eat what they leave. Do the same with your vineyard and your olive grove.

Questions:

1. What are the authority and principles on which this law code is based?
2. How are the law codes similar to Hammurabi's Law Code in document 1.5? How are they different?
3. What do these two law codes reveal about the social structure, family, and the position of women in each society?

1.7 The Instruction of the Ptah-hotep

No Law codes survive from the Egyptian Old Kingdom (2700-2200 B.C.E.). Worldly wisdom and clues to its culture's basic principles and ethics emerge from the texts inscribed in the tombs of the kings and of nobles such as Ptah-hotep, a vizier (chief minister) who lived around 2450 B.C.E. He addressed these instructions to his son, setting forth rules of appropriate behavior. The term "maat" in this text carries with it the meaning of accepted tradition and truth that has always worked and produced harmony.

Source: Readings in Ancient History: Thought and Experience from Gilgamesh to St. Augustine, Fifth Edition, ed. Nels M. Bailkey, (Lexington, MA: DC Heath and Company, 1996), pp. 38-42. (Based on a translation by F.L. Griffith in A Library of the World's Best Literature, XIII, pp. 5329-40).

PREFACE: ROYAL APPROVAL

The mayor and vizier Ptah-hotep said: "O king, my lord, years come on, old age is here, decrepitude arrives, weakness is renewed.... Let it be commanded of your servant to make a staff of old age: let my son be set in my place. Let me tell him the sayings of those who obeyed, the conduct of them of old, of them who listened to the gods....

Said the majesty of this god [the king]: "Instruct him in the sayings of the past.... Speak to him, for no one is born wise."

TITLE AND AIM

Beginning of the maxims of good words spoken by the... mayor and vizier, Ptah-hotep, teaching the ignorant to know according to the standard of good words, expounding the profit to him who shall listen to it, and the injury to him who shall transgress it. He said to his son:

INTELLECTUAL SNOBBERY

Be not arrogant because of your knowledge, and be not puffed up because you are a learned man. Take counsel with the ignorant as with the learned, for the limits of art cannot be reached, and no artist is perfect in his skills. Good speech is more hidden than the precious greenstone, and yet it is found among slave girls at the millstones....

LEADERSHIP AND "MAAT"

If you are a leader, commanding the conduct of many, seek out every good aim, so that your policy may be without error. A great thing is truth *[maat]*, enduring and surviving; it has not been upset since the time of Osiris. He who departs from its laws is punished. It is the right path for him who knows nothing. Wrongdoing has never brought its venture safe to port. Evil may win riches, but it is the strength of truth that it endures long, and a man can say, "I learned it from my father."...

CONDUCT AS A GUEST AT TABLE

If you are a guest at the table of one who is greater than you, take what he offers as it is set before you. Fix your gaze upon what is before you, and pierce not your host with many glances, for it is an abomination to force your attention upon him. Speak not to him until he calls, for no one knows what may be offensive; speak when he addresses you, for then your words will give satisfaction. Laugh when he laughs; that will please him, and then whatever you do will please him....

PATIENCE WITH SUPPLIANTS

If you are a leader be kind in hearing the speech of a suppliant. Treat him not roughly until he has unburdened himself of what he was minded to tell you. The compliant sets greater store by the easing of his mind than by the accomplishment of that for which he came. As for him who deals roughly with a petition, men say, "Why, pray, has he ignored it?" Not all that men plead for ever comes to pass, but to listen kindly soothes the heart.

RELATIONS WITH WOMEN

If you wish to prolong friendship in a house into which you enter as master, brother or friend, or any place that you enter, beware of approaching the women. No place in which that is done prospers. There is no wisdom in it. A thousand men are turned aside from their own good because of a little moment, like a dream, by tasting which death is reached.... He who... lusts after women, no plan of his will succeed.

GREED

If you want your conduct to be good, free from every evil, then beware of greed. It is an evil and incurable sickness. No man can live with it; it causes divisions between fathers and mothers, and between brothers of the same mother; it parts wife and husband; it is a gathering of every evil, a bag of everything hateful. A man thrives if his conduct is right. He who follows the right course wins wealth thereby. But the greedy man has no tomb....

MARRIAGE

If you are prosperous you should establish a household and love your wife as is fitting. Fill her belly and clothe her back. Oil is the tonic for her body. Make her heart glad as long as you live. She is a profitable field for her lord....

CONDUCT IN COUNCIL

If you are a worthy man sitting in the council of his lord, confine your attention to excellence. Silence is more valuable than chatter. Speak only when you know you can resolve difficulties. He who gives good counsel is an artist, for speech is more difficult than any craft....

Behavior in Changed Circumstances

If you are now great after being humble and rich after being poor in the city that you know, do not boast because of what happened to you in the past. Be not miserly with your wealth, which has come to you by the god's [the king's] gift. You are no different from another to whom the same has happened.

OBEDIENCE TO A SUPERIOR

Bend your back to him who is over you, your superior in the administration; then your house will endure by reason of its property, and your reward will come in due season. Wretched is he who opposes his superior, for one lives only so long as he is gracious....

EXHORTATION TO LISTEN

If you listen to my sayings, then all your affairs will go forward. They are precious; their memory goes on in the speech of men because of their excellence. If each saying is carried on, they will never perish in this land....

If the son of a man accepts what his father says, no plan of his will fail.... Failure follows him who does not listen. He who hears is established; he who is a fool is crushed....

A son who hears is a follower of Horus: there is good for him who listens. When he reaches old age and attains honor, he tells the like to his children, renewing the teaching of his father. Every man teaches as he has acted. He speaks to his children so that they may speak to their children....

CONCLUSION

May you succeed me, may your body be sound, may the king be well pleased with all that is done, and may you spend many years of life! It is no small thing that I have done on earth; I have spent one hundred and ten years of life, which the king gave me, and with rewards greater than those of the ancestors, by doing right for the king until death.

Questions:
1. *What are the guiding principles of behavior revealed in these instructions?*
2. *Keeping in mind that these are a parent's advice rather than enforced law, how do they differ from the ethical principles set forth in Hammurabi's and the Hebrew's laws above?*
3. *What does this document reveal about Egyptian society during this period?*

PART 2
Ancient Greece

2.1 Laws Relating to Women: Excerpts from the Gortyn Law Code

These laws that date from the fifth century B.C.E. provide the women of Gortyn in Crete with more independent legal rights in property and marriage than Athenian women enjoyed.

> **Source:** Women's Life in Greece and Rome. A Source Book in Translation, ed. Mary R. Lefkowitz and Maureen B. Fant. 2nd ed., (Baltimore: Johns Hopkins University Press, 1992). This selection was found at their internet site: [http://www.uky.edu/ArtsSciences/Classics/wlgr/wlgr-greeklegal76.html]

SEXUAL OFFENCES

If a person rapes a free person, male or female, he shall pay 100 staters, and if [the victim] is from the house of an *apetarios*,[1] 10 staters; and if a slave rapes a free person, male or female, he shall pay double. If a free man rapes a serf, male or female, he shall pay 5 drachmas. If a male serf rapes a serf, male or female, he shall pay five staters.

If a person deflowers a female household serf, he shall pay 2 staters. If she has already been deflowered, 1 obol if in day-time, 2 obols if at night. The female slave's oath takes precedence.[2]

If anyone makes an attempt to rape a free woman under the guardianship of a relative, he shall pay 10 staters, if a witness testifies.

If someone is taken in adultery with a free woman in her father's house, or her brother's or her husband's, he is to pay 10 staters; if in another man's house, 50 staters; if with the wife of an apetairos, 10 staters. But if a slave is taken in adultery with a free woman, he must pay double. If a slave is taken in adultery with a slave, 5 staters.

DISPOSITION OF PROPERTY IN DIVORCE

If a husband and wife divorce, she is to keep her property, whatever she brought to the marriage, and one-half the produce (if there is any) from her own property, and half of whatever she has woven within the house; also she is to have 5 staters if her husband is the cause of the divorce. If the husband swears that he is not the cause of the divorce, the judge is to take an oath and decide. If the wife carries away anything else belonging to the husband, she must pay 5 staters and whatever she carries away from him, and whatever she has stolen she must return to him. About what she denies [having taken], the judge is to order that she must swear by Artemis before the statue of [Artemis] Archeress in the Amyclean temple. If anyone takes anything from her after she has made her denial, he is to pay 5 staters and return the thing itself. If a stranger helps her to carry anything away, he must pay 10 staters and double the amount of whatever the judge swears that he helped her to take away.

WIDOWHOOD

If a man dies and leaves children behind, if the wife wishes, she may marry, keeping her own property and whatever her husband gave her according to an agreement written in the presence of three adult free witnesses. If she should take anything away that belongs to her children, that is grounds for a trial. If the husband leaves her without issue, she is to have her own property and half of whatever she has woven within the house, and she is to get her portion of the produce in the house along with the lawful heirs, and whatever her husband may have given her according to written agreement. But if she should take away anything else, it is grounds for a trial.

If a woman dies without issue the husband is to give her property back to her lawful heirs and half of what she has woven within and half of the produce if it comes from her property. If the husband or wife wishes to pay for its transport, it is to be in clothing or twelve staters or something worth 12 staters, but not more.

If a female serf is separated from a male serf while he is alive or if he dies, she is to keep what she has. If she takes anything else away, it is grounds for a trial.

---

[1] A free man, but not a citizen, perhaps roughly equivalent in status to the Attic *metoikos*, 'resident alien,' who had more rights than a slave but fewer than a citizen.

[2] Here and elsewhere in the Code, if oaths are sworn by both sides, the oath that has precedence wins by default; presumably, the oath was not merely an asseveration that one is telling the truth, but a solemn demand that the gods punish the swearer for lying.

PROVISIONS FOR CHILDREN IN CASE OF DEATH OR DIVORCE

If a wife who is separated from her husband should bear a child, it is to be brought to the husband in his house in the presence of three witnesses. If he does not receive it, it is up to the mother to raise or expose the child. The oath of relatives and witnesses is to have preference, if they brought it.

If a female serf should bear a child while separated [from her husband], she is to bring it to the master of the man who married her, in the presence of two witnesses. If he does not receive the child, it is to belong to the master of the female serf, but if she marries the same man again before the end of the year, the child shall belong to the master of the male serf. The oaths of person who brought the child and of the witnesses shall have preference.

If a divorced woman should expose her child before presenting it according to the law, she shall pay 50 staters for a free child, and 5 for a slave, if she is convicted. If the man to whom she brings the child has no house, or she does not see him, she shall not pay a penalty if she exposes the child.

If a female serf who is not married conceives and bears a child, the child shall belong to the master of her father. If the father is not alive then to the masters of her brothers.

The father has power over the children and division of property, and the mother over her own possessions. So long as [the father and mother] are alive, the property is not to be divided. But if one of them is fined, the person who is fined shall have his share reduced proportionately according to the law.

If a father dies, the city dwellings and whatever is inside the houses in which a serf who lives in the country does not reside, and the cattle which do not belong to a serf, shall belong to the sons. The other possessions shall be divided fairly, and the sons shall each get two parts, however many they are, and the daughters each get one part, however many they are.

The mother's property shall also be divided if she dies, in the same way as prescribed for the father's. But if there is no property other than the house, the daughters shall receive their share as prescribed. If the father during his lifetime should give to a married daughter, let him give her share as prescribed, but not more. The daughter to whom he gave or promised her share shall have it, but no additional possessions from her father's property.

If any woman does not have property either from a gift by her father or brother or from a pledge or from an inheritance given when the Aithalian clan consisting of Cyllus and his colleagues [where in power], these women are to have a portion, but it will not be lawful to take away gifts given previously.

If a mother dies leaving children, the father has power over the mother's estate, but he should not sell or mortage it, unless the children are of age and give their consent. If he marries another wife, the children are to have power over their mother's estate.

DETERMINATION OF SOCIAL STATUS

If a slave goes to a free woman and marries her, the children shall be free. If a free woman goes to a slave, the children shall be slaves.

HEIRESSES[3]

The heiress is to marry the oldest of her father's living brothers. If her father has no living brothers but there are sons of the brothers, she is to marry the oldest brother's son. If there are more heiresses and sons of brothers, the [additional heiress] is to marry the next son after the son of the oldest. The groom-elect is to have one heiress, and not more.

If the heiress is too young to marry, she is to have the house, if there is one, and the groom-elect is to have half of the revenue from everything.

If he does not wish to marry her as prescribed by law, the heiress is to take all the property and marry the next one in succession, if there is one. If there is no one, she may marry whomever she wishes to of those who ask her from the same phratry.[4] If the heiress is of age and does not wish to marry the intended bridgeroom, or the intended groom is too young and the heiress is unwilling to wait, she is to have the house, if there is one in the city, and whatever is in the house, and taking half of the remaining property she is to marry another of those from the phratry who ask her, but she is to give a share of the property to the groom [whom she rejected].

If there are no kinsmen as defined for the heiress, she is to take all the property and marry from the phratry whomever she wishes.

If no one from the phratry wishes to marry her, her relations should announce to the tribe 'does anyone want to marry her?' If someone wants to, it should be within thirty days of the announcement. If not, she is free to marry another man, whomever she can.

RESTRICTIONS CONCERNING ADOPTION

A woman is not to adopt [a child] nor a man under age.

Questions:
1. What rights did husbands and fathers have over their families in Crete?
2. Read document 2.5 "Education and Family Life in Sparta" and describe how these two documents illiustrate the differences in the lives of women and the institution of marriage in these Greek city-states?
3. What do these documents reveal about the lives of servants or slaves in these societies?

2.2 Homer from the *Iliad*

Homer's Iliad, written around 800 B.C.E., tells the story of the Trojan War. In Homer's telling, the Trojan war was not just a conflict between the armies of the Achaens and the Trojans, but a test of individual heroism, honor, and virtue. The passage included below explores the feud between Agamemnon, leader of the Achaens, and Achilles, his most powerful warrior.

Source: The *Iliad*, translation by Robert Fagles (New York: Viking Press, 1990), p. 77–80.

> Rage—Goddess, sing the rage of Peleus' son Achilles,
> murderous, doomed, that cost the Achaeans countless losses,
> hurling down to the House of Death so many sturdy souls,
> great fighters' souls, but made their bodies carrion,
> feasts for the dogs and birds,
> and the will of Zeus was moving toward its end.
> Begin, Muse, when the two first broke and clashed,
> Agamemnon lord of men and brilliant Achilles.
>
> What god drove them to fight with such a fury?
> Apollo the son of Zeus and Leto. Incensed at the king he
> swept a fatal plague through the army—men were dying
> and all because Agamemnon spurned Apollo's priest.
> Yes, Chryses approached the Achaeans' fast ships
> to win his daughter back, bringing a priceless ransom
> and bearing high in hand, wound on a golden staff,
> the wreaths of the god, the distant deadly Archer.
> he begged the whole Achaean army but most of all
> the two supreme commanders, Atreus' two sons,
> "Agamemnon, Menelaus—all Argives geared for war!
> May the Gods who hold the halls of Olympus give you
> Priam's city to plunder, then safe passage home.
> Just set my daughter free, my dear one . . . here,
> accept these gifts, this ransom. Honor the god
> who strikes from worlds away—the son of Zeus, Apollo!"
>
> And all ranks of Achaeans cried out their assent:
> "Respect the priest, accept the shining ransom!"
> But it brought no joy to the heart of Agamemnon.
> The king dismissed the priest with a brutal order
> ringing in his ears: "Never again, old man,
> let me catch sight of you by the hollow ships!

---

[3] Special provisions were made for daughters when no brothers were available to inhereit.
[4] The father's kinship group, sometimes translated 'tribe' or 'clan.'

Not loitering now, not slinking back tomorrow.
The staff and the wreaths of god will never save you then.
The girl—I won't give up the girl. Long before that,
old age will overtake her in *my* house, in Argos,
far from her fatherland, slaving back and forth
at the loom, forced to share my bed!

No go,
don't tempt my wrath—and you may depart alive."

The old man was terrified. He obeyed the order,
turning, trailing away in silence down the shore
where the roaring battle lines of breakers crash and drag.
And moving off to a safe distance, over and over
the old priest prayed to the son of sleek-haired Leto,
lord Apollo, "Hear me, Apollo! God of the silver bow
who strides the walls of Chryse and Cilla sacrosanct—
lord in power of Tenedos—Smintheus,
god of the plague!
If I ever roofed a shrine to please your heart,
ever burned the long rich bones of bulls and goats
on your holy altar, now, now bring my prayer to pass.
Pay the Danaans back—your arrows for my tears!"

His prayer went up and Phoebus Apollo heard him.
Down he strode from Olympus' peaks, storming at heart
with his bow and hooded quiver slung across his shoulders.
The arrows clanged at his back at the god quaked with rage,
the god himself on the march and down he came like night.
Over against the ships he dropped to a knee, let fly a shaft
and a terrifying clash rang out from the great silver bow.
First he went for the mules and circling dogs but then,
launching a piercing shaft at the men themselves,
he cut them down in droves—
and the corpse-fires burned on, night and day,
no end in sight.

Nine days the arrows of god swept through the army.
On the tenth Achilles called all ranks to muster—
the impulse seized him, sent by white-armed Hera
grieving to see Achaean fighters drop and die.
Once they'd gathered, crowding the meeting grounds,
the swift runner Achilles rose and spoke among them:
"Son of Atreus, now we are beaten back, I fear,
the long campaign is lost. So home we sail . . .
if we can escape our death—if war and plague
are joining forces now to crush the Argives.
But wait: let us question a holy man,
a prophet, even a man skilled with dreams—
dreams as well can come our way from Zeus—
come, someone to tell us why Apollo rages so,
whether he blames us for a vow we failed, or sacrifice.
If only the god would share the smoky savor of limbs
and full-grown goats, Apollo might be willing, still,
somehow, to save us from this plague."

So he proposed
and down he sat again as Calchas rose among them,
Thestor's son, the clearest by far of all the seers
who scan the flight of birds. He knew all things that are,
all things that are past and all that are to come,
the seer who had led the Argive ships to Troy
with the second sight that god Apollo gave him.
For the armies' good the seer began to speak:
"Achilles, dear to Zeus . . .
you order me to explain Apollo's anger,
the distant deadly Archer? I will tell it all.
But strike a pact with me, swear you will defend me
with all your heart, with words and strength of hand.
For there is a man I will enrage—I see it now—
a powerful man who lords it over all the Argives,
one the Achaeans must obey . . . A mighty king,
raging against an inferior, is too strong.
Even if he can swallow down his wrath today,
still he will nurse the burning in his chest
until, sooner or later, he sends it bursting forth.
Consider it closely, Achilles. Will you save me?"

And the matchless runner reassured him: "Courage!
Out with it now, Calchas. Reveal the will of god,
whatever you may know. And I swear by Apollo
dear to Zeus, the power you pray to, Calchas,
when you reveal god's will to the Argives—no one,
not while I am alive and see the light on earth, no one will
lay his heavy hands on you by the hollow ships.
None among all the armies. Not even if you mean
Agamemnon here who now claims to be, by far,
the best of the Achaeans."
The seer took heart
and this time he spoke out, bravely: "Beware—
he casts no blame for a vow we failed, a sacrifice.
The god's enraged because Agamemnon spurned his priest,
he refused to free his daughter, he refused the ransom.
That's why the Archer sends us pains
and he will send us more
and never drive this shameful destruction from the Argives,
not till we give back the girl with sparkling eyes
to her loving father—no price, no ransom paid—
and carry a sacred hundred bulls to Chryse town.
Then we can calm the god, and only then appease him."

Questions:
1. What is the role of the Gods in this reading?
2. What virtues are important to the ancient Greeks?

2.3 Historical Methods: Thucydides

Thucydides' great historical work was his History of the Peloponnesian Wars that he experienced first-hand. Here he explains his reason for writing about them and the method he pursued in the task.

Source: Thucydides, *History of the Peloponnesian Wars,* trans. Rex Warner, (New York: Penguin, 1954, revised 1972), pp. 35-39, 45-48.

Book One: Introduction

Thucydides the Athenian wrote the history of the war fought between Athens and Sparta, beginning the account at the very outbreak of the war, in the belief that it was going to be a great war and more worth writing about than any. of those which had taken lace in the past. My belief was based on the fact that the two sides were at the very height of their power and preparedness and I saw, too, that the rest of the Hellenic world was committed to one side or the other; even those who were not immediately engaged were deliberating on the courses which they were to take later. This was the greatest disturbance in the history of the Hellenes,1 affecting also a large part of the non-Hellenic world, and indeed, I might almost say, the whole of mankind. For though I have found it impossible, because of its remoteness in time, to acquire a really precise knowledge of the distant past or even of the history preceding our own period, yet, after looking back into it as far as I can, all the evidence leads me to conclude that these periods were not great periods either in warfare or in anything else.

It appears, for example, that the country now called Hellas had no settled population in ancient times; instead there was a series of migrations, as the various tribes, being under the constant pressure of invaders who were stronger than they were, were always prepared to abandon their own territory. There was no commerce, and no safe communication either by land or sea; the use they made of their land was limited to the production of necessities; they had no surplus left over for capital, and no regular system of agriculture, since they lacked the protection of fortifications and at any moment an invader might appear and take their land away from them. Thus, in the belief that the day-to-day necessities of life could be secured just as well in one place as in another, they showed no reluctance in moving from their homes, and therefore built no cities of any size or strength, nor acquired any important resources....

In investigating past history, and in forming the conclusions which I have formed, it must be admitted that one cannot rely on every detail which has come down to us by way of tradition. People are inclined to accept all stories of ancient times in an uncritical way-even when these stories concern their own native countries. Most people in Athens, for instance, are under the impression that Hipparchus, who was killed by Harmodius and Aristogiton, was tyrant at the time, not realizing that it was Hippias who was the eldest and the chief of the sons of Pisistratus, and that Hipparchus and Thessalus were his younger brothers. What happened was this; on the very day that had been fixed for their attempt, indeed at the very last moment, Harmodius and Aristogeiton had reason to believe that Hippias had been informed of the plot by some of the conspirators. Believing him to have been forewarned, they kept away from him, but, as they wanted to perform some daring exploit before they were arrested themselves, they killed Hipparchus when they found him by the Leocorium organizing the Panathenaic procession.

The rest of the Hellenes, too, make many incorrect assumptions not only about the dimly remembered past, but also about contemporary history. For instance, there is a general belief that the kings of Sparta are each entitled to two votes, whereas in fact they have only one; and it is believed, too, that the Spartans have a company of troops called 'Pitanate'. Such a company has never existed. Most people in fact, will not take trouble in finding out the truth, but are much more inclined to accept the first story they hear.

However, I do not think that one will be far wrong in accepting the conclusions I have reached from the evidence which I have put forward. It is better evidence than that of the poets, who exaggerate the importance of their themes, or of the prose chroniclers, who are less interested in telling the truth than in catching the attention of their public, whose authorities cannot be checked, and whose subject-matter, owing to the passage of time, is mostly lost in the unreliable streams of mythology. We may claim instead to have used only the plainest evidence and to have reached conclusions which are reasonably accurate, considering that we have been dealing with ancient history. As for this present war, even though people are apt to think that the war in which they are fighting is the greatest of all wars and, when it is over, to relapse again into their admiration of the past, nevertheless, if one looks at the facts themselves, one will see that this was the greatest war of all.

In this history I have made use of set speeches some of which were delivered just before and others during the war. I have found it difficult to remember the precise words used in the speeches which I listened to myself and my various informants have experienced the same difficulty; so my method has been, while keeping as closely as possible to the general sense of the words that were actually used, to make the speakers say what in my opinion, was called for by each situation....

And with regard to my factual reporting of the events of the war I have made it a principle not to write down the first story that came my way, and not even to be guided by my own general impressions; either I was present myself at the events which I have described or else I heard of them from eye-witnesses whose reports I have checked with as much thoroughness as possible, Not that even so the truth was easy to discover: different eye-witnesses give different accounts of the same events, speaking out of partiality for one side or the other or else from imperfect memories. And it may well be that my history will seem less easy to read because of the absence in it of a romantic element. It will be enough for me, however, if these words of mine are judged useful by those who want to understand clearly the events which happened in the past and which (human nature being what it is) will, at some time or other and in much the same ways, be repeated in the future. My work is not a piece of writing designed to meet the taste of an immediate public, but was done to last forever.

Questions:
1. What is Thucydides' goal and what method did he use to reach it?
2. If Thucydides were to apply his method of examination to our own state and history, how do you think he would be regarded by the public?

2.4 Tyrtaeus, *The Spartan Creed*

Tyrtaeus (7th Century B.C.E.) was a Greek poet who lived in Sparta. Many of his poems were meant to inspire the Spartans to victory in war. Some say he was a Spartan general, but according to Athenian legend he was a lame schoolmaster.

Source: *The Norton Book of Classical Literature,* ed. Bernard Knox (New York: W. W. Norton & Co., 1993), pp. 211–212.

I would not say anything for a man nor take account of him for any speed of his feet or
    wrestling skill he might have,
not if he had the size of a Cyclops and strength to go with it, not if he could outrun
    Bóreas, the North Wind of Thrace,
not if he were more handsome and gracefully formed than Tithónos, or had more riches
    than Midas had, or Kínyras too,
not if he were more of a king than Tantalid Pelops, or had the power of speech and per-
    suasion Adrastos had,
not if he had all splendors except for a fighting spirit. For no man ever proves himself a
    good man in war
unless he can endure to face the blood and the slaughter, go close against the enemy
    and fight with his hands.
Here is courage, mankind's finest possession, here is the noblest prize that a young man
    can endeavor to win,
and it is a good thing his city and all the people share with him when a man plants his
    feet and stands in the foremost spears
relentlessly, all thought of foul flight completely forgotten, and has well trained his
    heart to be steadfast and to endure,
and with words encourages the man who is stationed beside him. Here is a man who
    proves himself to be valiant in war.
With a sudden rush he turns to flight the rugged battalions of the enemy, and sustains
    the beating waves of assault.
And he who so falls among the champions and loses his sweet life, so blessing with
    honor his city, his father, and all his people,
with wounds in his chest, where the spear that he was facing has transfixed
that massive guard of his shield, and gone through his breastplate as well,
why, such a man is lamented alike by the young and the elders, and all his city goes
    into mourning and grieves for his loss.
His tomb is pointed to with pride, and so are his children, and his children's children,
    and afterward all the race that is his.
His shining glory is never forgotten, his name is remembered, and he becomes an
    immortal, though he lies under the ground,
when one who was a brave man has been killed by the furious War God
standing his ground and fighting hard for his children and land.
But if he escapes the doom of death, the destroyer of bodies, and wins his battle, and
    bright renown for the work of his spear,
all men give place to him alike, the youth and the elders, and much joy comes his way
    before he goes down to the dead.
Aging, he has reputation among his citizens. No one tries to interfere with his honors or
    all he deserves;

all men withdraw before his presence, and yield their seats to him, the youth, and the
men his age, and even those older than he.
Thus a man should endeavor to reach this high place of courage with all his heart, and,
so trying, never be backward in war.

Translated by Richmond Lattimore.

Question:
1. What is the main virtue of the Spartan citizen?

2.5 Education and the Family in Sparta

By the fifth century B.C.E. in Athens, young men of respectable family were educated at schools and by tutors to be good citizens and daughters were rarely educated beyond their domestic duties in the household. All children's lives and their educations remained under the control of their fathers. Sparta developed an entirely different system for raising their next generation of citizens.

Source: *Plutarch's Lives,* trans. John Dryden, revised by A.H. Clough, Vol. 1. (New York: Little, Brown and Company, 1909), pp. 100-119.

In order to the good education of their youth (which, as I said before, he thought the most important and noblest work of a lawgiver), [Lycurgus] went so far back as to take into consideration their very conception and birth, by regulating their marriages. For Aristotle is wrong in saying, that, after he had tried all ways to reduce the women to more modesty and sobriety, he was at last forced to leave them as they were, because that, in the absence of their husbands, who spent the best part of their lives in the wars, their wives, whom they were obliged to leave absolute mistresses at home, took great liberties and assumed the superiority; and were treated with overmuch respect and called by the title of lady or queen. The truth is, he took in their case, also, all the care that was possible; he ordered the maidens to exercise themselves with wrestling, running, throwing the quoit, and casting the dart, to the end that the fruit they conceived might, in strong and healthy bodies, take firmer root and find better growth, and withal that they, with this greater vigor, might be the more able to undergo the pains of child-bearing. And to the end he might take away their over-great tenderness and fear of exposure to the air, and all acquired womanishness, he ordered that the young women should go naked in the processions, as well as the young men, and dance, too, in that condition, at certain solemn feasts, singing certain songs, whilst the young men stood around, seeing and hearing them. On these occasions, they now and then made, by jests, a befitting reflection upon those who had misbehaved themselves in the wars; and again sang encomiums upon those who had done any gallant action, and by these means inspired the younger sort with an emulation of their glory. Those that were thus commended went away proud, elated, and gratified with their honor among the maidens; and those who were rallied were as sensibly touched with it 'As if they had been formally reprimanded; and so much the more, because the kings and the elders, as well as the rest of the city, saw and heard all that passed. Nor was there any thing shameful in this nakedness of the young women; modesty attended them, and all wantonness was excluded. It taught them simplicity and a care for good health, and gave them some taste of higher feelings, admitted as they thus were to the field of noble action and glory. Hence it was natural for them to think and speak as Gorgo, for example, the wife of Leonidas, is said to have done, when -some foreign lady, as it would seem, told her that the women of Lacedæmon were the only women of the world who could rule men; "With good reason," she said, "for we are the only women who bring forth men."

These public processions of the maidens, and their appearing naked in their exercises and dancings, were incitements to marriage, operating upon the young with the rigor and certainty, as Plato says, of love, if not of mathematics. But besides all this, to promote it yet more effectually, those who continued bachelors were in a degree disfranchised by law; for they were excluded from the sight of those public processions in which the young men and maidens danced naked, and, in wintertime, the officers compelled them to march naked themselves round the market-place, singing as they went a certain song to their own disgrace, that they justly suffered this punishment for disobeying the laws. Moreover, they were denied that respect and observance which the younger men paid their elders; and no man, for example, found fault with what was said to Dercyllidas, though so eminent a commander; upon whose approach one day, a young man, instead of rising, retained his seat, remarking, "No child of yours will make room for me."

In their marriages, the husband carried off his bride by a sort of force; nor were their brides ever small and of tender years, but in their full bloom and ripeness. After this, she who superintended the wedding comes and clips the hair of the bride close round her head, dresses her up in man's clothes, and leaves her upon a mattress in the dark; afterwards comes the bridegroom, in his every-day clothes, sober and composed, as having supped at the common table, and, entering privately into the room where the bride lies, unties her virgin zone, and takes her to himself; and, after staying some time together, he returns composedly to his own apartment, to sleep as usual with the other young men. And so he continues to do, spending his days, and, indeed, his nights with them, visiting his bride in fear and shame, and with circumspection, when he thought he should not be observed; she, also, on her part, using her wit to help and find favorable opportunities for their meeting, when company was out of the way. In this manner they lived a long time, insomuch that they sometimes had children by their wives before ever they saw their faces by daylight. Their interviews, being thus difficult and rare, served not only for continual exercise of their self-control, but brought them together with their bodies healthy and vigorous, and their affections fresh and lively, unsated and undulled by easy access and long continuance with each other; while their partings were always early enough to leave behind unextinguished in each of them some remainder fire of longing and mutual delight. After guarding marriage with this modesty and reserve, he was equally careful to banish empty and womanish jealousy. For this object, excluding all licentious disorders, he made it, nevertheless, honorable for men to give the use of their wives to those whom they should think fit, that so they might have children by them; ridiculing those in whose opinion such favors are so unfit for participation as to fight and shed blood and go to war about it. Lycurgus allowed a man who was advanced in years and had a young wife to recommend some virtuous and approved young man, that she might have a child by him, who might inherit the good qualities of the father, and be a son to himself. On the other side, an honest man who had love for a married woman upon account of her modesty and the wellfavoredness of her children, might, without formality, beg her company of her husband, that he might raise, as it were, from this plot of good ground, worthy and well-allied children for himself. And, indeed, Lycurgus was of a persuasion that children were not so much the property of their parents as of the whole commonwealth, and, therefore, would not have his citizens begot by the first comers, but by the best men that could be found; the laws of other nations seemed to him very absurd and inconsistent, where people would be so solicitous for their dogs and horses as to exert interest and pay money to procure fine breeding, and yet kept their wives shut up, to be made mothers only by themselves, who might be foolish, infirm, or diseased; as if it were not apparent that children of a bad breed would prove their bad qualities first upon those who kept and were rearing them, and well-born children, in like manner, their good qualities.

... Nor was it in the power of the father to dispose of the child as he thought fit; he was obliged to carry it before certain triers at a place called Lesche ; these were some of the elders of the tribe to which the child belonged; their business it was carefully to view the infant, and, if they found it stout and well made, they gave order for its rearing, and allotted to it one of the nine thousand shares of land above mentioned for its maintenance, but, if they found it puny and ill-shaped, ordered it to be taken to what was called the Apothetæ, a sort of chasm under Taygetus; as thinking it neither for the good of the child itself; nor for the public interest, that it should be brought up, if it did not, from the very outset, appear made to be healthy and vigorous. Upon the same account, the women did not bathe the new-born children with water, as is the custom in all other countries, but with wine, to prove the temper and complexion of their bodies; from a notion they had that epileptic and weakly children faint and waste away upon their being thus bathed, while, on the contrary, those of strong and vigorous habit acquire firmness and get a temper by it, like steel. There was much care and art, too, used by the nurses; they had no swaddling bands; the children grew up free and unconstrained in limb and form, and not dainty and fanciful about their food; not afraid in the dark, or of being left alone; without any peevishness or ill humor or crying....

... Nor was it lawful, indeed, for the father himself to breed up the children after his own fancy; but as soon as they were seven years old they were to be enrolled in certain companies and classes, where they all lived under the same order and discipline, doing their exercises and taking their play together. Of these, he who showed the most conduct and courage was made captain; they had their eyes always upon him, obeyed his orders, and underwent patiently whatsoever punishment he inflicted; so that the whole course of their education was one continued exercise of a ready and perfect obedience. The old men, too, were spectators of their performances, and often raised quarrels and disputes among them, to have a good opportunity of finding out their different characters, and of seeing which would be valiant, which a coward, when they should come to more dangerous encounters. Reading and writing they gave them, just enough to serve their turn; their chief care was to make them good subjects, and to teach them to endure pain and conquer in battle. To this end, as they grew in years, their discipline was proportionally increased; their heads were close-clipped, they were accustomed to go bare-foot, and for the most part to play naked.

After they were twelve years old, they were no longer allowed to wear any under-garment; they had one coat to serve them a year; their bodies were hard and dry, with but little acquaintance of baths and unguents; these human indulgences they were allowed only on some few particular days in the year. They lodged together in little bands upon beds made of the rushes which grew by the banks of the river Eurotas, which they were to break off with their hands without a knife; if it were winter, they mingled some thistle-down with their rushes, which it was thought had the property of giving warmth. By the time they were come to this age, there was not any of the more hopeful boys who had not a lover to bear him company. The old men, too, had an eye upon them, coming often to the grounds to hear and see them contend either in wit or strength with one another, and this as seriously and with as much concern as if they were their fathers, their tutors, or their magistrates; so that there scarcely was any time or place without some one present to put them in mind of their duty, and punish them if they had neglected it.

Besides all this, there was always one of the best and honestest men in the city appointed to undertake the charge and governance of them; he again arranged them into their several bands, and set over each of them for their captain the most temperate and boldest of those... who were usually twenty years old.... This young man, therefore, was their captain when they fought, and their master at home, using them for the offices of his house; sending the oldest of them to fetch wood, and the weaker and less able, to gather salads and herbs, and these they must either go without or steal; which they did by creeping into the gardens, or conveying themselves cunningly and closely into the eating-houses; if they were taken in the fact, they were whipped without mercy, for thieving so ill and awkwardly. They stole, too, all other meat they could lay their hands on, looking out and watching all opportunities, when people were asleep or more careless than usual. If they were caught, they were not only punished with whipping, but hunger, too, being reduced to their ordinary allowance, which was but very slender, and so contrived on purpose, that they might set about to help themselves, and be forced to exercise their energy and address. This was the principal design of their hard fare; there was another not inconsiderable, that they might grow taller; for the vital spirits, not being overburdened and oppressed by too great a quantity of nourishment, which necessarily discharges itself into thickness and breadth, do, by their natural lightness, rise; and the body, giving and yielding because it is pliant, grows in height. The same thing seems, also, to conduce to beauty of shape;...

They taught them, also, to speak with a natural and graceful raillery, and to comprehend much matter of thought in few words. For Lycurgus, who ordered, as we saw, that a great piece of money should be but of an inconsiderable value, on the contrary would allow no discourse to be current which did not contain in few words a great deal of useful and curious sense; children in Sparta, by a habit of long silence, came to give just and sententious answers; for, indeed, as loose and incontinent livers are seldom fathers of many children, so loose and incontinent talkers seldom originate many sensible words. King Agis, when some Athenian laughed at their short swords, and said that the jugglers on the stage swallowed them with ease, answered him, "We find them long enough to reach our enemies with;" and as their swords were short and sharp, so, it seems to me, were their sayings....

... Nor was their instruction in music and verse less carefully attended to than their habits of grace and good breeding in conversation. And their very songs had a life and spirit in them that inflamed and possessed men's minds with an enthusiasm and ardor for action; the style of them was plain and without affectation; the subject always serious and moral; most usually, it was in praise of such men as had died in defence of their country, or in derision of those that had been cowards; the former they declared happy and glorified; the life of the latter they described as most miserable and abject. There were also vaunts of what they would do and boasts of what they had done...

Their discipline continued still after they were full-grown men. No one was allowed to live after his own fancy; but the city was a sort of camp, in which every man had his share of provisions and business set out, and looked upon himself not so much born to serve his own ends as the interest of his country. Therefore, if they were commanded nothing else, they went to see the boys perform their exercises, to teach them something useful, or to learn it themselves of those who knew better. And, indeed, one of the greatest and highest blessings Lycurgus procured his people was the abundance of leisure, which proceeded from his forbidding to them the exercise of any mean and mechanical trade. Of the money-making that depends on troublesome going about and seeing people and doing business, they had no need at all in a state where wealth obtained no honor or respect. The Helots tilled their ground for them, and paid them yearly in kind the appointed quantity, without any trouble of theirs.... So much beneath them did they esteem the frivolous devotion of time and attention to the mechanical arts and to money-making.

... To conclude, he bred up his citizens in such a way that they neither would nor could live by themselves; they were to make themselves one with the public good, and, clustering like bees around their commander, be by their zeal and public spirit carried all but out of themselves, and devoted wholly to their country....

He filled Lacedæmon all through with roofs and examples of good conduct; with the constant sight of which from their youth up, the people would hardly fail to be gradually formed and advanced in virtue.

And this was the reason why he forbade them to travel abroad, and go about acquainting themselves with foreign rules of morality, the habits of ill-educated people, and different views of government.... He was as careful to save his city from the infection of foreign bad habits, as men usually are to prevent the introduction of a pestilence.

Questions:
1. What rights did husbands and fathers have over their families in Sparta?
2. Read document 2.1, "Laws Relating to Women: Excerpts from the Gortyn Law Code" and describe how these documents illustrate the differences in the lives of women and the institution of marriage in Crete and Sparta.
3. What do these documents reveal about the lives of servants or slaves in these societies?

2.6   Poetry: Sappho

Sappho, believed to have been born about 612 B.C.E., wrote exquisite poetry praised throughout the ages for its perfection. Mother, wife, poet, dancer, teacher, Sappho's character has long been a subject for debate. In her sixth century B.C.E. society, respectable women attended school and enjoyed far more freedoms than their nearly cloistered fifth century Athenian sisters.

Source: Sappho, Poems: Containing nearly all the Fragments printed from the restored Greek texts, trans. P. Maurice Hill, (London: Staples, 1953), pp. 9, 19, 25, 43, 55, 63.

24 REVERENCE FOR BEAUTY

For when I look upon you face to face, then I see in you
such beauty as not even Hermione possessed,
but I compare you with auburn-haired Helen,
rather than with mortal maids-though even
that is only a guess.

But understand this, that I am so struck with
your beauty that I can only render honour to it with the
sacrifice of my mind, and reverence you with my desire
for your company.

77 SOCIAL CLIMBING (A LETTER TO HER BROTHER, CHARAXOS)

If you crawl round the feet of the great instead
of the beautiful and the good, and bid your friends farewell,
and in the swollen pride of your heart say that I have
become a disgrace to you-with such things you can
flatter your heart. Feed your fill! For my mind is not so softly moved
by the petulance of a child! But make no mistake. The snare never catches
the old bird. I have put two and two together and know well the depth
of your former villainy, and what sort of enemy I am up against. So turn
your mind to better thoughts.
For, assuredly, I know that having been brought up to be kindly of heart,
I have the Blessed Ones on my side.

35 TO HER PUPILS

You slight the fair gifts of the
deep-bosomed Muses, children,
when you say 'We will crown
you, dear [Sappho], as first of
singers with the clear sweet
voice'.

Do you not realise that age has
wrinkled all my skin, that my
hair has become white from
being black, and that I have
hardly any teeth left; or that my
knees can no longer carry my body back
again to the old days when
I joined in the dance, like
the fawns, the nimblest
of living things?

But what can I do? Not even
God himself can do what
cannot be done. And, for us, as
unfailingly as starry
night follows rosy-armed
morning, and brings darkness to the
furthest ends of the earth, so
death tracks down and
overtakes every living thing;
and as he himself would not
give Orpheus his dearest wife,
so is he ever used to keep
prisoner every woman whom
he overtakes, even if he should
make her follow her spouse with
his singing and piping.

But listen now-I love
delicate living, and for me
brightness and beauty and a longing
for the sunlight have been
given me as a protection.
And, therefore, I have no
intention of departing to the
Grace of God before I need,
but will lovingly pursue my
life with you who love me.

And now this is enough
for me that I have your
love, and I desire no more.

51 THE APPLE

As the sweet apple reddens on
the top of the bough,
On the very topmost twig,
Which the apple-pickers had forgotten-
No, not forgotten, but
they could not reach it!

52 THE BLUEBELLS

As on the slopes, shepherd-men
trampled the bluebells underfoot,
and the flowers stain the earth with
colour.

60 THE GIRDLE

She wore an embroidered leather
girdle, the ends of which reached
down to her feet, a beautiful
piece of Lydian workmanship.

61 LOVE-SICKNESS

Sweet Mother, I cannot play the loom,
For I am overcome by my desire for a boy;
And all the fault of tender Aphrodite!

62 SELF RESTRAINT

When anger spread through your
breast, guard your tongue
from nagging.

65 THE FISHERMAN

On the grave of Pelagon, the
fisherman, his father Meniscos placed
a net and oar-witnesses to his life
of toil.

66 EPITAPH

Here lies the dust of timas, who died
upon her wedding eve; Persephone took
her into her sea-dark chamber.
And when she died, all her companions
sheared their lovely locks with the
sharp steel
And placed them on her tomb.

67 DEATH

Death is an evil. The gods have judged
it so. For otherwise they had died themselves.

68 THE PHILISTINE

Thou shalt be dead for ever,
Nor shall anything be remembered
of thee either now or at any time.
For thou hast scorned the roses of Poetry;
Therefore shalt thou go wandering about
among the feeble ghosts in the halls of Death.

Question:
1. What are the themes and topics of Sappho's poetry? What do they reveal about her life?

2.7 Alcaeus, Late 7th Century—Middle 6th Century B.C.

A contemporary and associate of Sappho, Alcaeus of Lesbos was an aristocrat and poet. His work reflects the violence and chaos of the times in which he lived. His poetry ranged from political odes to drinking songs.

Source: *The Norton Book of Classical Literature,* ed. Bernard Knox (New York: W.W. Norton & Co., 1993) pp. 220–223.

1

Wash your gullet with wine for the Dog-Star returns
with the heat of summer searing a thirsting earth.

Cicadas cry softly under high leaves, and pour down
shrill song incessantly from under their wings.
The artichoke blooms, and women are warn and wanton—
but men turn lean and limp for the burning Dog-
Star parches their brains and knees.

2

Come with me now and leave the land of
Pelops, mighty sons of Zeus and Leda,
and in kindness spread your light on us,
Kastor and Polydeukes.
You who wander above the long earth
and over all the seas on swift horses,
easily delivering mariners
from pitiful death,
fly to the masthead of our swift ship,
and gazing over foremast and forestays,
light a clear path through the midnight gloom
for our black vessel.

3

You have come home from the ends of the earth,
Antimenidas, my dear brother; come
with a gold and ivory handle to your sword.
You fought alongside the Babylonians
and your prowess saved them from annihilation
when you battled and cut down a warrior giant
who was almost eight feet tall.

4

One and all,
you have proclaimed Pittakos, the lowborn,
to be tyrant of your lifeless and doomed
land. Moreover, you deafen him with praise.

Translated by Willis Barnstone

5

The great hall is aglare with bronze armament and the
whole inside made fit for war
with helms glittering and hung high, crested over with
white horse-manes that nod and wave
and make splendid the heads of men who wear them. Here
are shining greaves made out of bronze,
hung on hooks, and they cover all the house's side. They
are strong to stop arrows and spears.
Hear are war-jackets quilted close of new linen, with
hollow shields stacked on the floor,
with broad swords of the Chalkis make, many tunics and
many belts heaped close beside.
These shall not lie neglected, now we have stood to our
task and have this work to do.

6

I cannot understand how the winds are set
against each other. Now from the side and now from that
the waves roll. We between them run with the wind
in our black ship driven,
hard pressed and laboring under the giant storm.
All round the mast-step washes the sea we shipped.
You can see through the sail already
where there are opening rents within it.
The forestays slacken. . . .

7

Zeus rains upon us, and from the sky comes down
enormous winter. Rivers have turned to ice. . . .
Dash down the winter. Throw a log on the fire
and mix the flattering wine (do not water it
too much) and bind on round our foreheads
soft ceremonial wreaths of spun fleece.
We must not let our spirits give way to grief.
By being sorry we get no further on,
my Bukchis. Best of all defenses
is to mix plenty of wine, and drink it.

Translated by Richmond Lattimore

Question:
1. *Alcaeus was a member of the artistocracy writing during turbulent times. How is this reflected in this section?*

PART 3
Classical and Hellenistic Civilization

3.1 *The Apology* from Plato

A pupil of Socrates and Aristotle's teacher, Plato (c. 427-347 B.C.E.) is one of the most influential thinkers in the history of Western Civilization. His ideas about the nature of existence and virtue played important roles in the development of Western philosophy, science, and theology. In The Apology Plato presents a defense of his mentor Socrates.

> **Source:** *Plato: The Collected Dialogues*, Edith Hamilton and Huntington Cairns, eds. (Princeton: University Press, 1961), pp. 5–19.

Very well, then, I must begin my defense, gentlemen, and I must try, in the short time that I have, to rid your minds of a false impression which is the work of many years. I should like this to be the result, gentlemen, assuming it to be for your advantage and my own; and I should like to be successful in my defense, but I think that it will be difficult, and I am quite aware of the nature of my task. However, let that turn out as God wills. I must obey the law and make my defense.

Let us go back to the beginning and consider what the charge is that has made me so unpopular, and has encouraged Meletus to draw up this indictment. Very well, what did my critics say in attacking my character? I must read out their affidavit, so to speak, as though they were my legal accusers: Socrates is guilty of criminal meddling, in that he inquires into things below the earth and in the sky, and makes the weaker argument defeat the stronger, and teachers others to follow his example. It runs something like that. You have seen it for yourselves in the play by Aristophanes, where Socrates goes whirling round, proclaiming that he is walking on air, and uttering a great deal of other nonsense about things of which I know nothing whatsoever. I mean no disrespect for such knowledge, if anyone really is versed in it—I do not want any more lawsuits brought against me by answer questions for rich and poor alike, and I am equally ready if anyone prefers to listen to me and answer my questions. If any given one of these people becomes a good citizen or a bad one, I cannot fairly be held responsible, since I have never promised or imparted any teaching to anybody, and if anyone asserts that he has ever learned or heard from me privately anything which was not open to everyone else, you may be quite sure that he is not telling the truth.

But how is it that some people enjoy spending a great deal of time in my company? You have heard the reason, gentlemen; I told you quite frankly. It is because they enjoy hearing me examine those who think that they are wise when they are not—an experience which has its amusing side. This duty I have accepted, as I said, in obedience to God's commands given in oracles and dreams and in every other way that any other divine dispensation has ever impressed a duty upon man. This is a true statement, gentlemen, and easy to verify. If it is a fact that I am in process of corrupting some of the young, and have succeeded already in corrupting others, and if it were a fact that some of the latter, being now grown up, had discovered that I had ever given them bad advice when they were young, surely they ought now to be coming forward to denounce and punish me. And if they did not like to do it themselves, you would expect some of their families— their fathers and brothers and other near relations—to remember it now, if their own flesh and blood had suffered any harm from me. Certainly a great many of them have found their way into this court, as I can see for myself—first Crito over there, my contemporary and near neighbor, the father of this young man Critobulus, and then Lysanias of Sphettus, the father of Aeschines here, and next Antiphon of Cephisus, over there, the father of Epigenes. Then besides there are all those whose brothers have been members of our circle—Nicostratus, the son of Theozotides, the brother of Theodotus, but Theodotus is dead, so he cannot appeal to his brother, and Paralus here, the son of Demodocus, whose brother was Theages. And here is Adimantus, the son of Ariston, whose brother Plato is over there, and Aeantodorus, whose brother Apollodorus is here on this side. I can name many more besides, some of whom Meletus most certainly ought to have produced as witnesses in the course of his speech. If he forgot to do so then, let him do it now—I am willing to make way for him. Let him state whether he has any such evidence to offer. On the contrary, gentlemen, you will find that they are all prepared to help me—the corrupter and evil genius of their nearest and dearest relatives, as Meletus and Anytus say. The actual victims of my corrupting influence might perhaps be excused for helping me; but as for the uncorrupted, their relations of mature age, what other reason can they have for helping me except the right and proper one, that they know Meletus is lying and I am telling the truth?

Questions:
1. What is the mission of Socrates?
2. Why does it arouse such opposition?

3.2   Aristotle, *Nichomachean Ethics*

Aristotle (384-322 B.C.E.) was born in the Greek town of Stagira. After studying under Plato at the Academy, he tutored Alexander the Great and then opened a school of his own in the Lyceum in Athens. In the selection from the Nichomachean Ethics included below, Aristotle defines virtue and vice.

> **Source:** *Introduction to Aristotle*, (Modern Library Series), ed. Richard McKeon (New York: Random House, 1992), pp. 358–367.

5 Next we must consider what virtue is. Since things that are found in the soul are of three kinds—passions, faculties, states of character, virtue must be one of these. By passions I mean appetite, anger, fear, confidence, envy, joy, friendly feeling, hatred, longing, emulation, pity, and in general the feelings that are accompanied by pleasure or pain; by faculties the things in virtue of which we are said to be capable of feeling these, e. g. of becoming angry or being pained or feeling pity; by states of character the things in virtue of which we stand well or badly with reference to the *passions*, e. g. with reference to anger we stand badly if we feel it violently or too weakly, and well if we feel it moderately; and similarly with reference to the other passions.

Now neither the virtues nor the vices are passions, because we are not called good or bad on the ground of our passions, but are so called on the ground of our virtues and our vices, and because we are neither praised nor blamed for our passions (for the man who feels fear or anger is not praised, nor is the man who simply feels anger blamed, but the man who feels it in a certain way), but for our virtues and our vices are *are* praised or blamed.

Again, we feel anger and fear without choice, but the virtues are modes of choice or involve choice. Further, in respect of the passions we are said to be moved, but in respect of the virtues and the vices we are said not to be moved but to be disposed in a particular way.

For these reasons also they are not *faculties*; for we are neither called good nor bad, nor praised or blamed, for the simple capacity of feeling the passions; again, we have the faculties by nature, but we are not made good or bad by nature; we have spoken of this before.[1]

If, then, the virtues are neither passions nor faculties, all that remains is that they should be *states of character*.

Thus we have stated what virtue is in respect of its genus.

6 We must, however, not only describe virtue as a state of character, but also say what sort of state it is. We may remark, then, that every virtue or excellence both brings into good condition the thing of which it is the excellence and makes the work of that thing be done well; e. g. the excellence of the eye makes both the eye and its work good; for it is by the excellence of the eye that we see well. Similarly the excellence of the horse makes a horse both good in itself and good at running and at carrying its rider and at awaiting the attack of the enemy. Therefore, if this is true in every case, the virtue of man also will be the state of character which makes a man good and which makes him do his own work well.

How this is to happen we have stated already,[2] but it will be made plain also by the following consideration of the specific nature of virtue. In everything that is continuous and divisible it is possible to take more, less, or an equal amount, and that either in terms of the thing itself or relatively to us; and the equal is an intermediate between excess and defect. By the intermediate in the object I mean that which is equidistant from each of the extremes, which is one and the same for all men; by the intermediate relatively to us that which is neither too much nor too little—and this is not one, nor the same for all. For instance, if ten is many and two is few, six is the intermediate, taken in terms of the object; for it exceeds and is exceeded by an equal amount; this is intermediate according to arithmetical proportion. But the intermediate relatively to us is not to be taken so; if ten pounds are too much for a particular person to eat and two too little, it does not follow that the trainer will order six pounds; for this also is perhaps too much for the person who is to take it, or too little— too little for Milo,[3] too much for the beginner in athletic exercises. The same is true of running and wrestling. Thus a master of any art avoids excess and defect, but seeks the intermediate and chooses this—the intermediate not in the object but relatively to us.

If it is thus, then, that every art does its work well—by looking to the intermediate and judging its works by this standard (so that we often say of good works of art that it is not possible either to take away or to add anything, implying that excess and defect destroy the goodness of works of art, while the mean preserves it; and good artists, as we say, look to this in their work), and if, further, virtue is more exact and better than any art, as nature also is, then virtue must have the quality of aiming at the intermediate. I mean moral virtue; for it is this that is concerned with passions and actions, and

---

[1] 1103ª 18–ᵇ 2.
[2] 1104ª 11–27.
[3] A famous wrestler.

in these there is excess, defect, and the intermediate. For instance, both fear and confidence and appetite and anger and pity and in general pleasure and pain may be felt both too much and too little, and in both cases not well; but to feel them at the right times, with reference to the right objects, towards the right people, with the right motive, and in the right way, is what is both intermediate and best, and this is characteristic of virtue. Similarly with regard to actions also there is excess, defect, and the intermediate. Now virtue is concerned with passions and actions, in which excess is a form of failure, and so is defect, while the intermediate is praised and is a form of success; and being praised and being successful are both characteristics of virtue. Therefore virtue is a kind of mean, since, as we have seen, it aims at what is intermediate.

Again, it is possible to fail in many ways (for evil belongs to the class of the unlimited, as the Pythagoreans conjectured, and good to that of the limited), while to succeed is possible only in one way (for which reason also one is easy and the other difficult—to miss the mark easy, to hit it difficult); for these reasons also, then, excess and defect are characteristic of vice, and the mean of virtue;

For men are good in but one way, but bad in many.

Virtue, then, is a state of character concerned with choice, lying in a mean, i. e. the mean relative to us, this being determined by a rational principle, and by that principle by which the man of practical wisdom would determine it. Now it is a mean between two vices, that which depends on excess and that which depends on defect; and again it is a mean because the vices respectively fall short of or exceed what is right in both passions and actions, while virtue both finds and chooses that which is intermediate. Hence in respect of its substance and the definition which states its essence virtue is a mean, with regard to what is best and right an extreme.

But not every action nor every passion admits of a mean; for some have names that already imply badness, e. g. spite, shamelessness, envy, and in the case of actions adultery, theft, murder; for all of these and suchlike things imply by their names that they are themselves bad, and not the excesses or deficiencies of them. it is not possible, then, ever to be right with regard to them; one must always be wrong. Nor does goodness or badness with regard to such things depend on committing adultery with the right woman, at the right time, and in the right way, but simply to do any of them is to go wrong. it would be equally absurd, then, to expect that in unjust, cowardly, and voluptuous action there should be a mean, an excess, and a deficiency; for at that rate there would be a mean of excess and of deficiency, an excess of excess, and a deficiency of deficiency. But as there is no excess and deficiency of temperance and courage because what is intermediate is in a sense an extreme, so too of the actions we have mentioned there is no mean nor any excess and deficiency, but however they are done they are wrong; for in general there is neither a mean of excess and deficiency, nor excess and deficiency of a mean.

7 We must, however, not only make this general statement, but also apply it to the individual facts. For among statements about conduct those which are general apply more widely, but those which are particular are more genuine, since conduct has to do with individual cases, and our statements must harmonize with the facts in these cases. We may take these cases from our table. With regard to feelings of fear and confidence courage is the mean; of the people who exceed, he who exceeds in fearlessness has no name (many of the states have no name), while the man who exceeds in confidence is rash, and he who exceeds in fear and falls short in confidence is a coward. With regard to pleasures and pains—not all of them, and not so much with regard to the pains—the mean is temperance, the excess self-indulgence. Persons deficient with regard to the pleasures are not often found; hence such persons also have received no name. But let us call them 'insensible'.

With regard to giving and taking of money the mean is liberality, the excess and the defect prodigality and meanness. In these actions people exceed and fall short in contrary ways; the prodigal exceeds in spending and falls short in taking, while the mean man exceeds in taking and falls short in spending. (At present we are giving a mere outline or summary, and are satisfied with this; later these states will be more exactly determined.[4]) With regard to money there are also other dispositions—a mean, magnificence (for the magnificent man differs from the liberal man; the former deals with large sums, the latter with small ones), and excess, tastelessness and vulgarity, and a deficiency, niggardliness; these differ from the states opposed to liberality, and the mode of their difference will be stated later.[5]

With regard to honour and dishonour the mean is proper pride, the excess is known as a sort of 'empty vanity', and the deficiency is undue humility; and as we said[6] liberality was related to magnificence, differing from it by dealing with small sums, so there is a state similarly related to proper pride, being concerned with small honours while that is concerned with great. For it is possible to desire honour as one ought, and more than one ought, and less, and the man who exceeds in his desires is called ambitious, the man who falls short unambitious, while the intermediate person has no name. The dispositions also are nameless, except that that of the ambitious man is called ambition. Hence the people who are at the extremes lay claim to the middle place; and we ourselves sometimes call the intermediate person ambitious and sometimes unambitious, and sometimes praise the ambitious man and sometimes the unambitious. The reason of our doing this will be stated in what follows;[7] but now let us speak of the remaining states according to the method which has been indicated.

With regard to anger also there is an excess, a deficiency, and a mean. Although they can scarcely be said to have names, yet since we call the intermediate person good-tempered let us call the mean good temper; of the persons at the extremes let the one who exceeds be called irascible, and his vice irascibility, and the man who falls short an inirascible sort of person, and the deficiency inirascibility.

There are also three other means, which have a certain likeness to one another, but differ from one another: for they are all concerned with intercourse in words and actions, but differ in that one is concerned with truth in this sphere, the other two with pleasantness; and of this one kind is exhibited in giving amusement, the other in all the circumstances of life. We must therefore speak of these too, that we may the better see that in all things the mean is praiseworthy, and the extremes neither praiseworthy nor right, but worthy of blame. Now most of these states also have no names, but we must try, as in the other cases, to invent names ourselves so that we may be clear and easy to follow. With regard to truth, then, the intermediate is a truthful sort of person and the mean may be called truthfulness, while the pretence which exaggerates is boastfulness and the person characterized by it a boaster, and that which understates is mock modesty and the person characterized by it mock-modest. With regard to pleasantness in the giving of amusement the intermediate person is ready-witted and the disposition ready wit, the excess is buffoonery and the person characterized by it a buffoon, while the man who falls short is a sort of boor and his state is boorishness. With regard to the remaining kind of pleasantness, that which is exhibited in life in general, the man who is pleasant in the right way is friendly and the mean is friendliness, while the man who exceeds is an obsequious person if he has no end in view, a flatterer if he is aiming at his own advantage, and the man who falls short and is unpleasant in all circumstances is a quarrelsome and surly sort of person.

There are also means in the passions and concerned with the passions; since shame is not a virtue, and yet praise is extended to the modest man. For even in these matters one man is said to be intermediate, and another to exceed, as for instance the bashful man who is ashamed of everything; while he who falls short or is not ashamed of anything at all is shameless, and the intermediate person is modest. Righteous indignation is a mean between envy and spite, and these states are concerned with the pain and pleasures that are felt at the fortunes of our neighbours; the man who is character-ized by righteous indignation is pained at undeserved good fortune, the envious man, going beyond him, is pained at all good fortune, and the spiteful man falls so far short of being pained that he even rejoices. But these states there will be an opportunity of describing elsewhere;[8] with regard to justice, since it has not one simple meaning, we shall, after describ-ing the other states, distinguish its two kinds and say how each of them is a mean;[9] and similarly we shall treat also of the rational virtues.[10]

8 There are three kinds of disposition, then, two of them vices, involving excess and deficiency respectively, and one a virtue, viz. the mean, and all are in a sense opposed to all; for the extreme states are contrary both to the intermedi-ate state and to each other, and the intermediate to the extremes; as the equal is greater relatively to the less, less relatively to the greater, so the middle states are excessive relatively to the deficiencies, deficient relatively to the excesses, both in passions and in actions. For the brave man appears rash relatively to the coward, and cowardly relatively to the rash man; and similarly the temperate man appears self-indulgent relatively to the insensible man, insensible relatively to the self-indulgent, and the liberal man prodigal relatively to the mean man, mean relatively to the prodigal. Hence also the people at the extremes push the intermediate man each over to the other, and the brave man is called rash by the coward, cowardly by the rash man, and correspondingly in the other cases.

These states being thus opposed to one another, the greatest contrariety is that of the extremes to each other, rather than to the intermediate; for these are further from each other than from the intermediate, as the great is further from the small and the small from the great than both are from the equal. Again, to the intermediate some extremes show a certain likeness, as that of rashness to courage and that of prodigality to liberality; but the extremes show the greatest unlikeness to each other; now contraries are defined as the things that are furthest from each other, so that things that are further apart are more contrary.

To the mean in some cases the deficiency, in some the excess is more opposed; e. g. it is not rashness, which is an excess, but cowardice, which is a deficiency, that is more opposed to courage, and not insensibility, which is a deficiency, but self-indulgence, which is an excess, that is more opposed to temperance. This happens from two reasons, one being drawn from the thing itself; for because one extreme is nearer and liker to the intermediate, we oppose not this but rather its contrary to the intermediate. E. g., since rashness is thought liker and nearer to courage, and cowardice more unlike, we oppose rather the latter to courage; for things that are further from the intermediate are thought more contrary to it. This, then, is one cause, drawn from the thing itself; another is drawn from ourselves; for the things to which we ourselves more naturally tend seem more contrary to the intermediate. For instance, we ourselves tend more naturally to pleasures, and hence are more easily carried away towards self-indulgence than towards propriety. We describe as contrary to the mean, then, rather the directions in which we more often go to great lengths; and therefore self-indulgence, which is an excess, is the more contrary to temperance.

Question:
1. What are some difficulties in finding the mean between excess and deficiency?

3.3 Aristotle's Will

The great fourth-century Athenian philosopher Aristotle left this will when he died in 322 B.C.E.

Source: Diogenes Laertius, Lives of Eminent Philosophers, trans. R.D. Hicks, Vol. 1. (Cambridge, MA: Harvard University Press, 1959), pp. 455-59.

"All will be well; but, in case anything should happen, Aristotle has made these dispositions. Antipater is to be executor in all matters and in general; but, until Nicanor shall arrive, Aristomenes, Timarchus, Hipparchus, Dioteles and (if he consent and if circumstances permit him) Theophrastus shall take charge as well of Herphyllis and the children as of the property. And when the girl shall be grown up she shall be given in marriage to Nicanor; but if anything happen to the girl (which heaven forbid and no such thing will happen) before her marriage, or when she is married but before there are children, Nicanor shall have full powers, both with regard to the child and with regard to everything else, to administer in a manner worthy both of himself and of us. Nicanor shall take charge of the girl and of the boy Nicomachus as he shall think fit in all that concerns them as if he were father and brother. And if anything should happen to Nicanor (which heaven forbid!) either before he marries the girl, or when he has married her but before there are children, any arrangements that he may make shall be valid. And if Theophrastus is willing to live with her, <he shall have> the same rights as Nicanor. Otherwise the executors in consultation with Antipater shall administer as regards the daughter and the boy as seems to them to be best. The executors and Nicanor, in memory of me and of the steady affection which Herpyllis has borne towards me, shall take care of her in every other respect and, if she desires to be married, shall see that she be given to one not unworthy; and besides what she has already received they shall give her a talent of silver out of the estate and three handmaids whomsoever she shall choose besides the maid she has at present and the man-servant Pyrrhaeus; and if she chooses to remain at Chalcis, the lodge by the garden, if in Stagira, my father's house. Whichever of these two houses she chooses, the executors shall furnish with such furniture as they think proper and as Herpyllis herself may approve. Nicanor shall take charge of the boy Myrmex, that he be taken to his own friends in a manner worthy of me with the property of his which we received. Ambracis shall be given her freedom, and on my daughter's marriage shall receive 500 drachmas and the maid whom she now has. And to Thale shall be given, in addition to the maid whom she has and who was bought, a thousand drachmas and a maid. And Simon, in addition to the money before paid to him towards another servant, shall either have a servant purchased for him or receive a further sum of money. And Tycho, Philo, Olympius and his child shall have their freedom when my daughter is married. None of the servants who waited upon me shall be sold but they shall continue to be employed; and when they arrive at the proper age they shall have their freedom if they deserve it. My executors shall see to it, when the images which Gryllion has been commissioned to execute are finished, that they be set up, namely that of Nicanor, that of Proxenus, which it was my intention to have executed, and that of Nicanor's mother; also they shall set up the bust which has been executed of Arimnestus, to be a memorial of him seeing that he died childless, and shall dedicate my mother's statue to Demeter at Nemea or wherever they think best. And wherever they bury me, there the bones of Pythias shall be laid, in accordance with her own instructions. And to commemorate Nicanor's safe return, as I vowed on his behalf, they shall set up in Stagira stone statues of life size to Zeus and Athena the Saviours."

Such is the tenor of Aristotle's will. It is said that a very large number of dishes belonging to him were found, and that Lyco mentioned his bathing in a bath of warm oil and then selling the oil. Some relate that he placed a skin of warm oil on his stomach, and that, when he went to sleep, a bronze ball was placed in his hand with a vessel under it, in order that, when the ball dropped form his hand into the vessel, he might be waked up by the sound.

Questions:
1. *What rights did husbands and fathers have over their families in Athens?*
2. *How does this document illustrate the lives of women and the institution of marriage in Athens?*
3. *What does this document reveal about the lives of servants or slaves in Athens?*

3.4   Drama: *Antigone* by Sophocles

Antigone, written in the fifth century B.C.E. by Sophocles, deals with the children of Oedipus, the king who could not escape his fate. Antigone focuses on the meaning of honor and duty. Gender issues are also involved. Before the play begins, the sons of Oedipus, cursed by their father, have quarreled over royal power in Thebes. Eteocles drove his brother Polyneices from Thebes to the city-state of Argos where he married the daughter of the king. Polyneices then marched on Thebes to recover the throne. During the battle, the two brothers meet and kill each other. Their uncle, Creon, became king and imme-diately forbid the burial of Polyneices.

> **Source:** Dudley Fitts, *Greek Plays in Modern Translation,* (New York: Dial Press, 1947), pp. 459-62, 464-65, 469-77.

Scene:Before the palace of Creon, King of Thebes. . . .
Time:dawn of the day after the repulse of the Argive army from the assault of Thebes.

PROLOGUE

[ANTIGONE and ISMENE enter from the central door of the Palace.

ANTIG.   Ismenê, dear sister,
You would think that we had already suffered enough
For the curse on Oedipus:
I cannot imagine any grief
That you and I have not gone through. And now-
Have they told you the new decree of our King Creon?

ISMENE   I have heard nothing: I know
That two sisters lost two brothers, and double death
In a single hour; and I know that the Argive army
Fled in the night; but beyond this, nothing.

ANTIG.   I thought so. And that is why I wanted you To come
out here with me. There is something we must do.

ISMENE   Why do you speak so strangely?

ANTIG.   Listen, Ismenê:
Creon buried our brother Eteoclês
With military honours, gave him a soldier's funeral,
And it was right that he should; but Polyneicês,
Who fought as bravely and died as miserably,-
They say that Creon has sworn
No one shall bury him, no one mourn for him,
But his body must lie in the fields, a sweet treasure
For carrion birds to find as they search for food.
That is what they say, and our good Creon is

38

coming here
To announce it publicly; and the penalty-
Stoning to death in the public square!
There it is,
And now you can prove what you are:
A true sister, or a traitor to your family.

ISMENE   Antigonê, you are mad! What could I possibly do?

ANTIG.   You must decide whether you will help me or not.

ISMENE   I do not understand you. Help you in what?

ANTIG.   Ismenê, I am going to bury him. Will you come?

ISMENE   Bury him! You have just said the new law forbids it.

ANTIG.   He is my brother. And he is your brother, too.

ISMENE   But think of the danger! Thank what Creon will do!

ANTIG.   Creon is not strong enough to stand in my way.

ISMENE   Ah sister!
Oedipus died, everyone hating him
For what his own search brought to light, his eyes
Ripped out by his own hand; and Iocastê died,
His mother and wife at once: she twisted the cords
That strangled her life; and our two brothers died,
Each killed by the other's sword. And we are left:
But oh, Antigonê,
Think how much more terrible than these
Our own death would be if we should go against Creon
And do what he has forbidden! We are only women,
We cannot fight with men, Antigonê!
The law is strong, we must give in to the law
In this thing, and in worse. I beg the Dead
To forgive me, but I am helpless: I must yield
To those in authority. And I think it is dangerous business
To be always meddling.

ANTIG.   If that is what you think,
I should not want you, even if you asked to come.
You have made your choice, you can be what you want to be.
But I will bury him; and if I must die,
I say that this crime is holy: I shall lie down
With him in death, and I shall be as dear
To him as he to me.
It is the dead,
Not the living, who make the longest demands:
We die for ever...
You may do as you like,
Since apparently the laws of the gods mean nothing to you.

ISMENE   They mean a great deal to me; but I have no strength
To break laws that were made for the public good.

39

ANTIG.   That must be your excuse, I suppose. But as for me,
            I will bury the brother I love.

ISMENE   Antigonê,
            I am so afraid for you!

ANTIG.   You need not be:
            You have yourself to consider, after all.

ISMENE   But no one must hear of this, you must tell no one!
            I will keep it a secret, I promise!

ANTIG.   Oh tell it! Tell everyone!
            Think how they'll hate you when it all comes out
            If they learn that you knew about it all the time!

ISMENE   So fiery! You should be cold with fear.

ANTIG.   Perhaps. But I am doing only what I must.

ISMENE   But can you do it? I say that you cannot.

ANTIG.   Very well: when my strength gives out, I shall do no
                more.

ISMENE   Impossible things should not be tried at all.

ANTIG.   Go away, Ismenê:
            I shall be hating you soon, and the dead will too,
            For your words are hateful. Leave me my foolish plan:
            I am not afraid of the danger; if it means death,
            It will not be the worst of deaths-death without honour.

ISMENE   Go then, if you feel that you must.
            You are unwise,
            But a loyal friend indeed to those who love you.

            [Exit into the Palace. ANTIGONE goes off, L.
Enters the Chorus.

SCENE I

CHORAG.   But now at last our new King is coming:
            Creon of Thebes, Menoiceus' son.
            In this auspicious dawn of his reign
            What are the new complexities
            That shifting Fate has woven for him?
            What is his counsel? Why has he summoned
            The old men to hear him?

            [Enter Creon from the Palace. He addresses the
                Chorus from the top step.

CREON   Gentlemen: I have the honour to inform you that our
                Ship of State, which recent storms have threatened
                to destroy, has come safely to harbour at last,

40

guided by the merciful wisdom of Heaven. I have summoned you here this morning because I know that I can depend upon you: your devotion to King Laïos was absolute; you never hesitated in your duty to our late ruler Oedipus; and when Oedipus died, your loyalty was transferred to his children. Unfortunately, as you know, his two sons, the princes Eteoclês and Polyneicês, have killed each other in battle; and I, as the next in blood, have succeeded to the full power of the throne.

I am aware, of course, that no Ruler can expect complete loyalty from his subjects until he has been tested in office. Nevertheless, I say to you at the very outset that I have nothing but contempt for the kind of Governor who is afraid, for whatever reason, to follow the course that he knows is best for the State; and as for the man who sets private friendship above the public welfare,-I have no use for him, either. I call God to witness that If I saw my country headed for ruin, I should not be afraid to speak out plainly; and I need hardly remind you that I would never have any dealings with any enemy of the people. No one values friendship more highly than I; but we must remember that friends made at the risk of wrecking our Ship are not real friends at all.

These are my principles, at any rate, and that is why I have made the following decision concerning the sons of Oedipus: Eteoclès, who died as a man should die, fighting for his country, is to be buried with full military honours, with all the ceremony that is usual when the greatest heroes dies; but his brother Polyneicês, who broke his exile to come back with fire and sword against his native city and the shrines of his father's god, whose one idea was to spill the blood of his blood and sell his own people into slavery-Polyneicês, I say, is to have no burial: no man is to touch him or say the least prayer for him; he shall lie on the plain, unburied; and the birds and the scavenging dogs can do with him whatever they like.

This is my command, and you can see the wisdom behind it. As long as I am king, no traitor is going to be honoured with the loyal man. But whoever shows by word and deed that he is on the side of the State,-he shall have my respect while he is living, and my reverence when he is dead.

CHORAG. If that is your will, Creon son of Menoiceus,
You have the right to enforce it; we are yours.

CREON That is my will. Take care that you do your part.

CHORAG. We are old men: let the younger ones carry it out.

CREON I do not mean that: the sentries have been appointed.

41

CHORAG.   Then what is it that you would have us do?

CREON   You will give no support to whoever breaks the law.

CHORAG.   Only a crazy man is in love with death!

CREON   And death it is; yet money talks, and the wisest
Have sometimes been known to count a few coins too many.

A sentry discovers Antigone burying her brother's body and brings
her to King Creon.

SCENE II

[Re-enter Sentry leading Antigone.

CHORAG.   What does this mean? Surely this captive woman
Is the Princess, Antigonê. Why should she be taken?

SENTRY   Here is the one who did it! We caught her
In the very act of burying him.-Where is Creon?

CHORAG.   Just coming from the house.

[Enter Creon, C.

CREON   What has happened?
Why have you come back so soon?

***

SENTRY   ... Here is this woman. She is the guilty one:
We found her trying to bury him.
Take her, then; question her; judge her as you will.
I am though with the whole thing now, and glad of it.

CREON   But this is Antigonê! Why have you brought her here?

SENTRY   She was burying him, I tell you!

[Severely.

CREON   Is this the truth?

SENTRY   I saw her with my own eyes. Can I say more?

***

[Slowly, dangerously.

CREON   And you, Antigonê,
You with your head hanging,-do you confess this thing?

ANTIG.   I do. I deny nothing.
[To Sentry:

CREON   You may go.

[Exit Sentry.

42

[To Antigone:
Tell me, tell me briefly:
Had you heard my proclamation touching this matter?

ANTIG.   It was public. Could I help hearing it?

CREON   And yet you dared defy the law.

ANTIG.   I dared.
It was not God's proclamation. That final Justice
That rules the world below makes no such laws.
Your edict, King, was strong,
But all your strength is weakness itself against
The immortal unrecorded laws of God.
They are not merely now: they were, and shall be,
Operative for ever, beyond man utterly.
I knew I must die, even without your decree:
I am only mortal. And if I must die
Now, before it is my time to die,
Surely this is no hardship: can anyone
Living, as I live, with evil all about me,
Think Death less than a friend? This death of mine
Is of no importance; but if I had left my brother
Lying in death unburied, I should have suffered.
Now I do not.
                        You smile at me. Ah Creon,
Think me a fool, if you like; but it may well be
That a fool convicts me of folly.

CHORAG.   Like father, like daughter: both headstrong, deaf to reason!
She has never learned to yield.

CREON   She has much to learn.
The inflexible heart breaks first, the toughest iron
Cracks first, and the wildest horses bend their necks
At the pull of the smallest curb.
                         Pride? In a slave?

This girl is guilty of a double insolence,
Breaking the given laws and boasting of it.
Who is the man here,
She or I, if this crime goes unpunished?
Sister's child, or more than sister's child,
Or closer yet in blood-she and her sister
Win bitter death for this!

                           [To servants:
                     Go, some of you,

Arrest Ismenê. I accuse her equally.
Bring her: you will find her sniffling in the house there.
Her mind's a traitor: crimes kept in the dark
Cry for light, and the guardian brain shudders;
But how much worse than this
Is brazen boasting of barefaced anarchy!

ANTIG.   Creon, what more do you want than my death?

CREON   Nothing.

43

                 That gives me everything.

ANTIG.   Then I beg you: kill me.
This talking is a great weariness: your words
Are distasteful to me, and I am sure that mine
Seem so to you. And yet they should not seem so:
I should have praise and honour for what I have done.
All these men here would praise me
Were their lips not frozen shut with fear of you.

                                   [Bitterly.

Ah the good fortune of kings,
Licensed to say and do whatever they please!

CREON   You are alone here in that opinion.

ANTIG.   No, they are with me. But they keep their tongues in leash.

CREON   Maybe. But you are guilty, and they are not.

ANTIG.   There is no guilt in reverence for the dead.

CREON   But Eteoclês-was he not your brother too?

ANTIG.   My brother too.

CREON   And you insult his memory?

                                   [Softly.

ANTIG.   The dead man would not say that I insult it.

CREON   He would: for you honour a traitor as much as him.

ANTIG.   His own brother, traitor or not, and equal in blood.

CREON   He made war on his country. Eteoclês defended it.

ANTIG.   Nevertheless, there are honours due all the dead.

CREON   But not the same for the wicked as for the just.

ANTIG.   Ah Creon, Creon,
Which of us can say what the gods hold wicked?

CREON   An enemy is an enemy, even dead.

ANTIG.   It is my nature to join in love, not hate.

                           [Finally losing patience.

CREON   Go join them, then; if you must have your love,
Find it in hell!

CHORAG.   But see, Ismenê comes:

                         [Enter Ismene, guarded.

Those tears are sisterly, the cloud
That shadows her eyes rains down gentle sorrow.

44

CREON   You too, Ismenê,
Snake in my ordered house, sucking my blood
Stealthily-and all the time I never knew
That these two sisters were aiming at my throne!

                                                   Ismenê,
Do you confess your share in this crime, or deny it?
Answer me.

ISMENE   Yes, if she will let my say so. I am guilty.

                                                   [Coldly.

ANTIG.   No, Ismenê. You have no right to say so.
You would not help me, and I will not have you help me.

ISMENE   But now I know what you meant; and I am here
To join you, to take my share of punishment.

ANTIG.   The dead man and the gods who rule the dead
Know whose act this was. Words are not friends.

ISMENE   Do you refuse me, Antigonê? I want to die with you:
I too have a duty that I must discharge to the dead.

ANTIG.   You shall not lessen my death by sharing it.

ISMENE   What do I care for life when you are dead?

ANTIG.   Ask Creon. You're always hanging on his opinions.

ISMENE   You are laughing at me. Why, Antigonê?

ANTIG.   It's a joyless laughter, Ismenê.

ISMENE   But can I do nothing?

ANTIG.   Yes. Save yourself. I shall not envy you.
There are those who will praise you; I shall have honour, too.

ISMENE   But we are equally guilty!

ANTIG.   No, more, Ismenê.
You are alive, but I belong to Death.

CREON   [To the Chorus:
Gentlemen, I beg you to observe these girls:
One has just now lost her mind; the other
It seems, has never had a mind at all.

ISMENE   Grief teaches the steadiest minds to waver, King.

CREON   Yours certainly did, when you assumed guilt with the guilty!

ISMENE   But how could I go on living without her?

CREON   You are.

She is already dead.

ISMENE   But your own son's bride!

CREON   There are places enough for him to push his plow.
I want no wicked women for my sons!

ISMENE   O dearest Haimon, how your father wrongs you!

CREON   I've had enough of your childish talk of marriage!

CHORAG.   Do you really intend to steal this girl from your son?

CREON   No; Death will do that for me.

CHORAG.   Then she must die?

CREON   You dazzle me.
—But enough of this talk!

                                [To Guards:

You, there, take them away and guard them well:
For they are but women, and even brave men run
When they see Death coming.

                [Exeunt Ismente, Antigone, and Guards.

Questions:
1. Why is Antigone willing to defy the king's decree and give her brother burial?
2. What arguments to Ismene and Creon use to oppose her action?
3. What can you conclude about the way men and women were regarded in this society?

3.5 *Pericles' Funeral Oration* by Thucydides

Pericles (c. 495 - 429 B.C.E.) was an Athenian statesman. Included in Thucydides' (460-400 B.C.E.) History of the Peloponnesian War, his funeral oration is a classic statement of Athenian values. In it, he reminds his countrymen of the deeds of the honored dead, the values for which they died, and the unique qualities of Athenian society.

Source: *History of the Peloponnesian War*, translation by Rex Warner (New York: Penguin Books, 1986), pp. 143–151.

In the same winter the Athenians, following their annual custom, gave a public funeral for those who had been the first to die in the war. These funerals are held in the following way: two days before the ceremony the bones of the fallen are brought and put in a tent which has been erected, and people make whatever offerings they wish to their own dead. Then there is a funeral procession in which coffins of cypress wood are carried on wagons. There is one coffin for each tribe, which contains the bones of members of that tribe. One empty bier is decorated and carried in the procession: that is for the missing, whose bodies could not be recovered. Everyone who wishes to, both citizens and foreigners, can join in the procession, and the women who are related to the dead are there to make their laments at the tomb. The bones are laid in the public burial-place, which is in the most beautiful quarter outside the city walls. Here the Athenians always bury those who have fallen in war. The only exception is those who died at Marathon, who, because their achievement was considered absolutely outstanding, were buried on the battlefield itself.

    When the bones have been laid in the earth, a man chosen by the city for his intellectual gifts and for his general reputation makes an appropriate speech in praise of the dead, and after the speech all depart. This is the procedure at these burials, and all through the war, when the time came to do so, the Athenians followed this ancient custom. Now, at the burial of those who were the first to fall in the war Pericles, the son of Xanthippus, was chosen to make the speech. When the moment arrived, he came forward from the tomb and, standing on a high platform, so that he might be heard by as many people as possible in the crowd, he spoke as follows:

'Many of those who have spoken here in the past have praised the institution of this speech at the close of our ceremony. It seemed to them a mark of honour to our soldiers who have fallen in war that a speech should be made over them. I do not agree. These men have shown themselves valiant in action, and it would be enough, I think, for their glories to be proclaimed in action, as you have just seen it done at this funeral organized by the state. Our belief in the courage and manliness of so many should not be hazard on the goodness or badness of one man's speech. Then it is not easy to speak with a proper sense of balance, when a man's listeners find it difficult to believe in the truth of what one is saying. The man who knows the facts and loves the dead may well think that an oration tells less than what he knows and what he would like to hear: others who do not know so much may feel envy for the dead, and think the orator over-praises them, when he speaks of exploits that are beyond their own capacities. Praise of other people is tolerable only up to a certain point, the point where one still believes that one could do oneself some of the things one is hearing about. Once you get beyond this point, you will find people becoming jealous and incredulous. However, the fact is that this institution was set up and approved by our forefathers, and it is my duty to follow the tradition and do my best to meet the wishes and the expectations of every one of you.

'I shall begin by speaking about our ancestors, since it is only right and proper on such an occasion to pay them the honour of recalling what they did. In this land of ours there have always been the same people living from generation to generation up till now, and they, by their courage and their virtues, have handed it on to us, a free country. They certainly deserve our praise. Even more so do our fathers deserve it. For to the inheritance they had received they added all the empire we have now, and it was not without blood and toil that they handed it down to us of the present generation. And then we ourselves, assembled here today, who are mostly in the prime of life, have, in most directions, added to the power of our empire and have organized our State in such a way that it is perfectly well able to look after itself both in peace and in war.

'I have no wish to make a long speech on subjects familiar to you all: so I shall say nothing about the warlike deeds by which we acquired our power or the battles in which we or our fathers gallantly resisted our enemies, Greek or foreign. What I want to do is, in the first place, to discuss the spirit in which we faced our trials and also our constitution and the way of life which has made us great. After that I shall speak in praise of the dead, believing that this kind of speech is not inappropriate to the present occasion, and that this whole assembly, of citizens and foreigners, may listen to it with advantage.

'Let me say that our system of government does not copy the institutions of our neighbours. It is me the case of our being a model to others, than of our imitating anyone else. Our constitution is called a democracy because power is in the hands not of a minority but of the whole people. When it is a question of settling private disputes, everyone is equal before the law; when it is a question of putting one person before another in positions of public responsibility, what counts is not membership of a particular class, but the actual ability which the man possesses. No one, so long as he has it in him to be of service to the state, is kept in political obscurity because of poverty. And, just as our political life is free and open, so is our day-to-day life in our relations with each other. We do not get into a state with our next-door neighbour if he enjoys himself in his own way, nor do we give him the kind of black looks which, though they do no real harm, still do hurt people's feelings. We are free and tolerant in our private lives; but in public affairs we keep to the law. This is because it commands our deep respect.

'We give our obedience to those whom we put in positions of authority, and we obey the laws themselves, especially those which are for the protection of the oppressed, and those unwritten laws which it is an acknowledged shame to break.

'And here is another point. When our work is over, we are in a position to enjoy all kinds of recreation for our spirits. There are various kinds of contests and sacrifices regularly throughout the year; in our own homes we find a beauty and a good taste which delight us every day and which drive away our cares. Then the greatness of our city brings it about that all the good things from all over the world flow in to us, so that to us it seems just as natural to enjoy foreign goods as our own local products.

'Then there is a great difference between us and our opponents, in our attitude towards military security. Here are some examples: Our city is open to the world, and we have no periodical deportations in order to prevent people observing or finding out secrets which might be of military advantage to the enemy. This is because we rely, not on secret weapons, but on our own real courage and loyalty. There is a difference, too, in our educational systems. The Spartans, from their earliest boyhood, are submitted to the most laborious training in courage; we pass our lives without all these restrictions, and yet are just as ready to face the same dangers as they are. Here is a proof of this: When the Spartan's invade our land, they do not come by themselves, but bring all their allies with them; whereas we, when we launch an attack abroad, do the job by ourselves, and, though fighting on foreign soil, do not often fail to defeat opponents who are fighting for their own hearths and homes. As a matter of fact none of our enemies have ever yet been confronted with our total strength, because we have to divide our attention between our navy and the many missions on which our troops are sent on land. Yet, if our enemies engage a detachment of our forces and defeat it, they give themselves credit for having thrown back our entire army; or, if they lose, they claim that they were beaten by us in full strength. There are certain advantages, I think, in our way of meeting danger voluntarily, with an easy mind, instead of with a laborious training, with natural rather than with state-induced courage. We do not have to spend our time practising to meet sufferings which are still in the future; and when they are actually upon us we show ourselves just as brave as these others who are always in strict training. This is one point in which, I think, our city deserves to be admired. There are also others:

'Our love of what is beautiful does not lead to extravagance; our love of the things of the mind does not make us soft. We regard wealth as something to be properly used, rather than as something to boast about. As for poverty, no one need be ashamed to admit it: the real shame is in not taking practical measures to escape from it. Here each individual is interested not only in his own affairs but in the affairs of the state as well: even those who are mostly occupied with their own business are extremely well-informed on general politics—This is a peculiarity of ours: we do not say that a man who takes no interest in politics is a man who minds his own business; we say that he has no business here at all. We Athenians, in our own persons, take our decisions on policy or submit them to proper discussions: for we do not think that there is an incompatibility between words and deeds; the worst thing is to rush into action before the consequences have been properly debated. And this is another point where we differ from other people. We are capable at the same time of taking risks and of estimating them beforehand. Others are brave out of ignorance; and, when they stop to think, they begin to fear. But the man who can most truly be accounted brave is he who best knows the meaning of what is sweet in life and of what is terrible, and then goes out undeterred to meet what is to come.

'Again, in questions of general good feeling there is a great contrast between us and most other people. We make friends by doing good to others, not by receiving good from them. This makes our friendship all the more reliable, since we want to keep alive the gratitude of those who are in our debt by showing continued good-will to them: whereas the feelings of one who owes us something lack the enthusiasm, since he knows that, when he repays our kindness, it will be more like paying back a debt than giving something spontaneously. We are unique in this. When we do kindnesses to others, we do not do them out of any calculations of profit or loss: we do them without afterthought, relying on our free liberality. Taking everything together then, I declare that our city is an education to Greece, and I declare that in my opinion each single one of our citizens, in all the manifold aspects of life, is able to show himself the rightful lord and owner of his own person, and do this, moreover, with exceptional grace and exceptional versatality. And to show that this is no empty boasting for the present occasion, but real tangible fact, you have only to consider the power which our city possesses and which has been won by those very qualities which I have mentioned. Athens, alone of the states we know, comes to her testing time in a greatness that surpasses what was imagined of her. In her case, and in her case alone, no invading enemy is ashamed at being defeated, and no subject can complain of being governed by people unfit for their responsibilities. Mighty indeed are the marks and monuments of our empire which we have left. Future ages will wonder at us, as the present age wonders at us now. We do not need the praises of a Homer, or of anyone else whose words may delight us for the moment, but whose estimation of facts will fall short of what is really true. For our adventurous spirit has forced an entry into every sea and into every land; and everywhere we have left behind us everlasting memorials of good done to our friends or suffering inflicted on our enemies.

'This, then, is the kind of city for which these men, who could not bear the thought of losing her, nobly fought and nobly died. It is only natural that every one of us who survive them should be willing to undergo hardships in her service. And it was for this reason that I have spoken at such length about our city, because I wanted to make it clear that for us there is more at stake than there is for others who lack our advantages; also I wanted my words of praise for the dead to be set in the bright light of evidence. And now the most important of these words has been spoken. I have sung the praises of our city; but it was the courage and gallantry of these men, and of people like them, which made her splendid. Nor would you find it true in the case of many of the Greeks, as it is true of them, that no words can do more than justice to their deeds.

'To me it seems that the consummation which has overtaken these men show us the meaning of manliness in its first revelation and in its final proof. Some of them, no doubt, had their faults; but what we ought to remember first is their gallant conduct against the enemy in defence of their native land. They have blotted out evil with good, and done more service to the commonwealth than they ever did harm in their private lives. No one of these men weakened because he wanted to go on enjoying his wealth: no one put off the awful day in the hope that he might live to escape his poverty and grow rich. More to be desired than such things, they chose to check the enemy's pride. This, to them, was a risk most glorious, and they accepted it, willing to strike down the enemy and relinquish everything else. As for success or failure, they left that in the doubtful hands of Hope, and when the reality of battle was before their faces, they put their trust in their own selves. In the fighting, they thought it more honourable to stand their ground and suffer death than to give in and save their lives. So they fled from the reproaches of men, abiding with life and limb the brunt of battle; and, in a small moment of time, the climax of their lives, a culmination of glory, not of fear, were swept away from us.

'So and such they were, these men—worthy of their city. We who remain behind may hope to be spared their fate, but must resolve to keep the same daring spirit against the foe. It is not simply a question of estimating the advantages in theory. I could tell you a long story (and you know it as well as I do) about what is to be gained by beating the enemy back. What I would prefer is that you should fix your eyes every day on the greatness of Athens as she really is, and should fall in love with her. When you realize her greatness, then reflect that what made her great was men with a spirit of adventure, men who knew their duty, men who were ashamed to fall below a certain standard. If they ever failed in an enterprise, they made up their minds that at any rate the city should not find their courage lacking to her, and they gave to her the best contribution that they could. They gave her their lives, to her and to all of us, and for their own selves they won praises that never grow old, the most splendid of sepulchres—not the sepulchre in which their bodies are laid, but where their glory remains eternal in men's minds, always there on the right occasion to stir others to speech or to action. For famous men have the whole earth as their memorial: it is not only the inscriptions on their graves in their own country that mark them out; no, in foreign lands also, not in any visible form but in people's hearts, their memory abides and grows. It is for you to try to be like them. Make up your minds that happiness depends on being free, and freedom depends on being courageous. Let there be no relaxation in face of the perils of the war. The people who have most excuse for despising death are not the wretched and unfortunate, who have no hope of doing well for themselves, but those who run the risk of a complete reversal in their lives, and who would feel the difference most intensely, if things went wrong for them. Any intelligent man would find a humiliation caused by his own slackness more painful to bear than death, when death comes to him unperceived, in battle, and in the confidence of his patriotism.

'For these reasons I shall not commiserate with those parents of the dead, who are present here. Instead I shall try to comfort them. They are well aware that they have grown up in a world where there are many changes and chances. But this is good fortune—for men to end their lives with honour, as these have done, and for you honourable to lament them: their life was set to a measure where death and happiness went hand in hand. I know that it is difficult to convince you of this. When you see other people happy you will often be reminded of what used to make you happy too. One does not feel sad at not having some good thing which is outside one's experience: real grief is felt at the loss of something which one is used to. All the same, those of you who are of the right age must bear up and take comfort in the thought of having more children. In your own homes these new children will prevent you from brooding over those who are no more, and they will be a help to the city, too, both in filling the empty places, and in assuring her security. For it is impossible for a man to put forward fair and honest views about our affairs if he has not, like everyone else, children whose lives may be at stake. As for those of you who are now too old to have children, I would ask you to count as gain the greater part of your life, in which you have been happy, and remember that what remains is not long, and let your hearts be lifted up at the thought of the fair fame of the dead. One's sense of honour is the only thing that does not grow old, and the last pleasure, when one is worn out with age, is not, as the poet said, making money, but having the respect of one's fellow men.

'As for those of you here who are sons or brothers of the dead, I can see a hard struggle in front of you. Everyone always speaks well of the dead, and, even if you rise to the greatest heights of heroism, it will be a hard thing for you to get the reputation of having come near, let alone equalled, their standard. When one is alive, one is always liable to the jealousy of one's competitors, but when one is out of the way, the honour one receives is sincere and unchallenged.

'Perhaps I should say a word or two on the duties of women to those among you who are now widowed. I can say all I have to say in a short word of advice. Your great glory is not to be inferior to what God has made you, and the greatest glory of a woman is to be least talked about by men, whether they are praising you or criticizing you. I have now, as the law demanded, said what I had to say. For the time being our offerings to the dead have been made, and for the future their children will be supported at the public expense by the city, until they come of age. This is the crown and prize which she offers, both to the dead and to their children, for the ordeals which they have faced. Where the rewards of valour are the greatest, there you will find also the best and bravest spirits among the people. And now, when you have mourned for your dear ones, you must depart.'

Questions:
1. *What are the main virtues of Athens as described by Pericles?*
2. *What is his purpose in stating them?*

3.6   On the Murder of Eratosthenes: A Husband's Defense

This is a transcript of a trial before the citizen's assembly at Athens around 400 B.C.E. Euphiletus defends himself on a charge of murdering Eratosthenes, his wife's lover.

Source: W.R.M. Lamb, trans., Lysias, (Cambridge: Harvard University Press, 1960), pp. 5-21, 27.

... When I, Athenians, decided to marry, and brought a wife into my house, for some time I was disposed neither to vex her nor to leave her too free to do just as she pleased; I kept a watch on her as far as possible, with such observation of her as was reasonable. But when a child was born to me, thence-forward I began to trust her, and placed all my affairs in her hands, presuming that we were now in perfect intimacy. It is true that in the early days, Athenians, she was the most excellent of wives; she was a clever, frugal housekeeper, and kept everything in the nicest order. But as soon as I lost my mother, her death became the cause of all my troubles. For it was in attending her funeral that my wife was seen by this man [Eratosthenes], who in time corrupted her. He looked out for the servant-girl who went to market, and so paid addresses to her mistress by which he wrought her ruin.

Now in the first place I must tell you, sirs (for I am obliged to give you these particulars), my dwelling is on two floors, the upper being equal in space to the lower, with the women's quarters above and the men's below. When the child was born to us, its mother suckled it; and in order that, each time that it had to be washed, she might avoid the risk of descending by the stairs, I used to live above, and the women below. By this time it had become such an habitual thing that my wife would often leave me and go down to sleep with the child, so as to be able to give it the breast and stop its crying. Things went on in this way for a long time, and I never suspected, but was simpleminded enough to suppose that my own was the chastest wife in the city.

Time went on, sirs; I came home unexpectedly from the country, and after dinner the child started crying in a peevish way, as the servant-girl was annoying it on purpose to make it so behave; for the man was in the house,-I learnt it all later. So I bade my wife go and give the child her breast, to stop its howling. At first she refused, as though delighted to see me home again after so long; but when I began to be angry and bade her go,

"Yes, so that you," she said, "may have a try here at the little maid. Once before, too, when you were drunk, you pulled her about." At that I laughed, while she got up, went out of the room, and closed the door, feigning to make fun, and she turned the key in the lock. I, without giving a thought to the matter, or having any suspicion, went to sleep in all content after my return from the country.

Towards daytime she came and opened the door. I asked why the doors made a noise in the night; she told me that the child's lamp had gone out, and she had lit it again at our neighbour's. I was silent and believed it was so. But it struck me, sirs, that she had powdered her face, though her brother had died not thirty days before; even so, however, I made no remark on the fact, but left the house in silence.

After this, sirs, an interval occurred in which I was left quite unaware of my own injuries; I was then accosted by a certain old female, who was secretly sent by a woman with whom that man was having an intrigue, as I heard later. This woman was angry with him and felt herself wronged, because he no longer visited her so regularly, and she kept a close watch on him until she discovered what was the cause. So the old creature accosted me where she was on the look-out, near my house, and said, "Euphiletus, do not think it is from any meddlesomeness that I have approached you; for the man who is working both your and your wife's dishonour happens to be our enemy. If, therefore, you take the servant-girl who goes to market and waits on you, and torture her, you will learn all. It is," she said, "Eratosthenes of Oë who is doing this; he has debauched not only your wife, but many others besides; he makes an art of it."

With these words, sirs, she took herself off; I was at once perturbed; all that had happened came into my mind, and I was filled with suspicion,-reflecting first how I was shut up in my chamber, and then remembering how on that night the inner and outer doors made a noise, which had never occurred before, and how it struck me that my wife had put on powder. All these things came into my mind, and I was filled with suspicion. Returning home, I bade the servant-girl follow me to the market, and taking her to the house of an intimate friend, I told her I was fully informed of what was going on in my house.

"So it is open to you," I said, "to choose as you please between two things,-either to be whipped and thrown into a mill, never to have any rest from miseries of that sort, or else to speak out the whole truth and, instead of suffering any harm, obtain my pardon for your transgressions. Tell no lies, but speak the whole truth."

The girl at first denied it, and bade me do what I pleased, for she knew nothing; but when I mentioned Eratosthenes to her, and said that he was the man who visited my wife, she was dismayed, supposing that I had exact knowledge of everything. At once she threw herself down at my knees, and having got my pledge that she should suffer no harm, she accused him, first, of approaching her after the funeral, and then told how at last she became his messenger; how my wife in time was persuaded, and by what means she procured his entrances, and how at the Thesmophoria,[11] while I was in the country, she went off to the temple with his mother. And the girl gave an exact account of everything else that had occurred.

When her tale was all told, I said, "Well now, see that nobody in the world gets knowledge of this; otherwise, nothing in your arrangement with me will hold good. And I require that you show me their guilt in the very act; I want no words, but manifestation of the fact, if it really is so."

She agreed to do this. Then came an interval of four or five days...[12]. But first I wish to relate what took place on the last day. I had an intimate friend named Sostratus. After sunset I met him as he came from the country. As I knew that, arriving at that hour, he would find none of his circle at home, I invited him to dine with me ; we came to my house, mounted to the upper room, and had dinner. When he had made a good meal, he left me and departed ; then I went to bed. Eratosthenes, sirs, entered, and the maidservant roused me at once, and told me that he was in the house. Bidding her look after the door, I descended and went out in silence; I called on one friend and another, and found some of them at home, while others were out of town. I took with me as many as I could among those who were there, and so came along. Then we got torches from the nearest shop, and went in; the door was open, as the girl had it in readiness.

We pushed open the door of the bedroom, and the first of us to enter were in time to see him lying down by my wife; those who followed saw him standing naked on the bed. I gave him a blow, sirs, which knocked him down, and pulling round his two hands behind his back, and tying them, I asked him why he had the insolence to enter my house. He admitted his guilt; then he besought and implored me not to kill him, but to exact a sum of money.

To this I replied, "It is not I who am going to kill you, but our city's law, which you have transgressed and regarded as of less account than your pleasures, choosing rather to commit this foul offence against my wife and my children than to obey the laws like a decent person."

Thus it was, sirs, that this man incurred the fate that the laws ordain for those who do such things; he had not been dragged in there from the street, nor had he taken refuge at my hearth, as these people say.[13] For how could it be so, when it was in the bedroom that he was struck and fell down then and there, and I pinioned his arms, and so many persons were in the house that he could not escape them, as he had neither steel nor wood nor anything else with which he might have beaten off those who had entered? But, sirs, I think you know as well as I that those whose acts are against justice do not acknowledge that their enemies speak the truth, but lie themselves and use other such devices to foment anger in their hearers against those whose acts are just. So, first read the law.

He did not dispute it, sirs: he acknowledged his guilt, and besought and implored that he might not be killed, and was ready to pay compensation in money. But I would not agree to his estimate, as I held that our city's law should have higher authority; and I obtained that satisfaction which you deemed most just when you imposed it on those who adopt such courses. Now, let my witnesses come forward in support of these statements.

[Witnesses are called and heard supporting his statements.]

I therefore, sirs, do not regard this requital as having been exacted in my own private interest, but in that of the whole city. For those who behave in that way, when they see the sort of prizes offered for such transgressions, will be less inclined to trespass against their neighbours, if they see that you also take the same view. Otherwise it were better far to erase our established laws, and ordain others which will inflict the penalties on men who keep watch on their own wives, and will allow full immunity to those who would debauch them. This would be a far juster way than to let the citizens be entrapped by the laws; these may bid a man, on catching an adulterer, to deal with him in whatever way he pleases, but the trials are found to be more dangerous to the wronged parties than to those who, in defiance of the laws, dishonour the wives of others. For I am now risking the loss of life, property and all else that I have, because I obeyed the city's laws.

Questions:
1. What rights did husbands and fathers have over their families in Athens?
2. How does this document illustrate the lives of women and the institution of marriage in Athens?
3. What does this document reveal about the lives of servants or slaves in Athens?

---

[11] A festival in honour of Demeter, celebrated by Athenian matrons in October
[12] Some words are missing here in the text.
[13] Witnesses for the prosecution. To kill someone on the hearth, the center of the family religion, would be sacrilege.

PART 4
Rome: Republic to Empire

4.1 The Speech of Camillus: *"All Things Went Well When We Obeyed the Gods, but Badly When We Disobeyed Them"*

Marcus Furius Camillus (d. c. 365 B.C.E.) was a patrician whose success as a general led to his election as dictator. Perhaps his greatest victory was his conquest of the Etruscan city of Veii. In the speech included here, attributed to Camillus by the Roman historian Titus Livius, he argues against the colonization of the captured city.

> **Source:** *The Ancient World: Readings in Social and Cultural History*, by D. Brendan Nagle and Stanley M. Burstein (Englewood Cliffs: Prentice Hall, 1995), pp. 184–186.

"When you see such striking stances of the effects of honoring or neglecting the divine, do you not see what an act of impiety you are about to perpetrate, and indeed, just at the moment we are emerging from the shipwreck brought about by our former irreligiosity? We have a city founded with all due observance of the auspices and augury. Not a spot in it is without religious rites and gods. Not only are the days for our sacrifices fixed, but also the places where they are to be performed.

"Romans, would you desert all these gods, public as well as private? Contrast this proposal with the action that occurred during the siege and was beheld with no less admiration by the enemy than by yourselves? This was the deed performed by Gaius Fabius, who descended from e citadel, braved Gallic spear, and performed on the Quirinal Hill the solemn rites of the Fabian family. Is it your wish that the family religious rites should not be interrupted even during war but that the public rites and the gods of Rome should be deserted in time of peace? Do you want the Pontiffs and Flamens to be more negligent of public ritual than a private individual in the anniversary rite of a particular family?

"Perhaps someone may say that either we will perform these duties at Veii or we will send our priests from there to perform the rituals here—but neither can be done without infringing on the established forms of worship. For not to enumerate all the sacred rites individually and all the gods, is it possible at the banquet of Jupiter for the *lectisternium* [*see* pp. 196–97, *"Steadiness of the Romans"*] to be set up anywhere else other than the Capitol? What shall I say of the eternal fire of Vesta, and of the statue which, as the pledge of empire, is kept under the safeguard of the temple [*the statue of Athena, the Palladium, supposed to have been brought by Aeneas from Troy*]? What, O Mars Gradivus, and you, Father Quirinus—what of your sacred shields? Is it right that these holy things, some as old as the city itself, some of them even more ancient, be abandoned on unconsecrated ground?

"Observe the difference existing between us and our ancestors. They handed down to us certain sacred rites to be performed by us on the Alban Mount and at Lavinium. It was felt to be impious to transfer these rites from enemy towns to Rome—yet you think you can transfer them to Veii, an enemy city, without sin! . . .

"We talk of sacred rituals and temples—but what about priests? Does it not occur to you what a sacrilege you are proposing to commit in respect of them? The Vestals have but one dwelling place which nothing ever caused them to leave except the capture of the city. Shall your Virgins forsake you, O Vesta? And shall the Flamen by living abroad draw on himself and on his country such a weight of guilt every night [*the Flamen was supposed to never leave Rome*]? What of the other things, all of which we transact under auspices within the Pomerium [*the sacred boundary around Rome*]? To what oblivion, to what neglect do we consign them? The Curiate Assembly, which deals with questions of war; the Centuriate Assembly at which you elect consuls and military tribunes—when can they be held under auspices except where they are accustomed to be held? Shall we transfer them to Veii? Or shall the people, for the sake of the assemblies, come together at great inconvenience in this city, deserted by gods and men? . . .

"Not without good cause did gods and men select this place for the founding of a city. These most healthful hills, a convenient river by means of which the produce of the soil may be conveyed from the inland areas, by which supplies from overseas may be obtained, close enough to the sea for all purposes of convenience, yet not exposed by being too close to the danger of foreign fleets. Situated in the center of Italy, it is singularly adapted by nature for the growth of a city. The very size of so new a city is itself proof. Citizens, it is now in its three hundred and sixty fifth year. Throughout those years you have been at war with many ancient nations. Not to mention single states, neither the Volscians combined with the Aequi, together with all their powerful towns, not all Etruria, so powerful by land and sea, occupying the breadth of Italy between the Tyrrhenian and Adriatic seas, have been a match for you in war. Since this is so, why in the name of goodness do you want to experiment elsewhere when you had such good fortune here? Though your courage may go with you, the fortune of this place certainly cannot be transferred. here is the Capitol, where a Human head was found which foretold that in that place would be the head of the world, the chief seat of empire [*a play on words; head in Latin is* caput].

Here, when the Capitol was being cleared with augural rites, the gods Juventas and Terminus, to the great joy of your fathers, refused to be moved. here is the fire of Vesta, here the sacred shields of Mars which fell from heaven. Here the gods will be propitious to you—if you stay."

Question:
1. What are the similarities between this speech and Pericles' Funeral Oration?

4.2   Women in Roman Politics: Manipulators or Manipulated?

Cleopatra (d. 31 B.C.E.), the most famous woman in Roman politics, was not even Roman, but was the last Ptolemy to rule Egypt. Some historians have argued that the liaison between Cleopatra and Antony was purely for political advantage, but contemporaries and ancient historians did not. Antony's passion for Cleopatra was obvious to them. Although Roman women did not have an official role in public life, they were often used as the cement in political alliances, such as when Antony married Octavia, the sister of Caesar [Octavian, later known as Augustus].

> **Source:** Plutarch, *Parallel Lives,* trans. John Dryden and modernized by A.H. Clough, Vol. V, (New York: Little, Brown and Company, 1909), pp. 189-213.

Antony first entertained Caesar, this also being a concession on Caesar's part to his sister; and when at length an agreement was made between them, that Caesar should give Antony two of his legions to serve him in the Parthian war, and that Antony should in return leave with him a hundred armed galleys, Octavia further obtained of her husband, besides this, twenty light ships for her brother, and of her brother, a thousand foot for her husband. So, having parted good friends, Caesar went immediately to make war with Pompey to conquer Sicily. And Antony, leaving in Caesar's charge his wife and children, and his children by his former wife Fulvia set sail for Asia.

But the mischief that thus long had lain still, the passion for Cleopatra, which better thoughts had seemed to have lulled and charmed into oblivion, upon his approach to Syria, gathered strength again, and broke out into a flame. And, in fine, like Plato's restive and rebellious horse of the human soul, flinging off all good and wholesome counsel, and breaking fairly loose, he sends Fonteius Capito to bring Cleopatra into Syria. To whom at her arrival he made no small or trifling present, Phoenicia, Coele-Syria, Cyprus, great part of Cilicia, that side of Judaea which produces balm, that part of Arabia where the Nabathaeans extend to the outer sea; profuse gifts, which much displeased the Romans.

... But Octavia, in Rome, being desirous to Antony, asked Caesar's leave to go to him; which he gave her, not so much, say most authors, to gratify his sister, as to obtain a fair pretence to begin the war upon her dishonorable reception. She no sooner arrived at Athens, but by letters from Antony she was informed of his new expedition, and his will that she should await him there. And, though she were much displeased, not being ignorant of the real reason of this usage, yet she wrote to him to know of what place he would be pleased she should send the things she had brought with her for his use; for she had brought clothes for his soldiers, baggage, cattle, money, and presents for his friends and officers, and two thousand chosen soldiers sumptuously armed, to form praetorian cohorts. This message was brought from Octavia to Antony by Niger, one of his friends, who added to it the praises she deserved so well. Cleopatra, feeling her rival already, as it were, at hand, was seized with fear, lest if to her noble life and her high alliance, she once could add the charm of daily habit and affectionate intercourse, she should become irresistible, and be his absolute mistress for ever. So she feigned to be dying for love of Antony, bring her body down by slender diet; when he entered the room, she fixed her eyes upon him in a rapture, and when he left, seemed to languish and half faint away. She took great pains that he should see her in tears, and, as soon as he noticed it, hastily dried them up and turned away, as if it were her wish that he should know nothing of it. All this was acting while he prepared for Media; and Cleopatra's creatures were not slow to forward the design, upbraiding Antony with his unfeeling, hard-hearted temper, thus letting a woman perish whose soul depended upon him and him alone. Octavia, it was true, was his wife, and had been married to him because it was found convenient for the affairs of her brother that it should be so, and she had the honor of the title; but Cleopatra, the sovereign queen of many nations, had been contented with the name of his mistress, nor did she shun or despise the character whilst she might see him, might live with him, and enjoy him; if she were bereaved of this, she would not survive the loss. In fine, they so melted and unmanned him, that, fully believing she would die if he forsook her, he put off the war and returned to Alexandria, deferring his Median expedition until next summer, though news came of the Parthians being all in confusion with intestine disputes. Nevertheless, he did some time after go into that country, and made an alliance with the king of Media, by marriage of a son of his by Cleopatra to the king's daughter, who was yet very young; and so returned, with his thoughts taken up about the civil war.

When Octavia returned from Athens, Caesar, who considered she had been injuriously treated, commanded her to live in a separate house; but she refused to leave the house of her husband, and entreated him, unless he had already resolved, upon other motives, to make war with Antony, that he would on her account let it alone; it would be intolerable to have it said of the two greatest commanders in the world, that they had involved the Roman people in a civil war, the one out of passion for the other out of resentment about, a woman. And her behavior proved her words to be sincere. She remained in Antony's house as if he were at home in it, and took the noblest and most generous care, not only of his children by her, but of those by Fulvia also. She received all the friends of Antony that came to Rome to seek office or upon any business, and did her utmost to prefer their requests to Caesar; yet this her honorable deportment did but, without her meaning it, damage the reputation of Antony; the wrong he did to such a woman made him hated. Nor was the division he made among his sons at Alexandria less unpopular; it seemed a theatrical piece of insolence and contempt of his country. For, assembling the people in the exercise ground, and causing two golden thrones to be placed on a platform of silver, the one for him and the other for Cleopatra, and at their feet lower thrones for their children, he proclaimed Cleopatra queen of Egypt, Cyprus, Libya, and Coele-Syria, and with her conjointly Caesarion, the reputed son of the former Caesar, who left Cleopatra with child. His own sons by Cleopatra were to have the style of kings of kings; to Alexander he gave Armenia and Media, with Parthia, so soon as it should be overcome; to Ptolemy, Phoenicia, Syria, and Cilicia. Alexander was brought out before the people in the Median costume, the tiara and upright peak, and Ptolemy, in boots and mantle and Macedonian cap done about with the diadem; for this was the habit of the successors of Alexander, as the other was of the Medes and Armenians. And, as soon as they had saluted their parents, the one was received by a guard of Macedonians, the other by one of Armenians. Cleopatra was then, as at other times when she appeared in public, dressed in the habit of the goddess Isis, and gave audience to the people under the name of the New Isis.

Caesar, relating these things in the senate, and often complaining to the people, excited men's minds against Antony. And Antony also sent messages of accusation against Caesar. The principal of his charges were these: first, that he had not made any division with him of Sicily, which was lately taken from Pompey; secondly, that he had retained the ships he had lent him for the war; thirdly, that after deposing Lepidus, their colleague, he had taken for himself the army, governments, and revenues formerly appropriated to him; and, lastly, that he had parcelled out almost all Italy amongst his own soldiers, and left nothing for his. Caesar's answer was as follows: that he had put Lepidus out of government because of his own misconduct; that what he had got in war he would divide with Antony, so soon as Antony gave him a share of Armenia; that Antony's soldiers had no claims in Italy, being in possession of Media and Parthia, the acquisitions which their brave actions under their general had added to the Roman empire.

Antony was in Armenia when this answer came to him, and immediately sent Canidius with sixteen legions towards the sea; but he, in the company of Cleopatra, went to Ephesus, whither ships were coming in from all quarters to form the navy, consisting, vessels of which Cleopatra furnished two hundred, together with twenty thousand talents, and provision for the whole army during the war. Antony, on the advice of Domitius and some others, bade Cleopatra return into Egypt, there to expect the event of the war; but she, dreading some new reconciliation by Octavia's means, prevailed with Canidius, by a large sum of money, to speak in her favor with Antony, pointing out to him that it was not just that one that bore so great a part in the charge of the war should be robbed of her share of glory in the carrying it on; nor would it be politic to disoblige the Egyptians, who were so considerable a part of his naval forces; nor did he see how she was inferior in prudence to any one of the kings that were serving with him; she had long governed a great kingdom by herself alone, and long lived with him, and gained experience in public affairs. These arguments (so the fate that destined all to Caesar would have it), prevailed; and when all their forces had met, they sailed together to Samos, and held high festivities....

This over, he gave Priene to his players for a habitation, and set sail for Athens, where fresh sports and play-acting employed him. Cleopatra, jealous of the honors Octavia had received at Athens (for Octavia was much beloved by the Athenians), courted the favor of the people with all sorts of attentions. The Athenians, in requital, having decreed her public honors, deputed several of the citizens to wait upon her at her house; amongst whom went Antony as one, he being an Athenian citizen, and he it was that made the speech. He sent orders to Rome to have Octavia removed out of his house. She left it, we are told, accompanied by all his children, except the eldest by Fulvia, who was then with his father, weeping and grieving that she must be looked upon as one of the causes of the war. But the Romans pitied, not so much her, as Antony himself, and more particularly those who had seen Cleopatra, whom they could report to have no way the advantage of Octavia either in youth or in beauty.

The speed and extent of Antony's preparations alarmed Caesar, who feared he might be forced to fight the decisive battle that summer. For he wanted many necessaries, and the people grudged very much to pay the taxes; freemen being called upon to pay a fourth part of their incomes, and freed slaves an eighth of their property, so that there were loud outcries against him, and disturbances throughout all Italy. And this is looked upon as one of the greatest of Antony's oversights, that he did not then press the war. For he allowed time at once for Caesar to make his preparations, and for the commotions to pass over. For while people were having their money called for, they were mutinous and violent; but, having paid it, they held their peace. Titius and Plancus, men of consular dignity and friends to Antony, having been ill used by Cleopatra, whom they had most resisted in her design of being present in the war came over to Caesar, and gave information of the contents of Antony's will, with which they were acquainted. It was deposited in the hands of the vestal virgins, who refused to deliver it up, and sent Caesar word, if he pleased, he should come and seize it himself, which he did. And, reading it over to himself, he noted those places that were most for his purpose, and, having summoned the senate, read them publicly. Many were scandalized at the proceeding, thinking it out of reason and equity to call a man to account for what was not to be until after his death. Caesar specially pressed what Antony said in his will about his burial; for he had ordered that even if he died in the city of Rome, his body, after being carried in state through the forum, should be sent to Cleopatra at Alexandria. Calvisius, a dependent of Caesar's, urged other charges in connection with Cleopatra against Antony; that he had given her the library of Pergamus, containing two hundred thousand distinct volumes; that at a great banquet, in the presence of many guests, he had risen up and rubbed her feet, to fulfil some wager or promise; that he had suffered the Ephesians to salute her as their queen; that he had frequently at the public audience of kings and princes received amorous messages written in tablets made of onyx and crystal, and read them openly on the tribunal; that when Furnius, a man of great authority and eloquence among the Romans, was pleading, Cleopatra happening to pass by in her chair, Antony started up and left them in the middle of their cause, to follow at her side and attend her home.

Calvisius, however, was looking upon as the inventor of most of these stories. Antony's friends went up and down the city to gain him credit, and sent one of themselves, Geminius, to him, to beg him to take heed and not allow himself to be deprived by yote of his authority, and proclaimed a public enemy to the Roman state. But Geminius no sooner arrived in Greece but he was looked upon as one of Octavia's spies; at their suppers he was made a continual butt for mockery, and was put to sit in the least honorable places; all which he bore very well, seeking only an occasion of speaking with Antony. So, at supper, being told to say what business he came about, he answered he would keep the rest for a soberer hour, but one thing he had to say, whether full or fasting, that all would go well if Cleopatra would return to Egypt. And on Antony showing his anger at it, "You have done well, Geminius," said Cleopatra, "to tell your secret without being put to the rack." So Geminius, after a few days, took occasion to make his escape and go to Rome. Many more of Antony's friends were drive from him by the insolent usage they had from Cleopatra's flatterers, amongst whom were Marcus Silanus and Dellius the historian. And Dellius says he was afraid of his life, and that Glaucus, the physician, informed him of Cleopatra's design against him. She was angry with him for having said that Antony's friends were served with sour wine, while at Rome Sarmentus, Caesar's little page (his *delicia,* as the Romans call it), drank Falernian.

As soon as Caesar had completed his preparations, he had a decree made, declaring war on Cleopatra, and depriving Antony of the authority which he had let a woman exercise in his place. Caesar added that he had drunk potions that had bereaved him of his senses, and that the generals they would have to fight with would be Mardion the eunuch, Pothinus, Iras, Cleopatra's hairdressing girl, and Charmion, who were Antony's chief state-councillors.

Questions:
1. What did Lucretia represent in this story about the relationship of the Roman Republic?
2. What is Plutarch's interpretation of the relationships between Antony, Cleopatra and Octavia?
3. How do Octavia and Lucretia each typify the ideal Roman woman?
4. How could one argue that these women were both manipulators or manipulated in this political/personal situation?

4.3   Slaves in the Roman Countryside

Slaves were an integral part of Roman society and economy. The number of slaves increased drastically in the last century of the Republic and during the early Empire as Roman territory expanded. Below are instructions and advice from three famous Roman writers about how to manage slaves used in agriculture.

> **Source:** Columella, On Agriculture 1.8.1, 2, 5, 6, 9, 10, 11, 16, 18, 19; Cato the Elder, On Agriculture, 56, 57, 58, 59; Varro, On Agriculture 1.17.1, 3-5, 7, printed in As the Romans Did: A Sourcebook in Roman Social History, Jo-Ann Shelton ed., (New York: Oxford University Press, 1998), pp. 169-72.

FROM COLUMBELLA, *ON AGRICULTURE*

A landowner must be concerned about what responsibility it is best to give each slave and what sort of work to assign to each. I advise that you not appoint a foreman from that type of slave who is physically attractive, and certainly not from the type who has been employed in the city, where all skills are directed toward increasing pleasure. This lazy and sleepy type of slave is accustomed to having a lot of time on his hands, to lounging around the Campus Martius, the Circus Maximus, the theaters, the gambling dens, the snack bars, and the brothels, and he is always dreaming of these same foolish pleasures. If a city slave continues to daydream when he has been transferred to a farm, the landowner suffers the loss not just of the slave but actually of his whole estate. You should therefore choose someone who has been hardened to farm work from infancy, and who has been tested by experience.

The foreman should be given a female companion both to keep him in bounds and also to assist him in certain matters.... He should not be acquainted with the city or the weekly market, except in regard to matters of buying and selling produce, which is his duty.[1]

The foreman should choose the slaves' clothing with an eye to utility rather than fashion, and he should take care to protect them from the wind, cold, and rain with long-sleeved leather tunics, patchwork cloaks, or hooded capes. All of these garments ward off the elements and thus no day is so unbearable that no out-of-doors work can be done. The foreman should not only be skilled in agricultural operations, but also be endowed with such strength and virtue of mind (at least as far as his slave's personality permits) that he may oversee men neither with laxity nor with cruelty.

There is no better method of maintaining control over even the most worthless of men than demanding hard labor.... After their exhausting toil, they will turn their attention to rest and sleep rather than to fun and games.

It should be an established custom for the landowner to inspect the slaves chained in the prison, to examine whether they are securely chained, whether their quarters are safe and well guarded, whether the foreman has put anyone in chains or released anyone from chains without his master's knowledge.

A diligent master investigates the quality of his slaves' food and drink by tasting it himself. He examines their clothing, hand-coverings, and foot-coverings. He should even grant them the opportunity of registering complaints against those who have harmed them either through cruelty or dishonesty.... I have given exemption from work and sometimes even freedom to very fertile female slaves when they have borne many children, since bearing a certain number of offspring ought to be rewarded. For a woman who has three sons, exemption from work is the reward; for a woman who has more, freedom.[2]

CATO THE ELDER, *ON AGRICULTURE*

When the master has arrived at his villa and has paid his respects to the household *lar*[3], he should walk around the whole farm, on the same day if possible; if not, on the next day. When he has learned how the farm is being looked after, what work has been done, and what has not been done, he should summon his foreman the next day and ask how much of the work has been completed, how much remains, whether the completed work was done pretty much on time, whether the remaining work can be finished, and how much wine, grain, and other products were produced. When he has received this information, he should calculate what was done in how many days, by how many workers. When the figures are not encouraging, the foreman usually claims that he has worked diligently but "the slaves have been ill," "the weather has been bad," the slaves have run away," etc., etc. When he has given these and many other excuses, call his attention again to your calculation of the work done and the workers used. If the weather has been rainy, remind him of the chores that could have been done on rainy days: washing out wine vats, sealing them with pitch, cleaning the villa, moving grain, hauling out manure, making a manure pit, cleaning seed, mending ropes, and making new ones. The slaves might also have repaired their cloaks and hats. On festival days, old ditches might have been cleaned out, the road repaired, brambles cut down, gardens dug, the meadow cleared, twigs bundled, thorn bushes uprooted, spelt ground, and general cleaning done. When the slaves were sick, he should not have given them so much food. When these things have been calmly pointed out, give orders for the remaining work to be completed. Look over his account books for ready cash, grain, fodder supplies, wine, oil-what has been sold, what payments have been collected, how much is left, and what remains to be sold. Order him to collect outstanding debts and to sell what remains. Order him to provide whatever is needed for the current year, and to sell off whatever is superfluous.... Tell him to scrutinize the herd and hold an auction. Sell your oil, if the price is right, and the surplus wine and grain. Sell off the old oxen, the blemished cattle and sheep, wool, hides, old wagons, old tools, old slaves, sick slaves, and whatever else is superfluous.

---

[1] The foreman obviously had some freedom of movement and could travel back and forth to the market, but was not to linger there to enjoy the attractions of the city.

[2] Although the mother might be set free, her children remained as slaves. We do not know whether Columella's willingness to free fertile female slaves was unusual among slave-owners.

[3] The *Lars Familiaris* was the spirit or deity who protected the household and its members. There was a shrine to this deity in the home, and sacrifices were made to it regularly.

Food rations for the slaves: For those who do hard labor, four measures of wheat in winter, four and one-half in the summer. For the foreman, the foreman's wife, the taskmaster, and the shepherd, three measures. For slaves working in chains, four pounds of bread in the winter, five when they begin to dig the vineyard, and back to four again when the figs appear.

. . . .

Clothing for the slaves: Provide a tunic weighing three and one-half pounds and a cloak every other year. Whenever you give a tunic or cloak to any of the slaves, first get the old one back; from it, patchwork coverings can be made. You ought to give the slaves sturdy wooden shoes every other year.

FROM VARRO, *ON AGRICULTURE*

The instruments by which the soil is cultivated: Some men divide these into three categories: (1) articulate instruments, i.e., slaves; (2) inarticulate instruments, i.e., oxen; and (3) mute instruments, i.e. carts....

Slaves should be neither timid nor brazen. They ought to have as overseers men who have knowledge of basic reading and writing skills and of some learning.... It is very important that the overseer be experienced in farming operations, for he must not only give orders but also perform the work, so that the other slaves may imitate him and understand that he has been made their overseer for good reason-he is superior to them in knowledge. However, overseers should not be allowed to force obedience with whips rather than words, if words can achieve the same result. Don't buy too many slaves of the same nationality, for this is very often accustomed to cause domestic quarrels. You should make your foremen more eager to work by giving them rewards and by seeing that they have [*monetary* rewards] and female companions from among their fellow slaves, who will bear them children.... Slaves become more eager to work when treated generously with respect to food or more clothing or time off or permission to graze some animal of their own on the farm, and other things of this kind. The result is that, when some rather difficult task is asked of them or some rather harsh punishment is meted out, their loyalty and good will toward their master is restored by the consolation of these former generosities.

Questions:
1. *How well or badly were slaves regarded and treated in Roman culture?*
2. *What differences can you see in the three writers' attitude toward slaves?*
3. *What differences appear between slaves who worked in the countryside on villas and those who lived in city households?*

4.4   Appian of Alexandria, *"War, Slaves, and Land Reform: Tiberius Gracchus"*

Appian of Alexandria was a second-century Roman historian. Over the course of his life, he held a variety of important political offices and was a supporter of Roman imperialism. The excerpt from his history of Rome included here describes the reform efforts of Tiberius Graccus.

> **Source:** *Readings in World Civilizations, Vol. 1*, by Kevin Reilly (New York: St. Martins Press, 1995), pp. 81–87.

The Romans, as they subdued the Italian nations successively in war, seized a part of their lands and built towns there, or established their own colonies in those already existing, and used them in place of garrisons. Of the land acquired by war they assigned the cultivated part forthwith to settlers, or leased or sold it. Since they had no leisure as yet to allot the part which then lay desolated by war (this was generally the greater part), they made proclamation that in the meantime those who were willing to work it might do so for a share of the yearly crops—a tenth of the grain and a fifth of the fruit. From those who kept flocks was required a share of the animals, both oxen and small cattle. They did these things in order to multiply the Italian race, which they considered the most laborious of peoples, so that they might have plenty of allies at home. But the very opposite thing happened; for the rich, getting possession of the greater part of the undistributed lands, and being emboldened by the lapse of time to believe that they would never be dispossessed, and adding to their holdings the small farms of their poor neighbors, partly by purchase and partly by force, came to cultivate vast tracts instead of single estates, using for this purpose slaves as laborers and herdsmen, lest free laborers should be drawn from agriculture into the army. The ownership of slaves itself brought them great gain from the multitude of their progeny, who increased because they were exempt from military service. Thus the powerful ones became enormously rich and the race of slaves multiplied throughout the country, while the Italian people dwindled in numbers and strength, being oppressed by penury, taxes, and military service. If they had any respite from these evils they passed their time in idleness, because the land was held by the rich, who employed slaves instead of freemen as cultivators.

For these reasons the people became troubled lest they should no longer have sufficient allies of the Italian stock, and lest the government itself should be endangered by such a vast number of slaves. Not perceiving any remedy, as it was not easy, nor exactly just, to deprive men of so many possessions they had held so long, including their own trees, buildings and fixtures, a law was once passed with difficulty at the instance of the tribunes, that nobody should hold more than 500 jugera of this land, or pasture on it more than 100 cattle or 500 sheep. To ensure the observance of this law it was provided also that there should be a certain number of freemen employed on the farms, whose business it should be to watch and report what was going on. Those who held possession of lands under the law were required to take an oath to obey the law, and penalties were fixed for violating it, and it was supposed that the remaining land would soon be divided among the poor in small parcels. But there was not the smallest consideration shown for the law or the oaths. The few who seemed to pay some respect to them conveyed their lands to their relations fraudulently, but the greater part disregarded it altogether.

At length Tiberius Sempronius Gracchus, an illustrious man, eager for glory, a most powerful speaker, and for these reasons well known to all, delivered an eloquent discourse, while serving as tribune, concerning the Italian race, lamenting that a people so valiant in war, and blood relations to the Romans, were declining little by little in the pauperism and paucity of numbers without any hope of remedy. He inveighed against the multitude of slaves as useless in war and never faithful to their masters, and adduced the recent calamity brought upon the masters by their slaves in Sicily, where the demands of agriculture had greatly increased the number of the latter; recalling also the war waged against them by the Romans, which was neither easy nor short, but long-protracted and full of vicissitudes and dangers. After speaking thus he again brought forward the law, providing that nobody should hold more than 500 jugera of the public domain. But he added a provision to the former law, that the sons of the present occupiers might each hold one-half of that amount, and that the remainder should be divided among the poor by triumvirs, who should be changed annually.

This was extremely disturbing to the rich because, on account of the triumvirs, they could no longer disregard the law as they had done before; nor could they buy the allotments of others, because Gracchus had provided against this by forbidding sales. They collected together in groups, and made lamentation, and accused the poor of appropriating the results of their tillage, their vineyards, and their dwellings. Some said that they had paid the price of the land to their neighbors. Were they to lose the money with the land? Others said that the graves of their ancestors were in the ground, which had been allotted to them in the division of their fathers' estates. Others said that their wives' dowries had been expended on the estates, or that the land had been given to their own daughters as dowry. Money-lenders could show loans made on this security. All kinds of wailing and expressions of indignation were heard at once. On the other side were heard the lamentations of the poor—that they had been reduced from competence to extreme penury, and from that to childlessness, because they were unable to rear their offspring. They recounted the military service they had rendered, by which this very land had been acquired, and were angry that they should be robbed of their share of the common property. They reproached the rich for employing slaves, who were always faithless and ill-tempered and for that reason unserviceable in war, instead of freemen, citizens, and soldiers. While these classes were lamenting and indulging in mutual accusations, a great number of others, composed of colonists, or inhabitants of the free towns, or persons otherwise interested in the lands and who were under like apprehensions, flocked in and took sides with their respective factions. Emboldened by numbers and exasperated against each other they attached themselves to turbulent crowds, and waited for the voting on the new law, some trying to prevent its enactment by all means, and others supporting it in every possible way. In addition to personal interest the spirit of rivalry spurred both sides in the preparations they were making against each other for the day of the comitia.

What Gracchus had in his mind in proposing the measure was not wealth, but an increase of efficient population. Inspired greatly by the usefulness of the work, and believing that nothing more advantageous of admirable could ever happen to Italy, he took no account of the difficulties surrounding it. When the time for voting came he advanced many other arguments at considerable length and also asked them whether it was not just to divide among the common people what belonged to them in common; whether a citizen was not worthy of more consideration at all times than a slave; whether a man who served in the army was not more useful than one who did not; and whether one who had a share in the country was not more likely to be devoted to the public interests. He did not dwell long on this comparison between freemen and slaves, which he considered degrading, but proceeded at once to a review of their hopes and fears for the country, saying that the Romans had acquired most of their territory by conquest, and that they had hopes of occupying the rest of the habitable world, but now the question of greatest hazard was, whether they should gain the rest by having plenty of brave men, or whether, through their weakness and mutual jealously, their enemies should take away what they already possessed. After exaggerating the glory and riches on the one side and the danger and fear on the other, he admonished the rich to take heed, and said that for the realization of these hopes they ought to bestow this very land as a free gift, if necessary, on men who would rear children, and not, by contending about small things, overlook larger ones; especially since they were receiving an ample compensation for labor expended in the undisputed title to 500 jugera each of free land, in a high state of cultivation, without cost, and half as much more for each son of those who had sons. After saying much more to the same purport and exciting the poor, as well as others who were moved by reason rather than by the desire for gain, he ordered the scribe to read the proposed law.

Marcus Octavius, another tribune, who had been induced by those in possession of the lands to interpose his veto (for among the Romans the tribune's veto always prevailed), ordered the scribe to keep silence. Thereupon Gracchus reproached him severely and adjourned the comitia to the following day. Then he stationed a sufficient guard, as if to force Octavius against his will, and ordered the scribe with threats to read the proposed law to the multitude. He began to read, but when Octavius again vetoed he stopped. Then the tribunes fell to wrangling with each other, and a considerable tumult arose among the people. The leading citizens besought the tribunes to submit their controversy to the Senate for decision. Gracchus seized on the suggestion, believing that the law was acceptable to all well-disposed persons, and hastened to the senate house. There, as he had only a few followers and was upbraided by the rich, he ran back to the forum and said that he would take the vote at the comitia of the following day, both on the law and on the magistracy of Octavius, to determine whether a tribune who was acting contrary to the people's interest could continue to hold his office. And so he did, for when Octavius, nothing daunted, again interposed, Gracchus distributed the pebbles to take a vote on him first. When the first tribe voted to abrogate the magistracy of Octavius, Gracchus turned to him and begged him to desist from his veto. As he would not yield, the votes of the other tribes were taken. There were thirty-five tribes at that time. The seventeen that voted first angrily sustained this motion. If the eighteenth should do the same it would make a majority. Again did Gracchus, in the sight of the people, urgently importune Octavius in his present extreme danger not to prevent this most pious work, so useful to all Italy, and not to frustrate the wishes so earnestly entertained by the people, whose desires he ought rather to share in his character of tribune, and not to risk the loss of his office by public condemnation. After speaking thus he called the gods to witness that he did not willingly do any despite to his colleague. As Octavius was still unyielding he went on taking the vote. Octavius was forthwith reduced to the rank of a private citizen and slunk away unobserved.

Quintus Mummius was chosen tribune in his place, and the agrarian law was enacted. The first triumvirs appointed to divide the land were Gracchus himself, the prosper of the law, his brother of the same name, and his father-in-law, Appius Claudius, since the people still feared that the law might fail of execution unless Gracchus should be put in the lead with his whole family. Gracchus became immensely popular by reason of the law and was escorted home by the multitude as though he were the founder, not of a single city or race, but of all the nations of Italy. After this the victorious party returned to the fields from which they had come to attend to this business. The defeated ones remained in the city and talked the matter over, feeling bitterly, and saying that as soon as Gracchus should become a private citizen he would be sorry that he had done despite to the sacred and inviolable office of tribune, and had opened such a fountain of discord in Italy.

At the advent of summer the notices for the election of tribunes were given, and as the day for voting approached it was very evident that the rich were earnestly promoting the election of those most inimical to Gracchus. The latter, fearing that evil would befall if he should not be reelected for the following year, summoned his friends from the fields to attend the comitia, but as they were occupied with their harvest he was obliged, when the day fixed for the voting drew near, to have recourse to the plebeians of the city. So he went around asking each one separately to elect him tribune for the ensuing year, on account of the danger he had incurred for them. When the voting took place the first two tribes pronounced for Gracchus. The rich objected that it was not lawful for the same man to hold the office twice in succession. The tribune Rubrius, who had been chosen by lot to preside over the comitia, was in doubt about it, and Mummius, who had been chosen in place of Octavius, urged him to turn over the comitia to his charge. This he did, but the remaining tribunes contended that the presidency should be decided by lot, saying that when Rubrius, who had been chosen in that way, resigned, the casting of lots ought to be done over again for all. As there was much strife over this question, Gracchus, who was getting the worst of it, adjourned the voting to the following day. In utter despair he clothed himself in black, while still in office, and led his son around the forum and introduced him to each man and committed him to their charge, as if he were about to perish at the hands of his enemies.

The poor were moved with deep sorrow, and rightly so, both on their own account (for they believed that they were no longer to live in a free state under equal laws, but were reduced to servitude by the rich), and on account of Gracchus himself, who had incurred such danger and suffering in their behalf. So they all accompanied him with tears to his house in the evening, and bade him be of good courage for the morrow. Gracchus cheered up, assembled his partisans before daybreak, and communicated to them a signal to be displayed in case of a fight. He then took possession of the template on the Capitoline hill, where the voting was to take place, and occupied the middle of the assembly. As he was obstructed by the other tribunes and by the rich, who would not allow the votes to be taken on this question, he gave the signal. There was a sudden shout from those who saw it, and a resort to violence in consequence. Some of the partisans of Gracchus took position around him like bodyguards. Others, having girded themselves, seized the fasces* and staves in the hands of the lictors and broke them in pieces. They drove the rich out of the assembly with such disorder and wounds that the tribunes fled from their places in terror, and the priests closed the doors of the temple. Many ran away pell-mell and scattered wild rumors. Some said that Gracchus had deposed all the other tribunes, and this was believed because none of them could be seen. Others said that he had declared himself tribune for the ensuing year without an election.

Under these circumstances the Senate assembled at the temple of Fides. It is astonishing to me that they never thought of appointing a dictator in this emergency, although they had often been protected by the government of a single ruler in such times of peril. Although this resource had been found most useful in former times few people remembered it, either then or later. After reaching the decision that they did reach, they marched up to the Capitol, Cornelius Scipio Nasica, the pontifex maximus [president of the guild of priests—Ed.], leading the way and calling out with a loud voice, "Let those who would save the country follow me." He wound the border of his toga about his head either to induce a greater number to go with him by the singularity of his appearance, or to make for himself, as it were, a helmet as a sign of battle for those who looked on, or in order to conceal from the gods what he was about to do. When he arrived at the temple and advanced against the partisans of Gracchus they yielded to the reputation of a foremost citizen, for they saw the Senate following with him. The latter wrested clubs out of the hands of the Gracchus themselves, or with fragments of broken benches or other apparatus that had been brought for the use of the assembly, began beating them, and pursued them, and drove them over the precipice. In the tumult many of the Gracchans perished, and Gracchus himself was caught near the temple, and was slain at the door close by the statues of the kings. All the bodies were thrown by night into the Tiber.

So perished on the Capitol, and while still tribune, Gracchus, the son of the Gracchus who was twice consul, and of Cornelia, daughter of that Scipio who subjugated Carthage. He lost his life in consequence of a most excellent design, which, however, he pursued in too violent a manner. This shocking affair, the first that was perpetrated in the public assembly, was seldom without parallels thereafter from time to time. On the subject of the murder of Gracchus the city was divided between sorrow and joy. Some mourned for themselves and for him, and deplored the present condition of things, believing that the commonwealth no longer existed, but had been supplanted by force and violence. Others considered that everything had turned out for them exactly as they wished.

Questions:
1. What are the virtues of the land reform plan?
2. Could it have worked?

4.5 Polybius: *"Why Romans and Not Greeks Govern the World"*

An influential Greek politician, Polybius (203 – c. 120 B.C.E.) was deported to Rome in 167 B.C.E. after the Roman defeat of Macedon. Under the protection and patronage of the Scipio family, he became a strong advocate of Roman power. His most famous work was a massive history of Rome in which he sought to explain Rome's rise to preeminence in the Mediterranean world.

> **Source:** Polybius, *Historiarum reliquiae* (Paris: Didot, 1839), VI, iii–xvii, pp. 338–48, *passim*; trans. and condensed by Henry A. Myers.

With those Greek states which have often risen to greatness and then experienced a complete change of fortune, it is easy to describe their past and to predict their future. For there is no difficulty in reporting the known facts, and it is not hard to foretell the future by inference from the past. But it is no simple matter to explain the present state of the Roman constitution, nor to predict its future owing to our ignorance of the peculiar features of Roman life in the past. Particular attention and study are therefore required if one wishes to survey clearly the distinctive qualities of Rome's constitution.

Most writers distinguish three kinds of constitutions: kingship, aristocracy, and democracy. One might ask them whether these three are the sole varieties or rather the best. In either case they are wrong. It is evident that the best constitution is one combining all three varieties, since we have had proof of this not only theoretically but by actual experience, Lycurgus having organized the Spartan state under a constitution based upon this principle. Nor can we agree that these three are the only kinds of states. We have witnessed monarchical and tyrannical governments, which differ sharply from true kingship, yet bear a certain resemblance to it. Several oligarchical constitutions also seem to resemble aristocratic ones. The same applies to democracies.

We must not apply the title of kingship to every monarchy, but must reserve it for one voluntarily accepted by willing subjects who are ruled by good judgment and not be terror and violence. Nor can we call every oligarchy an aristocracy, but only one where the government is in the hands of a selected body of the justest and wisest men. Similarly the name of democracy cannot be applied to a state in which the masses are free to do whatever they wish, but only to a community where it is traditional and customary to reverence the gods, honor one's parents, respect one's elders, and obey the laws. Such states, provided the will of the greater number prevails, are to be called democracies.

We should therefore recognize six kinds of governments: the three above mentioned, kingship, aristocracy, and democracy, and the three which are naturally related to them, monarchy, oligarchy, and ochlocracy (mob-rule). The first to arise was monarchy, its growth being natural and unaided: the next is true kingship born from monarchy by planning and reforms. Kingship is transformed into its vicious related form, tyranny; and next, the abolishment of both gives birth to aristocracy. Aristocracy by its very nature degenerates into oligarchy; and when the masses take vengeance on this government for its unjust rule, democracy is born: and in due course the arrogance and lawlessness of this form of government produces mob-rule to complete the cycle. Such is the recurring cycle of constitutions; such is the system devised by nature.

Rome, foreseeing the dangers presented by such a cycle, did not organize her government according to any one type, but rather tried to combine all the good features of the best constitutions. All three kinds of government shared in the control of the Roman state. Such fairness and propriety was shown in the use of these three types in drawing up the constitution, that it was impossible to say with certainty if the whole system was aristocratic, democratic, or monarchical. If one looked at the power of the Consuls, the constitution seemed completely monarchical; if at that of the Senate, it seemed aristocratic; and if at the power of the masses, it seemed clearly to be a democracy.

Roman Consuls exercise authority over all public affairs. All other magistrates except the tribunes are under them and bound to obey them, and they introduce embassies to the Senate. They consult the Senate on matters of urgency, they carry out in detail the provisions of its decrees, they summon assemblies, introduce measures, and preside over the execution of popular decrees. In war their power is almost uncontrolled; for they are empowered to make demands on allies, to appoint military tribunes, and to select soldiers. They also have the right of inflicting punishment on anyone under their command, and spending any sum they decide upon from the public funds. If one looks at this part of the administration alone, one may reasonably pronounce the constitution to be a pure monarchy or kingship.

To pass to the Senate: in the first place it has the control of the treasury, all revenue and expenditure being regulated by it; with the exception of payments made to the consuls, no disbursements are made without a decree of the Senate. Public works, whether constructions or repairs, are under the control of the Senate. Crimes such as treason, conspiracy, poisoning, and assassination, as well as civil disputes, are under the jurisdiction of the Senate. The Senate also sends all embassies to foreign countries to settle differences, impose demands, receive submission, or declare war; and with respect to embassies arriving in Rome it decides what reception and what answer should be given to them. All these matters are in the hands of the Senate, so that in these respects the constitution appears to be entirely aristocratic.

After this we are naturally inclined to ask what part in the constitution is left for the people. The Senate controls all the particular matters I mentioned and manages all finances, and the Consuls have uncontrolled authority as regards armaments and operations in the field. But there is a very important part left for the people. For the people alone have the right to confer honors and inflict punishment, the only bonds by which human society is held together. For where the distinction between rewards and punishment is overlooked, or is observed but badly applied, no affairs can be properly administered. For how can one expect rational administration when good and evil men are held in equal estimation? The people judge cases punishable by a fine, especially when the accused have held high office. In capital cases they are the sole judges. It is the people who bestow office on the deserving, the noblest reward of virtue in a state; the people have the power of approving or rejecting laws, and what is most important of all, they deliberate on questions of war and peace. Further in the case of alliances, terms of peace, and treaties, it is the people who ratify all these. Thus one might plausibly say that the people's share in the government is the greatest, and that the constitution is a democratic one.

Having stated how political power is distributed among the three constitutional forms, I will now explain how each of the three parts is enabled, if they wish, to oppose or cooperate with the other parts. The Consul, when he leaves with his army, appears to have absolute authority in all matters necessary for carrying out his purpose; however, in fact he really requires the support of the people and the Senate. For the legions require constant supplies, and without the consent of the Senate, neither grain, clothing, nor pay can be provided; so that the commander's plans come to nothing, if the Senate chooses to impede them. As for the people it is indispensable for the Consuls to conciliate them, however far away from home they may be; for it is the people who ratify or annual treaties, and what is most important, the Consuls are obliged to account for their actions to the people. So it is not safe for the Consuls to underestimate the importance of the good will of either the Senate or the people.

The Senate, which possess such great power, is obliged to respect the wishes of the people, and it cannot carry out inquiries into the most grave offenses against the state, unless confirmed by the people. The people alone have the power of passing or rejecting any law meant to deprive the Senate of some of its traditional authority. Therefore the Senate is afraid of the masses and must pay due attention to the popular will.

Similarly, the people are dependent on the Senate and must respect its members both in public and in private. Through the whole of Italy a vast number of contracts, which it would not be easy to enumerate, are given out by the Senate for the construction and repair of public buildings, and besides this there are many things which are farmed out, such as navigable rivers, harbors, gardens, mines, lands, in fact everything that forms part of the Roman domains. Now all these matters are undertaken by the people, and everyone is interested in these contracts and the work they involve. Certain people are the actual purchasers of the contracts, others are the partners of these first, others guarantee them, others pledge their own fortunes to the state for this purpose. In all these matters the Senate is supreme. It can grant extension of time; it can relieve the contractor if any accident occurs; and if the work proves to be absolutely impossible to carry out it can liberate him from his contract. There are many ways in which the Senate can either benefit or injure those who manage public property. What is even more important is that the judges in most civil trials are appointed from the Senate. As a result of the fact that all citizens are at the mercy of the Senate, and look forward with alarm to the uncertainty of litigation, they are very shy of obstructing or resisting its decisions. Similarly anyone is reluctant to oppose the projects of the Consuls as all are generally and individually under their authority when in the field.

Such being the power that each part has of hampering the others or cooperating with them, their union is adequate to all emergencies, so that it is impossible to find a better political system than this. Whenever the menace of some common danger from abroad compels them to act in concord and support each other, the strength of the state becomes great, as all are zealously competing in devising means of meeting the need of the hour. Consequently, this peculiar form of constitution posses an irresistible power of attaining every object upon which it is resolved. When they are freed from external menace, and reap the harvest of good fortune and affluence which is the result of their success, and in the enjoyment of this prosperity are corrupted by flattery and idleness and become insolent and overbearing, as indeed happens often enough, it is then especially that we see the state providing itself a remedy for the evil from which it suffers. For when one part having grown out of proportion to the others aims at supremacy and tends to become too predominant, it is evident that none of the three is absolute. The purpose of one can be offset and resisted by the others, and none of them will excessively outgrow the others or treat them with contempt. All parts abide by the traditional constitutional practices because any aggressive impulse is sure to be checked and because they fear from the outset the possibility of being interfered with by the others. . . .

Questions:

1. Why does Polybius think that checks and balances have given lasting stability to the Roman political system?
2. How does Polybius divide the Roman government into branches? How is his tripartite division both similar to and different from the system outlined in the U.S. Constitution?
3. How does aristocracy fit into the Roman system, according to Polybius? Does the concept of aristocracy play any part of the U.S. Constitution?

4.6 Marcus Tullius Cicero: *The Laws*

Marcus Tullius Cicero (106 – 43 B.C.E.) was the greatest of all Roman orators. An opponent of Julius Caesar, he was put to death when Octavius emerged triumphant in the civil war that followed Caesar's assassination. In the selection from his De legibus libri included here, Cicero argued that all true laws reflect nature.

Source: Marcus Tullius Cicero, *De legibus libri*, ed. J. Vahlen (Berlin: F. Vahlenum, 1883; I, vi, 18–19, I, xi, 33; II, iv, 9–v, 13) trans. Henry A. Myers. Dialogue-personage names omitted.

Those learned men appear to be right who say that law is the highest reason implanted in Nature, which commands what should be done and prohibits what should not be: when this same reason takes root and develops in the human mind it is law. Thus they consider law to be intelligence which has the power to command people to do what is right and to refrain from what is wrong. . . . The way Nature has made us let us share the concept of justice with each other and pass it on to all men. . . . Those human beings to whom Nature gave reason were also give *right* reason in matters of command and prohibition. . . .

From the time we were children, we have been calling rules that begin: "If a man makes a complaint in court" and similar things by the name "laws." It would be good now if we could establish that with commands to do things or refrain from doing them nations apply the power to steer people towards doing the right things and away from committing crimes; however, this power is not only older than peoples and governments but is of the same age as the God who protects and rules both Heaven and earth. You see, the divine mind cannot exist without reason, and divine reason must have the power to sanction what is right and wrong.

Nothing was ever written to say that one man alone on a bridge should face massed, armed forces of enemies and command the bridge behind him to be destroyed, but that fact should not mislead us into thinking that [Horatio] Cocles was not following to the utmost the law which summons us to deeds of bravery. If there has been no written law in Rome against rape back when Lucius Tarquin ruled as king, that would not mean that Sextus Tarquin was not breaking that eternal law when he took Lucretia by force. . . . The fact is that reason did exist, a gift of Nature, calling upon man to do right and abstain from wrong. It did not begin to be law when it first came into being, which it did at the same time as the divine mind. . . . The varied ordinances formulated for monetary needs of the peoples bear the name "laws" through being so favored by conventional usage rather than because they are really *laws*. . . . Men introduced such laws to insure the protection of citizens and states, as well as the peaceful and happy lot of mankind. Those who originated these sanctions persuaded their people that what they were writing down and putting into effect would—if the people lived by them—give them happiness and honor. When these sanctions were formulated and went into effect they were indeed called "laws."

How about all the pernicious and pestilential bits of legislation which nations have been known to enact? These no more deserve the name "laws" than the agreements that gangs of robbers might make among themselves. We know that if ignorant and inexperienced men should recommend poisons instead of medicines with the power to heal these would not be called "physicians' prescriptions." In the same way, nothing causing injury should be called a "law," no matter how it may have been enacted by a state or how the people may accept it. Thus we find that law reflects justice, distinct from injustice, and comes from that most ancient and rightfully dominant of all things: Nature, which all human laws reflect when they punish evildoers while defending and protecting good people.

Questions:
1. *Why does Cicero consider Natural Law to have greater power than man-made law? Do you? Why?*
2. *Why do you suppose that most twentieth-century lawyers prefer not to argue their cases in terms of Natural Law? Can you think of some cases in which Natural Law argumentation has won out?*

4.7   A Marriage Contract

The following marriage contract was drawn up in Egypt in 13 B.C.E. Since Egypt had only become a Roman province in 30 B.C.E., it is likely that it was as much [or more] influenced by Egyptian and Greek-Hellenistic procedure as by Roman practice.

> **Source:** *As the Romans Did: A Sourcebook in Roman Social History,* Jo-Ann Shelton ed., (New York: Oxford University Press, 1998), p 43.

To Protarchus, from Thermion daughter of Apion, accompained by her guardian Apollonius son of Chaereas, and from Apollonius son of Ptolemaeus:—

Thermion and Apollonius son of Ptolemaeus agree that they have come together for the purpose of sharing their lives with one another. The above-mentioned Apollonius son of Ptolemaeus agrees that he has received from Thermion, handed over from her household as a dowry, a pair of gold earrings.... From now on he will furnish Thermion, as his wedded wife, with all necessities clothing according to his means, and he will not mistreat her or cast her out or insult her or bring in another wife; otherwise he must at once return the dowry and in addition half again as much.

And Thermion will fulfill her duties toward her husband and her marriage, and will not sleep away from the house or be absent one day without the consent of Apollonius son of Ptolemaeus and will not damage or injure their common home and will not consort with another man; otherwise she, if judged guilty of these actions, will be deprived of her dowry, and in addition the transgressor will be liable to the prescribed fine. Dated the 17th year of Caesar [Augustus].

Questions:
1. *How does this marriage contract compare to Greek and Roman laws regarding women and marriage?*
2. *What is expected of the man and the woman in marriage?*
3. *What do these expectations tell us about the nature of marriage in Hellenistic/Roman Alexandria?*

PART 5
Imperial Rome

5.1   Augustus' Moral Legislation: Family Values

In 18 B.C.E. Augustus launched his program of social and moral reform. Concerned about public morality and worried about the continued domination of Italians in the Empire, he enacted laws curbing adultery, promoting marriage, and encouraging childbearing.

Source: Naphtali Lewis and Meyer Reinhold, ed., *Roman Civilization: Sourcebook I: The Republic,* (New York: Harper Torchbooks, 1966), pp. 48-52.

VARIOUS LEGAL SOURCES, COLLECTED IN REGIA ACADEMIA ITALICA, *ACTA DIVI AUGUSTI,* PARS PRIOR (ROME. 1945) *PP. 112-28* (ABRIDGED).

"No one shall hereafter commit debauchery or adultery knowingly and with malice aforethought." These words of the law apply to him who abets as well as to him who commits debauchery or adultery.

The Julian Law on Curbing Adultery punishes not only defilers of the marriages of others... but also the crime of debauchery when anyone without the use of force violates either a virgin or a widow of respectable character.

By the second section [of the law] a father, if he catches an adulterer of his daughter... in his own home or that of his son-in-law, or if the latter summons him in such an affair, is permitted to kill that adulterer with impunity, just as he may forthwith kill his daughter.

A husband also is permitted to kill an adulterer of his wife, but not anyone at all as is the father's right. For this law provides that a husband is permitted to kill [a procurer, actor, gladiator, convicted criminal, freedman, or slave] caught in the act of adultery with his wife in his own home (but not in that of his father-in-law). And it directs a husband who has killed any one of these to divorce his wife without delay. Moreover, he must make a report to the official who has jurisdiction in the place where the killing has occurred and he must divorce his wife; if he does not do this, he does not slay with impunity.

The law punishes as a procurer a husband who retains his wife after she has been caught in adultery and lets the adulterer go (for he ought to be enraged at his wife, who violated his marriage). In such a case the husband should be punished since he cannot claim the excuse of ignorance or feign patience on the pretext of not believing it.

He by whose aid or advice with malice aforethought it is made possible for a man or woman caught in adultery to evade punishment through bribe or any other collusion is condemned to the same penalty as is fixed for those who are convicted of the crime of procuring.

He who makes a profit from the adultery of his wife is scourged.

If a wife receives any profit from the adultery of her husband she is liable under the Julian Law as if she were an adultress.... Anyone who marries a woman convicted of adultery is liable under this law.

. . . .

It was enacted that women convicted of adultery be punished by confiscation of half of their dowry and a third of their property and by relegation to an island, and that the male adulterers be punished by like relegation to an island and by confiscation of half of their property, with the proviso that they be relegated to different islands.

SUETONIUS *LIFE OF AUGUSTUS* XXXIV

Among the laws which he revised or enacted were a sumptuary law and laws on adultery and chastity, on bribery, and on classes permitted to marry. The last of these he amended somewhat more severely than the others, but in the face of the clamor of opposition he was unable to push it through until he had withdrawn or mitigated some of the penalties and increased the rewards.... And when he saw that the intent of the law was being evaded by betrothal with immature girls and by frequent changes of wives, he shortened the duration of betrothals[1] and set a limit on divorces.

---

[1] He ordered that girls might not be bethrothed before the age of ten, and he limited the duration of bethrothals to a maximum of two years. Tacitus adds (*Annals,* xxviii) that the rewards offered for successful prosecution of evaders of these laws stimulated the rise of professional spies and informers.

DIO CASSIUS *ROMAN HISTORY* LIV. XV5. I–A

He laid heavier assessments upon the unmarried men and women and on the other hand offered prizes for marriage and the begetting of children. And since among the nobility there were far more males than females, he allowed all [free men] who wished, except senators, to marry freedwomen, and ordered that their offspring should be held legitimate.

TACITUS *ANNALS* III. XXV

Augustus in his old age supplemented the Julian Laws with the Papian-Poppaean Law in order to increase the penalties on celibacy and enrich the treasury. But people were not driven thereby to marriage and the rearing of children in any great numbers, so powerful were the attractions of the childless state. Instead the number of persons courting danger grew steadily greater, for every household was undermined by the denunciations of informers; and now the country suffered from its laws, as it had previously suffered from its vices.

VARIOUS LEGAL SOURCES, COLLECTED IN REGIA ACADEMIA ITALICA, *ACTA DIVI AUGUSTI,* PARS PRIOR (ROME, 1945) *PP. 112-28* (ABRIDGED IN THE COLLECTION CITED ABOVE).

The Julian Law provides as follows:

No one who is or shall be a senator, or a son, grandson born of a son, or great-grandson born of a son's son of any one of these, shall knowingly and with malice aforethought have as betrothed or wife a freedwoman or any woman who herself or whose father or mother is or has been an actor.

And no daughter of a senator or granddaughter born of a son or great-granddaughter born of a grandson (a son's son) shall knowingly and with malice aforethought be betrothed or married to a freedman or to a man who himself or whose father or mother is or has been an actor, and no such man shall knowingly and with malice aforethought have her as betrothed or wife.

Freeborn men are forbidden to marry a prostitute, a procuress, a woman manumitted by a procurer or procuress, one caught in adultery, one convicted in a public action, or one who has been an actress.

Conditions added contrary to laws and imperial decrees or to morality—such as, "if you do not marry," or "if you have no children"—carry no weight.

In the seventh section of the Julian Law priority in assuming the fasces[2] is given not to the consul who is older but to the one who has more children than his colleague either in his power[3] or lost in war.

.... But if both are married and the fathers of the same number of children, then the time-honored practice is restored and the one who is older assumes the fasces first.

• • • •

A freedwoman who is married to her patron shall not have the right of divorce,... as long as the patron wants her to be his wife.

A man or wife can, by virtue of marriage, inherit a tenth of the other's estate. But if they have living children from a previous marriage, in addition to the tenth which they take by virtue of marriage they receive as many tenths as the number of children. Likewise a common son or daughter lost after the day of naming adds one tenth, and two lost after the ninth day add two tenths. Besides the tenth they can receive also the usufruct of a third part of the estate, and whenever they have children the ownership of the same part.

Sometimes a man or wife can inherit the other's entire estate, for example, if both or either are not yet of the age at which the law requires children—that is, if the husband is under twenty-five and the wife under twenty; or if both have while married past the age prescribed by the Papian Law-that is, the man sixty, the woman fifty...

• • • •

Sometimes they inherit nothing from each other, that is, if they contract a marriage contrary to the Julian and Papian-Poppaean Law (for example if anyone marries a woman of ill repute or a senator marries a freedwoman).

---

[2] The ancient symbols of Roman imperium, power.
[3] That is, minors or unmarried females.

    Bachelors also are forbidden by the Julian Law to receive inheritances or legacies.... Likewise by the Papian Law childless persons, precisely because they have no children, lose one half of inheritances and legacies.

    The Julian Law exempted women from marriage for one year after the death of a husband and six months after a divorce; the Papian Law [raised these to] two years after the death of a husband and a year and six months after a divorce.

    In keeping with the thirty-fifth section of the Julian Law, those who without just cause prevent any children in their power from marrying or refuse to give a dowry... are compelled to give them in marriage and bestow dowry.

. . . .

If there is no one entitled to the possession of an estate, or if there is someone but he has failed to exercise his right, the estate passes to the public treasury.

Questions:
1. *How were men and women treated differently under this legislation?*
2. *From the opinions expressed in the readings, how effective do you think these laws were in achieving Augustus' goals?*

5.2   A Satirical View of Women

Juvenal (ca. 55–ca. 130 C.E.), called "the greatest satiric poet who ever lived," wrote sixteen Satires which luridly reveal the glaring vices and follies of Roman society at the end of the first century C.E. In his Sixth Satire, Juvenal denounces the emancipated upper-class women of Rome for breaching social conventions and moral standards.

Source: Peter Green, trans., *Juvenal: The Sixteen Satires,* (New York: Penguin Classics, 1967), pp. 142–44.

Yet a musical wife's not so bad as some presumptuous
Flat-chested busybody who rushes around the town
Gate-crashing all-male meetings, talking back straight-faced
To a uniformed general—and in her husband's presence.
She knows all the news of the world, what's cooking in
Thrace
Or China, just what the stepmother did with her stepson
Behind closed doors, who's fallen in love, which gallant
Is all the rage. She'll tell you who got the widow
Pregnant, and in which month; she knows each woman's
Pillow endearments, and all the positions she favors.
She's the first to spot any comet presaging trouble
For some eastern prince, in Armenia, maybe,
or Parthia.
She's on to the latest gossip and rumors as soon as
They reach the city-gates, or invents her own, informing
Everyone she meets that Niphates has overflowed
And is inundating whole countries—towns are cut off,
She says, and the land is sinking: flood and disaster! Yet
even this is not so insufferable
As her habit, when woken up, of grabbing some poor-class
Neighbor and belting into him with a whip. If her precious
Sleep is broken by barking, 'Fetch me the cudgels,'

She roars, 'and be quick about it!' The dog gets a

thrashing,
But its master gets one first. She's no joke to cross,
And her face is a grisly fright. Not till the evening
Does she visit the baths: only then are her oil-jars and
The rest of her clobber transferred there. First she works
out
With the weights and dumb-bells. Then, when her arms
are aching,
The masseur takes over, craftily slipping one hand
Along her thigh, and tickling her up till she comes.
Lastly she makes for the sweat-room. She loves to sit there
Amid all that hubbub, perspiring. Meanwhile at home
Her unfortunate guests are nearly dead with hunger.
At last she appears, all flushed, with a three-gallon thirst,
Enough to empty the brimming jar at her feet
Without assistance. She knocks back two straight pints
On an empty stomach, to sharpen her appetite: then
Throws it all up again, souses the floor with vomit
That flows in rivers across the terrazzo. She drinks
And spews by turns, like some big snake that's tumbled
Into a wine-vat, till her gilded jordan brims
Right over with sour and vinous slops. Quite sickened,
Eyes shut, her husband somehow holds down his bile.
Worse still is the well-read menace, who's hardly settled
for dinner
Before she starts praising Virgil, making a moral case
For Dido (death justifies all), comparing, evaluating
Rival poets, Virgil and Homer suspended
In opposite scales, weighed up one against the other.
Critics surrender, academics are routed, all
Fall silent, not a word from lawyer or auctioneer—
Or even another woman. Such a rattle of talk,
You'd think all the poets and bells were being clashed
together

Questions:
1. *How familiar do any of Juvenal's complaints about women and the city sound in the context of our times?*
2. *Written in satire, how seriously can we take Juvenal's descriptions and opinions of life and people?*
3. *What does this selection reveal about the tenor of Roman culture and society at the end of the first century C.E.?*

5.3 Traditional Roman Religious Practices

Roman religion was a religion of ritual and form, rather than of ideas and beliefs, and did not teach ethics or demand good works. Morality and ethical behavior were a family and civic responsibility, rather than a religious one. The first several selections illustrate common religious practices. By the fourth century C.E., however, Christianity began to win the support of the emperors, and in 392 the emperor Theodosius I banned all non-Christian rites. Christianity thus became the one official state religion. The last selection is an appeal to the Roman Emperor by Symmachus (ca. 340–402 C.E.), who had not converted from the old religion to Christianity. He requested that the altar of Victory erected by Augustus that had been removed from the Senate by the previous Christian Emperor be returned. He was unsuccessful.

Source: *As the Romans Did: A Sourcebook in Roman Social History,* ed. Jo-Ann Shelton, (New York:

Oxford University Press, 1998), pp. 366, 371–74, 379–80, 390–91.

A HYMN TO DIANA, BY CATULLUS, *POEMS*

Diana, we are in your care, we chaste girls and boys. Come, chaste boys and girls, let us sing in praise of Diana.

O daughter of Leto, mighty offspring of mightiest Jupiter, you who were born beside the Delian olive tree, queen of the mountains and the green forests and the trackless glens and the murmuring streams.

You are called Juno Lucina by women in the agony of childbirth. You are called powerful Trivia. You are called Luna, with your borrowed light.

You, goddess, measuring out the year's progress by your monthly phases, do fill the farmer's humble storerooms with fine produce.

Hallowed be thy name, whatever name it is that you prefer. And, as in years past you have been accustomed to do, so now, too, protect and preserve the race of Romulus with your kindly favor.

PLINY THE ELDER, *NATURAL HISTORY*

It apparently does no good to offer a sacrifice or to consult the gods with due ceremony unless you also speak words of prayer. In addition, some words are appropriate for seeking favorable omens, others for warding off evil, and still others for securing help. We notice, for example, that our highest magistrates make appeals to the gods with specific and set prayers. And in order that no word be omitted or spoken out of turn, one attendant reads the prayer from a book, another is assigned to check it closely, a third is appointed to enforce silence. In addition, a flutist plays to block out any extraneous sounds. There are recorded remarkable cases where either ill-omened noises have interrupted and ruined the ritual or an error has been made in the strict wording of the prayer.

CATO THE ELDER, *ON AGRICULTURE*

Before you harvest your crops, you should offer a sow as a preliminary sacrifice in the following manner. Offer a sow to Ceres before you store up the following crops: spelt, wheat, barley, beans, and rape seed. Before you slaughter the sow, invoke Janus,[1] Jupiter, and Juno, offering incense and wine.

Offer sacrificial crackers to Janus with the following words: "Father Janus, in offering to you these sacrificial crackers I humbly pray that you may be benevolent and well disposed toward me and my children and my home and my family."

Offer an oblation cracker to Jupiter and honor him with the following words: "Jupiter, in offering to you this oblation cracker I humbly pray that you may be benevolent and well disposed toward me and my children and my home and my family, being honored by this oblation cracker."

Afterward offer wine to Janus with the following words: "Father Janus, just as I humbly prayed when I offered to you the sacrificial crackers, so now for the same purpose be honored with sacrificial wine."

And afterward offer wine to Jupiter with the following words: "Jupiter, be honored by the oblation cracker, be honored by the sacrificial wine."

And then slaughter the sow as a preliminary sacrifice. When the internal organs have been cut out,[2] offer sacrificial crackers to Janus and honor him in the same terms as when you earlier offered him crackers. Offer an oblation cracker to Jupiter and honor him in the same terms as before. Likewise, offer wine to Janus and offer wine to Jupiter in the same terms as it was offered when you earlier offered the sacrificial crackers and the oblation crackers. Afterward offer the internal organs and wine to Ceres.

---

[1] Janus was the god of all beginnings (January) and thus appropriately invoked at the beginning of the harvest. He was also the god of doorways and was frequently represented as having two faces, each looking in the opposite direction, even as a door has two faces.

[2] The internal organs were first inspected carefully to ascertain the will of the gods [taking an augury] and then burned on the altar. The rest of the pig was eaten by the people who witnessed the sacrifice.

CATO THE ELDER, *ON AGRICULTURE* 141

It is necessary to purify your farmland in the following way. Have a pig-sheep-bull procession led around the land, while the following words are spoken: "With the benevolence of the gods, and hoping that everything may turn out well, I entrust to you the responsibility of having the pig-sheep-bull procession led around my farm, field, and land, wherever you decide the animals ought to be led or carried."

Invoke Janus and Jupiter with an offering of wine; then speak these words: 'Father Mars, I pray and entreat you to be benevolent and well disposed toward me and my home and my family. And for this reason I have ordered a pig-sheep-bull procession to be led around my field, land, and farm, so that you will hinder, ward off, and turn away diseases seen and unseen, barrenness and crop losses, disasters and storms; and so that you will allow the vegetable crops, the grain crops, the vineyards, and the orchards to grow and achieve a productive maturity; and so that you will protect the shepherds and the flocks and bestow safety and good health upon me and my home and my family. For these reasons, therefore, and because of the purifying of my farm, land, and field, and the offering of a sacrifice for purification, even as I have prayed, be honored by the sacrifice of the suckling pig-sheep-bull. For this reason, therefore, Father Mars, be honored by this suckling pig-sheep-bull sacrifice."

Slaughter the sacrificial animals with a knife. Bring forward sacrificial crackers, and an oblation cracker, and offer them. When you slaughter the pig, lamb, and calf, you must use these words:

"For this reason, therefore, be honored by the sacrifice of the pig-sheep-bull."... If all the sacrificial victims are not perfect, speak these words: "Father Mars, if somehow the suckling pig-sheep-bull sacrifice was not satisfactory to you, I offer this new pig-sheep-bull sacrifice as atonement." If there is doubt about only one or two of the animals, speak these words: "Father Mars, since that pig was not satisfactory to you, I offer this pig as atonement."

SYMMACHUS, *DISPATCHES TO THE EMPEROR*

Every man has his own customs and his own religious practices. Similarly, the divine mind has given to different cities different religious rites which protect them. And, just as each man receives at birth his own soul, so, too, does each nation receive a *genius*[3] which guides its destiny. We should also take into account the bestowal of favors, which, more than anything else, proves to man the existence of gods. For, since no human reasoning can illuminate this matter, from where else can knowledge of the gods come, and come more correctly, than from the recollection and evidences of prosperity? If the long passage of time gives validity to religious rites, we must keep faith with so many centuries and we must follow our fathers, who followed their fathers and therefore prospered.

Let us imagine that Rome herself is standing before us now and addressing these words to you:

"Best of emperors, fathers of the fatherland, respect my age! The dutiful performance of religious rites has carried me through many years. Let me enjoy the ancient ceremonies, for I do not regret them. Let me live in my own way, for I am free. This is the religion which made the whole world obedient to my laws. These are the rites which drove back Hannibal from my walls and the Senones from my Capitol. Have I been preserved only for this-to be rebuked in my old age? I will consider the changes which people think must be instituted, but modification, in old age, is humiliating and too late."

And so we are asking for amnesty for the gods of our fathers, the gods of our homeland. It is reasonable to assume that whatever each of us worships can be considered one and the same. We look up at the same stars, the same sky is above us all, the same universe encompasses us. What difference does it make which system each of us uses to find the truth? It is not by just one route that man can arrive at so great a mystery.

Questions:
1. What were the basic elements of Roman prayers and rituals?
2. How do the prayers and rituals illustrate the nature and characteristics of traditional Roman religion?
3. What argument does Symmachus use to support his request for the return of the altar of Victory? Why do you think the fourth-century Christians did not find this argument persuasive?

---

[3] Guardian Spirit.

5.4 *The Gospel According to Luke*

Written near the end of the first century, The Gospel According to Luke is thought to have been written by the physician Luke. Luke was Gentile convert and a friend of Paul's. In the selection included here, Luke tells the story of the life of Christ from Christ's birth to his baptism by John the Baptist.

Source: *The Bible: Revised Standard Version: Chapter 1–3, pp. 62–67.*

1 Inasmuch as many have undertaken to compile a narrative of the things which have been accomplished among us, 2 just as they were delivered to us by those who from the beginning were eyewitnesses and ministers of the world, 3 it seemed goo to me also, having followed all things closely [a] for some time past, to write an orderly account for you, most excellent. The-oph'ilus, 4 that you may know the truth concerning the things of which you have been informed.

5 In the days of Herod, king of Judea, there was a priest named Zechari'ah, [b] of the division of Abi'jah; and he had a wife of the daughters of Aaron, and her name was Elizabeth. 6 And they were both righteous before God, walking in all the commandments and ordinances of the Lord blameless. 7 But they had no child, because Elizabeth was barren, and both were advanced in years.

8 Now while he was serving as priest before God when his division was on duty, 9 according to the custom of the priesthood, it fell to him by lot to enter the temple of the Lord and burn incense. 10 And the whole multitude of the people were praying outside at the hour of incense. 11 And there appeared to him an angel of the Lord standing on the right side of the altar of incense. 12 And Zechari'ah was troubled when he saw him, and fear fell upon him. 13 But the angel said to him, "Do not be afraid, Zechari'ah, for your prayer is heard, and your wife Elizabeth will bear you a son, and you shall call his name John. 14 And you will have joy and gladness, and many will rejoice at his birth; 15 for he will be great before the Lord, and he shall drink no wine nor strong drink, and he will be filled with the Holy Spirit, even from his mother's womb. 16 And he will turn many of the sons of Israel to the Lord their God, 17 and he will go before him in the spirit and power of Eli'jah, to turn the hearts of the fathers to the children, and the disobedient to the wisdom of the just, to make ready for the Lord a people prepared."

18 And Zechari'ah said to the angel, "How shall I know this? For I am an old man and my wife is advanced in years." [19] And the angel answered him, "I am Gabriel, who stand in the presence of God; and I was sent to speak to you, and to bring you this good news. 20 And behold, you will be silent and unable to speak until the day that these things come to pass, because you did not believe my words, which will be fulfilled in their time." 21 And the people were waiting for Zechari'ah, and they wondered at this delay in the temple. 22 And when he came out, he could not speak to them, and they perceived that he had seen a vision in the temple; and he made signs to them and remained dumb. 23 And when his time of service was ended, he went to his home.

24 After these days his wife Elizabeth conceived, and for five months she hid herself, saying, 25 "Thus the Lord has done to me in the days when he looked on me, to take away my reproach among men."

26 In the sixth month the angel Gabriel was sent from God to a city of Galilee named Nazareth, 27 to a virgin betrothed to a man whose name was Joseph, of the house of David; and the virgin's name was Mary.

28 And he came to her and said, "Hail, O favored one, the Lord is with you!" [c] 29 But she was greatly troubled at the saying, and considered in her mind what sort of greeting this might be. 30 And the angel said to her, "Do not be afraid, Mary, for you have found favor with God. 31 And behold, you will conceive in your womb and bear a son, and you shall call his name Jesus. 32 He will be great, and will be called the Son of the Most High; and the Lord God will give to him the throne of his father David, 33 and he will reign over the house of Jacob for ever; and of his kingdom there will be no end." 34 And Mary said to the angel, "How can this be, since I have no husband?" 35 And the angel said to her, "The Holy Spirit will come upon you, and the power of the Most High will overshadow you; therefore the child to be born [d] will be called holy, the Son of God.

---

[a] *Or accurately*
[b] Greek Zacharias
[c] *Other ancient authorities add* "Blessed are you among women!"
[d] *Other ancient authorities add* of you
1. 2: 1 Jn. 1. 1; Acts 1. 21; Heb. 2, 3. 1. 3: Acts 1. 1. 2. 4: Jn. 20. 31. 1. 5: Mt. 2. 1; 1 Chron. 24. 10; 2 Chron. 31. 2. 1. 9: Ex. 30. 7. 1. 11: Lk. 2. 9; Acts 5. 19. 1. 13: Lk. 1. 30, 60. 1. 15: Num. 6. 3; Lk. 7. 33. 1. 17: Mt. 11. 14; 17. 13; Mal. 4. 5. 1. 18: K. 1. 34. 1. 19: Dan. 8. 16; 9. 21; Mt. 18. 10. 1. 25: Gen. 30. 23; Is. 4. 1.

36 And behold, your kinswoman Elizabeth in her old age has also conceived a son; and this is the sixth month with her who was called barren. 37 For with God nothing will be impossible." 38 And Mary said, "Behold, I am the handmaid of the Lord; let it be to me according to your word." And the angel departed from her.

39 In those days Mary arose and went with haste into the hill country, to a city of Judah, 40 and she entered the house of Zechari'ah and greeted Elizabeth. 41 And when Elizabeth heard the greeting of Mary, the babe leaped in her womb; and Elizabeth was filled with the Holy Spirit 42 and she exclaimed with a loud cry, "Blessed are you among women, and blessed is the fruit of your womb! 43 And why is this granted me, that the mother of my Lord should come to me? 44 For behold, when the voice of your greeting came to my ears, the babe in my womb leaped for joy. 45 And blessed is she who believed that there would be *e* a fulfillment of what was spoken to her from the Lord."

46 And Mary said, "My soul magnifies the Lord, 47 and my spirit rejoices in God my Savior, 48 for he has regarded the low estate of his handmaiden. For behold, henceforth all generations will call me blessed; 49 for he who is mighty has done great things for me, and holy is his name. 50 And his mercy is on those who fear him from generation to generation. 51 He has shown strength with his arm, he has scattered the proud in the imagination of their hearts, 52 he has put down the mighty from their thrones, and exalted those of low degree; 53 he has filled the hungry with good things, and the rich he has sent empty away. 54 He has helped his servant Israel, in remembrance of his mercy, 55 as he spoke to our fathers, to Abraham and to his posterity for ever."

56 And Mary remained with her about three months, and returned to her home.

57 Now the time came for Elizabeth to be delivered, and she gave birth to a son. 58 And her neighbors and kinsfolk heard that the Lord had shown great mercy to her, and they rejoiced with her. 59 And on the eighth day they came to circumcise the child; and they would have named him Zechari'ah after his father, 60 but his mother said, "Not so; he shall be called John." 61 And they said to her, "None of your kindred is called by this name." 62 And they made signs to his father, inquiring what he would have him called. 63 And he asked for a writing tablet, and wrote, "His name is John." And they all marveled. 64 And immediately his mouth was opened and his tongue loosed, and he spoke, blessing God.

65 And fear came on all their neighbors. And all these things were talked about through all the hill country of Judea; 66 and all who heard them laid them up in their hearts, saying, "What then will this child be?" For the hand of the Lord was with him.

67 And his father Zechari'ah was filled with the Holy Spirit, and prophesied, saying,

68 "Blessed be the Lord God of Israel, for he has visited and redeemed his people, 69 and has raised up a horn of salvation for us in the house of his servant David, 70 as he spoke by the mouth of his holy prophets from of old, 71 that we should be saved from other enemies, and from the hand of all who hate us; 72 to perform the mercy promised to our fathers, and to remember his holy covenant, 73 the oath which he swore to our father Abraham, 74 to grant us that we, being delivered form the hand of our enemies, might serve him without fear, 75 in holiness and righteousness before him all the days of our life. 76 And you, child, will be called the prophet of the Most High; for you will go before the Lord to prepare his ways, 77 to give knowledge of salvation to his people in the forgiveness of their sins, 78 through the tender mercy of our God, when the day shall dawn upon us *f* from on high 79 to give light to those who sit in darkness and in the shadow of death, to guide our feet into the way of peace."

80 And the child grew and became strong in spirit, and he was in the wilderness till the day of his manifestation to Israel.

2 In those days a decree went out from Caesar Augustus that all the world should be enrolled. 2 This was the first enrollment, when Quirin'i-us was governor of Syria. 3 And all went to be enrolled, each to his own city. 4 And Joseph also went up from Galilee, from the City of Nazareth, to Judea, to the city of David, which is called Bethlehem, because he was of the house and lineage of David, 5 to be enrolled with Mary, his betrothed, who was with child. 6 And while they were there, the time came for her to be delivered. 7 And she gave birth to her first-born son and wrapped him in swaddling cloths, and laid him in a manger, because there was no place for them in the inn.

8 And in that region there were shepherds out in the field, keeping watch over their flock by night. 9 And an angel of the Lord appeared to them, and the glory of the Lord appeared to them, and the glory of the Lord shone around them, and they were filled with fear.

10 And the angel said to them, "Be not afraid; for behold, I bring you good news of a great joy which will come to all the people; 11 for to you is born this day in the city of David a Savior, who is Christ the Lord. 12 And this will be a sign for you: you will find a babe wrapped in swaddling cloths and lying in a manger." 13 And suddenly there was with the angel a multitude of the heavenly host praising God and saying,

---

e Or believed, for there will be
f Or whereby the dayspring will visit. *Other ancient authorities read* since the dayspring has visited

14 "Glory to God in the highest, and on earth peace among men with whom he is pleased!" ᵍ

15 When the angels went away from them into heaven, the shepherds said to one another, "Let us go over to Bethlehem and see this thing that has happened, which the Lord has made known to us." ¹⁶ And they went with haste, and found Mary and Joseph, and the babe lying in a manger. ¹⁷ And when they saw it they made known the saying which had been told them concerning this child; ¹⁸ and all who heard it wondered at what the shepherds told them. ¹⁹ But Mary kept all these things, pondering them in her heart. ²⁰ And the shepherds returned, glorifying and praising God for all they had heard and seen, as it had been told them.

21 And at the end of eight days, when he was circumcised, he was called Jesus, the name given by the angel before he was conceived in the womb.

22 And when the time came for their purification according to the law of Moses, they brought him up to Jerusalem to present him to the Lord ²³ (as it is written in the law of the Lord, "Every male that opens the womb shall be called holy to the Lord") ²⁴ And to offer a sacrifice according to what is said in the law of the Lord, "a pair of turtledoves, or two young pigeons."

25 Now there was a man in Jerusalem, whose name was Simeon, and this man was righteous and devout, looking for the consolation of Israel, and the Holy Spirit was upon him. ²⁶ And it had been revealed to him by the Holy Spirit that he should not see death before he had seen the Lord's Christ. ²⁷ And inspired by the Spirit ʰ he came into the temple; and when the parents brought in the child Jesus, to do for him according to the custom of the law, ²⁸ he took him up in his arms and blessed God and said,

29 "Lord, now lettest thou thy servant depart in peace, according to thy word; ³⁰ for mine eyes have seen thy salvation ³¹ which thou has prepared in the presence of all peoples ³² a light for revelation to the Gentiles, and for glory to they people Israel."

33 And his father and his mother marveled at what was said about him; ³⁴ Simeon blessed them and said to Mary his mother, "Behold, this child is set for the fall and rising of many in Israel, and for a sign that is spoken against ³⁵ (and a sword will pierce through your own soul also), that thoughts out of many hearts may be revealed."

36 And there was a prophetess, Anna, the daughter of Phan'u-el, of the tribe of Asher; she was of a great age, having lived with her husband seven years from her virginity, ³⁷ and as a widow till she was eighty-four. She did not depart from the temple, worshipping with fasting and prayer night and day. ³⁸ And coming up at that very hour she gave thanks to God, and spoke of him to all who were looking for the redemption of Jerusalem.

39 And when they had performed everything according to the law of the Lord, they returned into Galilee, to their own city, Nazareth. ⁴⁰ And the child grew and became strong, filled with wisdom; and the favor of God was upon him.

41 Now his parents went to Jerusalem every year at the feast of the Passover. ⁴² And when he was twelve years old, they went up according to custom; ⁴³ and when the feast was ended, as they were returning, the boy Jesus stayed behind in Jerusalem. His parents did not know it, ⁴⁴ but supposing him to be in the company they went a day's journey, and they sought him among their kinsfolk and acquaintances; ⁴⁵ and when they did not find him, they returned to Jerusalem, seeking him. ⁴⁶ After three days they found him in the temple, sitting among the teachers, listening to them and asking them questions; ⁴⁷ and all who heard him were amazed at his understanding and his answers. ⁴⁸ And when they saw him they were astonished; and his mother said to him, "Son, why have you treated us so? Behold, your father and I have been looking for you anxiously." ⁴⁹ And he said to them, "How is it that you sought me? Did you not know that I must be in my Father's house?" ⁵⁰ And they did not understand the saying which he spoke to them. ⁵¹ And he went down with them and came to Nazareth, and was obedient to them; and his mother kept all these things in her heart.

52 And Jesus increased in wisdom and in stature, ⁱ and in favor with God and man.

3 In the fifteenth year of the reign of Tibe'ri-us Caesar, Pontius Pilate being governor of Judea, and Herod being tetrarch of Galilee, and his brother Philip tetrarch of the region of Iturae'a and Trachoni'tis, and Lysa'ni-as tetrarch of Abile'ne, ² in the high-priesthood of Annas and Ca'iaphas, the word of God came to John the son of Zechari'ah in the wilderness; ³ and he went into all the region about the Jordan, preaching a baptism of repentance for the forgiveness of sins. ⁴ As it is written in the book of the words of Isaiah the prophet, "The voice of one crying in the wilderness: Prepare the way of the Lord, make his paths straight. ⁵ Every valley shall be filled, and every mountain and hill shall be brought low, and the crooked shall be made straight, and the rough ways shall be made smooth; ⁶ and all flesh shall see the salvation of God."

ᵍ *Other ancient authorities read* peace, good will among men
ʰ *Or in the Spirit*
1. 30: Lk. 1. 13.   1. 31: Lk. 2. 21; Mt. 1. 21.   1. 33: Mt. 28. 18; Dan. 2. 44.   1. 34: Lk. 1. 18.   1. 35: Mt. 1. 20.   1. 37: Gen. 18. 14.   1. 42: Lk. 11. 27–28.   1. 46–55: 1 Sam. 2. 1–10.   1. 47: 1 Tim. 2. 3; Tit. 2. 10; Jude 25.   1. 55: Mic. 7. 20; Gen. 17. 7; 18. 18; 22. 17.   1. 59: Lev. 12. 3; Gen. 17. 12.   1. 63: Lk. 1. 13.   1. 76: Lk. 7. 26; Mal. 4. 5.   1. 77: Mk. 1. 4.   1. 78: Mal. 4. 2; Eph. 5. 14.   1. 79: Is. 9. 2; Mt. 4. 16.   1. 80: Lk. 2. 40; 2. 52.   2. 1: Lk. 3. 1.   2. 4: Lk. 1. 27.   2. 9: Lk. 1. 11; Acts 5. 19.
ⁱ *Or years*

7 He said therefore to the multitudes that came out to be baptized by him, "You brood of vipers! Who warned you to feel from the wrath to come? [8] Bear fruits that befit repentance, and do not begin to say to yourselves, 'We have Abraham as our father'; for I tell you, God is able from these stones to raise up children to Abraham. [9] Even now the axe is laid to the root of the trees; every tree therefore that does not bear good fruit is cut down and thrown into the fire."

10 And the multitudes asked him, "What then shall we do?" [11] And he answered them, "He who has two coats, let him share with him who has none; and he who has food, let him do likewise." [12] Tax collectors also came to be baptized, and said to him, "Teacher, what shall we do?" [13] And he said to them, "Collect no more than is appointed you." [14] Soldiers also asked him, "And we, that shall we do?" And he said to them, "Rob no one by violence or by false accusation, and be content with your wages."

15 As the people were in expectation, and all men questions in their hearts concerning John, whether perhaps he were the Christ, [16] John answered them all, "I baptize you with water; but he who is mightier than I is coming, the thong of whose sandals I am not worthy to untie; he will baptize you with the Holy Spirit and with fire. [17] His winnowing fork is in his hand, to clear his threshing floor, and to gather the wheat into his granary, but the chaff he will burn with unquenchable fire."

18 So, with many other exhortations, he preached good news to the people. [19] But Herod the tetrarch, who had been reproved by him for Hero'di-as, his brother's wife, and for all the evil things that Herod had done, [20] added this to them all, that he shut up John in prison.

21 Now when all the people were baptized, and when Jesus also had been baptized and was praying, the heaven was opened, [22] and the Holy Spirit descended upon him in bodily form, as a dove, and a voice came from heaven, "Thou art my beloved Son; [j] with thee I am well pleased." [k]

Questions:
1. *What does the birth story of Jesus and the story of his baptism tell us about how the early Church saw him and his mission?*
2. *How is Mary presented in the Gospel According to Luke? What parallels are there between the lives of Mary, mother of Jesus, and Elizabeth, mother of John the Baptist?*

5.5 *The Letter of Paul to the Romans*

Paul (d. c. 87 C.E.) was a Jewish convert to Christianity. He played a central role in preaching the message of the new faith to the Gentiles. In the excerpt included here, Paul declares the relevence of the Gospel to Gentiles and Jews alike and asserts the visible presence of God throughout the world.

Source: *The Bible: Revised Standard Version*, Chapter 1, p. 169.

---

[j] *Or* my Son, my (*or the*) Beloved
[k] *Other ancient authorities read* today I have begotten thee
2. 11 :Jn. 4. 42; Acts 5. 31; Mt. 16. 16; Acts. 2. 36.
2. 12: 1 Sam. 2. 34; 2 Kings 19. 29; Is. 7. 14.   2. 14: :k. 19. 38; 3. 22.   2. 19: Lk. 2. 51.
2. 21: Lk. 1. 59, 31; Mt. 1. 25.   2. 22–24: Lev. 12. 2–8.   2. 23: Ex. 13. 2, 12.
2. 25: Lk. 2. 38; 23. 51.   2. 30: Is. 52. 10; Lk. 3. 6.   2. 32: Is. 52. 6; 49. 6; Acts 13. 47; 26. 23.
2. 36: Acts 21. 9; Josh. 19. 24; 1 Tim. 5. 9.
2. 40: Judg. 13. 34; I Sam 2. 26.   2. 41: Deut. 16. 1–8; Ex. 23. 15.
2. 48: Mk. 3. 31–35.   2. 51: Lk 2. 19.   2. 52: Lk. 1. 80; 2. 40
3. 1: Lk. 23. 1; 9. 7; 13. 31; 23. 7.   3. 2: Jn. 18. 13; Acts 4. 6; Mt. 26. 3; Jn. 11. 49.
3. 3–9: Mt. 3. 1–10; Mk. 1. 1–5; Jn. 1. 6, 23.   3. 4–6: Is. 40. 3–5.   3. 6: Lk. 2. 30.
3. 7: Mt. 12. 34; 23. 33.   3. 8: Jn. 8. 33, 39.   3. 9: Mt. 7. 19; Heb. 6. 7–8.   3. 11: Lk. 6. 29.

1 Paul, a servant [a] of Jesus Christ, called to be an apostle, set apart for the gospel of God 2 which he promised beforehand through his prophets in the holy scriptures, 3 the gospel concerning his Son, who was descended from David according to the flesh 4 and designated Son of God in power according to the Spirit of holiness by his resurrection from the dead, Jesus Christ our Lord, 5 through whom we have received grace and apostleship to bring about the obedience of faith for the sake of his name among all the nations, 6 including yourselves who are called to belong to Jesus Christ;

7 To all God's beloved in Rome, who are called to be saints:

Grace to you and peace from God our Father and the Lord Jesus Christ.

8 First, I thank my God through Jesus Christ for all of you, because your faith is proclaimed in all the world. 9 For God is my witness, whom I serve with my spirit in the gospel of his Son, that without ceasing I mention you always in may prayers, 10 asking that somehow by God's will I may now at last succeed in coming to you. 11 For I long to see you, that I may impart to you some spiritual gift to strengthen you, 12 that is, that we may be mutually encouraged by each other's faith, both yours and mine. 13 I want you to know, brethren, that I have often intended to come to you (but thus far have been prevented), in order that I may reap some harvest among you as well as among the rest of the Gentiles. 14 I am under obligation both to Greeks and to barbarians, both to the wise and to the foolish: 15 so I am eager to preach the gospel to you also who are in Rome.

16 For I am not ashamed of the gospel: it is the power of God for salvation to every one who has faith, to the Jew first and also to the Greek. 17 For in it the righteousness of God is revealed through faith for faith; as it is written, "He who through faith is righteous shall live." [b]

18 For the wrath of God is revealed from heaven against all ungodliness and wickedness of men who by their wickedness suppress the truth. 19 For what can be known about God is plain to them, because God has shown it to them. 20 Ever since the creation of the world his invisible nature, namely, his eternal power and deity, has been clearly perceived in the things that have been made. So they are without excuse; 21 for although they knew God they did not honor him as God or give thanks to him, but they became futile in their thinking and their senseless minds were darkened. 22 Claiming to be wise, they became fools, 23 and exchanged the glory of the immortal God for images resembling mortal man or birds or animals or reptiles.

24 Therefore God gave them up in the lusts of their hearts to impurity, to the dishonoring of their bodies among themselves, 25 because they exchanged the truth about God for a lie and worshipped and served the creature rather than the Creator, who is blessed for ever! Amen.

Question:
1. What can we learn about the character and personality of Paul from this reading?

5.6 Defining the Christian Woman

Women had figured prominently in Jesus' ministry and life. Paul's instructions had circumscribed women's role in the Christian Church, and subsequent male church leaders tended to subordinate and reduce their role even further. Nevertheless, women continued to play an important role in spreading and nurturing the young Christian faith. Augustine, the greatest of all Christian writers (354–430 C.E.), discusses his relationship with his mother Monica and the role she filled in his conversion to the Christian faith.

Source: Saint Augustine, *Confessions*, trans. R.S. Pine-Coffin, (New York: Penguin Books, 1980, © 1961), pp. 67–69.

---

[a] *Or* slave
[b] *Or* The righteous shall live by faith
1. 1: Acts 9. 15; 13. 2; 1 Cor. 1. 1; 2 Cor. 1. 1; Gal. 1. 15.
1. 5: Acts 26. 16–18; Rom. 15. 18; Gal. 2. 7, 9.
1. 7: 1 Cor. 1. 3; 2 Cor. 1. 2; Gal. 1. 3; Eph. 1. 2; Phil. 1. 2; Col. 1. 2; 1 Thess. 1. 2; 2 Thess.
1. 2; 1 Tim. 1. 2; 2 Tim. 1. 2; Tit. 1. 4; Philem. 3; 2 Jn. 3.   1. 8: Rom. 16. 19.
1. 10: Rom. 15. 23, 32; Acts 19. 21.   1. 13: Rom. 15. 22.   1. 14: 1 Cor. 9. 16.
1. 16: 1 Cor. 1. 18, 24. 1. 17: Rom. 3. 21; Gal. 3. 11; Phil. 3. 9; Heb. 10. 38; Hab. 2. 4.
1. 18: Eph. 5. 6; Col. 3. 6.   1. 20: Ps. 19. 1–4.   1. 21: Eph. 4. 17–18.   1. 23: Acts 17. 29.

BOOK III-11

... You sent down your help from above[1] and rescued my soul from the depths of this darkness because my mother, your faithful servant, wept to you for me, shedding more tears for my spiritual death than other mothers shed for the bodily death of a son. For in her faith and in the spirit which she had from you she looked on me as dead. You heard her and did not despise the tears which streamed down and watered the earth in every place where she bowed her head in prayer. You heard her, for how else can I explain the dream with which you consoled her, so that she agreed to live with me and eat at the same table in our home? Lately she had refused to do this, because she loathed and shunned the blasphemy of my false beliefs.

She dreamed that she was standing on a wooden rule, and coming towards her in a halo of splendour she saw a young man who smiled at her in joy, although she herself was sad and quite consumed with grief. He asked her the reason for her sorrow and her daily tears, not because he did not know, but because he had something to tell her, for this is what happens in visions. When she replied that her tears were for the soul I had lost, he told her to take heart for, if she looked carefully, she would see that where she was, there also was I. And when she looked, she saw me standing beside her on the same rule.

Where could this dream have come from, unless it was that you listened to the prayer of her heart? For your goodness is almighty; you take good care of each of us as if you had no others in your care, and you look after all as you look after each. And surely it was for the same reason that, when she told me of the dream and I tried to interpret it as a message that she need not despair of being one day such as I was then, she said at once and without hesitation 'No! He did not say, "Where he is, you are," but "Where you are, he is."'

I have often said before and, to the best of my memory, I now declare to you, Lord, that I was much moved by this answer, which you gave me through my mother. She was not disturbed by my interpretation of her dream, plausible though it was, but quickly saw the true meaning, which I had not seen until she spoke. I was more deeply moved by this than by the dream itself, in which the joy for which this devout woman had still so long to wait was foretold so long before to comfort her in the time of her distress. For nearly nine years were yet to come during which I wallowed deep in the mire and the darkness of delusion. Often I tried to lift myself, only to plunge the deeper. Yet all the time this chaste, devout, and prudent woman, a widow such as is close to your heart, never ceased to pray at all hours and to offer you the tears she shed for me. The dream had given new spirit to her hope, but she gave no rest to her sighs and her tears. Her prayers reached your presence' and yet you still left me to twist and turn in the dark.

BOOK VI-1

O God, Hope of my youth,[2] where were you all this time? Where were you hiding from me? Were you not my Creator and was it not you who made me different from the beasts that walk on the earth and wiser than the birds that fly in the air? Yet I was walking on a treacherous path, in darkness. I was looking for you outside myself and I did not find the God of my own heart. I had reached the depths of the ocean. I had lost all faith and was in despair of finding the truth.

By now my mother had come to me, for her piety had given her strength to follow me over land and sea, facing all perils in the sure faith she had in you. When the ship was in danger, it was she who put heart into the crew, the very men to whom passengers unused to the sea turn for reassurance when they are alarmed. She promised them that they would make the land in safety, because you had given her this promise in a vision. And she found that I too was in grave danger because of my despair of discovering the truth.

---

[1] Many Christian Churches use an adaptation of the Nicene Creed as it was accepted at the Second Council of Constantinople in 381 C.E.
[2] Psalm 143:7 (144:7)

I told her that I was not a Catholic Christian, but at least I was no longer a Manichee.[3] Yet she did not leap for joy as though this news were unexpected. In fact, to this extent, her anxiety for me had already been allayed. For in her prayers to you she wept for me as though I were dead, but she also knew that you would recall me to life. In her heart she offered me to you as though I were laid out on a bier, waiting for you to say to the widow's son, 'Young man, I say to you, stand up.' And he would get up and begin to speak, and you would give him back to his mother.[4] So she felt no great surge of joy and her heart beat none the faster when she heard that the tears and the prayers which she had offered you day after day had at last, in great part, been rewarded. For I had been rescued from falsehood, even if I had not yet grasped the truth. Instead, because she was sure that if you had promised her all, you would also give her what remained to be given, she told me quite serenely, with her heart full of faith, that in Christ she believed that before she left this life she would see me a faithful Catholic. This was what she said to me. But to you, from whom all mercies spring, she poured out her tears and her prayers all the more fervently, begging you to speed your help and give me light in my darkness. She hurried all the more eagerly to church, where she listened with rapt attention to all that Ambrose said. For her his words were like a spring of water within her, that flows continually to bring her everlasting life.[5] She loved him as God's angel,[6] because she had learnt that it was through him that I had been led, for the time being, into a state of wavering uncertainty. She had no doubt that I must pass through this condition, which would lead me from sickness to health....

My heart lies open before you, O Lord my God, and this is what I believe. Because he could show me the way of salvation she was greatly devoted to Ambrose, and his heart too had warmed to her for her truly pious way of life, her zeal in good works, and her regular churchgoing. Often, when he saw me, he would break out in praise of her, congratulating me on having such a mother.

Questions:

1. *What role did Monica play in the conversion of Augustine to Christianity?*
2. *From Augustine's description, what sort of person was Monica?*
3. *How does your impression of Monica compare with Paul's injunctions for Christian women in Document 3?*

5.7   "What Has Jerusalem to do with Athens?"

Tertullian (ca. 160 – ca. 240 C.E.), a native of Carthage, became a strong defender of Christian morals and wrote a series of attacks on heretics. In his Prescriptions Against Heretics, he vehemently warns that heresy arises out of a dependence on Greco-Roman philosophy.

> **Source:** *Sources of the Western Tradition: Volume I: From Ancient Times to the Enlightenment,* ed. Marvin Perry, Joseph R. Peden, and Theodore H. Von Laue, (Boston: Houghton Mifflin Co., 1995), p. 182. Reprinted from *Early Latin Theology,* translated and edited by S.I. Greenslade, Vol. V: The Library of Christian Classics, (Philadelphia: Westminster Press).

... Worldly wisdom culminates in philosophy with its rash interpretation of God's nature and purpose. It is philosophy that supplies the heresies1 with their equipment.... The idea of a mortal soul was picked up from the Epicureans, and the denial of the restitution of the flesh was taken from the common tradition of the philosophical schools.... Heretics and philosophers [ponder] the same themes and are caught up in the same discussions. What is the origin of evil and why? The origin of man, and how?... A plague on Aristotle, who taught them dialectic [logical argumentation], the art which destroys as much as it builds, which changes its opinions like a coat, forces its conjectures, is stubborn in argument, works hard at being contentious and is a burden even to itself. For it reconsiders every point to make sure it never finishes a discussion.

From philosophy come those fables and... fruitless questionings, those "words that creep like as doth a canker." To hold us back from such things, the Apostle [Paul] testifies expressly in his letter to the Colossians [Colossians 2:8} that we

---

[3] A Manichee was considered a heretic by Catholic Christians. Manichees explained evil in the world by believing in an evil god who had created the world, and that there was a good god who would save one's soul if one rejected the evil material world including the desires of the flesh.

[4] Luke 7:14, 15.

[5] John 4:14

[6] Galatians 4:14.

should beware of philosophy. "Take heed lest any man [beguile] you through philosophy or vain deceit, after the tradition of men," against the providence of the Holy Ghost. He had been at Athens where he had come to grips with the human wisdom which attacks and perverts truth, being itself divided up into its own swarm of heresies by the variety of its mutually antagonistic sects. What has Jerusalem to do with Athens, the Church with [Plato's] Academy, the Christian with the heretic? Our principles come from the Porch of Solomon,2 who had himself taught that the Lord is to be sought in simplicity of heart. I have no use for Stoic or a Platonic or a dialectic Christianity. After Jesus Christ we have no need of speculation, after the Gospel no need of research. When we come to believe, we have no desire to believe anything else; for we begin by believing that there is nothing else which we have to believe.

Question:

1. Why did Tertullian condemn the study of pagan literature and philosophy as dangerous for Christians?

PART 6
The Early Middle Ages

6.1 Portrait of a Visigothic King

Theodoric II reigned over the Visigoths in South Gaul from 453 to 466 C.E. This portrait of him is by a courtly Gallo-Roman bishop who had every reason to flatter this leader of the recent conquerors.

> **Source:** "A Letter of Sidonius Apollinaris," found abridged in William Stearns Davis, ed., *Readings in Ancient History: Illustrative Extracts from the Sources,* Volume II: Rome and the West, (New York: Allyn and Bacon, 1913), pp. 319–21.

He is a prince well worthy of being known even by those not admitted to his intimate acquaintance, to such a degree have Nature and God, the sovereign Arbiter of all things, accumulated in his person gifts of varied excellence. His character is such that even envy itself, that universal accompaniment of all royalty, could not defraud him of his due praise.

You ask me to describe his daily outdoor life. Accompanied by a very small suite he attends before daybreak the services of the Church in his own household; he is careful in his devotions, but although his tone is suppressed, you may perceive that this is more a matter of habit with him than of religious principle. The business of administration occupies the rest of the morning. An armed aide-de-camp stands beside his throne; his band of fur-clad bodyguards is admitted to the Palace in order that they may be near to the royal presence; while in order that there may not be too much noise, they are kept out of the room; and so they talk in murmurs, inside a railing and outside the hangings [of the hall of audience].

Envoys from foreign powers are then introduced. The King listens much and says little. If their business calls for discussion, he puts it off, if for prompt action, he presses it forward. At eight o'clock he rises, and proceeds to examine either his treasures, or his stables. When he goes to hunt, he does not deem it suitable to the royal dignity to carry his bow upon his own person; when, however, any one points out to him a wild animal or bird, he puts out his hand, and receives his bow unstrung from a page: for, just as he regards it as an undignified thing to carry the weapon in its case, so does he deem it unmanly it should be prepared by another for his use. He selects an arrow and lets fly, first asking what you wish him to strike. You make your choice and invariably he hits the mark; indeed if there is ever any mistake, it is oftener in the sight of him who points out the object than in the aim of him who shoots at it.

His banquets do not differ from those of a private gentleman. You never see the vulgarity of a vast mass of tarnished plate, heaped upon a groaning table by a puffing and perspiring slave. The only thing that is weighty is the conversation: for either serious subjects are discussed, or none at all. Sometimes purple, and sometimes fine silk are employed in adorning the furniture of the dining room. The dinner is recommended by the skill of the cookery, not by the costliness of the provisions—the plate by its brightness, not by its massive weight. The guests are much more frequently called upon to complain of thirst, from finding the goblet too seldom pressed, than to shun inebriety by refusing it. In brief, one sees there the elegance of Greece and promptness of Italy, the splendor of a public along with the personal attention of a private entertainment, likewise the regular order of a royal household. After dinner Theodoric either takes no siesta at all or a very short one. When he feels like it, he picks up the dice quickly, looks at them carefully, shakes them scientifically, throws them at once, jocularly addresses them, and awaits the result with patience. When the cast is a good one he says nothing: when bad, he laughs; good or bad he is never angry, and takes both philosophically.

About three in the afternoon again come the cares of government, back come the suitors, and back those whose duty it is to keep them at a distance. On all sides is heard a wrangling and intriguing crowd, which, prolonged to the royal dinner hour, then only begins to diminish; after that it disperses, every man to seek his own patron. Occasionally, though not often, jesters are admitted to the royal banquet, without, however, being permitted to vent their malicious raillery upon any persons present. When he has risen from table, the guard of the treasury commences its nightly vigil: armed men take their station at all approaches to the palace, whose duty it will be to watch there during the first hours of the night."

[Despite this eulogy, Theodoric II had climbed to power by the foul murder of his brother, the rightful king.]

Questions:
1. *What does this document tell us about the nature of Germanic kingship among the Visigoths?*
2. *How did Christianity affect that kingship?*
3. *How does the author's Christian point of view affect his interpretation of the king and political events?*

6.2 *Corpus Juris Civilis:* Prologue

Roman law grew from abstract principles of justice on which the actual rules of law were legislated. The Emperor Justinian ordered a codification of all these laws that had accumulated from the time of the Republic to his own decrees. He issued the Corpus Juris Civilis (Body of Civil Law) in Latin consisting of three parts, the Digest, the Institutes, and a textbook that eventually transmitted Roman legal principles to Western Europe during the twelfth century, influencing church and continental law.

Source: From *The Digest of Justinian*, C. H. Monro, ed. (Cambridge, MA: Cambridge University Press, 1904).

THE DIGEST: PROLOGUE

The Emperor Caesar, Flavius, Justinianus, Pious, Fortunate, Renowned, Conqueror, and Triumpher, Ever Augustus, to Tribonianus His Quaestor.,

Greeting:

With the aid of God governing Our Empire which was delivered to Us by His Celestial Majesty, We carry on war successfully. We adorn peace and maintain the Constitution of the State, and have such confidence in the protection of Almighty God that We do not depend upon Our arms, or upon Our soldiers, or upon those who conduct Our Wars, or upon Our own genius, but We solely, place Our reliance upon the providence of the Holy Trinity, from which are derived the elements of the entire world and their disposition throughout the globe.

Therefore, since there is nothing to be found in all things as worthy of attention as the authority of the law, which properly regulates all affairs both divine and human, and expels all injustice; We have found the entire arrangement of the law which has come down to us from the foundation of the City of Rome and the times of Romulus, to be so confused that it is extended to an infinite length and is not within the grasp of human capacity; and hence We were first induced to begin by examining what had been enacted by former most venerated princes, to correct their constitutions, and make them more easily understood; to the end that being included in a single Code, and having had removed all that is superfluous in resemblance and all iniquitous discord, they may afford to all men the ready assistance of true meaning.

After having concluded this work and collected it all in a single volume under Our illustrious name, raising Ourself above small and comparatively insignificant matters, We have hastened to attempt the most complete and thorough amendment of the entire law, to collect and revise the whole body of Roman jurisprudence, and to assemble in one book the scattered treatises of so many authors which no one else has heretofore ventured to hope for or to expect and it has indeed been considered by Ourselves a most difficult undertaking, nay, one that was almost impossible; but with Our hands raised to heaven and having invoked the Divine aid, We have kept this object in Our mind, confiding in God who can grant the accomplishment of things which are almost desperate, and can Himself carry them into effect by virtue of the greatness of His power.

. . . .

We desire you to be careful with regard to the following: if you find in the old books anything that is not suitably arranged, superfluous, or incomplete, you must remove all superfluities, supply what is lacking, and present the entire work in regular form, and with as excellent an appearance as possible.

You must also observe the following, namely: if you find anything which the ancients have inserted in their old laws or constitutions that is incorrectly worded, you must correct this, and place it in its proper order, so that it may appear to be true, expressed in the best language, and written in this way in the first place; so that by comparing it with the original text, no one can venture to call in question as defective what you have selected and arranged.

Since by an ancient law, which is styled the Lex Regia, all the rights and power of the Roman people were transferred to the Emperor, We do not derive Our authority from that of other different compilations, but wish that it shall all be entirely Ours, for how can antiquity abrogate our laws?

Questions:
1. *How can you tell that the Roman Empire is now Christian?*
2. *Why was the compilation of law undertaken?*
3. *What were the instructions given to the scholars who codified the Law?*

6.3 The *Koran*

The Koran (Qur 'an) means "the recital" and is, according to Islamic belief, the direct words of God as told to his prophet Muhammad through the angel Gabriel. It is the sacred text for Muslims. Excerpts from one of the books, entitled "The Cow," are reproduced below.

Source: *The Koran,* trans. N.J. Dawood, (New York: Penguin Books, 1990), pp. 11-42 passim.

THE COW

In the Name of God, the Compassionate, the Merciful

Alif *l-am m-_m.* This Book is not to be doubted. It is a guide for the righteous, who have faith in the unseen and are steadfast in prayer; who bestow in charity a part of what We have given them; who trust what has been revealed to you[1] and to others before you, and firmly believe in the life to come. These are rightly guided by their Lord; these shall surely triumph.

As for the unbelievers, it is the same whether or not you forewarn them; they will not have faith. God has set a seal upon their hearts and ears; their sight is dimmed and grievous punishment awaits them.

There are some who declare: 'We believe in God and the Last Day,' yet they are no true believers. They seek to deceive God and those who believe in Him: but they deceive none save themselves, though they may not perceive it. There is a sickness in their hearts which God has aggravated: they shall be sternly punished for the lies they told.

. . . .

Proclaim good tidings to those who have faith and do good works. They shall dwell in gardens watered by running streams: whenever they are given fruit to eat they will say: 'This is what we used to eat before,' for they shall be given the like. Wedded to chaste virgins, they shall abide therein for ever.

. . . .

To Adam We said: 'Dwell with your wife in Paradise and eat of its fruits to your hearts' content wherever you will. But never approach this tree or you shall both become transgressors.'

But Satan removed them thence and brought about their banishment. 'Go hence,' We said, 'and be enemies to each other. The earth will for a while provide your dwelling and sustenance.'

Then Adam received commandments from his Lord, and his Lord relented towards him. He is the Forgiving One, the Merciful.

'Go down hence, all,' We said. 'When our guidance is revealed those that accept it shall have nothing to fear or to regret; but those that deny and reject Our revelations shall be the heirs of Hell, and there they shall abide for ever.'

Children of Israel, remember the blessing I have bestowed on you, and that I have exalted you above the nations. Guard yourselves against the day on which no soul shall avail another: when neither intercession nor ransom shall be accepted from it, nor any help be given it.

. . . .

To Moses We gave the Scriptures and after him We sent other apostles. We gave Jesus the son of Mary veritable signs and strengthened him with the Holy Spirit. Will you then scorn each apostle whose message does not suit your fancies, charging some with imposture and slaying others?

. . . .

And now that a Book confirming their own has come to them from God, they deny it, although they know it to be the truth and have long prayed for help against the unbelievers. God's curse be upon the infidels! Evil is that for which they have bartered away their souls. To deny God's own revelation, grudging that He should reveal His bounty to whom He chooses from among His servants! They have incurred God's most inexorable wrath. An ignominious punishment awaits the unbe-

---

[1] Cereal grain. What we know as corn originated in the Western Hemisphere.

lievers.

· · · ·

Say: 'Whoever is an enemy of Gabriel' (who has by God's grace revealed to you[2] the Koran as a guide and joyful tidings for the faithful, confirming previous scriptures) 'whoever is an enemy of God, His angels, or His apostles, or of Gabriel or Michael, will surely find that God is the enemy of the unbelievers.'

· · · ·

When his Lord put Abraham to the proof by enjoying on him certain commandments and Abraham fulfilled them, He said: 'I have appointed you a leader of mankind.'
    'And what of my descendants?' asked Abraham.
    'My covenant,' said He, 'does not apply to the evil-doers.'
    We made the House[3] a resort and a sanctuary for mankind, saying: 'Make the place where Abraham stood a house of worship.' We enjoined Abraham and Ishmael to cleanse Our House for those who walk round it, who meditate in it, and who kneel and prostrate themselves.

· · · ·

Who but a foolish man would renounce the faith of Abraham? We chose him in this world, and in the world to come he shall abide among the righteous. When his Lord said to him: 'Submit,' he answered: 'I have submitted to the Lord of the Universe.'

· · · ·

They say: 'Accept the Jewish or the Christian faith and you shall be rightly guided.'
    Say: 'By no means! We believe in the faith of Abraham, the upright one. He was no idolater.'
    Say: 'We believe in God and that which is revealed to us; in what was revealed to Abraham, Ishmael, Isaac, Jacob, and the tribes; to Moses and Jesus and the other prophets by their Lord. We make no distinction among any of them, and to God we have surrendered ourselves.'

· · · ·

Righteousness does not consist in whether you face towards the East or the West. The righteous man is he who believes in God and the Last Day, in the angels and the Book and the prophets, who, though he loves it dearly, gives away his wealth to kinsfolk, to orphans, to the helpless, to the traveller in need and to beggars, and for the redemption of captives; who attends to his prayers and renders the alms levy; who is true to his promises and steadfast in trial and adversity and in times of war. Such are the true believers; such are the God-fearing.

Believers, retaliation is decreed for you in bloodshed: a free man for a free man, a slave for a slave, and a female for a female. He who is pardoned by his aggrieved brother shall be prosecuted according to usage and shall pay him a liberal fine. This is a merciful dispensation from your Lord. He that transgresses thereafter shall be sternly punished.

· · · ·

Believers, fasting is decreed for you as it was decreed for those before you; perchance you will guard yourselves against evil. Fast a certain number of days, but if any one among you is ill or on a journey, let him fast a similar number of days later; and for those that cannot endure it there is a ransom: the feeding of a poor man. He that does good of his own accord shall be well rewarded; but to fast is better for you, if you but knew it.
    In the month of Ramad-an the Koran was revealed, a book of guidance with proofs of guidance distinguishing right from wrong. Therefore whoever of you is present in that month let him fast. But he who is ill or on a journey shall

---

[2] Muhammad
[3] The Ka'bah at Mecca.

fast a similar number of days later on.

God desires your well-being, not your discomfort. He desires you to fast the whole month so that you may magnify Him and render thanks to Him for giving you His guidance.

. . . .

It is now lawful for you to lie with your wives on the night of the fast; they are a comfort to you as you are to them. God knew that you were deceiving yourselves. He has relented towards you and pardoned you. Therefore you may now lie with them and seek what God has ordained for you. Eat and drink until you can tell a white thread from a black one in the light of the coming dawn. Then resume the fast till nightfall and do not approach them, but stay at your prayers in the mosques.

. . . .

Do not devour one another's property by unjust means, nor bribe with it the judges in order that you may wrongfully and knowingly usurp the possessions of other men.

. . . .

Fight for the sake of God those that fight against you, but do not attack them first. God does not love the aggressors.

Slay them wherever you find them. Drive them out of the places from which they drove you. Idolatry is worse than carnage. But do not fight them within the precincts of the Holy Mosque unless they attack you there; if they attack you put them to the sword. Thus shall the unbelievers be rewarded: but if they mend their ways, know that God is forgiving and merciful.

. . . .

Make the pilgrimage and visit the Sacred House for His sake. If you cannot, send such offerings as you can afford and do not shave your heads until the offerings have reached their destination. But if any of you is ill or suffers from an ailment of the head, he must pay a ransom either by fasting or by almsgiving or by offering a sacrifice.

. . . .

Make the pilgrimage in the appointed months. He that intends to perform it in those months must abstain from sexual intercourse, obscene language, and acrimonious disputes while on pilgrimage. God is aware of whatever good you do. Provide well for yourselves: the best provision is piety. Fear Me, then, you that are endowed with understanding.

It shall be no offence for you to seek the bounty of your Lord.

. . . .

There are some who say: 'Lord, give us abundance in this world.' These shall have no share in the world to come. But there are others who say: 'Lord, give us what is good both in this world and in the hereafter and keep us from the torment of the Fire.' These shall have a share, according to what they did. Swift is God's reckoning.

. . . .

They ask you about drinking and gambling. Say: 'There is great harm in both, although they have some benefit for men; but their harm is far greater than their benefit.'

They ask you what they should give in alms. Say: 'What you can spare.' Thus God makes plain to you His revelations so that you may reflect upon this world and the hereafter.

They question you concerning orphans. Say: 'To deal justly with them is best. If you mix their affairs with yours, remember they are your brothers. God knows the just from the unjust. If God pleased, He could afflict you. He is mighty and wise.'

. . . .

You shall not wed pagan women, unless they embrace the Faith. A believing slave-girl is better than an idolatress, although she may please you. Nor shall you wed idolaters, unless they embrace the Faith. A believing slave is better than an idolater, although he may please you. These call you to Hell-fire; but God calls you, by His will, to Paradise and to forgiveness. He makes plain His revelations to mankind, so that they may take heed.

They ask you about menstruation. Say: 'It is an indisposition. Keep aloof from women during their menstrual periods and do not touch them until they are clean again. Then have intercourse with them in the way God enjoined you. God loves those that turn to Him in repentance and strive to keep themselves clean.'

Women are your fields: go, then, into your fields whence you please. Do good works and fear God. Bear in mind that you shall meet Him. Give good tidings to the believers.

. . . .

Those that renounce their wives on oath must wait four months. If they change their minds, God is forgiving and merciful; but if they decide to divorce them, know that God hears all and knows all.

Divorced women must wait, keeping themselves from men, three menstrual courses. It is unlawful for them, if they believe in God and the Last Day, to hide what God has created in their wombs: in which case their husbands would do well to take them back, should they desire reconciliation.

Women shall with justice have rights similar to those exercised against them, although men have a status above women. God is almight and wise.

Divorce[4] may be pronounced twice, and then a woman must be retained in honour or allowed to go with kindness. It is unlawful for husbands to take from them anything they have given them, unless both fear that they may not be able to keep within the bounds set by God; in which case it shall be no offence for either of them if the wife ransom herself.

. . . .

Mothers shall give such to their children for two whole years if the father wishes the sucking to be completed. They must be maintained and clothed in a reasonable manner by the child's father. None should be charged with more than one can bear. A mother should not be allowed to suffer on account of her child, nor should a father on account of his child. The same duties devolve upon the father's heir. But if, after consultation, they choose by mutual consent to wean the child, they shall incur no guilt. Nor shall it be any offence for you if you prefer to have a nurse for your children, provided that you pay her what you promise, according to usage. Have fear of God and know that God is cognizant of all your actions.

Widows shall wait, keeping themselves apart from men for four months and ten days after their husbands' death. When they have reached the end of their waiting period, it shall be no offence for you to let them do whatever they choose for themselves, provided that it is decent. God is cognizant of all your actions.

. . . .

You shall bequeath your widows a year's maintenance without causing them to leave their homes; but if they leave of their own accord, no blame shall be attached to you for any course they may deem fit to pursue. God is mighty and wise. Reasonable provision shall also be made for divorced women. That is incumbent on righteous men.

. . . .

There shall be no compulsion in religion. True guidance is now distinct from error. He that renounces idol-worship and puts his faith in God shall grasp a firm handle that will never break. God hears all and knows all.

God is the Patron of the faithful. He leads them from darkness to the light. As for the unbelievers, their patrons are false gods, who lead them from light to darkness. They are the heirs of Hell and shall abide in it for ever.

. . . .

Satan threatens you with poverty and orders you to commit what is indecent. But God promises you His forgiveness and His bounty. God is munificent and all-knowing.

He gives wisdom to whom He will; and he that receives the gift of wisdom is rich indeed. Yet none except men

---

[4] Revocable divorce, or the renunciation of one's wife on oath.

83

of sense bear this in mind.

Whatever alms you give and whatever vows you make are known to God. The evil-doers shall have none to help them.

To be charitable in public is good, but to give alms to the poor in private is better and will atone for some of your sins. God has knowledge of all your actions.

It is not for you to guide them. God gives guidance to whom He will.

Whatever alms you give shall rebound to your own advantage, provided that you give them for the love of God. And whatever alms you give shall be paid back to you in full: you shall not be wronged.

. . . .

Those that live on usury shall rise up before God like men whom Satan has demented by his touch; for they claim that trading is no different from usury. But God has permitted trading and made usury unlawful. He that has received an admonition from his Lord and mended his ways may keep his previous gains; God will be his judge. Those that turn back shall be the inmates of the Fire, wherein they shall abide for ever.

God has laid His curse on usury and blessed almsgiving with increase. God bears no love for the impious and the sinful.

. . . .

Believers, when you contract a debt for a fixed period, put it in writing. Let a scribe write it down for you with fairness; no scribe should refuse to write as God has taught him.

. . . .

Call in two male witnesses from among you, but if two men cannot be found, then one man and two women whom you judge fit to act as witnesses; so that if either of them commit an error, the other will remember. Witnesses must not refuse to give evidence if called upon to do so...

. . . .

'This is more just in the sight of God; it ensures accuracy in testifying and is the best way to remove all doubt. But if the transaction in hand be a bargain concluded on the spot, it is no offence for you if you do not commit it to writing.

See that witnesses are present when you barter with one another, and let no harm be done to either scribe or witness.

Questions:
1. *According to the Koran, what are the relations between Muslims and the Jews and Christians?*
2. *What are the requirements of the believers? What if one does not follow them? Are there exceptions?*
3. *In what ways does the Koran provide guidelines in the realm of society, economics, and politics?*
4. *What does the Koran say about fighting against unbelievers, often called Jihad (holy wars)?*
5. *How are women and relations between men and women treated in the Koran?*

6.4 Baghdad: City of Wonders

This description of Baghdad is by an unknown Persian nobleman (perhaps a student at the university in Baghdad) in a letter to his father, written during the reign of Haroun al-Rashid (786–809). The nobleman is describing the city only fifty years after it was built to be the capital of the Abbasid Caliphate. The city was built as a walled fortress town with the caliphate's residence in the center of town behind its own ninety foot wall and moat. As can be seen by this description, it quickly became a prosperous town at the center of Islamic trade, with a population close to one million (this is less than the number cited in the document, but numbers tend to be exaggerated in such documents).

Source: *Primary Source Document Workbook to Accompany World Civilizations,* by Philip J. Adler; prepared by Robert Welborn, (New York: West Publishing Company, 1996), pp. 29-30. (Introduction based on Welborn's introduction to the Document.)

THE BAGHDAD OF HAROUN AL-RASHID

When I wandered about in the city after a long absence, I found it in an expansion of prosperity that I had not observed before this time. The resplendent buildings that rose in the city... were not sufficient for its wealthy people until they extended to the houses in this eastern quarter known as Rusafa. They built high castles and ornamented houses in this quarter, and set up markets, mosques, and public baths. The attention of al-Rashid... was directed toward adorning it with public buildings, until the old Baghdad became like an ancient town whose beauties were assembled in a section of the city which was created near by it.

I admired the arrival of buildings in Baghdad because of the over crowdedness of the people I had seen in its sections. Their billowing is like the sea in its expanses; their number is said to exceed 1,500,000, and no other city in the world has such a sum or even half its amount....

It is difficult for me, with this pen which is of limited substance, to describe the glorious qualities of the city which are but a small part of the honor it achieves, such that it prides itself in the splendor of power.... The people of wealth walk with slave boys and and retinue whose number the listener will fancy to be far from the truth. I witnessed at Attabiyya station a prince who was riding with a hundred horsemen and was surrounded by slave boys, even filling the road and blocking the path of the people until they passed.... Nor was any Caliph ever known to be more generous than he (Haroun al-Rashid) in the handing out of wealth. It is said that he spends ten thousand dirhams (a silver coin) every day for his food, and perhaps the cooks would prepare for him thirty kinds of food. Abu Yusuf informed me that when the Caliph consummated his marriage to Zubaida, the daughter of Ja'far the Barmakid, he gave a banquet unprecedented in Islam. He gave away unlimited presents at this banquet, even giving containers of gold filled with silver, containers of silver filled with gold, bags of musk, and pieces of ambergris. The total expenditure on this banquet reached 55,000,000 dirhams. The Caliph commanded that Zubaida be presented in a gown of pearls whose price no one was able to appraise. He adorned her with pieces of jewelry, so much so that she was not able to walk because of the great number of jewels which were upon her. This example of extravagance had no precedent among the kings of Persia, the emperors of Byzantium, or the princes of the Umayyads, despite the great amounts of money which they had at their disposal.

Affluence is abundant among the upper rank of those who are masters of the state. It then diminishes little by little among those of lesser rank, until only a small amount remains for the general public. As for those who do not enjoy the exalted power and breadth of bounty of the kings, they begin to equip themselves with all the good things after they have gone on journeys which gain them experience, show them wondrous things, and give them profits. The people in the provinces come to them with the grandest of all types of their wares, until markets have become plentiful in Baghdad. They have advanced from requesting necessities to the acquisition of things for beautification and decoration. This may be seen in the case of their purchase of arms inlaid with gold, their competing in costly jewels, ornamented vessels, and splendid furniture, and their acquisition of a large number of slave boys, female singers, and those things which they send out their retainers to seek in the provinces. When every expensive and rare thing in the country was brought to them, I realized that the beauties of the world had been assembled in Baghdad....

Questions:
1. *How would you characterize Baghdad based on this description? Consider wealth, social classes/occupations, kinds of goods available.*
2. *Why do you think the city is so prosperous only fifty years after its creation?*
3. *What does the description of the caliph reveal about the time, the city, the religion, social practices, etc?*

6.5   A Christian's Description of the Mongols

The Europeans came in contact with the Mongols while they were fighting the Muslims in the Crusades in the thirteenth century. In 1245, Pope Innocent IV sent a Christian missionary to the Mongols to try to convince them not to attack Europe and to convert to Christianity (See Chapter 10, Document 1 for the

Pope's bull and the Mongol leader's response). The Missionary provided the following description of the Mongols.

Source: John of Piano Carpini, *History of the Mongols,* IV, in *The Mongol Mission. Narratives and Letters of the Franciscan Missionairies* (sic) *in Mongolia and China in the Thirteenth and Fourteenth Centuries,* trans. A nun of Stanbrook Abbey, ed. C. Dawson, (New York: Sheed and Ward, 1955, pp. 32–38); reprinted in *The Crusades: A Documentary Survey,* ed. James A. Brundage, (Milwaukee, WI: The Marquette University Press, 1976, c. 1962), pp. 254–57.

These men, that is to say the Tartars, are more obedient to their masters than any other men in the world, be they religious or seculars; they show great respect to them nor do they lightly lie to them. They rarely or never contend with each other in word, and in action never. Fights, brawls, wounding, murder are never met with among them. Nor are robbers and thieves who steal on a large scale found there; consequently their dwellings and the carts in which they keep their valuables are not secured by bolts and bars. If any animals are lost, whoever comes across them either leaves them alone or takes them to men appointed for this purpose; the owners of the animals apply for them to these men and they get them back without any difficulty. They show considerable respect to each other and are very friendly together, and they willingly share their food with each other, although there is little enough of it. They are also long-suffering. When they are without food, eating nothing at all for one or two days, they do not easily show impatience, but they sing and make merry as if they had eaten well. On horseback they endure great cold and they also put up with excessive heat. Nor are they men fond of luxury; they are not envious of each other; there is practically no litigation among them. No one scorns another but helps him and promotes his good as far as circumstances permit.

Their women are chaste, nor does one hear any mention among them of any shameful behavior on their part; some of them, however, in jest make use of vile and disgusting language. Discord among them seems to arise rarely or never, and although they may get very drunk, yet in their intoxication they never come to words or blows.

Now that the good characteristics of the Tartars have been described, it is time for something to be said about their bad. They are most arrogant to other people and look down on all, indeed they consider them as nought, be they of high rank or low born....

They are quickly roused to anger with other people and are of an impatient nature; they also tell lies to others and practically no truth is to be found among them. At first indeed they are smooth-tongued, but in the end they sting like a scorpion. They are full of slyness and deceit, and if they can, they get round everyone by their cunning. They are men who are dirty in the way they take food and drink and do other things. Any evil they intend to do to others they conceal in a wonderful way so that the latter can take no precautions nor devise anything to offset their cunning. Drunkenness is considered an honorable thing by them and when anyone drinks too much, he is sick there and then, nor does this prevent him from drinking again. They are exceedingly grasping and avaricious; they are extremely exacting in their demands, most tenacious in holding on to what they have and most niggardly in giving. They consider the slaughter of other people as nothing. In short, it is impossible to put down in writing all their evil characteristics on account of the very great number of them.

Their food consists of everything that can be eaten, for they eat dogs, wolves, foxes, and horses and, when driven by necessity, they feed on human flesh. For instance, when they were fighting against a city of the Kitayans, where the emperor was residing, they besieged it for so long that they themselves completely ran out of supplies and, since they had nothing at all to eat, they thereupon took out one of every ten men for food. They eat the filth which comes from mares when they bring forth foals. Nay, I have even seen them eating lice. They would say, "Why should I not eat them since they eat the flesh of my son and drink his blood?" I have also seen them eat mice.

They do not use tablecloths or napkins. They have neither bread nor herbs nor vegetables nor anything else, nothing but meat, of which, however, they eat so little that other people would scarcely be able to exist on it. They make their hands very dirty with the grease of the meat, but when they eat they wipe them on their leggings or the grass or some other such thing. It is the custom for the more respectable among them to have small bits of cloth with which to wipe their hands at the end when they eat meat. One of them cuts the morsels and another takes them on the point of a knife and offers them to each, to some more, to some less, according to whether they wish to show them greater or less honor. They do not wash their dishes, and, if occasionally they rinse them with the meat broth, they put it back with the meat into the pot. Pots also or spoons or other articles intended for this use, if they are cleaned at all, are washed in the same manner. They consider it a great sin if any food or drink is allowed to be wasted in any way; consequently they do not allow bones to be given to dogs until the marrow has been extracted. They do not wash their clothes nor allow them to be washed, especially from the time when thunderstorms begin until the weather changes. They drink mare's milk in very great quantities if they have it; they also drink the milk of ewes, cows, goats and even camels. They do not have wine, ale, or mead unless it is sent or given to them by other nations. In the winter, moreover, unless they are wealthy, they do not have mare's milk. They boil millet in water and make it so thin that they cannot eat it but have to drink it. Each one of them drinks one or two cups in the morning and they eat nothing more during the day; in the evening, however, they are all given a little meat, and they drink the meat broth. But in the summer, seeing they have plenty of mare's milk, they seldom eat meat, unless it happens to be given to them or they catch some animal or bird when hunting.

They also have a law or custom of putting to death any man and woman they find openly committing adultery; similarly if a virgin commits fornication with anyone, they kill both the man and the woman. If any is found in the act of plundering or stealing in the territory under their power, he is put to death without any mercy. Again, if anyone reveals their plans, especially when they intend going to war, he is given a hundred stripes on his back, as heavy as a peasant can give with a big stick. If any of the lower class offend in any way, they are not spared by their superiors, but are soundly beaten. There is no distinction between the son of a concubine and the son of a wife, but the father gives to each what he will; and if they are of a family of princes, then the son of a concubine is a prince just the same as the son of a legitimate wife. When a Tartar has many wives, each one has her own dwelling and her household, and the husband eats and drinks and sleeps one day with one, and the next with another. One, however, is chief among the others and with her he stays more often than with the others. In spite of their numbers, they never easily quarrel among themselves.

The men do not make anything at all, with the exception of arrows, and they also sometimes tend the flocks, but they hunt and practice archery, for they are all, big and little, excellent archers, and their children begin as soon as they are two or three years old to ride and manage horses and to gallop on them, and they are given bows to suit their stature and are taught to shoot; they are extremely agile and also intrepid.

Young girls and women ride and gallop on horseback with agility like the men. We even saw them carrying bows and arrows. Both the men and the women are able to endure long stretches of riding. They have very short stirrups; they look after their horses very well, indeed they take the very greatest care of all their possessions. Their women make everything, leather garments, tunics, shoes, leggings, and everything made of leather; they also drive the carts and repair them, they load the camels, and in all their tasks they are very swift and energetic. All the women wear breeches and some of them shoot like the men.

Questions:
1. *What characteristics does the European missionary use to describe the Mongols?*
2. *Given the way he describes the Mongols, how might he perceive the Europeans to be?*
3. *Based on this description, what do we learn about the culture of the Mongols? Is there room for misunderstanding or misrepresentation on the part of the missionary? Note that cannibalism was a*
   [illegible]

6.6 Contracts between Lords and Vassals

Every vassal in medieval society concluded a contract of mutual obligations with his lord who granted him possession of a fief, an estate in land. Vassals often held many fiefs, with conflicting obligations to various lords. Such overlapping jurisdictions, created by the custom of vassals making their own grants of fiefs to others (a process called subinfeudation), could and did cause conflict and warfare in Europe during the Middle Ages. Here are three records of such contractual agreements: the grant of a fief by King Louis VII of France to the Bishop of Beauvais in 1167, a grant by the Count of Troyes to Jocelyn d'Avalon in 1200, and a contract of 1221 between the Countess of Nevers and her lord, Philip II, King of France.

Source: *Translations and Reprints from the Original Sources of European History,* Edward P. Cheyney, ed., (Philadelphia: University of Pennsylvania, 1897), vol. IV, no. 3, pp. 15–16, 18–20, 24–25.

GRANT OF A FIEF, 1167 C.E.

In the name of the Holy and Undivided Trinity, Amen. I, Louis, by the grace of God, king of the French, make known to all present as well as to come, that at Mante in our presence, Count Henry of Champagne conceded the fief of Savigny to Bartholomew, bishop of Beauvais, and his successors. And for that fief the said bishop has made promise and engagement for one knight and justice and service to Count Henry; and he has also agreed that the bishops who shall come after him will do likewise. In order that this may be understood and known to posterity we have caused the present charter to be corroborated by our seal; done at Mante, in the year of the Incarnate Word 1167; present in our palace those whose names and seals are appended: seal of count Thiebault, our steward; seal of Guy, the butler; seal of Matthew, the chamberlain; seal of Ralph, the constable. Given by the hand of Hugh, the chancellor.

GRANT OF A FIEF, 1200 C.E.

I, Thiebault, count palatine of Troyes, make known to those present and to come that I have given in fee to Jocelyn d'Avalon and his heirs the manor which is called Gillencourt, which is of the castellanerie of La Ferte sur Aube; and whatever the same Jocelyn shall be able to acquire in the same manor I have granted to him arid his heirs in augmentation of that fief. I have granted, moreover, to him that in no free manor of mine will I retain men who are of this gift. The same Jocelyn, moreover, on account of this has become my liege man, saving, however, his allegiance to Gerard d'Arcy, and to the lord duke of Burgundy, and to Peter, count of Auxerre. Done at Chouaude, by my own witness, in the year of the Incarnation of our Lord 1200, in the month of January. Given by the hand of Walter, my chancellor.

AUTHORITY OF A LORD OVER TITLE MARRIAGE OF VASSALS, 1221 C.E.

Eventually women were allowed to hold and inherit fiefs. Because military service was a major obligation of the vassal, a lord would be concerned about whom the heiress married.

I, Matilda, countess of Nevers make known to all who see this present letter, that I have sworn upon the sacred gospels to my dearest lord, Philip, by the grace of God, the illustrious king of France, that I will do to him good and faithful service against all living men and women, and that I will not marry except by his will and grace. For keeping these agreements firmly I have given pledges to the same lord king from my men whom I had with me, on their oaths, in this wise, that if I should fail to keep the said agreements with the lord king, (though this shall not be), these are held to come to the lord king with all their lands and fiefs which are held from me, and shall take their oaths to him against me until it shall have been made good to him to his satisfaction. And whenever the lord king shall ask me I will cause him to have similar oaths from my men who were not present with me before the lord king, that is to say from all whom I may have, in good faith, and without evil intention, and similarly the fealty of my town. And in order that this may remain firm and stable, I have written the present letters supported by my seal. Given at Melun, in the year of the Lord 1221, in the month of February.

Questions:
1. *What are the obligations that each document requires of the parties involved?*
2. *In what ways did granting a fief to a member of the ecclesiastical hierarchy involve that spiritual vassal in secular politics and create the possibility of a conflict of loyalties?*
3. *When a man held fiefs from different lords, how did the feudal system resolve questions of divided loyalty and service?*
4. *Why would or could a lord reasonably demand the right to consent to the marriage of heiresses to the fief?*

6.7   *The Book of Emperors and Kings*, Charlemagne and Pope Leo III

In this excerpt from The Book of Emperors and Kings the author describes the early years of Charlemagne's kingship and the development of his relationship with Pope Leo III. The narrative culminates in the Pope's consecration of Charlemagne as Emperor in 800. Whether the events described really happened or not, the document sheds light on early medieval ideas about kingship, the papacy, and the relationship between secular and religious authorities.

Source: *The Book of Emperors and Kings (Der keiser und der kunige buoch). Trans. Henry A. Myers from text published as Die Kaiserchronik eines Regensburger Geistlichen, ed. Eduward Schröder, in Monumenta Germaniae Historica, Deutsche Chroniken (Hannover: Hahn, 1892), vol. 1, pp. 339–53, passim.*

The Empire remained without a head. The lords of Rome set the crown on Saint Peter's Altar. Meeting all together, they swore before the people that never again would they choose a king—nor judge, nor anyone else to rule them—from the kin of the preceding house, which had proven unable to maintain faith and honor with them. They wanted kings from other lands. . . .

According to a custom of those days, young princes from all over the Empire were raised and instructed with great care at the court in Rome. The Romans gave them the sword of knighthood when the time came . . . , sending the young heirs back to their homelands. This helped keep all the dominions mindful of serving Rome.

It came to pass that Pippin, a mighty king of Karlingen,[1] had two fine sons. One of them named Leo came to hold Saint Peter's throne after being raised in Rome, while Charles, the other, stayed home.

One night when Charles fell asleep, a voice called out to him three times: "Arise, beloved Charles, and hurry to Rome! Your brother Leo needs you!" And quickly Charles made ready, saying nothing to anyone about what he intended to do until he asked leave of the King to go. . . .

When the young Prince asked for leave, his father granted it to him gladly and bestowed gifts upon his son in a manner worthy of a mighty king. . . .

Charles really undertook his journey more for [the chance to pray at the tombs of] the divine Apostles than for his brother's sake. Early and late in the day his thoughts, which he revealed to no one, were filled with love of God. . . .

When Charles arrived in Rome, he was given a fine reception by old and young. . . . Pope Leo sang a mass then in honor of the Holy Ghost and to strengthen the Prince's spirit. Then he received God's Body. All who were there praised God, finding Charles so worthy and to their liking that the law should make him their ruler.

Charles did not listen to what was being said: He had made his journey for the sake of prayer, and he let no commotion distract him. He entered churches barefoot and, imploring God's mercy, he prayed for his soul. This steadfast devotion brought him every worldly honor, too. . . .

Thus he spent four weeks so wrapped in prayer and meditation that no one could approach him to speak, until once his brother, Pope Leo, and all the people fell at his feet. Charles pointed out to God in Heaven that if he were to prove unworthy he never should have made his journey. Then he received the royal emblems, and they set a magnificent crown on his head. All those there in Rome rejoiced that day, and all said, "Amen."

Then the King sat in judgment, and the Pope made complaint before him that church properties and the collection of tithes, entrusted to him by his predecessors for his use in the saving of souls, were being granted away from his jurisdiction, and that his benefices had been taken from him. His complaint angered a number of the nobles.

Then Charles spoke these true ruler's words: "Never in this world, I feel sure, did anyone make a gift to honor God in order that another might take it. That would clearly be robbery. . . . Whoever would take anything away from gifts bestowed on God's houses, through which God's work is furthered, would be despised of God and could not remain a good Christian. . . ." Then those nobles departed, full of resentment. Charles also had no desire to remain there any longer.

Charles returned to Ripuaria.[2] The Romans realized very well that he was their rightful judge, but stupid men among them ridiculed the others for ever having proclaimed him ruler. . . . In Saint Peter's Cathedral they caught the Pope and pushed his eyes out of their sockets. . . , and sent him blind to the King in Ripuaria.

Nothing remained for the Pope to do but set out on the journey in his hapless condition. He rode on a donkey and took with him two of his chaplains, desiring no other escort. . . .

The Pope arrived in Ingelheim with his two chaplains and rode into the King's courtyard. When the King saw him coming, he said to one of his men: "Someone has attacked this pilgrim, and we shall do justice in his cause if we can. He seems badly injured. Someone must have robbed him. . . ."

The King strode quickly across the courtyard . . . and said: "Good pilgrim, if you wish to stay here with me, I will gladly take you in. Tell me if your misfortune is such that I can help you with it. Why don't you dismount?"

The noble Pope wanted to draw closer to the King. His head hung at a strange angle, and his eyes stared askew. "That God should have granted me your presence!" he began. . . . "It has not been long since I sang a mass for you at Rome, when I could still see." As he spoke these words, the noble King recognized him and was so shocked that he could neither see nor hear. . . . His body went limp and he could not speak. . . .

When the Emperor had recovered, the Pope told him sorrowfully: "I have come here that you may take pity on me. It was because of you that I lost my eyes: they blinded me to get even with you. Still, Brother, you must pull yourself together, and weep no more. . . ."

The Emperor himself lifted him down and carried him across the courtyard into his private chamber. There they sat together, and Charles told his men to go outside. "Brother," he said, "how did this happen to you? Let me hear your complaint, and then my forces of justice will right the wrong."

Pope Leo answered the King: "Brother, after you left Rome, the Romans very soon betrayed their loyalty to me in a conspiracy. They caught me in the Cathedral and committed this terrible crime upon me. Brother, we must bear this

---

[1] "Karlingen," the name given by several medieval German writers to the domain of Charlemagne and his ancestors, is probably a derivation by analogy on the assumption that the name of the great Charles (Karl) was given to his whole family domain. Similarly, his grandson Lothar's name was applied to Lorraine (Lotharingen).

[2] Territorial home of one historic group of the Franks on the Rhine River; for the author, this location is sometimes synonymous with "Karlingen," sometimes one of its provinces.

patiently: I seek vengeance only in Heaven, and you must not injure any of them for this."

"It would be doing God a dishonor to spare those murderers!" the noble King replied. "Ah! How sorely that would injure Christendom. I am called 'Judge' and 'Ruler': and this means I have the duty of judging over the peoples. . . . I must defend Christendom with the sword. You will have them sorely regret their crime against you. I will avenge your eyes, or I will renounce my sword."

Then he dispatched messengers to King Pippin to tell him of his great need and let the nobles of Karlingen know that if they ever wanted to render God a loving service they should hurry to him. And there were none in Karlingen but who proclaimed all with one voice: "Woe to the fatal hour that Rome was ever founded!" . . .

The messengers galloped ceaselessly from land to land and from lord to vassal: all men were willing to come to the cause of Charles. Farmers and merchants, too—no one could hold them back. They left all their belongings and set out to join Charles. The mourning and grief over the news traveled through Christendom from people to people, and the streams of warriors converged like clouds over the Great Saint Bernard Pass. . . . The book does not give a number for the total army, but it was the greatest military expedition that ever descended on Rome.

When the army had advanced to within sight of the Aventine Hill in Rome, the worthy King asked three days and nights for himself. This annoyed his great lords, who went to him to say that it ill became his office to pause there, now that they had come so close that they could see the city which had aggrieved them.

"First we must pray to God, for we must gain His leave to carry through," answered the King. "Then we shall fight with ease. . . ."

Early one morning the voice of God spoke to him: "God in Heaven commands you, King, to remain here no longer. Ride on to Rome: God has rendered judgment, and just vengeance shall overtake them."

And so the King's banner was raised, and Charles let word pass through his whole army that when the knights were prepared for battle they should keep their eyes upon the banner and ride in close formation. hearts swelling with high spirits, Charles's men swarmed over the hill. . . .

Owî, what an army this was that besieged Rome and the Lateran for seven days and seven nights, so menacingly that no one would fight against it! On the eighth day—this is the truth I am telling you—the Romans ordered the city gates opened and offered to let the King enter with this condition: that any man who could prove himself innocent of committing, aiding, or advising the crime would remain in the King's favor, while the King would deal with the guilty ones after deciding on a just sentence. . . .

As the Emperor sat in judgment and the document naming the guilty men was read, the accused all fervently denied their guilt when they were called forward. The King ordered them to submit to trial by combat for their unwillingness to confess. But then the Romans objected that this was not according to their law, and that no Emperor had ever forced such treatment on them before; instead, they should prove their innocence by swearing with their two fingers.

Then King Charles spoke: "I doubt that any crime so great was ever committed before. Don't be overhasty now: I imagine my brother saw at the time who did it." Still, when so very many of the accused offered their oaths in the Cathedral, the King said: I will not deprive you of recourse to your own law any longer; however, I know of a youth here named Pancras. If you are willing to swear an oath at his grave and if he tolerates it, then I will be willing to believe you."

Icy fear seized the Romans at the mention of this test. As they came to the place sacred to Saint Pancras and were supposed to hold up their fingers and to keep asserting their innocence under oath, one man was overcome, and panic gripped all the rest. They retreated in fear and fled back over the bridge although a fair number went back to Saint Peter's Cathedral.

Charles hesitated no longer but rode after them angrily. For three days, he and his men struck them down, and for three days they carried them out. Then they washed down the floor stones. . . . Charles fell on his knees before Saint Peter's tomb and made his plea to Christ: "Lord God in Heaven, how can I be any good to You as King when You let such shame befall me? Sinner that I may be, I do make every attempt to judge the people in a manner worthy of You. The Romans swore allegiance to a Pope, and You granted him a portion of Your power that he might loose the people from their sins and bind them. I [ask] . . . that you give the evil people of Rome something to recognize Your hidden power by: then they will know for certain that You are a true God. Grant me this, Holy Christ!"

A second time Charles, the noble King, fell to the ground and said: "Hail noble Saint Peter! You are really a divine stalwart of God, a watchman of Christendom. Think now, my lord, what I am going through! You are a summoner of the Kingdom of Heaven. Just look at your Pope! I left him sound of body in your care. Blinded was how I found him, and if you do not heal the blind man today I shall destroy your Cathedral and ruin the buildings and grounds donated to you, and then I shall leave him for you blind as he is, and go back again to Ripuaria."

Quickly the noble Pope Leo made himself ready and said his confession. As he spoke the last word, he saw a heavenly light with both his eyes. Great are hidden powers of God.

The Pope turned around and spoke to the multitude: "My dearest children gathered from afar, be glad of heart, for the Kingdom of God is drawing near to you. God has heard you and because of your holy prayer has turned His face toward you. Here, at this very place, you are called to be public witnesses that a great miracle has happened. . . . I can see with both eyes better than I ever saw in this world." . . .

The Pope consecrated him as Emperor and granted absolution to all his comrades in arms. Owî, what joy there was in Rome then! The whole people rejoiced then and sang: *"Gloria in excelsis Deo."*

Then Charles laid down the Imperial Law, as an angel recited the true words of God to him. . . . And so the mighty Emperor left us many good laws, which God caused to be spoken before him. . . .

The very first laws the Emperor established dealt with what seemed to him to be the most exalted matters, those concerning bishops and priests, for the Imperial Law of Constantine had been sadly neglected. At the same time, he established laws governing tithes and gifts of property to the Church. . . .

Now I shall tell you about what the peasant is to wear according to the Imperial Law: his clothes may be black or gray, and he is allowed no other. . . . He is to have shoes of cow leather only and seven yards of towcloth for his shirt and breeches. He is to spend six days at the plow and doing plenty of other work; on Sunday he is to go to Church, carrying his animal goad openly in his hand. If a sword is found on a peasant, he is to be led bound to the churchyard fence, where he is to be tied and his skin and hair are to be flayed. If he is threatened by enemies, however, let him defend himself with a pitchfork. This law King Charles established for his peasants. . . .

Emperor Charles besieged a walled city called Arles [France], which actually took him more than seven years. The inhabitants had considered him unworthy of his office. By way of an underground canal, wine was conveyed to them in plentiful supply, but finally Charles's cunning succeeded in cutting off their source. When the inhabitants could not hold out any longer, they threw open the city gates and fought fiercely, offering no terms at all. So many were slain on both sides that there is no man who can tell another how many of either the Christians or the heathens were lying there dead after the battle. No one could tell the dead apart until the Emperor solved the problem with God's help: He found the Christians lying separately in well adorned coffins. Now that is a wonder really worth telling about. . . .

The Emperor and his men turned toward Galicia [in Spain], where the king of the heathens inflicted great losses upon them. The Christian soldiers were all slain, and Charles barely escaped from the battle. Today the stone stays wet on which Charles sat afterwards, weeping passionately as he lamented his sins, saying: "Hail to You, God sublime! Grant me mercy for my poor soul. Take me out of this world, so that my people will no longer be punished because of me. I can never be consoled again."

Then an angel comforted him, saying: "Charles, beloved of God, your joy will come to you quickly. Bid your messengers make haste to summon virgin women—leave the married ones at home—for God will reveal His power through them. If you will fear and love God, the maidens will win your honor back again for you."

The messengers made haste and thoroughly searched through all the lands. They gathered together the maidens and brought them together . . . where the Emperor was waiting for them. Many a young maid came to join the host, fifty-three thousand—I am telling you this as a fact—and sixty-six more. . . .

When all the maidens arrived in a valley since named for Charles, they readied themselves for battle in formations just like men. . . .

Each heathen sentry was struck by wonder as to who this people could be, for it all seemed very strange to them. They hurried back, and one of them said to their king: "Sire, even though we slew the old ones, we must tell you for a fact that the young ones have followed them here. I have the feeling they want to slake their thirst for vengeance. They are big around the chest. Sire, if you fight with them, it will not come to any good end. Their hair is long, and their gait is very graceful: They are fine knights indeed. They are a terrifying lot. . . . No force could ever be assembled on this earth to defeat them. . . ."

At the advice of his experienced counsellors, their king turned over hostages to the Emperor. The king then had himself baptized—how well he suddenly believed in God!—and all his people with him. . . . Thus God made Charles victorious without the thrust of a spear or the blow of a sword, and the maidens well realized that God in Heaven was with them.

Charles and his heroines returned to their own homes back in the Empire. On the way, the worthy maidens came to a green meadow. Tired from the expedition, the heroines stuck their spearshafts into the ground and stretched out their arms in the form of a cross, sleeping on the ground after praising God for the goodness which He had shown them. They stayed there overnight, and a great miracle occurred. Their spearshafts had turned green and had sent forth leaves and blossoms. That is why the place is called "Woods of the Spearshafts"; it can be seen to this day.

Charles, the rich and powerful, built a mighty and beautiful church for the praise of Holy Christ, the honor of Saint Mary and all God's maidens, and the solace of Christendom. Since through chastity and spiritual purity the maids achieved their victory, the church is called *Domini Sanctitas.*[3]

Questions:
1. *How does the author establish Charlemagne as a model Christian ruler?*
2. *What motivates the Romans to attack the Pope? Why is Charlemagne ultimately to blame for this conflict?*
3. *Why is the pope's requesting mercy for his assailants unacceptable to Charlemagne?*
4. *Does The Book of Emperors and Kings give any justification for identifying most of the inhabitants of Arles as "heathens"?*
5. *How does Charlemagne finally win his struggle in Spain?*

6.8 St. Patrick's Confession

St. Patrick (ca. 389-461 C.E.) was the son of a Christian Briton family who was seized in a raid by the Irish and taken back to their island as a slave. Escaping, he entered a monastery on the Continent and was ordained a missionary to Ireland in 432. Although there were some Irish Christians in the south before Patrick's mission, it is largely through his thirty years of missionary activity in Ireland that Christianity became established and systemized there. He left a Confession that includes a brief account of his life, of personal spiritual struggles, and of missionary activity.

Source: *The Book of Letters of Saint Patrick the Bishop,* ed. and trans. D.R. Howlett, (Dublin: Four Courts Press, 1994), pp. 53, 57-65, 67-69, 93.

PART I

I, Patrick, a sinner, very rustic, and the least of all the faithful, and very contemptible in the estimation of most men, had as father a certain man called Calpornius, a deacon, son of Potitus, a presbyter, who was in the town Bannaventa Berniae, for he had a little villa nearby, where I conceded capture. In years I was then almost sixteen. For I was ignorant of the true God, and I was led to Ireland in captivity with so many thousands of men according to our deserts, because we withdrew from God, and we did not keep watch over His precepts, and we were not obedient to our priests, who kept admonishing our salvation, and the Lord led down over us the wrath of His anger and dispersed us among many gentiles even as far as the furthest part of land, where now my insignificance is seen to be among members of a strange race. And there the Lord opened the consciousness of my unbelief so that, perhaps, late, I might remember my delicts, and that I might turn with a whole heart to the Lord my God, Who turned His gaze round on my lowliness and took pity on my adolescence and ignorance and kept watch over me before I knew Him and before I was wise or distinguished between good and bad, and He fortified me and consoled me as a father [consoles] a son.

. . . .

As an adolescent, more precisely, as an almost wordless boy, I conceded capture before I knew what I ought to seek or what to avoid. Whence therefore today I blush for shame and vehemently thoroughly fear to strip naked my unlearnedness, because I cannot unfold in speech to those learned in conciseness as, however, my spirit and mind longs, and the emotion of my consciousness suggests. But if, consequently, it had been given to me just as also to others, even so I would not be silent on account of what should be handed back [from me to God]. And if by chance it seems to certain men that I put myself forward in this, with my lack of knowledge and my rather slow tongue, but even so it is, however, written, "Stammering tongues will swiftly learn to speak peace." How much more ought we to seek, we who are, he affirms, The letter of Christ for salvation as far as the furthest part of land, and if not learned, yet valid and very vigorous, written in your hearts not with ink but by the Spirit of the living God, and again the Spirit testifies even rustic work created by the Most High. Whence I, the extreme rustic, a refugee, untaught, doubtless, who do not know how to look forward into the future, but that I do know most certainly, that indeed before I was humbled. I was like a stone that lies in deep mud, and He Who is powerful came and in His pity He raised me up and assuredly to be sure lifted me upward and placed me on the highest wall and therefore I ought forcefully to shout out for something that should be handed back to the Lord also for His benefits so great here and for eternity, which [benefits] the mind of men cannot estimate. Whence, moreover, be astonished,

---

[3] This church is the Emperor's Chapel, the main and oldest part of the Aachen Cathedral, also called Saint Mary's.

consequently, you great and small who fear God, and you, sirs [lords], clever rhetoricians hear therefore and examine who roused me up, a fool, from the midst of those who seem to be wise and learned by experience in law and powerful in speech and in everything and inspired me, assuredly, beyond the others of this execrable world..., in order even after my death to leave behind a legacy to my brothers and Sons whom I have baptized in the Lord, so many thousands of men....

PART II

But after I had come to Ireland, I was consequently pasturing domestic animals daily, and often in the day I was praying. More and more the love of God and fear of Him was approaching, and faith was being increased, and the Spirit was being stirred up, so that in a single day up to a hundred prayers, and in a night nearly the same, even as I was staying in forests and on the mountain, and before dawn I was roused up to prayer, through snow, through frost, through rain, and I was feeling nothing bad, nor was there any sloth in me, as I see now, because the Spirit was being fervent in me then, and there, to be sure, on a certain night in a dream I heard a voice saying to me, "It is well that you are fasting, bound soon to go to your fatherland." And again after a very little time I heard the answer saying to me, "Look, your ship is ready." And it was not near, but perhaps two hundred miles and I had never been there, nor did I have any single acquaintance among men there, and then later I turned to flight, and I abandoned the man with whom I had been for six years, and I came in the power of God, Who was directing my way toward the good, and I was fearing nothing until I came through to that ship, and on that day on which I came through the ship set out from its own place, and I spoke as I had the wherewithal to ship with them, and the captain, it displeased him, and he responded sharply with indignation, "By no means will you seek to go with us."

And when I heard these things I separated myself from them, so that I would come to the little hut where I was staying, and on the journey I began to pray, and before I could bring the prayer to the highest perfection I heard one of them, and he was shouting out vigorously after me, "Come soon, because these men are calling you", and immediately I returned to them, and they began to say to me, "Come, because we are receiving you on faith, make friendship with us in whatever way you will have wished" and on that day, to be sure, I refused to suck their nipples on account of the fear of God, but nevertheless I hoped to come by them to the faith of Jesus Christ, as they were gentiles, and because of this I got my way with them, and we shipped at once.

And after a three-day period we reached land, and for twenty-eight days we made a journey through the desert, and food was not forthcoming for them, and hunger prevailed over them, and on the next day the captain began to say to me, "What is it, Christian? You say your God is great and all-powerful. Why therefore can you not pray for us, because we are imperilled by hunger, for it is not likely that we may ever see any man."

But I said confidently to them, "Be turned in faith with a whole heart to the Lord my God, because nothing is impossible to Him, so that today He may dispatch food to you until you should be satisfied on your way, as there was abundance everywhere for Him." And with God helping it was made so.

Look, a flock of pigs appeared in the way before our eyes, and they killed many of them, and there they remained two nights and were well fed, and they were refilled with their flesh, because many of them fainted away, and were left behind half-alive along the way, and after this they gave the highest thanks to God, and I was made honourable in their eyes, and from this day they had food abundantly; they even discovered [lit. 'came upon'] forest honey, and they offered a part to me, and one of them said, "It is a [pagan] sacrifice." Thanks be to God, I tasted nothing from it.

· · · ·

And again after a few years in the Britains I was with my parents, who received me as a son, and in faith requested me whether now I, after such great tribulations which I bore, I should not ever depart from them. And there to be sure I saw in a vision of the night a man coming as if from Ireland, whose name [was] Victoricius, with innumerable epistles, and he gave me one of them, and I read the beginning of the epistle containing 'the Voice of the Irish', and while I was reciting the beginning of the epistle I kept imagining hearing at that very moment the voice of those very men who were beside the Forest of Foclut, which is near the Western Sea [lit. 'the sea of the setting (sc. of the sun)'], and thus they shouted out as if from one mouth, "We request you, holy boy, that you come and walk farther among us." And I was especially stabbed at heart, and I could not read further. And thus I have learned by experience, thanks be to God, that after very many years the Lord has supplied them according to their clamour.

· · · ·

PART V

Look, again and again briefly I will set out the words of my Confession.

I bear testimony in truth and in exultation of heart before God and His holy angels that I have never had any occasion besides the Gospel and His promises that I should ever go back to that gentile people whence earlier I had barely escaped.

But I beseech those believing and fearing God, whoever will have deigned to look on or receive this writing, which Patrick, a sinner, untaught, to be sure, wrote down in Ireland, that no man should ever say that by my ignorance, if I have accomplished or demonstrated any small thing according to the acceptable purpose of God, but that you judge and it must be most truly believed that it was the gift of God, and this is my Confession before I die.

Questions:
1. What were Patrick's first experiences in Ireland and how did he escape?
2. What problems did Patrick have to overcome to become a Christian missionary?
3. What is his own evaluation of his life and work?

PART 7
Church and State in the High Middle Ages

7.1 Gregory VII's Letter to the Bishop of Metz, *1081*

Gregory VII (pope 1073–1085) was one of the great medieval popes. An advocate of reform and a strengthened papacy, Gregory came into conflict with many of Europe's secular rulers, chief among them the Holy Roman Emperor Henry IV (1050–1106). In the letter included here, Gregory argued for the primacy of the pope over kings and other secular authorities.

> **Source:** *Documents of the Christian Church*, ed. Henry Bettenson (New York: Oxford University Press, 1970), pp. 104–110.

Bishop Gregory, servant of the servants of God, to his beloved brother in Christ, Hermann bishop of Metz, greeting and apostolic benediction. It is doubtless owing to a dispensation of God that, as we learn, thou art ready to endure trials and dangers in defence of the truth. For such is His ineffable grace and wonderful mercy that He never allows His chosen ones completely to go astray—never permits them utterly to fall or to be cast down. For, after they have been afflicted by a period of persecution—a useful term of probation as it were,—He makes them, even if they have been for a time faint-hearted, stronger than before. Since, moreover, manly courage impels one strong man to act more bravely than another and to press forward more boldly—even as among cowards fear induces one to flee more disgracefully than another,—we wish, beloved, with the voice of exhortation, to impress this upon thee: thou shouldst the more delight to stand in the army of the Christian faith among the first, the more thou art convinced that the conquerors are the most worthy and the nearest to God. Thy request, indeed, to be aided, as it were, by our writings and fortified against the madness of those who babble forth with impious tongue that the authority of the holy and apostolic see had no authority to excommunicate Henry—a man who despises the Christian law; a destroyer of the churches and of the empire; a patron and companion of heretics—or to absolve any one from the oath of fealty to him, seems to us to be hardly necessary when so many and such absolutely decisive warrants are to be found in the pages of Holy Scripture. Nor do we believe, indeed, that those who (heaping up for themselves damnation) impudently detract from the truth and contradict it have added these assertions to the audacity of their defence so much from ignorance as from a certain madness.

For, to cite a few passages from among many, who does not know the words of our Lord and Saviour Jesus Christ who says in the gospel: 'Thou art Peter and upon this rock will I build my church, and the gates of hell shall not prevail against it; and I will give unto thee the keys of the kingdom of Heaven; and whatsoever thou shalt bind upon earth shall be bound also in Heaven, and whatsoever thou shalt loose upon earth shall be loosed also in Heaven'? [Matthew xvi. 18, 19.] Are kings excepted here? Or are they not included among the sheep which the Son of God committed to St Peter? Who, I ask, in view of this universal concession of the power of binding and loosing, can think that he is withdrawn from the authority of St Peter, unless, perhaps, that unhappy man who is unwilling to bear the yoke of the Lord and subjects himself to the burden of the devil, refusing to be among the number of Christ's sheep? It will help him little to his wretched liberty that he shake from his proud neck the divinely granted power of Peter. For the more any one, through pride, refuses to bear it, the more heavily shall it press upon him unto damnation at the judgement.

The holy fathers, as well in general councils as in their writings and doings, have called the Holy Roman Church the universal mother, accepting and serving with great veneration this institution founded by the divine will, this pledge of a dispensation to the church, this privilege entrusted in the beginning and confirmed to St Peter the chief of the apostles. And even as they accepted its statements in confirmation of their faith and of the doctrines of holy religion, so also they received its judgements—consenting in this, and agreeing as it were with one spirit and one voice: that all greater matters and exceptional cases, and judgements over all churches, ought to be referred to it as to a mother and a head; that from it there was no appeal; that no one should or could retract or reverse its decisions. . . .

. . . Shall not an authority founded by laymen—even by those who do not know God,—be subject to that authority which the providence of God Almighty has for His own honour established and in his mercy given to the world? For His Son, even as He is undoubtingly believed to be God and man, so is He considered the highest priest, the head of all priests, sitting on the right hand of the Father and always interceding for us. Yet He despised a secular kingdom, which makes the sons of this world swell with pride, and came of His own will to the priesthood of the cross. Who does not know that kings and leaders are sprung from men who were ignorant of God, who by pride, robbery, perfidy, murders—in a word, by almost every crime at the prompting of the devil, who is the prince of this world—have striven with blind cupidity and intolerable presumption to dominate over their equals, that is, over mankind?

To whom, indeed, can we better compare them, when they seek to make the priests of God bend to their feet, than to him who is head over all the sons of pride[1] and who, tempting the Highest Pontiff Himself, the Head of priests, the Son of the Most High, and promising to Him all the kingdoms of the world, said: 'All these I will give unto Thee if Thou wilt fall down and worship me'?[2] who can doubt but that the priests of Christ are to be considered the fathers and masters of kings and princes and of all the faithful? Is it not clearly pitiful madness for a son to attempt to subject to himself his father, a pupil his master; and for one to bring into his power and bind with iniquitous bonds him by whom he believes that he himself can be bound and loosed not only on earth but also in Heaven? This the emperor Constantine the Great, lord of all the kings and princes of nearly the whole world, plainly understood—as the blessed Gregory reminds us in a letter to the emperor Maurice, when, sitting last after all the bishops, in the holy council of Nicaea, he presumed to give no sentence of judgement over them, but addressed them as gods and decreed that they should not be subject to his judgement but that he should be dependent upon their will. . . .

. . . Many pontiffs have excommunicated kings or emperors. For, if particular examples of such princes is needed, the blessed pope Innocent excommunicated the emperor Arcadius for consenting that St John Chrysostom should be expelled from his see. Likewise another Roman pontiff, Zacchary, deposed a king of the Franks, not so much for his iniquities as because he was not fitted to exercise so great power. And in his stead he set up Pepin, father of the emperor Charles the Great, in his place—releasing all the Franks from the oath of fealty which they had sworn him. As, indeed, the holy church frequently does by its authority when it absolves servitors from the fetters of an oath sworn to such bishops as, by apostolic sentence, are deposed from their pontifical rank. And the blessed Ambrose—who, although a saint, was still not bishop over the whole church—excommunicated and excluded from the church the emperor Theodosius the Great for a fault[3] which, by other priests, was not regarded as very grave. He shows, too, in his writings that gold does not so much excel lead in value as the priestly dignity transcends the royal power; speaking thus towards the beginning of his pastoral letter: 'The honour and sublimity of bishops, brethren, is beyond all comparison. If one should compare them to resplendent kings and diademed princes it would be far less worthy than if one compared the base metal lead to gleaming gold. For, indeed, one can see how the necks of kings and princes are bowed before the knees of priests; and how, having kissed their right hands, they believe themselves strengthened by their prayers.' And a little later: 'Ye should know, brethren, that we have mentioned all this to show that nothing can be found in this world more lofty than priests or more sublime than bishops.'

Furthermore every Christian king, when he comes to die, seeks as a pitiful suppliant the aid of a priest, that he may escape hell's prison, may pass from the darkness into the light, and at the judgement of God may appear absolved from the bondage of his sins. Who, in his last hour (what layman, not to speak of priests), has ever implored the aid of an earthly king for the salvation of his soul? And what king or emperor is able, by reason of the office he holds, to rescue a Christian from the power of the devil through holy baptism, to number him among the sons of God, and to fortify him with the divine unction? Who of them can by his own words make the body and blood of our Lord,—the greatest act in the Christian religion? Or who of them possesses the power of binding and loosing in heaven and on earth? From all of these considerations it is clear how greatly the priestly office excels in power.

Who of them can ordain a single clerk in the holy Church, much less depose him for any fault? For in the orders of the Church a greater power is needed to depose than to ordain. Bishops may ordain other bishops, but can by no means depose them without the authority of the apostolic see. Who, therefore, of even moderate understanding, can hesitate to give priests the precedence over kings? Then, if kings are to be judged by priests for their sins, by whom can they be judged with better right than by the Roman pontiff?

In short, any good Christians may far more properly be considered kings than may bad princes. For the former, seeking the glory of God, strictly govern themselves, whereas the latter, seeking the things which are their own and not the things of God, are enemies to themselves and tyrannical oppressors of others. Faithful Christians are the body of the true king, Christ; evil rulers, that of the devil. The former rule themselves in the hope that they will eternally reign with the Supreme Emperor, but the sway of the latter ends in their destruction and eternal damnation with the prince of darkness, who is king over all the sons of pride.

It is certainly not strange that wicked bishops are of one mind with a bad king, whom they love and fear for the honours which they have wrongfully obtained from him. Such men simoniacally ordain whom they please and sell God even for a paltry sum. As even the elect are indissolubly united with their Head, so also the wicked are inescapably leagued

---

[1] Job xli. 34.
[2] Matt. iv. 9.
[3] A savage massacre in Thessalonica, 390, as a reprisal for a riot.

with him who is the head of evil, their chief purpose being to resist the good. But surely we ought not so much to denounce them as to mourn for them with tears and lamentations, beseeching God Almighty to snatch them from the snares of Satan in which they are held captive, and after their peril to bring them at last to a knowledge of the truth.

We refer to those kings and emperors who, too much puffed up by worldly glory, rule not for God but for themselves. Now, since it belongs to our office to admonish and encourage every one according to the rank or dignity which he enjoys, we endeavour, by God's grace, to arm emperors and kings and other princes with the weapon of humility, that they may be able to allay the waves of the sea[5] and the floods of pride. For we know that earthly glory and the cares of this world usually tempt men to pride, especially those in authority. So that they neglect humility and seek their own glory, desiring to lord it over their brethren. Therefore it is of especial advantage for emperors and kings, when their minds tend to be puffed up and to delight in their own glory, to discover a way of humbling themselves, and to realize that what causes their complacency is the thing which should be feared above all else. Let them, therefore, diligently consider how perilous and how much to be feared is the royal or imperial dignity. For very few are saved of those who enjoy it; and those who, through the mercy of God, do come to salvation are not so glorified in the Holy Church by the judgement of the Holy Spirit as are many poor people. For, from the beginning of the world until our own times, in the whole of authentic history we do not find seven emperors or kings whose lives were as distinguished for religion and so adorned by miracles of power as those of an innumerable multitude who despised the world—although we believe many of them to have found mercy in the presence of God Almighty. For what emperor or king was ever so distinguished by miracles as were St Martin, St Antony and St Benedict—not to mention the apostles and martyrs? And what emperor or king raised the dead, cleansed lepers, or healed the blind? See how the Holy Church praises and venerates the Emperor Constantine of blessed memory, Theodosius and Honorius, Charles and Louis as lovers of justice, promoters of the Christian religion, defenders of the churches: it does not, however, declare them to have been resplendent with such glorious miracles. Moreover, to how many kings or emperors has the holy church ordered chapels or altars to be dedicated, or masses to be celebrated in their honour? Let kings and other princes fear lest the more they rejoice at being placed over other men in this life, the more they will be subjected to eternal fires. For of them it is written: 'The powerful shall powerfully suffer torments.'[6] And they are about to render account to God for as many men as they have had subjects under their dominion. But if it be no little task for any private religious man to guard his own soul: how much labour will there be for those who are rulers over many thousands of souls? Moreover, if the judgement of the Holy Church severely punishes a sinner for the slaying of one man, what will become of those who, for the sake of worldly glory, hand over many thousands to death? And such persons, although after having slain many they often say with their lips 'I have sinned,' nevertheless rejoice in their hearts at the extension of their (so-called) fame. They do not regret what they have done. Nor are they grieved at having sent their brethren down to Tartarus. As long as they do not repent with their whole heart, nor agree to give up what they have acquired or kept through bloodshed, their repentance remains without the true fruit of penitence before God.

Therefore they should greatly fear and often call to mind what we have said above, that out of the innumerable host of kings in all countries from the beginning of the world, very few are found to have been holy; whereas in one single see—the Roman—of the successive bishops from the time of blessed Peter the Apostle, nearly one hundred are counted amongst the most holy. And why is this, unless because kings and princes, enticed by vain glory, prefer, as has been said, their own things to things spiritual, whereas the bishops of the Church, despising vain glory, prefer God's will to earthly things? The former are quick to punish offences against themselves, but lightly tolerate those who sin against God. The latter readily pardon those who sin against themselves, but do not readily forgive offenders against God. The former, too bent on earthly achievements, think little of spiritual ones; the latter, earnestly meditating on heavenly, things, despise the things of earth. . . .

Therefore let those whom Holy Church, of its own will and after proper counsel, not for transitory glory but for the salvation of many, calls to have rule or dominion, humbly obey. And let them always beware in that point as to which St Gregory in that same pastoral book[7] bears witness: 'Indeed, when a man disdains to be like to men, he is made like to an apostate angel. Thus Saul, after having possessed the merit of humility, came to be swollen with pride when at the summit of power. Through humility, indeed, he was advanced; through pride, rejected—God being witness who said:

---

[5] Psalm xciii. 4.
[6] Wisdom vi. 6. Greek, 'Mighty men shall be searched out mightily.'
[7] Reg. Past. II. vi.

"When thou wast small in thine own eyes, did I not make thee head over the tribes of Israel?"[8] And a little further on: 'Moreover, strange to say, when he was small in his own eyes he was great in the eyes of God; but when he seemed great his own eyes he was small in the eyes of God.' Let them also carefully retain what God says in the gospel: 'I seek not my own glory'; and, 'He who will be the first among you shall be the servant of all.'[9] Let them always prefer the honour of God to their own; let them cherish and guard justice by observing the rights of every man; let them not walk in the counsel of the ungodly but, with an assenting heart, always consort with good men. Let them not seek to subject to themselves or to subjugate the Holy Church as a handmaid; but above all let them strive, by recognizing the teachers and fathers, to render due honour to the eyes of the Church—the priests of God. For if we are ordered to honour our fathers and mothers after the flesh—how much more our spiritual ones! And if he who has cursed his father or mother after the flesh is to be punished with death—what does he merit who curses his spiritual father or mother? Let them not, led astray by wordly love, strive to place one of their own sons over the flock for which Christ poured forth His blood, if they can find some one who is better and more useful than he: lest, loving their son more than God, they inflict the greatest damage on the Holy Church. For he who neglects to provide to the best of his ability for such a want—and, one might say, necessity—of Holy Mother Church is openly convicted of not loving God and his neighbour as a Christian should.

For if this virtue, love, has been neglected, no matter what good any one does he shall be without any fruit of salvation. And so by humbly doing these things, and by observing the love of God and of their neighbour as they ought, they may hope for the mercy of Him who said: 'Learn of Me, for I am meek and lowly of heart.'[10] If they have humbly imitated Him they shall pass from this servile and transitory kingdom to a true kingdom of liberty and eternity.

Question:
1. Why is Papal authority so important to Gregory and the Church? Could he have compromised?

7.2   Benedict of Nursia: *The Rule of St. Benedict*

Benedict of Nursia (d. c. 547) played a key role in shaping the development of monasticism in the West. In 529, Benedict founded the monastery at Monte Casino in central Italy. The Rule of St. Benedict would become the model for life in many future monastic communities.

> **Source:** *Documents of the Christian Church*, ed. Henry Bettenson (New York: Oxford University Press, 1970), pp. 116–128.

    I.   *Of the Kinds of Monks.*

   II.   *Of the Character of the Abbot.*

  III.   *Of calling the Brethren to Counsel.*— Whenever matters of importances have to be dealt with in the monastery, let the abbot summon the whole congregation and himself put forward the question that has arisen. Then, after hearing the advice of the brethren let him think it over by himself and do what he shall judge most advantageous. Now we have said that all should be summoned to take counsel for this reason, that it is often to the younger that the Lord reveals what is best. But let the brethren give advice with all subjection of humility, so as not to presume obstinately to defend their own opinions; rather let the matter depend on the abbot's judgement, so that all should submit to whatever he decide to be best. Yet, just as it becomes the disciples to obey their master, so it behoves him to order all things with prudence and justice.

And in all things let all follow the Rule as their guide: and let no one diverge from it without good reason. Let no one in the monastery follow his own inclinations, and let no one boldly presume to dispute with his abbot, whether within or without the monastery. If anyone so presume, let him be subject to the discipline of the Rule. The abbot, for his part, should do everything in the fear of the Lord and in observance of the Rule; knowing that he will surely have to give account to God for all his decisions, as to a most impartial judge. If it happen that matters of less moment have to be dealt with, let him avail himself of the advice of the seniors only; as it is written: 'Do all things with counsel, and thou shalt not thereafter repent' [Ecclus. xxxii. 19.]

VIII. *Of the Divine Office at Night.*—In the winter time, that is from the First of November until Easter, according to what is reasonable, they must rise at the eighth hour of the night, so that they rest a little more than half the night,

---

[8] I Sam. xv. 17.

[9] Jn. viii, 50, Matt. xx. 27.

[10] Matt. xi. 29.

and rise when they have had their full sleep. But let the time that remains after vigils be spent in study by those brothers who have still to learn any part of the psalter or lessons. From Easter, moreover, until the aforesaid First of November, let the hour of keeping vigils be so arranged that, after a short interval, in which the brethren may go out for the necessities of nature, lauds, which are always to be said at break of day, may follow immediately.

XVI. *How Divine Office shall be said in the Daytime.*—As the prophet says: 'Seven times in the day do I praise Thee.' This sacred number seven will thus be fulfilled by us if, at lauds, at the first, third, sixth, ninth hours, at vesper time and at 'completorium' we perform the duties of our service; for it is of these hours of the day that he said: 'Seven times in the day do I praise Thee' [Ps. cxix. 164]. For, concerning the night hours, the same prophet says: 'At midnight I arose to confess unto thee' [*ibid.* 62]. Therefore, at these times, let us give thanks to our Creator concerning the judgements of his righteousness; that is, at matins, etc. . . . and at night we will rise and confess to him. . . .

XX. *Of Reverence in Prayer.*—When we make application to men in high positions we do not presume to do so without reverence and humility; how much more, then, are we bound to entreat God, the Lord of all, with all humility and devout purity of heart. And we must recognize that we are heard not for our much speaking, but for our purity of heart and tears of contrition. Therefore our prayer must be brief and pure—unless it chance to be prolonged with the inspiration of God's grace. When we assemble together, let the prayer be quite brief; and let us all rise together, when the Prior gives the signal.

XXI. *Of the Deans of the Monastery.*—If the congregation be a larger one, let there be chosen from it brothers of good reputation and of godly life; and let them be made deans. And they shall be watchful over their deaneries in all things, according to the commands of God and the precepts of their abbot. And the deans elected shall be such that the abbot may with confidence share his burdens with them. And they shall not be elected according to seniority, but according to the merit of their life and their learning and wisdom. And, should any one of these deans be found to be blameworthy, being puffed up by pride; and if, after being admonished once and again and a third time, he be unwilling to amend—let him be deposed; and let another, who is worthy, be chosen in his place.

XXII. *How the Monks are to sleep.*—Let them sleep in separate beds, and let their beds be suitable to their manner of life, as the Abbot shall appoint. If possible, let them all sleep in one room. But if there be too many for this, let them take their rest in groups of 10 or 20, with seniors in charge of each group. Let a candle be kept burning in the cell until morning. Let them sleep clothed, girdled with belts or cords—but without knives at their sides, lest they injure themselves in sleep. And thus let the monks be always ready; and, when the signal is given, let them rise without delay and rival one another in their haste to the service of God, yet with all reverence and modesty.

Let not the younger brothers have beds by themselves, but dispersed among the seniors. And when they rise for the service of God let them gently encourage one another, because the sleepy ones are apt to make excuses.

XXIII. *Of Excommunication for Faults.*—If a brother be found contumacious or disobedient, proud or a grumbler, or in any way acting contrary to the holy Rule and despising the orders of his seniors, let him, according to the Lord's commandment, be privately admonished once and twice by his seniors. If he do not then amend, let him be publicly rebuked before all. But if even then he do not correct himself, let him be subjected to excommunication, if he understands the gravity of this penalty. If, however, he is incorrigible, let him undergo corporal chastisement.

XXIV. *Of the Extent of Excommunication.*—The extent of the excommunication or discipline is to be regulated according to the gravity of the fault; and this is to be decided by the abbot's discretion. If a brother be found guilty of a lighter fault, he shall be excluded from the common table; he shall also intone neither psalm nor antiphon in the oratory, or read a lesson, until he has atoned. He shall take his meals alone, after those of the brethren; if, for example, the brothers have their meal at the sixth hour, he shall have his at the ninth. . . .

XXV. *Of Grave Faults.*—The brother who is held guilty of a graver fault shall be suspended both from table and from the oratory. None of the brothers may in any way consort with him, or have speech with him. He shall be alone at the labour enjoined upon him, and continue in the sorrow of penitence; knowing that terrible sentence of the Apostle who said that such a man was given over to the destruction of the flesh in order that his soul might be saved at the day of the Lord [I Cor. v. 5]. His portion of food he shall take alone, in the measure and at the time that the abbot shall appoint as suitable for him. Nor shall he be blessed by any one who passes by, nor the food that is given him.

XXVI. *Of those who, without being ordered by the Abbot, consort with the Excommunicated.*—If any brother presume, without an order of the abbot, in any way to associate with an excommunicated brother, or to speak with him, or to give an order to him: he shall suffer the same penalty of excommunication.

XXVII. *What care the Abbot should exercise with regard to the Excommunicated.*—The abbot shall show the utmost solicitude and care towards brothers that offend: 'They that be whole need not a physician, but they that are sick [Matt. ix. 12]. And therefore he ought to use every means, as a wise physician; to send 'playmates,' i.e. older and wiser brothers, who, as it were secretly, shall console the wavering brother and lead him to the atonement of humility. And they shall comfort him lest he be overwhelmed by excess of sorrow. But rather, as the same apostle says [2 Cor. ii. 8], charity shall be confirmed in him, and he shall be prayed for by all. For the abbot should employ the utmost solicitude, and take care with all prudence and diligence, lest he lose any of the sheep entrusted to him. For he should know that he has undertaken the care of weak souls, not the tyranny over the strong. And he shall fear the threat of the prophet through whom the Lord says: 'Ye did take that which ye saw to be strong, and that which was weak ye did cast out' [? cf. Ezek. xxxiv]. And let him imitate the pious example of the good Shepherd, who, leaving the ninety and nine sheep upon the mountains, went out to seek the one sheep that had gone astray: and He had such compassion upon its infirmity, that He deigned to place it upon His sacred shoulders, and thus to carry it back to the flock.

XXVIII. *Of those who, being often rebuked, do not amend.*—If any brother, having frequently been rebuked for any fault, do not amend even after he has been excommunicated, a more severe chastisement shall fall upon him; that is, the punishment of the lash shall be inflicted upon him. But if he do not even then amend; or, if perchance (which God forbid) puffed up with pride he try even to defend his deeds: then the abbot shall act as a wise physician. If he have applied the fomentations, the ointments of exhortation, the medicaments of the Divine Scriptures; if he have proceeded to the last cauterization of excommunication, or flogging, and if he see that his efforts avail nothing: let him also (what is more powerful) call in the prayer of himself and all the brothers for him: that God who can do all things may work a cure upon a sick brother. But if he be not healed, even in this way, then at last the abbot may use the surgeon's knife, as the apostle says: 'Remove evil from, you' [I Cor. v. 13], lest one diseased sheep contaminate the whole flock.

XXIX. *Whether Brothers who leave the Monastery ought again to be received.*— A brother who goes out, or is cast out, of the monastery for his own fault, if he wish to return, shall first promise every amends for the fault on account of which he departed; and thus he shall be received into the lowest degree—so that thereby his humility may be proved. But if he again depart, up to the third time he shall be received. Knowing that after this every opportunity of return is denied to him.

XXX. *Concerning Boys under Age, how they shall be corrected.*—Every age or intelligence ought to have its proper bounds. Therefore as often as boys or youths, or those who are less able to understand how great is the punishment of excommunication; as often as such persons offend, they shall either be punished with extra fasts, or coerced with severe blows, that they may be healed.

XXXIII. *Whether the Monks should have anything of their own.*—More than any thing else is this vice of property to be cut off root and branch from the monastery. Let no one presume to give or receive anything without the leave of the abbot, or to retain anything as his own. He should have nothing at all: neither a book, nor tablets, nor a pen—nothing at all. For indeed it is not allowed to the monks to have bodies or wills in their own power. But for all things necessary they must look to the Father of the monastery; nor is it allowable to have anything which the abbot has not given or permitted. All things shall be common to all, as it is written: 'Let not any man presume or call anything his own' [Acts iv. 32]. But if any one is found delighting in this most evil vice: being warned once and again, if he do not amend, let him be subjected to punishment.

XXXIV. *Whether all ought to receive Necessaries equally.*—As it is written: 'It was divided among them singly, according as each had need' [Acts iv. 35]: whereby we do not say—far from it—that there should be respect of persons, but a consideration for infirmities. Wherefore he who needs less, let him thank God and not be grieved; but he who needs more, let him be humiliated on account of his weakness, and not made proud on account of the indulgence that is shown him. And thus all members will be in peace. Above all, let not the evil of grumbling appear, on any account, by the least word or sign whatever. But, if such a grumbler is discovered, he shall be subjected to stricter discipline.

XXXV. *Of the Weekly Officers of the Kitchen.*—The brothers shall wait on each other in turn that no one shall be excused from the kitchen-work, unless he be prevented by sickness, or by preoccupation with some matter of great necessity whereby is gained a greater reward and increase of charity. . . . An hour before each meal the weekly servers are to receive a cup of drink and a piece of bread over and above their ration, so that they may wait on their brethren without grumbling or undue fatigue. But on solemn days they shall fast till after Mass. . . .

XXXVI. *Of the Sick Brethren.*—Before all things, and above all things, care must be taken of the sick; so that the brethren shall minister to them as they would to Christ himself; for he said: 'I was sick and ye visited me' [Matt. xxv. 36], and 'Inasmuch as, etc.' [*ibid.* 40]. But let the sick, on their part, remember that they are being cared for to the honour of God; and let them not by their abundance offend the brothers who serve them: which (offences) nevertheless are patiently to be borne, for, from such, a greater reward is acquired. Wherefore let the abbot take the greatest care that they suffer no neglect. And for these infirm brothers a cell shall be set apart, and a servitor, God-fearing, and diligent and careful. The use of baths shall be offered to the sick as often as is necessary: to the healthy, and especially to youths, more rarely. The eating of meat also shall be allowed to the sick, and to the delicate, to assist their recovery. But when they have grown better, they shall all, in the usual manner, abstain from flesh. The abbot, moreover, shall take the greatest care that the sick be not neglected by the cellarer or by the servitors: for whatever fault is committed by the disciples recoils upon him.

XXXVII. *Of the Old and Young.*—Although human nature itself is prone to have consideration for these ages—that is, old age and infancy,—nevertheless the authority of the Rule also should provide for them. Their weakness shall always be taken into account, and in the matter of food, the strict tenor of the Rule shall by no means be observed, as far as they are concerned; but they shall be treated with kind consideration, and may anticipate the regular (canonical) hours [*sc.* of meals].

XXXVIII. *Of the Weekly Reader.*—At the meal times of the brothers there should always be reading; no one may dare to take up the book at random and begin to read there; but he who is about to read for the whole week shall begin his duties on Sunday. And, entering upon his office after Mass and Communion, he shall ask all to pray for him, that God may avert from him the spirit of elation. And this verse shall be said in the oratory three times by all, he however beginning it: 'O Lord, open Thou my lips, and my mouth shall show forth Thy praise.' And thus, having received the benediction, he shall enter upon his duties as reader. And there shall be the greatest silence at table, so that no whispering or any voice save the reader's may be heard. And whatever is needed, in the way of food, the brethren should pass to each other in turn, so that no one need ask for anything. But if anything should be wanted let them ask for it by means of a sign rather than by speech. . . .

XXXIX. *Of the Amount of Food.*—We think it sufficient for the daily meal, either at the sixth or the ninth hour, that there be, at all seasons, two cooked dishes. And this because of the weaknesses of different people, so that he who happens not to be able to eat of one may make his meal of the other. Let two dishes, then, suffice for the brethren: or if fruits or fresh vegetables are obtainable, a third may be added. Let one pound of bread suffice for a day, whether there be one principal meal, or both dinner and supper. If there is to be supper, the cellarer must keep back a third of the pound, to be given out at supper. But if unusually heavy work has been done it shall be in the discretion and power of the abbot to make some addition; avoiding excess, above all things, that no monk be overtaken by indigestion. . . . All must abstain from the flesh of four-footed beasts, except the delicate and the sick.

XL. *Of the Amount of Drink.*—Each one has his own gift from God, the one in this way, the other in that [I Cor. ix. 17]. Therefore it is with some hesitation that the amount of daily sustenance for others is fixed by us. Nevertheless, in view of the weakness of the infirm we believe that one pint of wine a day is enough for each one. Let those to whom God gives the ability to endure abstinence know that they will have their reward. But the prior shall judge if either the nature of the locality or labour, or the heat of summer, requires more; taking care in all things lest satiety or drunkenness creep in. Indeed we read that wine is not suitable for monks at all. But because, in our day, it is not possible to persuade the monks of this, let us agree at least as to the fact that we should not drink to excess, but sparingly. For wine can make even the wise to go astray. Where, moreover, owing to local conditions, the amount aforesaid cannot be provided,—but much less or nothing at all—those who live there shall bless God and shall not grumble. And we admonish them as to this above all: that they be without grumbling.

XLI. *At what Hours the Brothers ought to take their Refection.*—From the holy Easter time until Pentecost the brothers shall have their refection at the sixth hour; and at evening they shall sup. From Pentecost, moreover, through the whole summer—unless the monks have hard labour in the fields, or the extreme heat of the summer oppress them—they shall fast on Wednesday and Friday until the ninth hour: but on the other days they shall have their meal at the sixth hour. Which sixth hour, if they have ordinary work in the fields, or if the heat of summer is not great, shall be kept to for the meal; and it shall be for the abbot to decide. And he shall so arrange all things, that their souls may be saved on the one hand; and that, on the other, what the brothers do they shall do without any justifiable grumbling. Moreover, from the 13th of September to the beginning of Lent they shall have their meal at the ninth hour. But during Lent they shall have the meal in the evening, at such time as enables them to finish in daylight. . . .

XLII. *Of Silence after Compline.*—Monks should practise silence at all times, but especially in the hours of night. Therefore on all days, whether fasting days or otherwise, let them sit together as soon as they have risen from supper (if it be not a fast day) and let one of them read the 'Collations' ['Selections'] or 'Lives of the Fathers,' or something, else which may edify the hearers. But not the Heptateuch, or 'Kings'; for it will not profit weak intellects to listen to that part of Scripture at that hour; but they may be read at other times. . . . At the end of the reading . . . let them say Compline [*Completorium*] and when that is over, let no one be allowed to speak to anyone. If anyone be found breaking this law of silence he shall undergo severe punishments. Unless the presence of guests should require speech, or the abbot should chance to issue some order. But, even so, let it be done with the utmost gravity and moderation.

XLVIII. *Of the daily Manual Labour.*—Idleness is enemy of the soul. And therefore, at fixed times, the brothers ought to be occupied in manual labour; and again, at fixed times, in sacred reading. Therefore we believe that both these ought to be arranged thus: from Easter until the 1st of October, on coming out of Prime they shall do what labour may be necessary until the fourth hour. From the fourth hour until about the sixth, they shall apply themselves to reading. After the meal of the sixth hour, moreover, rising from table, they shall rest in their beds in complete silence; or, perchance, he that wishes to read may read to himself in such a way as not to disturb any other. And None shall be said rather before the time, about the middle of the eighth hour; and again they shall work at their tasks until evening. But, if the needs of the place or poverty demand that they labour at the harvest, they shall not grieve at this: for then they are truly monks if they live by the labours of their hands; as did also our fathers and the apostles. Let all things be done with moderation, however, on account of the fainthearted. From the 1st of October, moreover, until the beginning of Lent they shall be free for reading

101

until the end of the second hour. At the second hour Terce shall be said, and all shall labour at the task which is enjoined upon them until the ninth. The first signal of None having been given, they shall each one leave off his work; and be ready when the second signal strikes. After the meal they shall be free for their readings or for psalms. But in the days of Lent, from dawn until the end of the third hour, they shall be free for their readings; and, until the end of the tenth hour, they shall do the labour that is enjoined on them. In which days of Lent they shall each receive a book from the library; which they shall read entirely through in order. These books are to be given out on the first day of Lent. Above all there shall certainly be appointed one or two elders, who shall go round the monastery at the hours in which the brothers are engaged in reading, and see to it that no troublesome brother chance to be found who is engaged in idleness or gossip instead of reading. . . . On Sunday all shall be occupied in reading, except those who are assigned to various duties. But if any is so negligent or slothful that he lacks the will or the ability to read, let some task within his capacity be given him, that he be not idle. For the weak or delicate brethren some work or craft must be found to keep them from idleness while not overwhelming them with such heavy labour as to drive them away. The abbot is to take their infirmity into consideration.

XLIX. *Of the Observance of Lent.*—The life of a monk should be always as if Lent were being kept. But few have virtue enought for this, and so we urge that during Lent he shall utterly purify his life, and wipe out, in that holy season, the negligence of other times. This is duly performed if we abstain from vices and devote ourselves to prayer with weeping, to study and heartfelt contrition and to abstinence. And so, in those days, let us of ourselves make some addition to our service—special prayers, and special abstinence in food and drink; so that each of us shall offer, over and above his appointed portion, a freewill offering to God, with the joy of the Holy Spirit. Let him discipline his body in respect of food, drink, sleep, chatter, and mirth; and let him look forward to holy Easter with the joy of spiritual longing. And let each announce his offering to the abbot that it may be done with his prayers and with his approval. For whatever is done without the leave of the spiritual father is to be set down to presumption and pride, and not to the credit of a monk.

L. *Of those who work away from the Monastery, or those on a Journey.* [They must observe the Hours.]

LI. *Of those who go on Short Journeys.* [They must not eat outside, without leave of the abbot.]

LIII. *Of the Reception of Guests.*—All guests are to be received as Christ himself; for He Himself said: 'I was a stranger and ye took Me in' [Mt. xxv. 35]. And to all, fitting honour shall be shown; but, most of all, to servants of the faith and to pilgrims. When, therefore, a guest is announced, the prior or the brothers shall run to meet him, with every service of love. And first they shall pray together; and thus they shall be joined together in peace. Which kiss of peace shall not first be offered, unless a prayer have preceded, on account of the wiles of the devil. In the salutation itself, moreover, all humility shall be shown. In the case of all guests arriving or departing: with inclined head, or with prostrating of the whole body upon the ground, Christ, who is also received in them, shall be adored. The guests moreover, having been received, shall be conducted to prayer; and afterwards the prior, or one whom he himself orders, shall sit with them. The law of God shall be read before the guest that he may be edified; and, after this, every kindness shall be shown. A fast may be broken by the prior on account of a guest; unless, perchance, it be a special day of fast which cannot be violated. The brothers, moreover, shall continue their customary fasts. The abbot shall give water into the hands of his guests; and the abbot as well as the whole congregation shall wash the feet of all guests. This being done, they shall say this verse: 'We have received, O Lord, Thy loving-kindness in the midst of Thy temple' [Ps. xlvii. 8, Vulgate=xlviii. 9, E.V.]. Chiefly in the reception of the poor and of pilgrims shall care be most anxiously shown: for in them Christ is received the more. For the very fear of the rich exacts honour for them. The kitchen of the abbot and the guests shall be by itself; so that guests coming at uncertain hours, as is always happening in a monastery, may not disturb the brothers. Into the control of this kitchen, two brothers, who can well fulfil that duty, shall enter yearly; and to them, according as they shall need it, help shall be administered; so that they may serve without grumbling. And again, when they are less occupied they shall go out where they are commanded to, and labour. . . .

LIV. *Whether a Brother may receive Letters or Gifts.* [No; except by leave of the abbot.]

LV. *Of Clothing.*—Clothing shall be given to the brothers according to the nature of the places where they dwell, or the climate. For in cold regions more is required; but in warm, less. This is a matter for the abbot to decide. We nevertheless consider that for temperate places a cowl and tunic apiece shall suffice—the cowl in winter hairy, in summer fine or worn—and a scapular for work. And for the feet, shoes and stockings. Concerning the colour and size of all of which things the monks shall not talk; but they shall be such as can be found in the province where they are or as can be bought the most cheaply. The abbot, moreover, shall provide, as to the measure, that those vestments be not short for those using them; but of suitable length. And, when new ones are received, they shall always straightway return the old ones, to be kept in the wardrobe for the benefit of the poor. It is enough, moreover, for a monk to have two tunics and two cowls; a spare one for nights, and to permit them to wash the things themselves. Everything, then, that is over this is superfluous, and ought to be removed. And the shoes, and whatever is old, they shall return when they receive something new. And those who are sent on a journey shall receive cloths for the loins from the wardrobe; which on their return they shall restore, having washed them. And there shall be cowls and tunics somewhat better than those which they have ordinarily: which, when they start on a journey, they shall receive from the wardrobe, and, on returning, shall restore. For bedding, a mattress, a woollen blanket, a woollen under-blanket, and a pillow shall suffice. And these beds are frequently to be searched by the abbot for private property. And, if anything is found belonging to any one which he did not receive from the abbot, he shall be subjected to the most severe discipline. And, in order that this vice of property may be cut off at the roots, all things which are necessary shall be given by the abbot: that is, a cowl, a tunic, shoes, stockings, girdle, a knife, a pen, a needle, a handkerchief, tablets: so that all excuse of necessity shall be removed.

LVIII. *Concerning the Manner of receiving Brothers.*—When any new comer applies for admission, an easy entrance shall not be granted him: but, as the Apostle says, 'Try the spirits if they be of God' [I John iv. I]. Therefore, if he who comes perseveres in knocking, and is seen after four or five days to endure with patience the insults inflicted upon him, and the difficulty of entrance, and to persist in his demand, entrance shall be allowed him, and he shall remain for a few days in the cell of the guests. After this he shall be in the cell of the novices, where he shall meditate and eat and sleep. And an elder brother shall be appointed for him who shall be capable of saving souls, who shall watch him with the closest scrutiny, and make it his care to see if he reverently seek God, if he be zealous in the service of God, in obedience, in suffering shame. And all the harshness and roughness of the means through which God is approached shall be told him in advance. If he promise perseverance in his steadfastness, after the lapse of two months this Rule shall be read to him in order, and it shall be said to him: 'Behold the law under which thou dost wish to serve; if thou canst observe it, enter; but if thou canst not, depart freely.' If he have stood firm thus far, then he shall be taken into the aforesaid cell of the novices; and again he shall be tried with every kind of endurance. And, after the lapse of six months, the Rule shall be read to him; that he may know upon what he is entering. And, if he stand firm thus far, after four months the same Rule shall again be re-read to him. And if, having deliberated with himself, he shall promise to keep everything, and to obey all the commands that are laid upon him: then he shall be received in the congregation; knowing that it is decreed, by the law of the Rule, that from that day he shall not be allowed to depart from the monastery, nor to free his neck from the yoke of the Rule, which, after such long deliberation, he was at liberty either to refuse or receive. He who is to be received, moreover, shall, in the oratory, in the presence of all, make promise concerning his steadfastness and the change in his manner of life and his obedience to God and to His saints; so that if, at any time, he act contrary, he shall know that he shall be condemned by Him whom he mocks. . . .

LXIV. *Of the Appointing of an Abbot.*—In appointing an abbot this principle shall always be observed: that such a one shall be put into office as the whole congregation, according to the fear of God, with one heart—or even a part, however small, of the congregation with more prudent counsel—shall have chosen. He who is to be ordained, moreover, shall be elected for merit of life and learnedness in wisdom; even though he be the lowest in rank in the congregation. But even if the whole congregation with one consent shall have elected a person willing to connive at their vices (which God forbid), and those vices shall in any way come clearly to the knowledge of the bishop to whose diocese that place pertains, or to the neighbouring abbots or Christians: the latter shall not allow the consent of the wicked to prevail, but shall set up a worthy steward of the house of God; knowing that they will receive a good reward for this, if they do it in pureness of heart and with zeal for God. Just so they shall know, on the contrary, that they have sinned if they neglect it. The abbot who is ordained, moreover, shall reflect always what a burden he is undertaking, and to whom he is to render account of his stewardship. He shall know that he ought rather to be of help than to command. He ought, therefore, to be learned in the divine law, that he may know how to bring forth both the new and the old; chaste, sober, merciful. He shall always exalt mercy over judgement, that he may obtain the same. He shall hate vice, he shall love the brethren. In his blame itself he shall act prudently and do nothing excessive; lest, while he is too desirous of removing the rust, the vessel be broken. And he shall always suspect his own frailty; and shall remember that bruised reed is not to be crushed. By which we do not say that he shall permit vice to be nourished; but prudently, and with charity, he shall remove it, according as he finds it to be expedient in the case of each one, as we have already said. And he shall strive rather to be loved than feared. He shall not be troubled and anxious; he also shall not be too obstinate; he shall not be jealous and too suspicious; for then he will have no rest. In his commands he shall be prudent, and shall consider whether they be of God or of the world. He shall use discernment and moderation with regard to the labours which he enjoins, thinking of the discretion of holy Jacob who said: 'if I overdrive my flocks they will die all in one day.' [Gen. xxxiii. 13]. Accepting therefore this and other testimony of discretion the mother of the virtues, he shall so temper all things that there may be both what the strong desire, and the weak do no shrink from. And, especially, he shall keep the present Rule in all things; . . .

LXV. *Of the Provost.*—[Not to consider himself a 'second abbot.']

LXVI. *Concerning the Doorkeepers of the Monastery.*—At the door of the monastery shall be placed a wise old man who shall know how to receive a reply and to return one; whose ripeness of age will not permit him to gossip. The doorkeeper ought to have a cell next to the door; so that those arriving may always find one present from whom they may receive a reply. And straightway, when any one has knocked, or a poor man has called out, he shall answer, 'Thanks be to God!' or shall give the blessing; and with all the gentleness of the fear of God he shall quickly give a reply with the fervour of charity. And if this doorkeeper need assistance he may receive a younger brother.

A monastery should, if possible, be so arranged that everything necessary—that is, water, a mill, a garden, a bakery—may be available, and different trades be carried on, within the monastery; so that there shall be no need for the monks to wander about outside. For this is not at all good for their souls. We wish, moreover, that this Rule be read very often in the congregation; lest any of the brothers excuse himself on account of ignorance.

LXVIII. *If Impossibilities are enjoined.*—If it happen that any overwhelming or impossible task is set him, a brother should receive the command of one in authority with all meekness and obedience. But if he sees that the weight of the burden is utterly beyond his strength, let him, with patience and at a convenient time, suggest to his Superior what makes it impossible—without presumption or obstinacy or answering back. If. after this suggestion, the command of the superior stand as it was first given, the subordinate shall realize that thus it is expedient for him: and he shall obey, with all charity, and will trust in God's help.

LXIX. *No one shall take it on himself to take another's part.*

LXX. *No one shall take it on himself to strike another without orders.*

LXXI. *Monks shall obey each other.*

LXXII. *Of the Good Zeal which the Monk, should have.*—[A zeal mingled with charity, patience, and tolerance for others.]

LXX. *Concerning the Fact that not every Righteous Observance is decreed in this Rule.*—We have written out this Rule that we may show those observing it in the monasteries how to have some honesty of character, or the beginning of conversion. But for those who hasten to the perfection of living, there are the teachings of the holy Fathers; the observance of which leads a man to the heights of perfection. For what page, or what discourse, of Divine authority in the Old or the New Testament does not contain a most perfect rule for human life? Or what book of the holy Catholic Fathers does not tell us with the voice of a trumpet how by the right path we may come to our Creator? And the reading aloud of the Fathers, and their decrees, and their lives; also the Rule of our holy Father Basil—what else are they except instruments of virtue for well-living and obedient monks? We blush with shame for the idle, and the evil-living and the negligent. Thou that hastenest to the heavenly country, perform with Christ's aid this Rule which is written down as the least of beginnings: and then at length, under God's protection, thou wilt come to the greater things that we have mentioned; to the heights of learning and virtue.

Question:

1. *Compare and contrast the role and powers of the Abbot with that of the Pope, as described by Gregory.*

7.3 Duke William of Aquitane: *Foundation Charter for the Abbey of Cluny*, 909

The abbey of Cluny was founded in 910 by the monk Berno and Duke William of Aquitane. Cluny became the center of the Clunaic order and, in time, Abbots of Cluny would come to control some 1,000 monastic communities. The wealth and power of Cluny made it a target for twelfth-century advocates of church reform.

Source: *The Tenth Century*, ed. R. S. Lopez; New York, Holt, Rinehart & Winston, 1959, pp. 14–15; by permission.

It is clear to all men of sane mind that the providence of God so decrees for any rich man that he may be able to deserve everlasting rewards by means of the goods he transitorily possesses, if he uses them well. . . .

And I, William, count [of Auvergne] and duke [of Aquitaine] by the gift of God, carefully pondering this, and desiring to provide for my own salvation while it is permissible for me, have considered it proper, nay, most necessary, that from the goods which have been temporarily conferred upon me, I am to give a small portion for the gain of my soul. . . . And in order to make this deed not a temporary but lasting one, I am to support at my own expense a congregation of monks, trusting and hoping that even though I myself am unable to despise all things, nevertheless, by taking charge of despisers of the world whom I deem to be righteous, "I may receive the reward of the righteous" [Matthew 10, 41].

Therefore. . . . I hand over from my own domains to the holy apostles, Peter and Paul, the following goods legally held by me: the vill of Cluny with the court and demesne manor, and the chapel in honor of Saint Mary, mother of God, and of Saint Peter, prince of the apostles, together with all the goods pertaining to it, namely, the vills, the chapels, the serfs of both sexes, the vines, the fields, the meadows, the waters and their courses, the mills, the entrances and exits, what is cultivated and what is not, all in their entirety. . . . [I give all this] with this understanding, that a regular monastery be constructed in Cluny in honor of the holy apostles Peter and Paul, and that there the monks shall congregate and live according to the rule of the blessed Benedict. . . .

And let the monks, as well as all the aforesaid possessions, be under the power and authority of the Abbot Bemon [d. 926], who shall regularly preside over them, as long as he lives, according to his knowledge and ability. But after his death, the same monks are to have power and permission to elect as abbot and rector any one of their order whom they will choose, in keeping with the will of God and the rule promulgated by Saint Benedict, so that they may not be impeded from making a canonical election by our opposition or that of any other power. Every five years, then, the aforesaid monks are to pay ten shillings to the church of the apostles for their lights. . . . We further will that every day they perform works of mercy toward the poor, the needy, the stranger and the pilgrim. . . .

The same monks there congregated are to be subject neither to our sway nor to that of our relatives, nor to the splendor of the royal greatness, nor to that of any earthly power. And I warn and beseech, through God and all His saints, and by the terrible Day of Judgment, that no one of the secular princes, no count whatever, no bishop at all, nor the pontiff of the aforesaid Roman See, is to invade the property of these servants of God, or alienate it, or impair it, or give it as a benefice to any one, or appoint any prelate over them against their will. . . . And I beseech you, Oh Peter and Paul, holy apostles and glorious princes of the earth, and you, Pontiff of the pontiffs of the apostolic see, that . . . you remove from the community of the holy church of God and of life eternal the robbers and invaders and alienators of these goods.

Question:
1. What elements of the Rule of St. Benedict are adopted by the Order of the Cluny?

7.4 Behâ-ed-Din: *Richard I Massacres Prisoners after Taking Acre, 2–20 August 1191*

The recapture of Jerusalem by the Muslim leader Saladin in 1187 sparked the Third Crusade. At the key point in the campaign, Richard I of England and King Philip II of France led a successful siege of the city of Acre. As part of the terms of surrender, the Crusaders held 2,700 Muslims as hostages against Saladin's completion of the remainder of the terms. When Saladin failed to fulfill his part of the bargain, Richard ordered the execution of the hostages. Behâ-ed-Din, a member of Saladin's court, was a witness to the massacre.

Source: *Eyewitness to History*, ed. John Casey (New York: Avon, 1997), pp. 35–37.

The same day Hossâm ad-Din Ibn Barîc, an interpreter working with the English, issued from Acre accompanied by two officers of the King of England [Richard I]. He brought news that the King of France had set out for Tyre, and that they had come to talk over the matter of a possible exchange of prisoners and to see the true cross of the Crucifixion if it were still in the Mussulman camp, or to ascertain if it really had been sent to Baghdad. The True Cross was shown to them, and on beholding it they showed the profoundest reverence, throwing themselves on the ground till they were covered with dust, and humbling themselves in token of devotion. These envoys told us that the European princes had accepted the Sultan's [Saladin's] proposition, viz., to deliver all that was specified in the treaty by three instalments at intervals of a month. The Sultan then sent an envoy to Tyre with rich presents, quantities of perfumes, and fine raiment—all of which were for the King of the French.

In the morning of the tenth day of Ralab, [3 August] Ibn Barîc and his comrades returned to the King of England while the Sultan went off with his bodyguard and his closest friends to the hill that abuts on Shefa'Amr . . . Envoys did not cease to pass from one side to the other in the hope of laying the foundation of a firm peace. These negotiations continued till our men had procured the money and the number of prisoners that they were to deliver to the Christians at the end of the first period in accordance with the treaty. The first instalment was to consist of the Holy Cross, 100,000 dinars and 1,600 prisoners. Trustworthy men sent by the Christians to conduct the examination found it all complete saving only the prisoners who had been demanded by name, all of whom had not yet been gathered together. And thus the negotiations continued to drag on till the end of the first term. On this day, the 18th of Rajah [11 August], the enemy sent demanding what was due.

The Sultan replied as follows: 'Choose one of two things. Either send us back our comrades and receive the payment fixed for this term, in which case we will give hostages to ensure the full execution of all that is left. Or accept what we are going to send you today, and in your turn give us hostages to keep until those of our comrades whom you hold prisoners are restored.' To this the envoys made answer: 'Not so. Send us what is due for this term and in return we will give our solemn oath that your people shall be restored you.'

This proposition the Sultan rejected, knowing full well that if he were to deliver the money, the Cross, and the prisoners, while our men were still kept captive by the Christians, he would have no security against treachery on the part of the enemy, and this would be a great disaster to Islam.

Then the King of England, seeing all the delays interposed by the Sultan to the execution of the treaty, acted perfidiously as regards his Mussulman prisoners. On their yielding the town of Acre he had engaged to grant them life, adding that if the Sultan carried out the bargain he would give them freedom and suffer them to carry off their children and wives; if the Sultan did not fulfil his engagements they were to be made slaves. Now the King broke his promises to them and made open display of what he had till now kept hidden in his heart, by carrying out what he had intended to do after he had received the money and the Christian prisoners. It is thus that people in his nation ultimately admitted.

In the afternoon of Tuesday, 27 Rajah [20 August], about four o'clock, he came out on horseback with all the Christian army, knights, footmen, Turcopoles [light-armed soldiers of the Order of St John of Jerusalem] and advanced to the pits at the foot of the hill of Al 'Ayâdîyeh, to which place he had already sent on his tents. The Christians, on reaching the middle of the plain that stretches between this hill and that of Keisân, close to which place the Sultan's advanced guard had drawn back, ordered all the Mussulman prisoners, whose martyrdom God had decreed for this day, to be brought before him. They numbered more than three thousand and were all bound with ropes. The Christians then flung themselves upon them all at once and massacred them with sword and lance in cold blood. Our advanced guard had already told the Sultan of the enemy's movements and he sent it some reinforcements, but only after the massacre. The Mussulmans, seeing what was being done to the prisoners, rushed against the Christians and in the combat, which lasted till nightfall, several were slain and wounded on either side. On the morrow morning our people gathered at the spot and found the Mussulmans stretched out upon the ground as martyrs for the faith. They even recognized some of the dead, and the sight was a great affliction to them. The enemy had only spared the prisoners of note and such as were strong enough to work.

The motives of this massacre are differently told; according to some, the captives were slain by way of reprisal for the death of those Christians whom the Mussulmans had slain. Others again say that the King of England, on deciding to attempt the conquest of Ascalon, thought it unwise to leave so many prisoners in the town after his departure. God alone knows what the real reason was.

Question:
1. What does this account say about the nature of both sides during the Crusades?

7.5 *Unam Sanctam:* Two Swords

Pope Boniface VIII had tried to limit the fighting within Europe, particularly between the English and the French, by issuing a bull in 1296, that prohibited monarchs from taxing the clergy without papal authorization. King Philip the Fair of France and Edward I of England rejected this bull; they needed those taxes to fund their war efforts. When they retaliated in ways that sharply diminished the papacy's finances, the Pope retreated. After continued dispute, the Pope issued another bull, the Unam Sanctam, excerpted below. Philip responded to this bull by having the Pope captured in order to put him on trial. Instead, he quickly released him, but not before the Pope had suffered both physically and in terms of his pride. When he died a few weeks later, he was replaced by a French pope, Clement V (1305–1314), who soon moved the papacy to Avignon, France.

> **Source:** "The Bull Unam Sanctam of Boniface VIII," in Translations and Reprints from the Original Sources of European History, vol. III, no. 6, (Philadelphia: The Department of History of the University of Pennsylvania, 1912), pp. 20–23; reprinted in ed. John L. Beatty and Oliver A. Johnson, Heritage of Western Civilization, vol. 1, 7th edition, (Englewood Cliffs, NJ: Prentice Hall, 1991), pp. 319–21.

That there is one Holy Catholic and Apostolic Church we are impelled by our faith to believe and to hold—this we do firmly believe and openly confess—and outside of this there is neither salvation or remission of sins, as the bridegroom proclaims in Canticles, "My dove, my undefiled is but one; she is the only one of her mother; she is the choice one of her that bare her." The Church represents one mystic body and of this body Christ is the head; of Christ, indeed. God is the head. In it is one Lord, and one faith, and one baptism. In the time of the flood, there was one ark of Noah, prefiguring the one Church, finished in one cubit, having one Noah as steersman and commander. Outside of this, all things upon the face of the earth were, as we read, destroyed. This Church we venerate and this alone, the Lord saying through his prophets, "Deliver my soul, O God, from the sword; my darling from the power of the dog." He prays thus for his soul, that is for Himself, as head, and also for the body, which He calls one, namely, the Church on account of the unity of the bridegroom, of the faith, of the sacraments, and of the charity of the Church. It is that seamless coat of the Lord, which was not rent, but fell by lot. Therefore, in this one and only Church, there is one body and one head—not two heads as if it were a monster—namely, Christ and Christ's Vicar. Peter and Peter's successor, for the Lord said to Peter himself, "Feed my sheep": my sheep, he said, using a general term and not designating these or those sheep, so that we must believe that all the sheep were committed to him. If, then, the Greeks or others, shall say that they were not entrusted to Peter and his successors, they must perforce admit that they are not of Christ's sheep, as the Lord says in John, "there is one fold, and one shepherd."

In this Church and in its power are two swords, to wit, a spiritual and a temporal, and this we are taught by the words of the Gospel, for when the Apostles said, "Behold, here are two swords" (in the Church, namely, since the Apostles were speaking), the Lord did not reply that it was too many, but enough. And surely he who claims that the temporal sword is not in the power of Peter has but ill understood the word of our Lord when he said, "Put up the sword in its scabbard." Both, therefore, the spiritual and material swords, are in the power of the Church, the latter indeed to be used for the Church, the former by the Church, the one by the priest, the other by the hand of kings and soldiers, but by the will and sufferance of the priest. It is fitting, moreover, that one sword should be under the other, and the temporal authority subject to the spiritual power. For when the Apostle said "there is no power but of God and the powers that are of God are ordained," they would not be ordained unless one sword were under the other, and one, as inferior, was brought back by the other to the highest place. For, according to the Holy Dionysius, the law of divinity is to lead the lowest through the intermediate to the highest. Therefore, according to the law of the universe, things are not reduced to order directly, and upon the same footing, but the lowest through the intermediate and the inferior through the superior. It behooves us, therefore, the more freely to confess that the spiritual power excels in dignity and nobility any form whatsoever of earthly power, as spiritual interests exceed the temporal in importance. All this we see fairly from the giving of tithes, from the benediction and sanctification, from the recognition of this power and the control of the same things. For the truth bearing witness, it is for the spiritual power to establish the earthly power and judge it, if it be not good. Thus, in the case of the Church and the power of the Church, the prophecy of Jeremiah is fulfilled: "See, I have this day set thee over the nations and over the kingdoms"—and so forth. Therefore, if the earthly power shall err, it shall be judged by the spiritual power: if the lesser spiritual power err, it shall be judged by the higher. But if the supreme power err, it can be judged by God alone and not by man, the apostles bearing witness saying, the spiritual man judges all things but he himself is judged by no one. Hence this power, although given to man and exercised by man, is not human, but rather divine power, given by the divine lips to Peter, and founded on a rock for Him and his successors in Him whom he confessed, the Lord saying to Peter himself, "Whatsoever thou shalt bind," etc. Whoever, therefore, shall resist this power, ordained by God, resists the ordination of God, unless there should be two beginnings, as the Manichaean imagines. But this we judge to be false and heretical, since, by the testimony of Moses, not in the *beginnings*, but in the *beginning,* God created the heaven and the earth. We, moreover, proclaim, declare, and pronounce that it is altogether necessary to salvation for every human being to be subject to the Roman Pontiff.

Given at the Lateran the twelfth day before the Kalends of December, in our eighth year, as a perpetual memorial of this matter.

Questions!
1. What are the two swords?
2. What does Boniface claim is the relationship between the two swords? Based on what justification or principles?

7.6 Penitentials

Penitentials were issued to help priests learn and understand their duties as confessors. Confession with penance had been imposed on parishioners at least once a year in the Fourth Lateran Council in 1215. The following penitential was issued by Cardinal St. Charles Borromeo (1538–84), who pushed for Church reform and discipline during the Counter-Reformation. The excerpt includes the introduction which outlines the purpose of the penitential and a selection of penances required for various sins listed under each commandment.

> **Source:** "The Milan Penitential of Cardinal Borromeo (ca. 1565–82)"; reprinted in *Medieval Handbooks of Penance: A Translation of the principal libri poenitentiales* and selections from related documents, ed. John T. McNeill and Helena M. Gamer, (New York: Octagon Books, Inc., 1965) pp. 364–68.

Penitential Canons, Knowledge of Which Is Necessary for Parish Priests and Confessors, Set Forth according to the Plan and Order of the Decalog

The fathers taught how very necessary for priests who are engaged in hearing the confessions of penitents is a knowledge of the penitential canons. And indeed if all things that pertain to the method of penance are to be administered not only with prudence and piety but also with justice, assuredly the pattern of this ought to be taken from the penitential canons. For there are, so to speak, two rules by which priests and confessors are so directed as both to discern the gravity of an offense committed and in relation to this to impose a true penance: that they severally accurately investigate both the things that pertain to the greatness of the sin and those that pertain to the status, condition, and age of the penitent and the inmost sorrow of the contrite heart—and then, that they temper the penance with their own justice and prudence. And indeed the method explained by the fathers so disposed these things and everything else that is complicated of this necessary knowledge, that, as was said above in its proper place, the penitential canons set forth according to the plan of the Decalog are held over to the last part of the book, whence some knowledge of them can be drawn by the confessor-priests themselves....

The chief penitential canons collected according to the order of the Decalog from various councils and penitentiary books in the Instruction of St. Charles B[orromeo]

On the First Commandment of the Decalog

1. He who falls away from the faith shall do penance for ten years.
2. He who observes auguries and divinations [and] he who makes diabolical incantations, seven years. One who beholds things to come in an astrolabe, two years.
3. If anyone makes knots or enchantments, two years.
4. He who consults magicians, five years.

On the Second Commandment

1. Whoever knowingly commits perjury, shall do penance for forty days on bread and water, and seven succeeding years; and he shall never be without penance. And he shall never be accepted as a witness; and after these things he shall take communion.
2. He who commits perjury in a church, ten years.
3. If anyone publicly blasphemes God or the Blessed Virgin or any saint, he shall stand in the open in front of the doors of the church on seven Sundays, while the solemnities of the masses are performed, and on the last of these days, without robe and shoes, with a cord tied about his neck; and on the seven preceding Fridays he shall fast on bread and water; and he shall then by no means enter the church. Moreover, on each of these seven Sundays he shall feed three or two or one, if he is able. Otherwise he shall do another penance; if he refuses, he shall be forbidden to enter the church; in [case of] his death he shall be denied ecclesiastical burial.
4. He who violates a simple vow shall do penance for three years.

On the Third Commandment

1. He who does any servile work on the Lord's day or on a feast day shall do penance for seven days on bread and water.
2. If anyone violates fasts set by Holy Church, he shall do penance for forty days on bread and water.
3. He who violates the fast in Lent shall do a seven-day penance for one day.
4. He who without unavoidable necessity eats flesh in Lent shall not take communion at Easter and shall thereafter abstain from flesh.

On the Fourth Commandment

1. He who reviles his parents shall be a penitent for forty days on bread and water.
2. He who does an injury to his parents, three years.
3. He who beats [them], seven years.
4. If anyone rises up against his bishop, his pastor and father, he shall do penance in a monastery all the days of his life.
5. If anyone despises or derides the command of his bishop, or of the bishop's servants, or of his parish priest, he shall do penance for forty days on bread and water.

On the Fifth Commandment

1. He who kills a presbyter shall do penance for twelve years.
2. If anyone kills his mother, father, or sister, he shall not take the Lord's body throughout his whole life, except

at his departure; he shall abstain from flesh and wine, while he lives; he shall fast on Monday, Wednesday, and Friday.

3. If anyone kills a man he shall always be at the door of the church, and at death he shall receive communion. [Sections 4–10 omitted.]

On the Sixth Commandment

[Sections 1–6 omitted.]

7. If any woman paints herself with ceruse or other pigment in order to please men, she shall do penance for three years.

8. If a priest is intimate with his own spiritual daughter, that is, one whom he has baptized or who has confessed to him, he ought to do penance for twelve years; and if the offense is publicly known, he ought to be deposed and do penance for twelve years on pilgrimage, and thereafter enter a monastery to remain there throughout his life. For adultery penances of seven, and of ten, years, are imposed; for unchaste kissing or embracing a penance of thirty days is commanded.

On the Seventh Commandment

1. If anyone commits a theft of a thing of small value he shall do penance for a year.

2. He who steals anything from the furniture of a church or from the treasury, or ecclesiastical property, or offerings made to the church shall be a penitent for seven years.

3. He who retains to himself his tithe or neglects to pay it, shall restore fourfold and do penance for twenty days on bread and water.

4. He who takes usury commits robbery; he shall do penance for three years on bread and water.

On the Eighth Commandment

1. He who conspires in falsification of evidence shall be a penitent for five years.

2. A forger shall do penance on bread and water as long as he lives.

3. If anyone slanders his neighbor, he shall be a penitent for seven days on bread and water.

On the Ninth and Tenth Commandments

1. He who basely covets another's goods and is avaricious shall be a penitent for three years.

2. If anyone desires to commit fornication, if a bishop, he shall be a penitent for seven years; if a presbyter, five; if a deacon or monk three; if a cleric or layman, two years.

Questions:
1. What role did the priest have in applying the penitentials?
2. With what kind of sins were the penitentials concerned, and which were considered the worst?

7.7 The Siege of Lisbon

On the way to join the Second Crusade in 1147, Crusading knights from England, Germany, Flanders, and Normandy interrupted their voyage to assist King Alfonso of Castile besiege Lisbon, held by Muslim rulers since the eighth century. In return for their help, the king promised that they could plunder and pillage the city when it fell.

> **Source:** *Medieval Iberia: Readings from Christian, Muslim and Jewish Sources*, ed. Olivia Remie Constable, (Philadelphia: University of Pennsylvania Press, 1997), pp. 135-36.

Then our men, attending more strictly to the siege, began to dig a subterranean mine between the tower and the Porta do Ferro in order that they might bring down the wall. When this had been discovered, for it was quite accessible to the enemy, it proved greatly to our detriment after the investment of the city, for many days were consumed in its vain defense. Besides, two Balearic mangonels were set up by our forces-one on the river bank which was operated by seamen, the other in front of the Porta do Ferro, which was operated by the knights and their table companions. All these men having been divided into groups of one hundred, on a given signal the first hundred retired and another took their places, so that within the space of ten hours five thousand stones were hurled. And the enemy were greatly harassed by this action. Again the Normans and the English and those who were with them began the erection of a movable tower eighty-three feet in height. Once more, with a view to bringing down the wall, the men of Cologne and the Flemings began to dig a mine beneath the wall of the stronghold higher up-a mine which, marvelous to relate, had five entrances and extended inside to a depth of forty cubits from the front; and they completed it within a month.

Meanwhile, hunger and the stench of corpses greatly tormented the enemy, for there was no burial space within the city. And for food they collected the refuse which was thrown out from our ships and borne up by the waves beneath their walls. A ridiculous incident occurred as a result of their hunger when some of the Flemings, while keeping guard among the ruins of houses, were eating figs and, having had enough, left some lying about unconsumed. When this was discovered by four of the Moors, they came up stealthily and cautiously like birds approaching food. And when the Flemings observed this, they frequently scattered refuse of this sort about in order that they might lure them on with bait. And, finally, having set snares in the accustomed places, they caught three of the Moors in them and thereby caused enormous merriment among us.

When the wall had been undermined and inflammable material had been placed within the mine and lighted, the same night at cockcrow about thirty cubits of the wall crumbled to the ground. Then the Moors who were guarding the wall were heard to cry out in their anguish that they might now make an end of their long labors and that this very day would be their last and that it would have to be divided with death, and that this would be their greatest consolation for death, if, without fearing it, they might exchange their lives for ours. For it was necessary to go yonder whence there was no need of returning; and, if a life were well ended, it would nowhere be said to have been cut short. For what mattered was not how long but how well a life had been lived; and a life would have lasted as long as it should, even though not as long as it naturally could, provided it closed in a fitting end. And so the Moors gathered from all sides for the defense of the breach in the wall, placing against it a barrier of beams. Accordingly, when the men of Cologne and the Flemings went out to attempt an entrance, they were repulsed. For, although the wall had collapsed, the nature of the situation [on the steep hillside] prevented an entry merely by the heap [of ruins]. But when they failed to overcome the defenders in a hand-to-hand encounter, they attacked them furiously from a distance with arrows, so that they looked like hedgehogs as, bristling with bolts, they stood immovably at the defense and endured as if unharmed. Thus the defense was maintained against the onslaught of the attackers until the first hour of the day, when the latter retired to camp. The Normans and the English came under arms to take up the struggle in place of their associates, supposing that an entrance would be easy now that the enemy were wounded and exhausted. But they were prevented by the leaders of the Flemings and the men of Cologne, who assailed them with insults and demanded that we attempt an entrance in any way it might be accomplished with our own engines; for they said that they had prepared the breach which now stood open for themselves, not for us. And so for several days they were altogether repulsed from the breach.

Questions:
1. *How did the Crusaders prepare before battle?*
2. *What machines and techniques did they use in besieging and taking the cities?*
3. *How were the city's inhabitants and defenders treated by the Christian knights?*
4. *What sort of cooperation was there between different nationalities of Crusaders?*

PART 8
Society and Culture in the High Middle Ages

8.1 Manorial Court Records

The lord of the manor held a court for his tenants, both free and unfree, regulating rights in land and settling disputes according to local custom. For the unfree serfs, this was their only court for legal redress. In England, the manorial courts sometimes absorbed the local "hundred courts" over which the county sheriff theoretically ought to have presided. As a result, the jurisdiction of the manorial court was quite varied. Below are some thirteenth-century records of manorial courts held by the Abbey of Bec in England.

> **Source:** Maitland, F. W., ed. *Select Pleas in Manorial and Other Seignorial Courts* (Publications of the Selden Society: London, 1889), pp. 6–9, 11–13.

PLEAS OF THE MANORS IN ENGLAND OF THE ABBEY OF BEC FOR THE HOKEDAY TERM, 1246

Bledlow [Buckinghamshire]. Saturday before Ascension Day.

1 The court has presented that Simon Combe has set up a fence on the lord's land. Therefore let it be abated.[1]

2 Simone Combe gives 18 d[2]. for leave to compromise with Simon Besmere. Pledges, John Sperling and John Harding.

3 A day is given to Alice of Standen at the next court to produce her charter and her heir.

4 John Sperling complains that Richard of Newmere on the Sunday next before S. Bartholomew's day last past with his cattle, horses and pigs wrongfully destroyed the corn on his [John's] land to his damage to the extent of one thrave of wheat, and to his dishonour to the extent of two shillings; and of this he produces suit. And Richard comes and defends all of it. Therefore let him go to the law six-handed.[3] His pledges, Simon Combe and Hugh Frith.

Swincombe [Oxfordshire]. Sunday before Ascension Day.

5 Richard Rastold [essoins himself][4] of the general summons by William Henry's son.

6 Hugh Pike and Robert his son are in mercy for wood of the lord thievishly carried away. The fine for each, 6 s. 8 d. Pledges, Richard Mile and William Shepherd.

7 Peter Alexander's son in mercy for the same. Fine, 2 s. Pledge, Alexander his father.

8 Henry Mile in mercy for waste of the lord's corn. Pledges, Richard Mile and William Shepherd.

9 John Smith in mercy for not producing what he was pledge to produce. Pledges, Richard Etys and Hugh Wood. Fine, 12 d.

10 Roger Abovewood and William Shepherd in mercy for not producing what they were pledges to produce.... Fine, half a sextary of wine.

Tooting [Surrey]. Sunday after Ascension Day.

11 The court presented that the following had encroached on the lord's land, to wit,[5] William Cobbler, Maud Robin's widow (fined 12 d.), John Shepherd (fined 12 d.), Walter Reeve (fined 2 s.), William of Moreville (fined 12 d.), Hamo of Hageldon (fined 12 d.), Mabel Spendlove's widow (fined [6] d.). Therefore they are in mercy.

12 ... Roger Rede in mercy for detention of rent. Pledge, John of Stratham. Fine, 6 d.

13 William of Streatham is in mercy for not producing what he was pledge to produce. Fine, 12d.

---

[1] Removed.

[2] The abbreviations for coins were: d. = pence, s. = shilling, and l = pound. Twelve pence = 1 shilling and 20 shillings = 1 pound. The amount 6s.8d.was equal to 1 mark which was not a coin, but an amount of money. (For example: The old expression "2 bits" equals a quarter coin, but there was never coin minted that equaled one "bit") Three marks = 1 pound.

[3] To "make his law" or "go to the law six-handed" means that he must bring five men of lawful reputation to swear with him that they believe he is a man who is telling the truth.

[4] Presents a legal excuse for himself for not appearing in court when summoned to do so.

[5] Namely.

[6] All adult free males in England became a member of a "tithing" about the age 14. A tithing was a group of about ten men who were legally responsible for one another's actions. At the "Hundred" court, the local court like a township court, the sheriff would question the members of a tithing to report crimes and problems as well as locate people when they were needed in court.

Ruislip [Middlesex]. Tuesday after Ascension Day.

14 The court presents that Nicholas Brakespeare is not in a tithing and holds land. Therefore let him be distrained.[7]

15 Breakers of the assize[8]: Alice Salvage's widow (fined 12 d.), Agnotta the Shepherd's mistress, Roger Canon (fined 6 d.), the wife of Richard Chayham, the widow of Peter Beyondgrove, the wife of Ralph Coke (fined 6 d.), Ailwin (fined 6 d.), John Shepherd (fined 6 d.), Geoffrey Carpenter, Roise the Miller's wife (fined 6 d.), William White, John Carpenter, John Bradif.

16 Roger Hamo's son gives 20 s. to have seisin[9] of the land which was his father's and to have an inquest of twelve as to a certain croft which Gilbert Bisuthe holds. Pledges, Gilbert Lamb, William John's son and Robert King.

17 Isabella Peter's widow is in mercy for a trespass which her son John had committed in the lord's wood. Fine, 18 d. Pledges, Gilbert Bisuthe and Richard Robin.

18 Richard Maleville is at his law against the lord [to prove] that he did not take from the lord's servants goods taken in distress to the damage and dishonour of his lord [to the extent of] 20 s. Pledges, Gilbert Bisuthe and Richard Hubert.

19 Hugh Tree in mercy for his beasts caught in the lord's garden. Pledges, Walter Hill and William Slipper. Fine, 6 d.

20 [The] twelve jurors say that Hugh Cross has right in the bank and hedge about which there was a dispute between him and William White. Therefore let him hold in peace and let William be distrained for his many trespasses. (Afterwards he made fine[10] for 12 s.) They say also that the hedge which is between the Widow Druet and William Slipper so far as the bank extends should be divided along the middle of the bank, so that the crest of the bank should be the boundary between them, for the crest was thrown up along the ancient boundary.

21 [The roll is torn in places for the next two entries]... son of Roger Clerk gives 20 s. to have seisin of the land which was his father's. Pledges, Gilbert...and Hugh Cross.

22 [Name missing] gives 13 s. 4d. to have seisin of the land which was his mother's beyond the wood. Pledges, William... and Robert Mareleward.

PLEAS OF THE MANORS OF THE ABBEY OF BEC FOR THE MARTINMAS TERM A.D. 1247.

Weedon Beck [Northamptonshire]. Vigil of St. Michael.

23 Richard le Boys of Aldeston has sworn fealty for the land which was his father's and has found pledges for 4 s. as his relief, to wit, William Clerk of the same place, Godfrey Elder and Roger Smith.

24 Elias Deynte in full court resigned his land and William Deynte his son was put in seisin of it and swore fealty and found the same pledges for 5 s. as his relief. Afterwards he paid.

25 The township presents that they suspect Robert Dochy and William Tale because they made fine with the knights, [who formed the jury] before the justices [in eyre][11] when they were accused of larceny.

26 Breakers of the assize: William Paris, Richard Cappe, Maud widow of Robert Carter, Walter Carter, Roger Smith, Richard Guy's son, William Green, Gilbert Vicar's son, Guy Lawman.

27 William Green and Guy Lawman have gallons which are too small.

28 John Mercer will give three chickens yearly at Martinmas for having the lord's patronage and he is received into a tithing.

Wretham [Norfolk]. Friday after the feast of S. Michael.

30 Gilbert Richard's son gives 5 s. for license to marry a wife. Pledge, Seaman. Term [for payment,] the Purification.

Tooting [Surrey]. Tuesday after the feast of S. Denis.

31 William Jordan in mercy for bad ploughing on the lord's land. Pledge, Arthur. Fine, 6 d.

32 John Shepherd in mercy for encroaching beyond the boundary of his land. Pledge, Walter Reeve. Fine, 6 d.

33 ... Elias of Streatham in mercy for default of service in the autumn. Fine, 6 d.

---

[7] "Distrained" means that some part of Nicholas' property will be taken into the custody of the court to motivate him to join a tithing like any law abiding landholder ought to.

[8] "Breakers of the assize" sold ale or bread that did not meet the established standards of quality and price.

[9] Lawful possession.

[10] Made Payment.

[11] The Justices in eyre were the king's justices that went from county to county in England on a regular circuit.

34 Bartholomew Chaloner who was at his law against Reginald Swain's son has made default in his law. Therefore he is in mercy and let him make satisfaction to Reginald for his damage and dishonour with 6 s. Pledges, William Cobbler and William Spendlove. Fine, 6 gallons.

35 Ralph of Morville gives a half-mark on the security of Jordan of Streatham and William Spendlove to have a jury to inquire whether he be the next heir to the land which William of Morville holds. And [the] twelve jurors come and say that he has no right in the said land but that William Scot has greater right in the said land than any one else. And the said William [Scot] gives 1 mark on the security of Hamo of Hageldon, William of Morville, Reginald Swain and Richard Leaware that he may have seisin of the said land after the death of William of Morville in case he [William Scot] shall survive him [William of Morville].

36 Afterwards came the said William Scot and by the lord's leave quit-claimed all the right that he had in the said land with its appurtenances to a certain William son of William of Morville, who gives 20 s. to have seisin of the said land and is put in seisin of it and has sworn fealty. Walter the serjeant is to receive the pledges.

Deverill [Wiltshire]. Saturday after the feast of S. Leonard.

37 ... Arnold Smith is in mercy for not producing the said William Scut whose pledge he was.

38 The parson of the church is in mercy for his cow caught in the lord's meadow. Pledges, Thomas Guner and William Coke.

39 From William Cobbe, William Coke and Walter Dogskin 2 s. for the ward of seven pigs belonging to Robert Gentil and for the damage that they did in the lord's corn. [Maitland believes that they were amerced for not guarding the lord's crops]

40 From Martin Shepherd 6 d. for the wound that he gave Pekin.

Questions:
1. What range of cases and business was heard at these manorial courts?
2. What do you think a "pledge" did? What does "in mercy" mean?
3. How did the court determine the facts in disputes?
4. What sort of penalties did the court lay on the guilty?
5. What happened when a juvenile did something wrong?

8.2 "The Sports of the City"

In the late twelfth century traveler William FitzStephen writes in his description of London, "Furthermore let us consider also the sports of the City, since it is not meet that a city should only be useful and sober, unless it also be pleasant and merry."

Source: William FitzStephen, A Description of London, prefixed to his *Life of Thomas a Becket,* trans. H. E. Butler, (Historical Association, 1934) reprinted in *Everyone a Witness: The Plantagenet Age,* ed. Arthur S. Finlay, (New York: Thomas Y. Crowell, 1976), pp. 112–14.

London in place of shows in the theatre and stage-plays has holier plays, wherein are shown forth the miracles wrought by Holy Confessors or the sufferings which glorified the constancy of Martyrs.

Moreover, each year upon the day called Carnival—to begin with the sports of boys (for we were all boys once)—boys from the schools bring fighting-cocks to their master, and the whole forenoon is given up to boyish sport; for they have a holiday in the schools that they may watch their cocks do battle. After dinner all the youth of the City goes out into the fields in a much-frequented game of ball. The scholars of each school have their own ball, and almost all the workers of each trade have theirs also in their hands. Elder men and fathers and rich citizens come on horseback to watch the contests of their juniors and after their fashion are young again with the young; and it seems that the motion of their natural heat is kindled by the contemplation of such violent motion and by their partaking in the joys of untrammelled youth.

Every Sunday in Lent after dinner a 'fresh swarm of young gentles' goes forth on war-horses, 'steeds skilled in the contest, of which each is 'apt and schooled to wheel in circles round'. From the gates burst forth in throngs the lay sons of citizens, armed with lance and shield, the younger with shafts forked at the end, but with steel point removed. 'They wake war's semblance' and in mimic contest exercise their skill at arms. Many courtiers come too, when the King is in residence; and from the households of Earls and Barons come young men not yet invested with the belt of knighthood, that they may there contend together. Each one of them is on fire with hope of victory. The fierce horses neigh, 'their limbs tremble; they champ the bit; impatient of delay they cannot stand still'. When at length 'the hoof of trampling steeds careers along', the youthful riders divide their hosts; some pursue those that fly before, and cannot overtake them; others unhorse their comrades and speed by.

At the feast of Easter they make sport with naval tourneys, as it were. For a shield being strongly bound to a stout pole in mid-stream, a small vessel, swiftly driven on by many an oar and by the river's flow, carries a youth standing at the prow, who is to strike the shield with his lance. If he break the lance by striking the shield and keep his feet unshaken, he has achieved his purpose and fulfilled his desire. If, however, he strike it strongly without splintering his lance, he is thrown into the rushing river, and the boat of its own speed passes him by. But there are on each side of the shield two vessels moored, and in them are many youths to snatch up the striker who has been sucked down by the stream, as soon as he emerges into sight or 'once more bubbles on the topmost wave'. On the bridge and the galleries above the river are spectators of the sport 'ready to laugh their fill'.

On feast-days throughout the summer the youths exercise themselves in leaping, archery and wrestling, putting the stone, and throwing the thonged javelin beyond a mark, and fighting with sword and buckler. 'Cytherea leads the dance of maidens and the earth is smitten with free foot at moonrise.'

In winter on almost every feast-day before dinner either foaming boars and hogs, armed with 'tusks lightning-swift', themselves soon to be bacon, fight for their lives, or fat bulls with butting horns, or huge bears, do combat to the death against hounds let loose upon them.

When the great marsh that washes the northern walls of the City is frozen, dense throngs of youths go forth to disport themselves upon the ice. Some gathering speed by a run, glide sidelong, with feet set well apart, over a vast space of ice. Others make themselves seats of ice like millstones and are dragged along by a number who run before them holding hands. Sometimes they slip owing to the greatness of their speed and fall, every one of them, upon their faces. Others there are, more skilled to sport upon the ice, who fit to their feet the shin-bones of beasts, lashing them beneath their ankles, and with ironshod poles in their hands they strike ever and anon against the ice and are borne along swift as a bird in flight or a bolt shot from a mangonel. But sometimes two by agreement run one against the other from a great distance and, raising their poles, strike one another. One or both fall, not without bodily hurt, since on falling they are borne a long way in opposite directions.

Many of the citizens delight in taking their sport with birds of the air, merlins and falcons and the like, and with dogs that wage warfare in the woods. The citizens have the special privilege of hunting in Middlesex, Hertfordshire and all Chiltern, and in Kent as far as the river Cray.

Questions:
1. What kind of sports were popular in London?
2. Who is missing from this description of public play in London? Why?

8.3   College Life: Between Students and Their Fathers

European universities first emerged in the middle ages and western universities today are descended from them. The administrative structure, system of degrees, and even the robes worn at graduation are vestiges of the twelfth century. The following selections reveal the personal and social aspect of college life.

Source: *Sources of the Western Tradition: Volume I: From Ancient Times to the Enlightenment,* ed. Marvin Perry, Joseph R. Peden, and Theodore H. Von Laue, (Boston: Houghton Mifflin Co., 1995), p. 182. Used with permission from G.G. Coulton, *Life in the Middle Ages,* Vol. 3, (Cambridge: Cambridge University Press, 1928/29).

FATHERS TO SONS

I

I have recently discovered that you live dissolutely and slothfully, preferring license to restraint and play to work and strumming a guitar while the others are at their studies, whence it happens that you have read but one volume of law while your more industrious companions have read several. Wherefore I have decided to exhort you herewith to repent utterly of your dissolute and careless ways, that you may no longer be called a waster and your shame may be turned to good repute.

II

I have learned—not from your master, although he ought not to hide such things from me, but from a certain trustworthy source—that you do not study in your room or act in the schools as a good student should, but play and wander about, disobedient to your master and indulging in sport and in certain other dishonorable practices which I do not now care to explain by letter.

SONS TO FATHERS

I

"Well-beloved father, I have not a penny, nor can I get any save through you, for all things at the University are so dear: nor can I study in my Code or my Digest, for they are all tattered. Moreover, I owe ten crowns in dues to the Provost, and can find no man to lend them to me; I send you word of greetings and of money.

The Student hath need of many things if he will profit here; his father and his kin must needs supply him freely, that he be not compelled to pawn his books, but have ready money in his purse, with gowns and furs and decent clothing, or he will be damned for a beggar; wherefore, that men may not take me for a beast, I send you word of greetings and of money.

Wines are dear, and hostels, and other good things; I owe in every street, and am hard bested to free myself from such snares. Dear father, design to help me! I fear to be excommunicated; already have I been cited, and there is not even a dry bone in my larder. If I find not the money before this feast of Easter, the church door will be shut in my face: wherefore grant my supplication, for I send you word of greetings and of money.

L'Envoy

Well-beloved father, to ease my debts contracted at the tavern, at the baker's, with the doctor and the bedells [a minor college official], and to pay my subscriptions to the laundress and the barber, I send you word of greetings and of money."

II

Sing unto the Lord a new song, praise him with stringed instruments and organs, rejoice upon the high-sounding cymbals, for your son has held a glorious disputation, which was attended by a great number of teachers and scholars. He answered all questions without a mistake, and no one could get the better of him or prevail against his arguments. Moreover he celebrated a famous banquet, at which both rich and poor were honoured as never before, and he has duly begun to give lectures which are already so popular that others' classrooms are deserted and his own are filled.

Questions:
1. *How do the relationships between these fathers and sons resemble those of the present day?*
2. *From these letters, can you discern any major differences between college life today and 500 years ago?*

8.4   St. Thomas Aquinas: *The Summa against the Gentiles (Summa Contra Gentiles, 1259–1264)*

St. Thomas Aquinas (1225–1274) was perhaps the most important medieval theologian. As a leading proponent of scholasticism, he was deeply interested in the problem of reconciling Christian theology and classical philosophy. In the excerpt from his Summa Contra Gentiles included here, Aquinas defined the relationship between truths known by reason and truths known by faith.

Source: *St. Thomas Aquinas on Politics and Ethnics* (Norton Critical Editions), translated and edited by Paul Sigmund (New York: W. W. Norton & Co., 1983), pp. 3–5.

BOOK 1

CHAPTER 3

The Two Ways of Knowing the Truth about God.
There are two ways of knowing what we hold to be true about God. There are some truths about God that exceed

the capacity of human reason—for example the fact that God is three and one. There are also some truths that natural reason can attain, such as that God exists, that he is one, and other truths of this kind. These are truths about God that have been conclusively proved by philosophers making use of their natural reason.

It is evident that there are some things to be known about God that completely exceed the capacity of human reason. Since all the knowledge that a person has about a thing is based on his understanding of its substance (according to the Philosopher [Aristotle] the basis for any argument is "what a thing is"),[1] the way the substance of a thing is understood must determine what is known about it. Thus if the human intellect comprehends the substance of, say, a stone or a triangle, no intelligible aspect of that thing is beyond the capacity of the human reason. However this is not the case for us with God. The human intellect can not achieve the understanding of God's substance by means of its natural capacity because in this life all knowledge that is in our intellects originates in the senses. Hence things that are not perceived by the senses cannot be grasped by the human intellect except in so far as knowledge of them is gathered from the senses. But the objects of the senses cannot lead the human intellect to the point that in them it can see the divine substance as it is, for they are effects that are not equal in power to their cause. However our intellect is led from the objects of the senses to the knowledge of the existence of God—as well as to other attributes of the First Principle.[2] Therefore there are some things that can be known about God that are available to human reason, but there are others that totally exceed its power.

CHAPTER 4

Truths about God that are Known by Reason are also Properly Made Available to Man by Faith.

If it were left solely to reason to seek the truth about God, few men would possess a knowledge of God. There are three reasons why most men are prevented from carrying out the diligent inquiry that leads to the discovery of truth. Some are prevented from doing so because of their physical disinclination—as a result of which many men by nature are not disposed to learning. And so however earnest they are, they cannot attain the highest level of human knowledge which consists in knowing God. Others are prevented from doing so by the pressures of family life. Some men must devote themselves to managing temporal affairs and thus are not able to spend time in leisurely contemplative inquiry, so as to reach the highest point of human inquiry—the knowledge of God. Laziness prevents others. To know what reason can investigate concerning God requires that one already have a knowledge of many things, since almost all of philosophy is directed towards the knowledge of God. This is why we learn metaphysics, which is concerned with the divine, last among the subjects in the field of philosophy. The study of truth requires a considerable effort—which is why few are willing to undertake it out of love of knowledge—despite the fact that God has implanted a natural appetite for such knowledge in the minds of men.

CHAPTER 7

Truths Based on Reason Are Not Contrary to the Truth of the Christian Faith.

Although the truth of the Christian faith exceeds the capacity of human reason, truths that reason is fitted by nature to know cannot be contrary to the truth of faith. The things that reason is fitted by nature to know are clearly most true, and it would be impossible to think of them as false.[3] It is also wrong to think that something that is held by faith could be false since it is clearly confirmed by God. Since we know by definition that what is false is contrary to the truth, it is impossible for the principles that reason knows by nature to be contrary to the truth of faith.

. . . .

We conclude therefore that any arguments made against the doctrines of faith are incorrectly derived from the self-evident first principles of nature. Such conclusions do not have the force of proofs, but are either doubtful opinions or sophistries, and so it is possible to answer them.

CHAPTER 8

The Relationship between the Human Reason and the Primary Truth of Faith.

There is a further point to be considered. The objects of the senses on which human reason bases its knowledge retain some traces of likeness to God, since they exist and are good. This resemblance is inadequate because it is completely

---

[1] Aristotle, *Posterior Analytics*, II, 3. For medieval philosophy, *substantia* is the underlying reality that distinguishes a thing from others and gives it independent existence.

[2] First Principle—God as the Foundation of all creation. For Aquinas's argument that reason can lead us to the knowledge of the existence of God, see *Summa Theologiae*, I, qu. 2, a. 3. (p. 30).

[3] Nature, for Aquinas, is purposive and man's intellect is directed by nature to the knowledge of truth.

insufficient to manifest the substance of God. Effects possess a resemblance to causes in their own particular way because everything that acts does so in ways like itself, but effects do not always exhibit a perfect likeness to their cause. Now human reason is related to the knowledge of the truth of faith—which can only be known fully by those who see the divine substance—in such a way that reason can attain likenesses of it that are true but not sufficient to comprehend the truth conclusively or as known in itself. Yet it is useful for the human mind to exercise its powers of reasoning, however weak, in this way provided that there is no presumption that it can comprehend or demonstrate [the substance of the divine]. For it is most pleasing to be able to see some aspect of the loftiest things, however weak and inadequate our consideration of them may be.

Question:
1. What truths about God are reserved to faith? What can reason tell us about God?

8.5   Guilds: Regulating the Craft

Tradesmen, craftsmen, and merchants organized themselves into guilds, associations that maintained a monopoly, guaranteed quality, and regulated prices and standards of production. The following articles regulated the Spurriers (1345) in London and illustrate the guild principle as it applied to the industrial trade of making spurs.

> **Source:** Articles of the Spurriers" in Henry Thomas Riley, ed., *Memorials of London and London Life, A.D. 1276-1419* (London: Longmans, Green, and Co., 1868), pp. 226–28, 239–40.

ARTICLES OF THE LONDON SPURRIERS, 1347

Be it remembered, that on Tuesday, the morrow of St. Peter's Chains [1 August], in the 19th year of the reign of King Edward the Third etc., the Articles underwritten were read before John Hamond, Mayor, Roger de Depham, Recorder, and the other Aldermen; and seeing that the same were deemed befitting, they were accepted and enrolled, in these words:

"In the first place,—that no one of the trade of Spurriers shall work longer than from the beginning of the day until curfew rung out at the Church of St. Sepulchre, without Neugate; by reason that no man can work so neatly by night as by day.

And many persons of the said trade, who compass how to practise deception in their work, desire to work by night rather than by day: and then they introduce false iron, and iron that has been cracked, for tin, and also, they put gilt on false copper, and cracked.

And further, many of the said trade are wandering about all day, without working at all at their trade; and then, when they have become drunk and frantic, they take to their work, to the annoyance of the sick and of all their neighbourhood, as well as by reason of the broils that arise between them and the strange folks who are dwelling among them.

And then they blow up their fires so vigorously, that their forges begin all at once to blaze; to the great peril of themselves and of all the neighbourhood around. And then too, all the neighbours are much in dread of the sparks, which so vigorously issue forth in all directions from the mouths of the chimneys in their forges.

By reason whereof, it seems unto them that working by night [should be put an end to,] in order such false work and such perils to avoid; and therefore, the Mayor and Aldermen do will, by assent of the good folks of the said trade, and for the common profit, that from henceforth such time for working, and such false work made in the trade, shall be forbidden.

And if any person shall be found in the said trade to do to the contrary hereof, let him be amerced1, the first time in 40 d [pence]., one half thereof to go to the use of the Chamber of the Guildhall of London, and the other half to the use of the said trade; the second time, in half a mark, and the third time, in 10 s. [shillings], to the use of the same Chamber and trade; and the fourth time, let him forswear the trade for ever.

"Also,—that no one of the said trade shall hang his spurs out on Sunday, or on other days that are Double Feasts; but only a sign indicating his business: and such spurs as they shall so sell, they are to show and sell within their shops, without exposing them without, or opening the doors or windows of their shops, on the pain aforesaid"Also,—that no one of the said trade shall keep a house or shop to carry on his business, unless he is free of the City;2 and that no one shall cause to be sold, or exposed for sale, any manner of old spurs for new ones; or shall garnish them, or change them for new ones.

"Also,—that no one of the said trade shall take an apprentice for a less term than seven years; and such apprentice shall be enrolled, according to the usages of the said city.

"Also,—that if any one of the said trade, who is not a freeman, shall take an apprentice for a term of years, he shall be amerced, as aforesaid.

"Also,—that no one of the said trade shall receive the apprentice, serving-man, or journeyman, of another in the same trade, during the term agreed upon between his master and him; on the pain aforesaid.

"Also,—that no alien of another country, or foreigner of this country, shall follow or use the said trade, unless he is enfranchised before the Mayor, Aldermen, and Chamberlain; and that, by witness and surety of the good folks of the said trade, who will undertake for him as to his loyalty and his good behaviour.

"Also,—that no one of the said trade shall work on Saturdays, after None has been rung out in the City; and not from that hour until the Monday morning following."

Questions:
The following questions pertain to documents 8.5 and 8.6.

1. *In what ways did their articles guarantee a monopoly to guild members? How did the guilds maintain quality and prevent fraud?*
2. *Who was eligible for membership in the guilds?*
3. *With what other activities besides regulation of their trade did the guilds concern themselves?*
4. *How did rivalry between guilds express itself in Florence?*

8.6 "For the Honor of the Guild," Social Responsibility

These documents each pertain to one of the various guilds in Florence. The first are the articles regulating the wine merchants; the second is a petition from the silk guild to the government of Florence; and the last is a decree passed by the Lana (Wool) guild. Each of these three sources reveals another dimension of the guilds that extended beyond simple regulation of their trade.

Source: *The Society of Renaissance Florence: A Documentary Study,* ed.Gene Brucker, (Harper and Row, Inc., 1972), pp. 90–94.

The Corporation of Wine Merchants

[Chapter 18] It is also decreed and ordained that the consuls [of the guild] are required, by their oath, to force all of the winesellers... who sell at retail in the city and *contado* of Florence to swear allegiance to this guild and for this guild. And for this purpose they must make a monthly search through the city and the suburbs of Florence, and if they find anyone who is not matriculated in the guild, they must require him to swear allegiance.... And whoever, as has been said, is engaged in this trade, even though he is not... matriculated in the guild... is considered to be a member of the guild.... And each newly matriculated wineseller... must pay... 5 lire to the guild treasurer... as his matriculation fee.... If, however, he is a father or son of a guild member, then he is not required to pay anything.

[Chapter 20] The consuls, treasurer, and notary of the guild are required to assemble together wherever they wish... to render justice to whoever demands it of the men of this guild, against any and all those... who sell wine at retail... in the city, *contado*, and district of Florence.

... [They must] hear, take cognizance of, make decisions, and act on everything which pertains to their office, and accept every appeal which is brought before them by whosoever has any claim upon any member of the guild.... They must record [these acts] in their protocols and render justice with good faith and without fraud on one day of each week.

With respect to these disputes, the consuls are required to proceed in the following manner. If any dispute or quarrel is brought against any member of the guild... and it involves a sum of 3 Florentine lire di piccolo or less, this dispute is to be decided summarily by the consuls, after the parties have sworn an oath, in favor of whoever appears to be more honest and of better reputation.... If the dispute involves 60 soldi or more, the consuls, after receiving the complaint, are required to demand that... the defendant appear to reply to the complaint.... [Witnesses are to be called and interrogated in such major disputes, and the consuls must announce their judgment within one month.]

[Chapter 21] It is decreed and ordained that each wine-seller shall come to the assembly of the guild as often as he is summoned by the consuls.... The consuls are required to levy a fine of 10 soldi... against whoever violates this [rule], and the same penalty is to be incurred by anyone who fails to respond to the consuls' order to come to the guild's offering in a church.... And if necessity requires that the members of the guild assemble under their banner to stand guard, or to go on a march, by day or night, in the city and *contado* of Florence or elsewhere, every member of the guild is required to appear in person, with or without arms as ordered, with their standard-bearer and under their banner, or pay a fine of 10 lire.

[Chapter 35] For the honor of the guild and of the members of the guild, it is decreed and ordained that whenever any member of the guild dies, all guild members in the city and suburbs who are summoned by the messenger of the guild... are required to go to the service for the dead man, and to stay there until he is buried.... And the consuls are required to send the guild messenger, requesting and inviting the members of the guild to participate in the obsequies for the dead.

A CHARITABLE ENTERPRISE, 1421

... This petition is presented with all due reverence to you, lord priors, on behalf of your devoted sons of the guild of Por Santa Maria [the silk guild] and the merchants and guildsmen of that association. It is well known to all of the people of Florence that this guild has sought, through pious acts, to conserve... and also to promote your republic and this guild. It has begun to construct a most beautiful edifice in the city of Florence and in the parish of S. Michele Visdomini, next to the piazza called the "Frati de' Servi." [This building is] a hospital called S.Maria degli Innocenti, in which shall be received those who, against natural law, have been deserted by their fathers or their mothers, that is, infants, who in the vernacular are called *gittatelli* [literally, castaways; foundlings]. Without the help and favor of your benign lordships, it will not be possible to transform this laudable objective into reality nor after it has been achieved, to preserve and conserve it.

And since [we] realized that your lordships and all of the people are, in the highest degree, committed to works of charity, [we have] decided to have recourse to your clemency, and to request, most devotedly, all of the things which are described below. So on behalf of the above-mentioned guild, you are humbly petitioned... to enact a law that this guild of Por Santa Maria and its members and guildsmen-as founders, originators, and principals of this hospital-are understood in perpetuity to be... the sole patrons, defenders, protectors, and supporters of this hospital as representatives of, and in the name of, the *popolo* and Commune of Florence.

Item, the consuls of the guild... have authority to choose supervisors and governors of the hospital and of the children and servants.

GUILD RIVALRY, 1425

The above-mentioned consuls, assembled together in the palace of the [Lana]1 guild in sufficient numbers and in the accustomed manner for the exercise of their office... have diligently considered the law approved by the captains of the society of the blessed Virgin Mary of Orsanmichele. This law decreed, in effect, that for the ornamentation of that oratory, each of the twenty-one guilds of the city of Florence... in a place assigned to each of them by the captains of the society, should construct... a tabernacle, properly and carefully decorated, for the honor of the city and the beautification of the oratory. The consuls have considered that all of the guilds have finished their tabernacles, and that those constructed by the Calimala and Cambio guilds, and by other guilds, surpass in beauty and ornamentation that of the Lana guild. So it may truly be said that this does not redound to the honor of the Lana guild, particularly when one considers the magnificence of that guild which has always sought to be the master and the superior of the other guilds.

For the splendor and honor of the guild, the lord consuls desire to provide a remedy for this.... They decree that through the month of August, the existing lord consuls and their successors in office, by authority of the present provision, are to construct, fabricate, and remake a tabernacle and a statue of the blessed Stephen, protomartyr, protector and defender of the renowned Lana guild, in his honor and in reverence to God. They are to do this by whatever ways and means they choose, which will most honorably contribute to the splendor of the guild, so that this tabernacle will exceed, or at least equal, in beauty and decoration the more beautiful ones. In the construction of this tabernacle and statue, the lord consuls... may spend... up to 1,000 florins. And during this time, the lord consuls may commission that statue and tabernacle to the person or persons, and for that price or prices, and with whatever agreement and time or times which seem to them to be most useful for the guild.

Questions:
The following questions pertain to documents 8.5 and 8.6.

1. *In what ways did their articles guarantee a monopoly to guild members? How did the guilds maintain quality and prevent fraud?*
2. *Who was eligible for membership in the guilds?*
3. *With what other activities besides regulation of their trade did the guilds concern themselves?*
4. *How did rivalry between guilds express itself in Florence?*

8.7   The Ideal Wife of a Merchant

Alberti, a Florentine Renaissance humanist, presents a picture of the ideal wife as described by a fictional, rich old Florentine merchant.

Source: *Not in God's Image: Women in History from the Greeks to the Victorian,* eds. Julia O'Faolain, and Lauro Martines, (New York: Harper and Row, 1973), pp. 187–89.

After my wife had been settled in my house a few days, and after her first pangs of longing for her mother and family had begun to fade, I took her by the hand and showed her around the whole house. I explained that the loft was the place for grain and that the stores of wine and wood were kept in the cellar. I showed her where things needed for the table were kept, and so on, through the whole house. At the end there were no household goods of which my wife had not learned both the place and the purpose. Then we returned to my room, and, having locked the door, I showed her my treasures, silver, tapestry, garments, jewels, and where each thing had its place....

Only my books and records and those of my ancestors did I determine to keep well sealed.... These my wife not only could not read, she could not even lay hands on them. I kept my records at all times... locked up and arranged in order in my study, almost like sacred and religious objects. I never gave my wife permission to enter that place, with me or alone. I also ordered her, if she ever came across any writing of mine, to give it over to my keeping at once. To take away any taste she might have for looking at my notes or prying into my private affairs, I often used to express my disapproval of bold and forward females who try too hard to know about things outside the house and about the concerns of their husband and of men in general....

[Husbands] who take counsel with their wives... are madmen if they think true prudence or good counsel lies in the female brain.... For this very reason I have always tried carefully not to let any secret of mine be known to a woman. I did not doubt that my wife was most loving, and more discreet and modest in her ways than any, but I still considered it safer to have her unable, and not merely unwilling, to harm me.... Furthermore, I made it a rule never to speak with her of anything but household matters or questions of conduct, or of the children. Of these matters I spoke a good deal to her....

When my wife had seen and understood the place of everything in the house, I said to her, 'My dear wife... you have seen our treasures now, and thanks be to God they are such that we ought to be contented with them. If we know how to preserve them, these things will serve you and me and our children. It is up to you, therefore, my dear wife, to keep no less careful watch over them than I.'

... She said she would be happy to do conscientiously whatever she knew how to do and had the skill to do, hoping it might please me. To this I said, 'Dear wife, listen to me. I shall be most pleased if you do just three things: first, my wife, see that you never want another man to share this bed but me. You understand.' She blushed and cast down her eyes. Still I repeated that she should never receive anyone into that room but myself. That was the first point. The second, I said, was that she should take care of the household, preside over it with modesty, serenity, tranquillity, and peace. That was the second point. The third thing, I said, was that she should see that nothing went wrong in the house.

... I could not describe to you how reverently she replied to me. She said her mother had taught her only how to spin and sew, and how to be virtuous and obedient. Now she would gladly learn from me how to rule the family and whatever I might wish to teach her.

Then she and I knelt down and prayed to God to give us the power to make good use of those possessions which he, in his mercy and kindness, had allowed us to enjoy. We also prayed... that he might grant us the grace to live together in peace and harmony for many happy years, and with many male children, and that he might grant to me riches, friendship, and honor, and to her, integrity, purity, and the character of a perfect mistress of the household. Then, when we had stood up, I said to her: 'My dear wife, to have prayed God for these things is not enough.... I shall seek with all my powers to gain what we have asked of God. You, too, must set your whole will, all your mind, and all your modesty to work to make yourself a person whom God has heard.... You should realize that in this regard nothing is so important for yourself, so acceptable to God, so pleasing to me, and precious in the sight of your children as your chastity. The woman's character is the jewel of her family; the mother's purity has always been a part of the dowry she passes on to her daughters; her purity has always far outweighed her beauty.... Shun every sort of dishonor, my dear wife. Use every means to appear to all people as a highly respectable woman. To seem less would be to offend God, me, our children, and yourself.'

.... Never, at any moment, did I choose to show in word or action even the least bit of self-surrender in front of my wife. I did not imagine for a moment that I could hope to win obedience from one to whom I had confessed myself a slave. Always, therefore, I showed myself virile and a real man.

Question:
1. What does the Florentine merchant expect of his wife?

PART 9
The Late Middle Ages

9.1 The Flagellants

Although flagellation (voluntary whipping) had been practiced in monastic communities long before, it does not emerge as a public group activity until the midthirteenth century. When Europe experienced the Black Death (1347–1350), the Brotherhood of Flagellants (it included women also) resorted to even more spectacular public flagellation. The movement probably originated in Eastern Europe and took root most deeply in German areas. As we see from the following report of Robert of Avesbury, however, they also crossed the English Channel.

> **Sources:** *Medieval England as Viewed by Contemporaries,* ed. W. O. Hassall, (New York: Harper Torch-books, 1965, © 1957), pp. 157–58.

About Michaelmas 1349 over six hundred men came to London from Flanders, mostly of Zeeland and Holland origin. Sometimes at St. Paul's and sometimes at other points in the city they made two daily public appearances wearing cloths from the thighs to the ankles, but otherwise stripped bare. Each wore a cap marked with a red cross in front and behind. Each had in his right hand a scourge with three tails. Each tail had a knot and though the middle of it there were sometimes sharp nails fixed. They marched naked in a file one behind the other and whipped themselves with these scourges on their naked and bleeding bodies. Four of them would chant in their native tongue and another four would chant in response like a litany. Thrice they would all cast themselves on the ground in this sort of procession, stretching out their hands like the arms of a cross. The singing would go on and, the one who was in the rear of those thus prostrate acting first, each of them in turn would step over the others and give one stroke with his scourge to the man lying under him. This went on from the first to the last until each of them had observed the ritual to the full tale of those on the ground. Then each put on his customary garments and always wearing their caps and carrying their whips in their hands they retired to their lodgings. It is said that every night they performed the same penance.

Questions:
1. What was the motivation behind the flagellant movement?
2. Why do you think most church authorities discouraged such activities? Why do you think secular and church authorities allowed them to continue?

9.2 Propositions of Wycliffe condemned at London, 1382, and at the Council of Constance, 1415

John Wycliffe (c. 1328–1384) taught theology and philosophy at Oxford and was a forceful advocate of church reform. He believed that the Bible was the highest spiritual authority and that the sacraments of the church were not necessary for salvation. The fact that he preached these beliefs in public and in English led to his condemnation as a heretic. He was not, however, executed but rather forced into retirement from public life.

> **Source:** *Documents of the Christian Church,* ed. Henry Bettenson (New York: Oxford University Press, 1970), pp. 172–173.

I.[1] That the material substance of bread and the material substance of wine remain in the Sacrament of the altar.
2. That the accidents of bread do not remain without a subject (substance) in the said Sacrament.
3. That Christ is not in the Sacrament essentially and really, in his own corporeal presence.
4. That if a bishop or priest be in mortal sin he does not ordain, consecrate or baptize.
5. That it is not laid down in the Gospel that Christ ordained the Mass.
6. That God ought to obey the devil.[2]

---

[1] The propositions are numbered as at Constance. *Fasc. Ziz.* give a different order.
[2] i.e. 'Dominion by grace' cannot be put into operation in the world as it is.

7. That if a man be duly penitent any outward confession is superfluous and useless.

10. That it is contrary to Holy Scripture that ecclesiastics should have possessions.

14. That any deacon or priest may preach the word of God apart from the authority of the Apostolic See or a Catholic bishop.

15. That no one is civil lord, or prelate, or bishop, while he is in mortal sin.

16. That temporal lords can at their will take away temporal goods from the church, when those who hold them are sinful (habitually sinful, not sinning in one act only).

17. That the people can at their own will correct sinful lords.

18. That tithes are mere alms, and that parishioners can withdraw them at their will because of the misdeeds of their curates.

20. That he who gives alms to friars is by that fact excommunicate.

21. That any one who enters a private religion (i.e. religious house], either of those having property or of mendicants, is rendered more inapt and unfit for the performance of the commands of God.

22. That holy men have sinned in founding private religions.

23. That the religious who live in private religions are not of the Christian religion.

24. That friars are bound to gain their livelihood by the labour of their hands, and not by begging.

28. That the confirmation of young men, the ordination of clerics, the consecration of places are reserved for the Pope and bishops on account of the desire for temporal gain and honour.

30. That the excommunication of the Pope or of any prelate is not to be feared, because it is the censure of antichrist.

34. That all of the order of mendicants are heretics.

35. That the Roman Church is the synagogue of Satan, and the Pope is not the next and immediate vicar of Christ and the Apostles.

42. That it is fatuous to believe in the indulgences of the Pope and the bishops.

43. That all oaths made to corroborate human contracts and civil business are unlawful.

Question:
1. Why were the ideas of Wycliffe so odious to the Church?

9.3 The Lollard Conclusions, 1394

Wycliffe's condemnation did not stop his followers, known as Lollards, from spreading his ideas. One of their chief accomplishments was the translation of the Bible from Latin into English. Many historians see the Lollard movement as a precursor to Protestantism.

Source: *Documents of the Christian Church*, ed. Henry Bettenson (New York: Oxford University Press, 1970), pp. 175–179.

1. That when the Church of England began to go mad after temporalities, like its great step-mother the Roman Church, and churches were authorized by appropriation in divers places, faith, hope, and charity began to flee from our Church, because pride, with its doleful progeny of moral sins, claimed this under title of truth. This conclusion is general, and proved by experience, custom, and manner or fashion, as you shall afterwards hear.

2. That our usual priesthood which began in Rome, pretended to be of power more lofty than the angels, is not that priesthood which Christ ordained for His apostles. This conclusion is proved because the Roman priesthood is bestowed with signs, rites, and pontifical blessings, of small virtue, nowhere exemplified in Holy Scripture, because the bishop's ordinal and the New Testament scarcely agree, and we cannot see that the Holy Spirit, by reason of any such signs, confers the gift, for He and all His excellent gifts cannot consist in any one with mortal sin. A corollary to this is that it is

a grievous play for wise men to see bishops trifle with the Holy Spirit in the bestowal for orders, because they give the tonsure in outward appearance in the place of white hearts[3]; and this is the unrestrained introduction of antichrist into the Church to give colour to idleness.

3. That the law of continence enjoined on priests, which was first ordained to the prejudice of women, brings sodomy into all the Holy Church, but we excuse ourselves by the Bible because the decree says that we should not mention it, though suspected. Reason and experience prove this conclusion: reason, because the good living of ecclesiastics must have a natural outlet or worse; experience, because the secret proof of such men is that they find delight in women, and when thou hast proved such a man mark him well, because he is one of them. A corollary to this is that private religions and the originators or beginning of this sin would be specially worthy of being checked, but God of His power with regard to secret sin sends open vengeance in His Church.

4. That the pretended miracle of the sacrament of bread drives all men, but a few, to idolatry, because they think that the Body of Christ which is never away from heaven could by power of the priest's word be enclosed essentially in a little bread which they show the people; but God grant that they might be willing to believe what the evangelical doctor[4] says in his Trialogus (iv. 7), that the bread of the altar is habitually the Body of Christ, for we take it that in this way any faithful man and woman can by God's law perform the sacrament of that bread without any such miracle. A final corollary is that although the Body of Christ has been granted eternal joy, the service of Corpus Christi, instituted by Brother Thomas [Aquinas], is not true but is fictitious and full of false miracles. It is no wonder; because Brother Thomas, at that time holding with the pope, would have been willing to perform a miracle with a hen's egg; and we know well that any falsehood openly preached turns to the disgrace of Him who is always true and without any defect.

5. That exorcisms and blessings performed over wine, bread, water and oil, salt, wax, and incense, the stones of the altar, and church walls, over clothing, mitre, cross, and pilgrims' staves, are the genuine performance of necromancy rather than of sacred theology. This conclusion is proved as follows, because by such exorcisms creatures are honoured as being of higher virtue than they are in their own nature, and we do not see any change in any creature which is so exorcized, save by false faith which is the principal characteristic of the Devil's art. A corollary: that if the book of exorcising holy water, read in church, were entirely trustworthy we think truly that the holy water used in church would be the best medicine for all kinds of illnesses—sores, for instance; whereas we experience the contrary day by day.

6. That king and bishop in one person, prelate and judge in temporal causes, curate and officer in secular office, puts any kingdom beyond good rule. This conclusion is clearly proved because the temporal and spiritual are two halves of the entire Holy Church. And so he who has applied himself to one should not meddle with the other, for no one can serve two masters. It seems that hermaphrodite or ambidexter would be good names for such men of double estate. A corollary is that we, the procurators of God in this behalf, do petition before Parliament that all curates, as well superior as inferior, be fully excused and should occupy themselves with their own charge and no other.

7. That special prayers for the souls of the dead offered in our Church, preferring one before another in name, are a false foundation of alms, and for that reason all houses of alms in England have been wrongly founded. This conclusion is proved by two reasons: the one is that meritorious prayer, and of any effect, ought to be a work proceeding from deep charity, and perfect charity leaves out no one, for 'Thou shalt love thy neighbour as thyself.' And so it is clear to us that the gift of temporal good bestowed on the priesthood and houses of alms is a special incentive to private prayer which is not far from simony. For another reason is that special prayer made for men condemned is very displeasing to God. And although it be doubtful, it is probable to faithful Christian people that founders of a house of alms have for their poisonous endowment passed over for the most part to the broad road. The corollary is: effectual prayer springing from perfect love would in general embrace all whom God would have saved, and would do away with that well-worn way or merchandise in special prayers made for the possessionary mendicants and other hired priests, who are a people of great burden to the whole realm, kept in idleness: for it has been proved in one book, which the king had, that a hundred houses of alms would suffice in all the realm, and from this would rather accrue possible profit to the temporal estate.

8. That pilgrimages, prayers, and offerings made to blind crosses or roods, and to deaf images of wood or stone, are pretty well akin to idolatry and far from alms, and although these be forbidden and imaginary, a book of error to the lay folk, still the customary image of the Trinity is specially abominable. This conclusion God clearly proves, bidding alms to be done to the needy man because they are the image of God, and more like than wood or stone; for God did not say, 'let us make wood or stone in our likeness and image,' but man; because the supreme honour which clerks call *latria* appertains to the Godhead only; and the lower honour which clerks call *dulia* appertains to man and angel and to no inferior creature. A corollary is that the service of the cross, performed twice in any year in our church, is full of idolatry, for if that should, so might the nails and lance be so highly honoured; then would the lips of Judas be relics indeed if any were

---

[3] *Alborum cervorum* = 'white harts'!

[4] I.e. Wycliffe, who in the *Trialogus* ('Three-cornered Discussion'—between Truth, Falsehood, and Prudence) expounded his views on the Eucharist.

able to possess them. But we ask you, pilgrim, to tell us when you offer to the bones of saints placed in a shrine in any spot, whether you relieve the saint who is in joy, or that almshouse which is so well endowed and for which men have been canonized, God knows how. And to speak more plainly, a faithful Christian supposes that the wounds of that noble man, whom men call St Thomas, were not a case of martyrdom.

9. That auricular confession which is said to be so necessary to the salvation of a man, with its pretended power of absolution, exalts the arrogance of priests and gives them opportunity of other secret colloquies which we will not speak of; for both lords and ladies attest that, for fear of their confessors, they dare not speak the truth. And at the time of confession there is a ready occasion for assignation, that is for 'wooing,' and other secret understandings leading to mortal sins. They themselves say that they are God's representatives to judge of every sin, to pardon and cleanse whomsoever they please. They say that they have the keys of heaven and of hell, and can excommunicate and bless, bind and loose, at their will, so much so that for a drink, or twelve pence, they will sell the blessing of heaven with charter and close warrant sealed with the common seal. This conclusion is so notorious that it needs not any proof. It is a corollary that the pope of Rome, who has given himself out as treasurer of the whole Church, having in charge that worthy jewel of Christ's passion together with the merits of all saints in heaven, whereby he grants pretended indulgence from penalty and guilt, is a treasurer almost devoid of charity, in that he can set free all that are prisoners in hell at his will, and cause that they should never come to that place. But in this any Christian can well see there is much secret falsehood hidden away in our Church.

10. That manslaughter in war, or by pretended law of justice for a temporal cause, without spiritual revelation, is expressly contrary to the New Testament, which indeed is the law of grace and full of mercies. This conclusion is openly proved by the examples of Christ's preaching here on earth, for he specially taught a man to love his enemies, and to show them pity, and not to slay them. The reason is this, that for the most part, when men fight, after the first blow, charity is broken. And whoever dies without charity goes the straight road to hell. And beyond this we know well that no clergyman can by Scripture or lawful reason remit the punishment of death for one mortal sin and not for another; but the law of mercy, which is the New Testament, prohibits all manner of manslaughter, for in the Gospel: 'It was said unto them of old time, Thou shalt not kill.' The corollary is that it is indeed robbery of poor folk when lords get indulgences from punishment and guilt for those who aid their army to kill a Christian people in distant lands for temporal gain, just as we too have seen soldiers who run into heathendom to get them a name for the slaughter of men; much more do they deserve ill thanks from the King of Peace, for by our humility and patience was the faith multiplied, and Christ Jesus hates and threatens men who fight and kill, when He says: 'He who smites with the sword shall perish by the sword.'

11. That the vow of continence made in our Church by women who are frail and imperfect in nature, is the cause of bringing in the gravest horrible sins possible to human nature, because, although the killing of abortive children before they are baptized and the destruction of nature by drugs are vile sins, yet connection with themselves or brute beasts of any creature not having fife surpasses them in foulness to such an extent as that they should be punished with the pains of hell. The corollary is that, widows and such as take the veil and the ring, being delicately fed, we could wish that they were given in marriage, because we cannot excuse them from secret sins.

12. That the abundance of unnecessary arts practised in our realm nourishes much sin in waste, profusion, and disguise. This, experience and reason prove in some measure, because nature is sufficient for a man's necessity with few arts. The corollary is that since St Paul says: 'having food and raiment, let us be therewith content,' it seems to us that goldsmiths and armourers and all kinds of arts not necessary for a man, according to the apostle, should be destroyed for the increase of virtue; because although these two said arts were exceedingly necessary in the old law, the New Testament abolishes them and many others.

This is our embassy, which Christ has bidden us fulfil, very necessary for this time for several reasons. And although these matters are briefly noted here they are however set forth at large in another book, and many others besides, at length in our own language, and we wish that these were accessible to all Christian people. We ask God then of His supreme goodness to reform our Church, as being entirely out of joint, to the perfectness of its first beginning.

[*Foxe's translation of some contemporary verses added to the foregoing document*]
The English nation doth lament of these vile men their sin,
Which Paul doth plainly dignify by idols to begin.
But Gehazites full ingrate from sinful Simon sprung,
This to defend, though priests in name, make bulwarks great and strong.
Ye princes, therefore, whom to rule the people God hath placed
With justice' sword, why see ye not this evil great defaced?

Question:
1. How do the Lollards carry the ideas of Wycliffe even further?

9.4 Individual Heretics: Saints and Witches

In the later middle ages (from the fourteenth century on) many changes rocked society, including the devastating mortality of the Black Death, rural migration to cities, disruption in the Church, new technology, discoveries, and ideas. Increasing uncertainty placed marginal people at further risk and made everyone more suspicious of others who threatened the accepted order and authority. The following two accounts reveal how some people were condemned in Florence for such dubious behavior or beliefs.

> **Source:** *The Society of Renaissance Florence: A Documentary Study*, ed.Gene Brucker, (Harper and Row, Inc., 1972), pp. 253–57, 270–73.

THE EXECUTION OF FRA MICHELE OF CALCI, 1389

[April 30, 1389] This is the condemnation of Giovanni, called Fra Michele di Berti of Calci, in the territory of Pisa, a man of low condition, evil conversation, life, and reputation, and a heretic against the Catholic faith, against whom we have proceeded by means of inquisition.... It has come to our attention that this Giovanni... with the spirit and intent of being a heretic, had relations with the Fraticelli, called the Little Brothers of Poverty, heretics and schismatics and denounced by the Holy Roman Church, and that he joined that depraved sect in a place called the grotto of the *Dieci Yoffensi,* in which place they congregated and stayed.... With the intention of proclaiming this heresy and of contaminating faithful Christians, the accused came to the city of Florence and in public places he did maintain, affirm, and preach the heretical teachings hereby stated:

Item, that Christ, our Redeemer, possessed no property either individually or in common but divested himself of all things, as the Holy Scripture testifies.

Item, that Christ and his Apostles, according to the Scriptures, denounced the taking, holding, or exchanging of goods as against divine law.

Item, that Pope John XXII [d. 1334] of blessed memory was a heretic and lost all power and ecclesiastical authority as pope and as a heretic had no authority to appoint bishops or prelates, and that all prelates so appointed by him do not legally hold their office and that they sin by pretending to do so.

Item, that all cardinals, prelates, and clerics who accepted the teaching of John XXII on apostolic poverty, and who should resist these teachings and who do not resist, are also heretics and have lost all authority as priests of Christ.

Item, that this Giovanni, a heretic and schismatic, not content with all this mentioned above, but desiring also the damnation of others, in the months of March and April sought to persuade many men and women of the city of Florence, to induce them to believe inland to enter the above-mentioned sect of the Fraticelli. He told them about the above-mentioned sect; with false words and with erroneous reasons he claimed that this sect was the true religion and the true observance of the rule and life of the blessed Francis; and that all those who observe this doctrine and life are in a state of grace, and that all other friars and priests are heretics and schismatics and are damned.

And since this Giovanni appeared before us and our court and confessed to the above-mentioned charges... and refused to recant or to reject these teachings, we hereby decree that unless this Giovanni gives up his false teaching and beliefs, that as an example to others, he be taken to the place of justice and there he is to be burned with fire and the flames of fire so that he shall die and his spirit be separated from his body.

Now everything which I here describe, I who write both saw or heard. Fra Michele, having come into the courtyard, waited attentively to hear the condemnation. And the vicar [general of the bishop] spoke: "The bishop and the Inquisitor have sent me here to tell you that if you wish to return to the Holy Church and renounce your errors, then do so, in order that the people may see that the church is merciful." And Fra Michele replied, "I believe in the poor crucified Christ, and I believe that Christ, showing the way to perfection, possessed nothing...." Having read his confession, the judge turned his back upon Fra Michele... and the guards seized him and with great force pushed him outside of the gate of the judge's palace. He remained there alone, surrounded by scoundrels, appearing in truth as one of the martyrs. And there was such a great crowd that one could scarcely see. And the throng increased in size, shouting: "You don't want to die!" And Fra Michele replied, "I will die for Christ." And the crowd answered: "Oh! You aren't dying for Christ! You don't believe in God!" And Fra Michele replied: "I believe in God, in the Virgin Mary, and in the Holy Church!" And someone said to him, "You wretch! The devil is pushing you from behind!"

And when he arrived in the district of the Proconsolo, there was a great press of people who came to watch. And one of the faithful cried: "Fra Michele! Pray to God for us...." When he arrived at S. Giovanni, they shouted to him: "Repent, repent! You don't want to die." And he said:

"I have repented of my sins...." And at the Mercato Vecchio, they shouted even louder: "Save yourself! Save yourself!" And he replied, "Save yourselves from damnation." And at the Mercato Nuovo, the shouts grew louder:

"Repent, repent!" And he replied, "Repent of your sins; repent of your usury and your false merchandising....And at the Piazza del Grano, there were many women in the windows of the houses who cried to him: "Repent, repent!" And he replied, "Repent of your sins, your usury, your gambling, your fornication...." When he arrived at S. Croce, near the gate of the friars, the image of St. Francis was shown to him and he raised his eyes to heaven and said, "St. Francis, my father, pray to Christ for me."

And then moving toward the gate of Justice, the crowd cried in unison: "Recant, recant! You don't want to die!" And he replied, "Christ died for us." And some said to him, mocking: "Ho, you're not Christ and you don't have to die for us." And he replied, "I wish to die for Him." And then another shouted, "Ho, you're not among pagans," and he answered, "I wish to die for the truth...."

And when he arrived at the gate near the place of execution, one of the faithful began to cry, "Remain firm, martyr of Christ, for soon you will receive the crown...." And arriving at the place of execution, there was a great turmoil and the crowd urged him to repent and save himself and he refused.... And the guards pushed the crowd back and formed a circle of horsemen around the pyre so that no one could enter. I myself did not enter but climbed upon the river bank to see, but I was unable to hear.... And he was bound to the stake... and the crowd begged him to recant, except one of the faithful, who comforted him. And they set fire to the wood... and Fra Michele began to recite the Te Deum.... And when he had said, "In your hands, 0 Lord, I commend my spirit," the fire burned the cords which bound him and he fell dead... to the earth.

And many of the onlookers said, "He seems to be a saint." Even his enemies whispered it... and then they slowly began to return to their homes. They talked about Michele and the majority said that he was wrong and that no one should speak such evil of the priests. And some said, "He is a martyr," and others said, "He is a saint," and still others denied it. And there was a greater tumult and disturbance in Florence than there had ever been.

CONDEMNATION OF A WITCH (JUNE 7, 1427)

...We condemn... Giovanna called Caterina, daughter of Francesco called El Toso, a resident of the parish of S. Ambrogio of Florence... who is a magician, witch, and sorceress, and a practitioner of the black arts.

It happened that Giovanni Ceresani of the parish of S. Jacopo tra le Fosse was passing by her door and stared at her fixedly. She thought that she would draw the chaste spirit of Giovanni to her for carnal purposes by means of the black arts.... She went to the shop of Monna Gilia, the druggist, and purchased from her a small amount of lead... and then she took a bowl and placed the lead in it and put it on the fire so that the lead would melt. With this melted lead she made a small chain and spoke certain words which have significance for this magical and diabolical art (and which, lest the people learn about them, shall not be recorded).... All this which was done and spoken against Giovanni's safety by Giovanna was so powerful that his chaste spirit was deflected to lust after her, so that willynilly he went several times to her house and there he fulfilled her perfidious desire.

With the desire of doing further harm to Giovanni's health through the black arts, and so persisting in what she had begun, she acquired a little gold, frankincense, and myrrh, and then took a little bowl with some glowing charcoal inside, and having prepared these ingredients and having lit the candle which she held in her left hand, she genuflected before the image and placed the bowl at the foot of the figure. Calling out the name of Giovanni, she threw the gold, frankincense, and myrrh upon the charcoal. And when the smoke from the charcoal covered the whole image, Giovanna spoke certain words, the tenor of which is vile and detestable, and which should be buried in silence lest the people be given information for committing sin.

When she realized that what she had done against Giovanni's health was not sufficient to satisfy completely her insatiable lust, she learned from a certain priest that... if water from the skulls of dead men was distilled and given with a little wine to any man, that it was a most valid test.... Night and day, that woman thought of nothing but how she could give that water to Giovanni to drink.... She visited the priest and bought from him a small amount of that water... and that accursed woman gave Giovanni that water mixed with wine to drink. After he drank it, Giovanni could think of nothing but satisfying his lust with Giovanna. And his health has been somewhat damaged, in the opinion of good and worthy [men].

In the time when Giovanna was menstruating, she took a little of her menses, that quantity which is required by the diabolical ceremonies, and placed it in a small beaker, and then poured it into another flask filled with wine and gave it to Giovanni to drink. And on account of this and the other things described above, Giovanni no longer has time for his affairs as he did in the past, and he has left his home and his wife and son... And does only what pleases Giovanna....

On several occasions, Giovanna had intercourse with a certain Jacopo di Andrea, a doublet-maker, of the parish of S. Niccolo. Desiring to possess his chaste spirit totally for her lust and against his health, Giovanna... thought to give Jacopo some of her menses, since she knew that it was very efficacious.... Having observed several diabolical rites, she took the beaker with the menses... and gave it to Jacopo to drink. After he had drunk, she uttered these words among others: "I will catch you in my net if you don't flee." ... When they were engaged in the act of intercourse, she placed her hand on her private parts... and after uttering certain diabolical words, she put a finger on Jacopo's lips.... Thereafter, in the opinion of everyone, Jacopo's health deteriorated and he was forced by necessity to obey her in everything.

Several years ago, Giovanna was the concubine of Niccolo di Ser Casciotto of the parish of S. Giorgio, and she had three children by him. Having a great affection for Niccolo, who was then in Hungary, she wanted him to return to her in Florence.... So she planned a diabolical experiment by invoking a demon, to the detriment of Niccolo's health.... She went to someone who shall not be identified... and asked him to go to another diabolical woman, a sorceress (whose name shall not be publicized, for the public good), and asked her to make for Giovanna a wax image in the form of a woman; and also some pins and other items required by this diabolical experiment.... Giovanna took that image and placed it in a chest in her house. When, a few days later, she had to leave that house and move to another, she left the image in the chest. Later it was discovered by the residents of that house, who burned it.

She collected nine beans, a piece of cloth, some charcoal, several olive leaves which had been blessed and which stood before the image of the Virgin Mary, a coin with a cross, and a grain of salt. With these in her hand she genuflected... [before the image] and recited three times the Pater Noster and the Ave Maria, spurning the divine prayers composed for the worship of God and his mother the Virgin Mary. Having done this, she placed these items on a piece of linen cloth and slept over them for three nights. And afterwards, she took them in her hand and thrice repeated the Pater Noster and the Ave Maria.... And thus Giovanna knew that her future husband would not love her. And so it happened, for after the celebration and the consummation of the marriage, her husband Giovanni stayed with her for a few days, and then left her and has not yet returned. [Giovanna confessed to these crimes and was beheaded.]

Questions:

1. Why would both church and civil authorities consider Fra Michele's teachings dangerous while others hailed him as a saint?
2. What role do you think gender played in the accusation and conviction of Giovanna?
3. How could her alleged behavior be considered threatening to the social order?
4. Do you think Giovanna and Giovanni were victims or guilty mischief-makers in Florence?

9.5   How They Died

The following selections are Coroner Reports from the City of London during the fourteenth century. The untimely death of these ordinary townspeople also reveals many details about their everyday lives.

> **Source:** *Calendar of Coroners Rolls of the City of London,* 1300–1378. ed. R. R. Sharpe, (London: Richard Clay and Sons, 1913), pp. 56–57, 63–69, 86–87, 127, 183. Language has been modernized by the editors.

1. ON THE DEATH OF ROBERT, SON OF JOHN DE ST. BOTULPH

Saturday before the Feast of St. Margaret [20 July] in the year [16 Edward II, A.D. 1322], information was given to the... Coroner and Sheriffs that a certain Robert, son of John de St. Botulph, a boy seven years old, lay dead of a death other than his rightful death in a certain shop which the said Robert held of Richard de Wirhale in the parish of St. Michael de Paternosterchurch in the Ward of Vintry. Thereupon the Coroner and Sheriffs proceeded there and, having summoned good men of that Ward and of the three nearest Wards, namely Douuegate, Queenhithe and Cordewanerstreet, they diligently inquired how it happened. The jurors say that when on the Sunday next before the Feast of St. Dunstan [19 May], [Robert son of] John, Richard son of John de Chesthunt, and two other boys, names unknown, were playing on certain pieces of timber in a lane called "Kyrounelane" in the Ward of Vintry, a certain piece fell on [Robert] and broke his right leg. In the course of time Johanna, his mother, arrived, and rolled the timber off him, and carried him to a shop where he lingered until

Friday... when he died at the hour of Prime of the broken leg and of no other felony, nor do they suspect anyone of the death, but only the accident and the fracture. Being asked who were present when it happened, they say the aforesaid Robert, Richard son of John de Chesthunt and two boys whose names they know not and no others.

Four neighbors attached, namely:
Richard Daske, by Peter Cosyn and Roger le Roper.
Anketin de Gisors, by Robert de Wynton and Andrew de Gloucester.
Thomas le Roper, by Richard de Colyngstoke and Thomas atte March.
John Amys, by John de Shirbourne and John de Lincoln.

2. ON THE DEATH OF NICHOLAS, SERVANT OF SIMON DE KNOTTYNGLEY

On Monday in Pentecost week the year [A.D. 1324], it happened that Nicholas, the servant of Simon de Knottyngley, lay killed before the gate of the house of William de Pomfreit in the high street in the parish of St. Botulph de Bisshopsgate.... On hearing this, the... Coroner and Sheriffs proceeded there, and having summoned good men of that Ward and of the three nearest Wards..., they diligently inquired how it happened. The jurors say that on that Monday, at break of day, William de la March, the late palfrey-man [a type of groom] of Henry de Percy, Thomas the servant of Henry de Percy's cook, John the servant to Henry Krok, who was Henry's esquire, assaulted, beat and wounded Nicholas in the house held by Alice de Witteney, a courtesan, whose landlord was John de Assheby.... William de la March struck Nicholas with a knife called an "Irishknife" under the right breast and penetrating to the belly, inflicting a wound an inch long and in depth half through the body. [Nicholas] thus wounded went from there to the place where he was found dead, where he died at daybreak of the same day. Being asked what became of the said William, Thomas and John, the jurors say that they immediately fled, but where they went or who received them they know not, nor do they suspect any one except those three. Being asked as to their goods and chattels, the jurors say that they had none, so far as could be ascertained. Being asked who first found the corpse, they say it was Thomas, son of John le Marshall, who raised the cry so that the country came. The corpse was viewed on which the wound appeared. [Order] to the Sheriff to attach the said William, Thomas and John as soon as they be found in their bailiwick.

Afterwards the William de la March was captured by Adam de Salisbury, the Sheriff and committed to Newgate [prison]. William has a surcoat which is confiscated [because of] his flight, worth two shillings, for which Adam de Salisbury the Sheriff [is responsible].

Four neighbors attached, namely:
John Assheby, by Thomas Starling and Walter de Stanes.
Walter de Bedefunte, by Walter de Northampton and John le Barber.
William de Pomfreit, by William de Chalke and Roger Swetyng.
Adam le Fuitz Robert, by Eustace le Hattere and Thomas de Borham.

3. ON THE DEATH OF THOMAS LE POUNTAGER

On Saturday the Feast of St. Laurence [10 Aug.] the year [A.D. 1325], it happened that a certain Thomas, son of John le Pountager, lay drowned in the water of the Thames before the wharf of Richard Dorking in the parish of St. Martin, in the Ward of Vintry. On hearing this, the Coroner and Sheriffs proceeded there, and having summoned good men of that Ward and of the three nearest Wards... they diligently inquired how it happened. The jurors say that when on the preceding Friday, at dusk, Thomas had placed himself on the quay of Edward le Blount to bathe in the Thames, he was accidentally drowned, no one being present; that he remained in the water until Saturday, when at the third hour John Fleg a boatman discovered his corpse and raised the cry so that the country came. The corpse viewed on which no wound or bruise appeared.
The above John Fleg, the finder of the body, attached by Robert de Lenne and Robert de Taunton.
Four neighbors attached [their names are listed in the report].

4. ON THE DEATH OF JOHANNA, DAUGHTER OF BERNARD OF IRLAUNDE

Friday after the Feast of St. Dunstan [19 May] the year [A.D. 1322], it happened that Johanna daughter of Bernard de Irlaunde, a child one month old, lay dead of a death other than her rightful death, in a shop held by the said Bernard... in the parish of St. Michael, in the Ward of Queenhithe. On hearing this, the Coroner and Sheriffs proceeded there, and having summoned good men of that Ward and of the three nearest Wards..., they diligently inquired how it happened. The jurors say that when on the preceding Thursday, before the hour of Vespers, Johanna was lying in her cradle alone, the shop door being open there entered a certain sow which mortally bit the right side of the head of Johanna. At length there came Margaret, ... Johanna's mother, and raised the cry and snatched up Johanna and kept her alive until midnight Friday when she died of the said bite and of no other felony. Being asked who were present, [the jurors] say, "No one except Margaret," nor do they suspect [any other cause] except the bite . the corpse of the said Johanna viewed on which no [other?] hurt appeared [sic]. The sow appraised by the jurors at 13 d. for which Richard Costantin, the Sheriff; [is responsible].

The above Margaret who found the body attached by John de Bedford and Andrew de Gloucester.

Four neighbors attached [their names are listed in the report].

5. ON THE DEATH OF MATILDA LA CAMBESTER AND MARGERY HER DAUGHTER

Friday after the Feast of St. Ambrose [4 April, 1337], information given to the Coroner and Sheriffs, that Matilda la Cambester and Margery her daughter aged one mouth, lay dead of a death other than their rightful death in a shop in the rent of the Prior of Tortyton in the parish of St Swythin in the Ward of Walbrok. Thereupon they proceeded there, and having summoned good men of that Ward, they diligently inquired how it happened. The jurors... say that on the preceding Thursday, after the hour of curfew when Matilda and Margery lay asleep in the shop a lighted candle which Matilda had negligently left on the wall, fell down among some straw and set fire to the shop so that the said Matilda and Margery were suffocated and burnt before the neighbors knew anything about it. The bodies viewed, &c.

Four neighbors attached [their names are listed in the report].

6. ON THE DEATH OF LUCY FAUKES

On Monday before the Feast of St. Michael [29 Sept., 1322], it happened that a certain Lucy Faukes lay dead of a death other than her rightful death in a certain shop which Richard le Sherman held of John Priour, senior, in the parish of St. Olave in the Ward of Alegate. On hearing this, the Coroner and Sheriffs proceeded thither, and having summoned good men of that Ward and of the three nearest Wards, ... they diligently inquired how it happened. The jurors say that on Sunday before the Feast of St. Matthew [2 Sept., 1322], about the hour of curfew, Lucy came to the shop in order to pass the night there with... Richard le Sherman and Cristina his wife, as she oftentimes was accustomed, and because Lucy was clad in good clothes, Richard and Cristina began to quarrel with her in order to obtain a reason for killing her for her clothes. At length Robert took up a staff called 'Balstaf;' and with the force and assistance of Cristina, struck her on the top of the head, and mortally broke and crushed the whole of her head, so that she died at once. Richard and Cristina stripped Lucy of her clothes, and immediately fled, but where they went or who received them, [the jurors] do not know. Being asked who were present when this happened, they say, "No one except the said Richard, Cristina and Lucy." Nor do they suspect anyone of the death except Richard and Cristina. Being asked about the goods and chattels of Richard and Cristina, the jurors say that they had nothing except what they took away with them. Being asked who found the dead Lucy's dead body, they say a certain Giles le Portor who raised the cry so that the country came. Order to the Sheriffs to attach the said Richard and Cristina when found in their bailiwick.

... Four neighbors attached [their names are listed in the report].

Questions:
1. *What role do members of the community have in the event of "a death other than a rightful death?"*
2. *What do these reports inform us about the living conditions in the city of London?*
3 *What do they reveal about the roles of male and female among working urban dwellers?*

9.6 Workers Revolt: The Demands of the Ciompi

The demographic disaster of the Black Death (1347–1350) and economic troubles of the fourteenth century deeply disturbed the social stability of Europe. Workers and peasants revolted against the ruling elites across Europe. In 1378 an urban revolt broke out in Florence, Italy. The revolutionaries, the Ciompi issued their demands to the Florentine Republic that was dominated by an oligarchy of wealthy merchants. Although concessions were initially granted, by 1382, the reforms were rescinded.

> **Source:** *The Society of Renaissance Florence: A Documentary Study*, ed.Gene Brucker, (New York: Harper and Row, 1971), pp. 236–39.

[July 21, 1378] When the *popolo* and the guildsmen had seized the palace [of the podestá], they sent a message to the Sig-

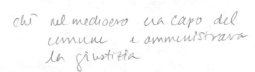

noría... that they wished to make certain demands by means of petitions, which were just and reasonable.... They said that, for the peace and repose of the city, they wanted certain things which they had decided among themselves... and they begged the priors to have them read, and then to deliberate on them, and to present them to their colleges.

The first chapter [of the petition] stated that the Lana guild[5] would no longer have a [police] official of the guild. Another was that the combers, carders, trimmers, washers, and other cloth workers would have their own [guild] consuls, and would no longer be subject to the Lana guild.

Another chapter [stated that] the Commune's funded debt would no longer pay interest, but the capital would be restored [to the shareholders] within twelve years.

Another chapter was that all outlaws and those who had been condemned by the Commune... except rebels and traitors would be pardoned. Moreover, all penalties involving a loss of a limb would be cancelled, and those who were condemned would pay a money fine.... Furthermore, for two years none of the poor people could be prosecuted for debts of 50 florins or less. For a period of six months, no forced loans were to be levied.... And within that six months' period, a schedule for levying direct taxes [*estimo*] was to be compiled....

The *popolo* entered the palace and [the podestá] departed, without any harm being done to him. They ascended the bell tower and placed there the emblem of the blacksmiths' guild, that is, the tongs. Then the banners of the other guilds, both great and small, were unfurled from the windows of the [palace of] the podestá, and also the standard of justice, but there was no flag of the Lana guild. Those inside the palace threw out and burned... every document which they found. And they remained there, all that day and night, in honor of God. Both rich and poor were there, each one to protect the standard of his guild.

The next morning the *popolo* brought the standard of justice from the palace and they marched, all armed, to the Piazza della Signoria, shouting: "Long live the *popolo minuto!*".... Then they began to cry "that the Signoria should leave, and if they didn't wish to depart, they would be taken to their homes." Into the piazza came a certain Michele di Lando, a wool-comber, who was the son of Monna Simona, who sold provisions to the prisoners in the Stinche... and he was seized and the standard of justice placed in his hands.... Then the *popolo* ordered the priors to abandon the palace. It was well furnished with supplies necessary [for defense] but they were frightened men and they left [the palace], which was the best course. Then the *popolo* entered, taking with them the standard of justice... and they entered all the rooms and they found many ropes which [the authorities] had bought to hang the poor people.... Several young men climbed the bell tower and rang the bells to signal the victory which they had won in seizing the palace, in God's honor. Then they decided to do everything necessary to fortify themselves and to liberate the *popolo minuto*. Then they acclaimed the woolcomber, Michele di Lando, as *signore* and standard-bearer of justice, and he was signore for two days.... Then [the *popolo*] decided to call other priors who would be good comrades and who would fill up the office of those priors who had been expelled. And so by acclamation, they named eight priors and the Twelve and the [Sixteen] standard-bearers.

When they wished to convene a council, these priors called together the colleges and the consuls of the guilds.... This council enacted a decree that everyone who had been proscribed as a Ghibelline since 1357 was to be restored to Guelf status[6].... And this was done to give a part to more people, and so that each would be content, and each would have a share of the offices, and so that all of the citizens would be united. Thus poor men would have their due, for they have always borne the expenses [of government], and only the rich have profited.

... And they deliberated to expand the lower guilds, and where there had been fourteen, there would now be seventeen, and thus they would be stronger, and this was done. The first new guild comprised those who worked in the woolen industry: factors, brokers in wool and in thread, workers who were employed in the dye shops and the stretching sheds, menders, sorters, shearers, beaters, combers, and weavers. These were all banded together, some nine thousand men.... The second new guild was made up of dyers, washers, carders, and makers of combs.... In the third guild were menders, trimmers, stretchers, washers, shirtmakers, tailors, stocking-makers, and makers of flags.... So all together, the lower guilds increased by some thirteen thousand men.

The lord priors and the colleges decided to burn the old Communal scrutiny lists, and this was done. Then a new scrutiny was held. The Offices were divided as follows: the [seven] greater guilds had three priors; the fourteen [lower] guilds had another three, and the three new guilds had three priors. And so a new scrutiny was completed, which satisfied many who had never before had any share of the offices, and had always borne the expenses.

Questions:
1. *Who were the workers who made up the Ciompi?*
2. *What were their demands for changes in the guilds and the government?*

---

[5] The Lana Guild is the Wool Guild dominated by the wool merchants.
[6] These were the two chief political groups fighting for control of the Florentine Republic.

PART 10
The Renaissance

10.1 Petrarch: Rules for the Ruler

Petrarch (1304–74) was one of the first humanists who made his living as a public writer, receiving patronage from the wealthy political leaders of the Italian city-states. His concerns, more than his medieval predecessors, were secular, though he did not entirely ignore religion, especially later in life. In this excerpt, he duly praises his patron and then speaks more generally about how one ought to rule a state. Like Dante a generation before him, he used the vernacular and helped to make Italian a literary language.

Source: Francesco Petrarca, *How a Ruler Ought to Govern His State,* trans. Benjamin G. Kohl, cited in *The Earthly Republic: Italian Humanists on Government and Society,* ed. Benjamin G. Kohl and Ronald G. Witt, (University of Pennsylvania Press, 1981, © 1978), pp. 35–80, passim.

. . . .

You ruled with such competence and such maturity that no rumor, no hint of rebellion, disturbed the city in that time of great change. Next, after a short time, you transformed into a large surplus the enormous deficit that debts to foreign powers had left in your treasury. And now the years and experience in government have so matured you that you are esteemed as an outstanding lord, not only by your own citizens but also by the lords of many other cities, who hold you up as a model. As a result, I have often heard neighboring peoples express the wish that they could be governed by you and nurture envy for your subjects. You have never devoted yourself to either the arrogance of pompous display or to the idleness of pleasure, but you have devoted yourself to just rule so that everyone acknowledges that you are peaceful without being feckless and dignified without being prideful. As a result, modesty coexists with magnanimity in your character. You are thus full of dignity. Although, because of your incredible humanity, you permit easy access to yourself even to the most humble, still one of your most outstanding acts is to have at the same time contracted for your daughters very advantageous marriages with noble families in distant lands.[1] And you have been, above all other rulers, a lover of public order and peace—a peace that was never thought possible by the citizen-body when Padua was ruled by a communal regime or by any of your family, no matter how long they held the power—you alone constructed many strong fortresses at suitable points along the Paduan frontiers. Thus you acted in every way so that the citizens felt free and secure with you as a ruler, and no innocent blood was spilled. You also have pacified all your neighbors either by fear or by love or by admiration for your excellence, so that for many years now you have ruled a flourishing state with serene tranquility and in continual peace. But at last the adversary of the human race, that enemy of peace [the Devil], suddenly stirred up a dangerous war with that power you never feared. Consequently, although you still loved peace, you fought with Venice bravely and with great determination over a long time, even though you lacked the aid from allies that you had hoped for. And when it seemed most advantageous to do so, you skillfully concluded peace so that at one stroke you won twofold praise both for your bravery and your political wisdom.[2] From these facts and from many others I shall omit, you have been viewed as vastly superior to all other rulers of your state and to all rulers of other cities, not only in the judgment of your own subjects but indeed in the opinion of the whole world as well.

. . . .

The first quality is that a lord should be friendly, never terrifying, to the good citizens, even though it is inevitable that he be terrifying to evil citizens if he is to be a friend to justice. "For he does not carry a sword without good cause, since he is a minister of God," as the Apostle says. Now nothing is more foolish, nothing is more destructive to the stability of the state, than to wish to be dreaded by everyone. Many princes, both in antiquity and in modern times, have wanted nothing more than to be feared and have believed that nothing is more useful than fear and cruelty in maintaining their power. Concerning this belief we have an example in the case of the barbaric emperor named Maximinus. In fact, nothing

---

[1] Francesco da Carrara contracted marriages for several of his daughters with the scions of noble houses in Italy and Germany, including the count of Oettingen, the count of Veglie, and the duke of Saxony.

[2] An allusion to the border war fought with Venice in 1372–73, which Francesco da Carrara ended by agreeing to the payment of an indemnity to Venice while he maintained substantially his original frontiers. See Paolo Sambin, "La guerra del 1372–73 tra Venezia e Padova," *Archivio Veneti* ser., 38–41 (1946–47):1–76.

is farther from the truth than these opinions; rather, it is much more advantageous to be loved than to be feared, unless we are speaking of the way in which a devoted child fears a good father. Any other kind of fear is diametrically opposed to what a ruler should desire. Rulers in general want to reign for a long time and to lead their lives in security, but to be feared is opposed to both of these desires, and to be loved is consistent with both.

· · · ·

What I can say is that the nature of public love is the same as private love. Seneca says: "I shall show you a love potion that is made without medicines, without herbs, without the incantations of any poison-maker. If you want to be loved, love." There it is. Although many other things could be said, this saying is the summation of everything. What is the need for magical arts, what for any reward or labor? Love is free; it is sought out by love alone. And who can be found with such a steely heart that he would not want to return an honorable love? "Honorable" I say, for a dishonorable love is not love at all, but rather hatred hidden under the guise of love. Now to return love to someone who loves basely is to do nothing other than to compound one crime with another and to become a part of another person's disgraceful deceit.

· · · ·

Indeed, from the discussion of this topic nothing but immense and honorable pleasure ought to come to you since you are so beloved by your subjects that you seem to them to be not a lord over citizens but the "father of your country." In fact this was the title of almost all of the emperors of antiquity; some of them bore the name justly, but others carried it so injustly that nothing more perverse can be conceived. Both Caesar Augustus and Nero were called "father of his country." The first was a true father, the second was an enemy of both his country and of religion. But this title really does belong to you.

· · · ·

You should know, moreover, that to merit this kind of esteem you must always render justice and treat your citizens with goodwill. Do you really want to be a father to your citizens? Then you must want for your subjects what you want for your own children.

· · · ·

Now I shall speak of justice, the very important and noble function that is to give to each person his due so that no one is punished without good reason. Even when there is a good reason for punishment you should incline to mercy, following the example of Our Heavenly Judge and Eternal King. For no one of us is immune from sin and all of us are weak by our very nature, so there is no one of us who does not need mercy.

· · · ·

Indeed, I do not deny, nor am I ignorant of, the fact that the lord of a city ought to take every precaution to avoid useless and superfluous expenditures. In this way he will not exhaust the treasury and have nothing left for necessary expenditures. Therefore, a lord should spend nothing and do nothing whatsoever that does not further the beauty and good order of the city over which he rules. To put it briefly, he ought to act as a careful guardian of the state, not as its lord. Such was the advice that the Philosopher gave at great length in his *Politics,* advice that is found to be very useful and clearly consistent with justice.[3] Rulers who act otherwise are to be judged as thieves rather than as defenders and preservers of the state.

· · · ·

From these concerns, however, derives not just the happiness of the people, but the security of the ruling class as well. For no one is more terrifying than a starving commoner of whom it has been said: "the hungry pleb knows no fear." Indeed, there are not just ancient examples but contemporary ones, especially from recent events in the city of Rome, which bear out this saying.[4]

---

[3] Aristotle *Politica* 5.9, 1314b40ff, which Petrarch knew only in medieval Latin translation.

[4] An allusion to a revolt—caused by famine—by the lower classes of Rome against the senatorial families in 1353, just before the return to the city of the demagogic Cola di Rienzo. See F. Gregorovius, *History of the City of Rome in the Middle Ages,* trans. A. Hamilton, 8 vols. (London, 1898), 6:337ff.

• • • •

Among those honored for their abilities in governing, the first place ought to go to learned men. And among these learned men, a major place should go to those whose knowledge in law is always very useful to the state. If, indeed, love of and devotion to justice is added to their knowledge of law, these citizens are (as Cicero puts it) "learned not just in the law, but in justice."[5] However, there are those who follow the law but do no justice, and these are unworthy to bear the name of the legal profession. For it is not enough simply to have knowledge; you must want to use it. A good lawyer adds good intentions to his legal knowledge. Indeed, there have been many lawyers who have added luster to ancient Rome and other places: Adrianus Julius Celsus, Salvius Julianus, Neratius Priscus, Antonius Scaevola, Severus Papinianus, Alexander Domitius Ulpianus, Fabius Sabinus, Julius Paulus, and many others.[6] And you too (as much as our own times permit) have by the patronage of your university added honor to your country. There are other kinds of learned men, some of whom you can depend on for advice and learned conversation, and (as Alexander used to say) invent literary tales.[7] One reads that Julius Caesar, in like fashion, used to confer Roman citizenship on doctors of medicine and on teachers of the liberal arts.[8] Now, among learned men there is no doubt that we ought to give preference to those who teach the knowledge of sacred things (or what we call theology), provided that these men have kept themselves free from any foolish sophistries.

That very wise emperor Augustus used to bestow patronage on learned men to encourage them to remain in Rome, and hope of such a reward stimulated others to study, for at that time Roman citizenship was a highly valued honor. Indeed, when St. Paul claimed that he was a Roman citizen, the tribune judging the case said to him: "I myself have at a high price obtained this status."[9]

• • • •

Even if it were not written in any book, still death is certain, as our common nature tells us. Now I do not know whether it is because of human nature or from some longstanding custom that at the death of our close friends and relatives we can scarcely contain our grief and tears, and that our funeral services are often attended by wailings and lamentations. But I do know that scarcely ever has this propensity for public grief been so deep-rooted in other cities as it is in yours. Someone dies—and I do not care whether he is a noble or a commoner, the grief displayed by the commoners is certainly no less manifest, and perhaps more so, than that of the nobles, for the plebs are more apt to show their emotions and less likely to be moved by what is proper; as soon as he breathes his last, a great howling and torrent of tears begins. Now I am not asking you to forbid expressions of grief. This would be difficult and probably impossible, given human nature. But what Jeremiah says is true: "You should not bemoan the dead, nor bathe the corpse in tears."[10] As the great poet Euripides wrote in Crespontes: "Considering the evil of our present existence, we ought to lament at our birth and rejoice at our death."[11] But these philosophic opinions are not well known, and, in any case, the common people would find them unthinkable and strange.

Therefore, I will tell you what I am asking. Take an example: [illegible] the streets and through the public squares accompanied by loud and indecent wailing so that someone who did not know what was happening could easily think that here was a madman on the loose or that the city was under enemy attack. Now, when the funeral cortege finally gets to the church, the horrible keening redoubles, and at the very spot where there ought to be hymns to Christ or devoted prayers for the soul of the deceased in a subdued voice or even silence, the walls resound with the lamentations of the mourners and the holy altars shake with the wailing of women. All this simply because a human being has died. This custom is contrary to any decent and honorable behavior and unworthy of any city under your rule. I wish you would have it changed. In fact, I am not just advising you, I am (if I may) begging you to do so. Order that wailing women should not be permitted to step outside their homes; and if some lamentation is necessary to the grieved, let them do it at home and do not let them disturb the public thoroughfares.

---

[5] Cicero *Orationes Philippicae* 9.5.10.

[6] Petrarch derived this list of famous legal experts from the time of the Roman Empire mainly from his reading of the *Scriptores historiae Augusta* passim.

[7] *Scriptores historiae Augustae* 18.34.6.

[8] Seutonius *Divus Julius* 42.

[9] Acts 22:28.

[10] Jeremiah 22:10.

[11] Cf. Cicero *Tusculane disputationes* 1.48.115, quoting Euripides.

I have said to you perhaps more than I should, but less than I would like to say. And if it seems to you, illustrious sir, that I am mistaken in one place or another, I beg your pardon, and I ask you to consider only the good advice. May you rule your city long and happily. Farewell. Arquà, the 28th of November.

Questions:
1. *What examples and sources are used to support various claims by this author?*
2. *What relation does this author have to the ancient authors of Rome and Greece?*
3. *What attitudes and aptitudes seem to describe the Renaissance man? How is Petrarch a Renaissance man?*
4. *What attitudes are expressed about the world and people about them?*
5. *What is the role of the patron in Renaissance society? How does this affect things?*

10.2 Machiavelli: from *The Discourses*

Niccolo Machiavelli's (1469–1527) political philosophy was shaped by humanism and practical experience. As a Florentine official and diplomat, Machiavelli had an opportunity to experience first hand the cut-throat world of fifteenth-century Italian politics. In the excerpt from his Discourses included here, Machiavelli used a discussion of Roman history as a vehicle for establishing general political principles.

Source: *The Discourses* (Penguin Classics), translation by Leslie Walker, ed. Bernard Crick (New York: Penguin Books, 1983), pp. 131–135.

That it is necessary to be the Sole Authority if one would constitute a Republic afresh or would reform it thoroughly regardless of its Ancient Institutions

To some it will appear strange that I have got so far in my discussion of Roman history without having made any mention of the founders of that republic or of either its religious or its military institutions. Hence, that I may not keep the minds of those who are anxious to hear about such things any longer in suspense, let me say that many perchance will think it a bad precedent that the founder of a civic state, such as Romulus, should first have killed his brother, and then have acquiesced in the death of Titus Tatius, the Sabine, whom he had chosen as his colleague in the kingdom. They will urge that, if such actions be justifiable, ambitious citizens who are eager to govern, will follow the example of their prince and use violence against those who are opposed to *their* authority. A view that will hold good provided we leave out of consideration the end which Romulus had in committing these murders.

One should take it as a general rule that rarely, if ever, does it happen that a state, whether it be a republic or a kingdom, is either well-ordered at the outset or radically transformed *vis-à-vis* its old institutions unless this be done by one person. It is likewise essential that there should be but one person upon whose mind and method depends any similar process of organization. Wherefore the prudent organizer of a state whose intention it is to govern not in his own interests but for the common good, and not in the interest of his successors but for the sake of that fatherland which is common to all, should contrive to be alone in his authority. Nor will any reasonable man blame him for taking any action, however extraordinary, which may be of service in the organizing of a kingdom or the constituting of a republic. It is a sound maxim that reprehensible actions may be justified by their effects, and that when the effect is good, as it was in the case of Romulus, it always justifies the action. For it is the man who uses violence to spoil things, not the man who uses it to mend them, that is blameworthy.

The organizer of a state ought further to have sufficient prudence and virtue not to bequeath the authority he has assumed to any other person, for, seeing that men are more prone to evil than to good, his successor might well make ambitious use of that which he had used virtuously. Furthermore, though but one person suffices for the purpose of organization, what he has organized will not last long if it continues to rest on the shoulders of one man, but may well last if many remain in charge and many look to its maintenance. Because, though the many are incompetent to draw up a constitution since diversity of opinion will prevent them from discovering how best to do it, yet when they realize it has been done, they will not agree to abandon it.

That Romulus was a man of this character, that for the death of his brother and of his colleague he deserves to be excused, and that what he did was done for the common good and not to satisfy his personal ambition, is shown by his having at once instituted a senate with which he consulted and with whose views his decisions were in accord. Also, a careful consideration of the authority which Romulus reserved to himself will show that all he reserved to himself was the command of the army in time of war and the convoking of the senate. It is clear, too, that when the Tarquins were expelled and Rome became free, none of its ancient institutions were changed, save that in lieu of a permanent king there were appointed each year two consuls. This shows that the original institutions of this city as a whole were more in conformity with a political and self-governing state than with absolutism or tyranny.

I might adduce in support of what I have just said numberless examples, for example Moses, Lycurgus, Solon and other founders of kingdoms and republics who assumed authority that they might formulate laws to the common good; but this I propose to omit since it is well known. I shall adduce but one further example, not so celebrated but worth considering by those who are contemplating the drawing up of good laws. It is this. Agis, King of Sparta, was considering how to confine the activities of the Spartans to the limits originally set for them by the laws of Lycurgus, because it seemed to him that it was owing to their having deviated from them in part that this city had lost a good deal of its ancient virtue, and, in consequence, a good deal of its power and of its empire. He was, however, while his project was still in the initial stage, killed by the Spartan ephors, who took him to be a man who was out to set up a tyranny. But Cleomenes, his successor in that kingdom, having learned from some records and writings of Agis which he had discovered, what was the latter's true mind and intention, determined to pursue the same plan. He realized, however, that be could not do this for the good of his country unless he became the sole authority there, and, since it seemed to him impossible owing to man's ambition to help the many against the will of the few, he took a suitable opportunity and had all the ephors killed and anybody else who might obstruct him. He then renewed in their entirety the laws of Lycurgus. By so doing he gave fresh life to Sparta, and his reputation might thereby have become as great as that of Lycurgus if it had not been for the power of the Macedonians and the weakness of other Greek republics. For, after Sparta had thus been reorganized, it was attacked by the Macedonians, and, since its forces proved to be inferior and it could get no outside help, it was defeated, with the result that Cleomenes' plans, however just and praiseworthy, were never brought to completion.

All things considered, therefore, I conclude that it is necessary to be the sole authority if one is to organize a state, and that Romulus' action in regard to the death of Remus and Titus Tatius is excusable, not blameworthy.

Question:
1. Does the end always justify the means?

10.3 Christopher Columbus: *The Letters of Columbus to Ferdinand and Isabel*

Historians debate whether Christopher Columbus (1451–1506) was or was not the first European to reach the Americas. What is beyond dispute, however, is that his voyages sparked an unprecedented period of European exploration and expansion. In his letter to Ferdinand and Isabel included here, Columbus painted a picture of the New World calculated to please his royal patrons.

Source: *The Journal of Christopher Columbus*, translation by Cecil Jane (London: Anthony Blond, 1968) pp. 191, 194, 196–198, 200–201.

SIR: Since I know that you will be pleased at the great victory with which Our Lord has crowned my voyage, I write this to you, from which you will learn how in thirty-three days I passed from the Canary Islands to the Indies, with the fleet which the most illustrious King and Queen, our Sovereigns, gave to me. There I found very many islands, filled with innumerable people, and I have taken possession of them all for their Highnesses, done by proclamation and with the royal standard unfurled, and no opposition was offered to me.

To the first island which I found I gave the name "San Salvador," in remembrance of the Divine Majesty, Who had marvellously bestowed all this; the Indians call it "Guanahani." To the second, I gave the name the island of "Santa Maria de Concepcion," to the third, "Fernandina," to the fourth, "Isabella," to the fifth island, "Juana," and so each received from me a new name. . . .

Española is a marvel. The sierras and the mountains, the plains, the champaigns, are so lovely and so rich for planting and sowing, for breeding cattle of every kind, for building towns and villages. The harbours of the sea here are such as cannot be believed to exist unless they have been seen, and so with the rivers, many and great, and of good water, the majority of which contain gold. In the trees, fruits and plants, there is a great difference from those of Juana. In this island, there are many spices and great mines of gold and of other metals.

The people of this island and of all the other islands which I have found and of which I have information, all go naked, men and women, as their mothers bore them, although some of the women cover a single place with the leaf of a plant or with a net of cotton which they make for the purpose. They have no iron or steel or weapons, nor are they fitted to use them. This is not because they are not well built and of handsome stature, but because they are very marvellously

135

timorous. They have no other arms than spears made of canes, cut in seeding time, to the ends of which they fix a small sharpened stick. Of these they do not dare to make use, for many times it has happened that I have sent ashore two or three men to some town to have speech with them, and countless people have come out to them, and as soon as they have seen my men approaching, they have fled, a father not even waiting for his son. This is not because ill has been done to any one of them; on the contrary, at every place where I have been and have been able to have speech with them, I have given to them of that which I had, such as cloth and many other things, receiving nothing in exchange. But so they are, incurably timid. It is true that, after they have been reassured and have lost this fear, they are so guileless and so generous with all that they possess, that no one would believe it who has not seen it. They refuse nothing that they possess, if it be asked of them; on the contrary, they invite any one to share it and display as much love as if they would give their hearts. They are content with whatever trifle of whatever kind that may be given to them, whether it be of value or valueless. I forbade that they should be given things so worthless as fragments of broken crockery, scraps of broken glass and lace tips, although when they were able to get them, they fancied that they possessed the best jewel in the world. So it was found that for a thong a sailor received gold to the weight of two and a half Castellanos, and others received much more for other things which were worth less. As for new blancas, for them they would give everything which they had, although it might be two or three castellanos' [gold coins] weight of gold or an arroba or two of spun cotton. They took even the pieces of the broken hoops of the wine barrels and, like savages, gave what they had, so that it seemed to me to be wrong and I forbade it. I gave them a thousand handsome good things, which I had brought, in order that they might conceive affection for us and, more than that, might become Christians and be inclined to the love and service of Your Highnesses and of the whole Castilian nation, and strive to collect and give us of the things which they have in abundance and which are necessary to us.

They do not hold any creed nor are they idolaters; but they all believe that power and good are in the heavens and were very firmly convinced that I, with these ships and men, came from the heavens, and in this belief they everywhere received me after they had mastered their fear. This belief is not the result of ignorance, for they are, on the contrary, of a very acute intelligence and they are men who navigate all those seas, so that it is amazing how good an account they give of everything. It is because they have never seen people clothed or ships of such a kind.

As soon as I arrived in the Indies, in the first island which I found, I took some of the natives by force, in order that they might learn and might give me information of whatever there is in these parts. And so it was that they soon understood us, and we them, either by speech or signs, and they have been very serviceable. At present, those I bring with me are still of the opinion that I come from Heaven, for all the intercourse which they have had with me. They were the first to announce this wherever I went, and the others went running from house to house, and to the neighbouring towns, with loud cries of, "Come! Come! See the men from Heaven!" So all came, men and women alike, when their minds were set at rest concerning us, not one, small or great, remaining behind, and they all brought something to eat and drink, which they gave with extraordinary affection. . . .

In all these islands, I saw no great diversity in the appearance of the people or in their manners and language. On the contrary, they all understand one another, which is a very curious thing, on account of which I hope that their Highnesses will determine upon their conversion to our holy faith, towards which they are very inclined.

I have already said how I went one hundred and seven leagues in a straight line from west to east along the seashore of the island of Juana, and as a result of this voyage I can say that this island is larger than England and Scotland together, for, beyond these one hundred and seven leagues, there remain to the westward two provinces to which I have not gone. One of these provinces they call "Avan," and there people are born with tails. These provinces cannot have a length of less than fifty or sixty leagues, as I could understand from those Indians whom I have and who know all the islands.

The other island, Española, has a circumference greater than all Spain from Collioure by the seacoast to Fuenterabia in Vizcaya, for I voyaged along one side for one hundred and eighty-eight great leagues in a straight line from west to east. It is a land to be desired and, when seen, never to be left. I have taken possession of all for their Highnesses, and all are more richly endowed than I know how or am able to say, and I hold all for their Highnesses, so that they may dispose of them as they do of the kingdoms of Castile and as absolutely. But especially, in this Española, in the situation most convenient and in the best position for the mines of gold and for all trade as well with the mainland here as with that there, belonging to the Grand Khan, where will be great trade and profit, I have taken possession of a large town, to which I gave the name "Villa de Navidad," and in it I have made fortifications and a fort, which will now by this time be entirely completed. In it I have left enough men for such a purpose with arms and artillery and provisions for more than a year, and a fusta, and one, a master of all seacraft, to build others, and I have established great friendship with the king of that land, so much so, that he was proud to call me "brother" and to treat me as such. . . .

In conclusion, to speak only of what has been accomplished on this voyage, which was so hasty, their Highnesses can see that I will give them as much gold as they may need, if their Highnesses will render me very slight assistance; presently, I will give them spices and cotton, as much as their Highnesses shall command; and mastic, as much as they shall order to be shipped and which, up to now, has been found only in Greece, in the island of Chios, and the Seignory sells it for what it pleases; and aloe, as much as they shall order to be shipped; and slaves, as many as they shall order, and who will be from the idolaters. I believe also that I have found rhubarb and cinnamon, and I shall find a thousand other things of value, which the people whom I have left there will have discovered, for I have not delayed at any point, so far as the wind allowed me to sail, except in the town of Navidad, in order to leave it secured and well established, and in truth I should have done much more if the ships had served me as reason demanded. . . .

This is an account of the facts, thus abridged.

Done in the caravel, off the Canary Islands, on the fifteenth day of February, in the year one thousand four hundred and ninety-three.

Question:
1. How could Columbus reconcile his views of the native peoples with his stated intention of taking their gold and enslaving them?

10.4 Bartholomew De Las Casas: *Amerindians and the "Garden of Eden"*

When Bartholomé De Las Casas (1474–1566) was twenty-eight years old, he made his first trip to the Americas. By 1514, he had committed himself to pressuring the Spanish government to improve the treatment of the Amerindians, to abolish slavery and forced labor, and to devote more resources to the spread of Catholicism in the New World. He would spend his entire life working towards these goals.

> **Source:** Bartholomew De Las Casas: *His Life, His Apostolate, and His Writings*, translation by Francis Augustus McNutt (New York, 1909), pp. 314–315.

God has created all these numberless people to be quite the simplest, without malice or duplicity, most obedient, most faithful to their natural Lords, and to the Christians, whom they serve; the most humble, most patient, most peaceful, and calm, without strife nor tumults; not wrangling, nor querulous, as free from uproar, hate and desire of revenge, as any in the world.

They are likewise the most delicate people, weak and of feeble constitution, and less than any other can they bear fatigue, and they very easily die of whatsoever infirmity; so much so, that not even the sons of our Princes and of nobles, brought up in royal and gentle life, are more delicate than they; although there are among them such as are of the peasant class. They are also a very poor people, who of worldly goods possess little, nor wish to possess: and they are therefore neither proud, nor ambitious, nor avaricious. . . .

They are likewise of a clean, unspoiled, and vivacious intellect, very capable, and receptive to every good doctrine; most prompt to accept our Holy Catholic Faith, to be endowed with virtuous customs; and they have as little difficulty with such things as any people created by God in the world.

Once they have begun to learn of matters pertaining to faith, they are so importunate to know them, and in frequenting the sacraments and divine service of the Church, that to tell the truth, the clergy have need to be endowed of God with the gift of preeminent patience to bear with them: and finally, I have heard many lay Spaniards frequently say many years ago, (unable to deny the goodness of those they saw) certainly these people were the most blessed of the earth, had they only knowledge of God.

THE "SINS" OF THE SPANISH INVASION

Militant friars like Las Casas and many of his fellow Dominicans also tried to picture the Spanish conquistadors and settlers as vicious and cruel exploiters. These tales had some basis in reality, but they were also aimed at convincing a European audience that the excesses of the conquest had to be curbed and the powers of the crown and the clergy expanded in the New World. Along with the images of the indigenous peoples as innocents reminiscent of the Garden of Eden, they created a powerful picture of European excesses. According to many friars, these abuses undermined the chances for salvation of all Christians who tolerated such "sins" against humanity. The selection below is taken from Bartolomé de las Casas, Very Brief Account of the Destruction of the Indies, *trans. Francis Augusts MacNutt in* Bartholomew De Las Casas, *319–20.*

The Christians, with their horses and swords and lances, began to slaughter and practise strange cruelty among them. They penetrated into the country and spared neither children nor the aged, nor pregnant women, nor those in child labour, all of whom they ran through the body and lacerated, as though they were assaulting so many lambs herded in their sheepfold.

They made bets as to who would slit a man in two, or cut off his head at one blow: or they opened up his bowels. They tore the babes from their mothers' breast by the feet, and dashed their heads against the rocks. Others they seized by the shoulders and threw into the rivers, laughing and joking, and when they fell into the water they exclaimed: "boil body of so and so!" They spitted the bodies of other babes, together with their mothers and all who were before them, on their swords.

They made a gallows just high enough for the feet to nearly touch the ground, and by thirteens, in honour and reverence of our Redeemer and the twelve Apostles, they put wood underneath and, with fire, they burned the Indians alive. . . .

And because all the people who could flee, hid among the mountains and climbed the crags to escape from men so deprived of humanity, so wicked, such wild beasts, exterminators and capital enemies of all the human race, the Spaniards taught and trained the fiercest boar-hounds to tear an Indian to pieces as soon as they saw him, so that they more willingly attacked and ate one, than if he had been a boar. These hounds made great havoc and slaughter.

Question:
1. What are the similarities between Columbus's view of the natives and that of Las Casas? What explains the dramatic difference in how they sought to treat the natives?

10.5   Cellini: The Artist

Cellini (1500–1571) was an artist who made his living as a goldsmith in the Italian city-states of Florence and Rome. He was also quite a talented musician. The following excerpt, from his autobiography, written between 1558–1562, describes his life and work as an artist. It was not published until the eighteenth century, when it became quite popular.

Source: Benvenuto Cellini, *The Life of Benvenuto Ceillini,* 4th edition, trans. J. A. Symonds, cited in ed. John L. Beatty and Oliver A. Johnson, *Heritage of Western Civilization,* vol. 1, 7th edition, (Englewood Cliffs, NJ: Prentice Hall, 1991), pp. 397–411, passim.

II

It is true that men who have laboured with some show of excellence, have already given knowledge of themselves to the world; and this alone ought to suffice them; I mean the fact that they have proved their manhood and achieved renown. Yet one must needs live like others; and so in a work like this there will always be found occasion for natural bragging, which is of divers kinds, and the first is that a man should let others know he draws his lineage from persons of worth and most ancient origin.

When I reached the age of fifteen, I put myself, against my father's will, to the goldsmith's trade with a man called Antonio, son of Sandro, known commonly as Marcone the goldsmith. He was a most excellent craftsman and a very good fellow to boot, high-spirited and frank in all his ways. My father would not let him give me wages like the other apprentices; for having taken up the study of this art to please myself, he wished me to indulge by whim for drawing to the full. I did so willingly enough; and that honest master of mine took marvellous delight in my performances. He had an only son, a bastard, to whom he often gave his orders, in order to spare me. My liking for the art was so great, or, I may truly say, my natural bias, both one and the other, that in a few months I caught up the good, nay, the best young craftsmen in our business, and began to reap the fruits of my labours. I did not, however, neglect to gratify my good father from time to time by playing on the flute or cornet. Each time he heard me, I used to make his tears fall accompanied with deep-drawn sighs of satisfaction. My filial piety often made me give him that contentment, and induced me to pretend that I enjoyed the music too.

XIV

[... Later, after traveling to Rome, he entered a new workshop]
"Welcome to my workshop; and do as you have promised; let your hands declare what man you are."

He gave me a very fine piece of silver plate to work on for a cardinal. It was a little oblong box, copied from the prophyry sarcophagus before the door of the Rotonda. Beside what I copied, I enriched it with so many elegant masks of my invention, that my master went about showing it through the art, and boasting that so good a piece of work had been turned out from his shop. It was about half a cubit in size, and was so constructed as to serve for a salt-cellar at table. This was the first earning that I touched at Rome, and part of it I sent to assist my good father; the rest I kept for my own use, living upon it while I went about studying the antiquities of Rome, until my money failed, and I had to return to the shop for work.

· · ·

After undertaking some new commissions, I took it into my head, as soon as I had finished them, to change my master; I had indeed been worried into doing so by a certain Milanese, called Pagolo Arsago. My first master, Firenzuola, had a great quarrel about this with Arsago, and abused him in my presence; whereupon I took up speech in defence of my new master. I said that I was born free, and free I meant to live, and that there was no reason to complain of him, far less of me, since some few crowns of wages were still due to me; also that I chose to go, like a free journeyman, where it pleased me, knowing I did wrong to no man. My new master then put in with his excuses, saying that he had not asked me to come, and that I should gratify him by returning to Firenzuola. To this I replied that I was not aware of wronging the latter in any way, and as I had completed his commissions, I chose to be my own master and not the man of others, and that he who wanted me must beg me of myself. Firenzuola cried: "I don't intend to beg you of yourself; I have done with you; don't show yourself again upon my premises." I reminded him of the money he owed me. He laughed me in the face; on which I said that if I knew how to use my tools in handicraft as well as he had seen, I could be quite as clever with my sword in claiming the just payment of my labour. While we were exchanging these words, an old man happened to come up, called Maestro Antonio, of San Marino. He was the chief among the Roman goldsmiths, and had been Firenzuola's master. Hearing what I had to say, which I took good care that he should understand, he immediately espoused my cause, and bade Firenzuola pay me. The dispute waxed warm, because Firenzuola was an admirable swordsman, far better than he was a goldsmith. Yet reason made itself heard; and I backed my cause with the same spirit, till I got myself paid. In course of time Firenzuola and I became friends, and at his request I stood godfather to one of his children.

XV

I went on working with Pagolo Arsago, and earned a good deal of money, the greater part of which I always sent to my good father. At the end of two years, upon my father's entreaty, I returned to Florence, and put myself once more under Francesco Salimbene, with whom I earned a great deal, and took continual pains to improve in my arts. I renewed my intimacy with Francesco di Filippo; and though I was too much given to pleasure, owing to that accursed music, I never neglected to devote some hours of the day or night to study.

. . .

XIX

. . .

During that time I went to draw sometimes in Michel Agnolo's chapel, and sometimes in the house of Agostino Chigi of Siena, which contained many incomparable paintings by the hand of that great master Raffaello., This I did on feast-days, because the house was then inhabited by Messer Gismondo, Agostino's brother. They plumed themselves exceedingly when they saw young men of my sort coming to study in their palaces. Gismondo's wife, noticing my frequent presence in that house, she was a lady as courteous as could be, and of surpassing beauty, came up to me one day, looked at my drawings, and asked me if I was a sculptor or a painter; to whom I said I was a goldsmith. She remarked that I drew too well for a goldsmith; and having made one of her waiting-maids bring a lily of the finest diamonds set in gold, she showed it to me, and bade me value it. I valued it at 800 crowns. Then she said that I had very nearly hit the mark, and asked me whether I felt capable of setting the stones really well. I said that I should much like to do so, and began before her eyes to make a little sketch for it, working all the better because of the pleasure I took in conversing with so lovely and agreeable a gentlewoman. When the sketch was finished, another Roman lady of great beauty joined us; she had been above, and now descending to the ground-floor, asked Madonna Porzia what she was doing there. She answered with a smile: "I am amusing myself by watching this worthy young man at his drawing; he is as good as he is handsome." I had by this time acquired a trifle of assurance, mixed, however, with some honest bashfulness; so I blushed and said: "Such as I am, lady, I shall ever be most ready to serve you." The gentlewoman, also slightly blushing, said: "You know well that I want you to serve me"; and reaching me the lily, told me to take it away; and gave me besides twenty golden crowns which she had in her bag, and added: "Set me the jewel after the fashion you have sketched, and keep for me the old gold in which it is now set." On this the Roman lady observed: "If I were in that young man's body, I should go off without asking leave." Madonna Porzia replied that virtues rarely are at home with vices, and that if I did such a thing, I should strongly belie my good looks of an honest man. Then turning round, she took the Roman lady's hand, and with a pleasant smile said: "Farewell, Benvenuto." I stayed on a short while at the drawing I was making, which was a copy of a Jove by Raffaello. When I had finished it and left the house, I set myself to making a little model of wax, in order to show how the jewel would look when it was completed. This I took to Madonna Porzia, whom I found with the same Roman lady. Both of them were highly satisfied with my work, and treated me so kindly that, being somewhat emboldened, I promised the jewel should be twice as good as the model. Accordingly I set hand to it, and in twelve days I finished it in the form of a fleur-de-lys, as I have said above, ornamenting it with little masks, children, and animals, exquisitely enamelled, whereby the diamonds which formed the lily were more than doubled in effect.

XX

While I was working at this piece, Lucagnolo, of whose ability I have before spoken, showed considerable discontent, telling me over and over again that I might acquire far more profit and honour by helping him to execute large plate, as I had done at first. I made him answer that, whenever I chose, I should always be capable of working at great silver pieces; but that things like that on which I was now engaged were not commissioned every day; and beside their bringing no less honour than large silver plate, there was also more profit to be made by them. He laughed me in the face, and said: "Wait and see Benvenuto; for by the time that you have finished that work of yours, I will make haste to have finished this vase, which I took in hand when you did the jewel; and then experience shall teach you what profit I shall get from my vase, and what you will get from your ornament." I answered that I was very glad indeed to enter into such a competition with so good a craftsman as he was, because the end would show which of us was mistaken. Accordingly both the one and the other of us, with a scornful smile upon our lips, bent our heads in grim earnest to the work, which both were now desirous of accomplishing; so that after about ten days, each had finished his undertaking with the great delicacy and artistic skill.

. . .

So he took his vase and carried it to the Pope, who was very well pleased with it, and ordered at once that he should be paid at the ordinary rate of such large plate. Meanwhile I carried mine to Madonna Porzia, who looked at it with astonishment, and told me I had far surpassed my promise. Then she bade me ask for my reward whatever I liked; for it seemed to her my desert was so great that if I craved a castle she could hardly recompense me; but since that was not in her hands to bestow, she added laughing that I must beg what lay within her power. I answered that the greatest reward I could desire for my labour was to have satisfied her ladyship. Then, smiling in my turn, and bowing to her, I took my leave, saying I wanted no reward but that. She turned to the Roman lady and said: "You see that the qualities we discerned in him are companied by virtues, and not vices." They both expressed their admiration, and then Madonna Porzio continued: "Friend Benvenuto, have you never heard it said that when the poor give to the rich, the devil laughs?" I replied: "Quite true! and yet, in the midst of all his troubles, I should like this time to see him laugh"; and as I took my leave, she said that this time she had no will to bestow on him that favour.

When I came back to the shop, Lucagnolo had the money for his vase in a paper packet; and on my arrive he cried out: "Come and compare the price of your jewel with the price of my plate." I said that he must leave things as they were till the next day, because I hoped that even as my work in its kind was not less excellent than his, so I should be able to show him quite an equal price for it.

XXI

On the following, Madonna Porzia sent a major-domo of hers to my shop, who called me out, and putting into my hands a paper packet full of money from his lady, told me that she did not choose the devil should have his whole laugh out; by which she hinted that the money sent me was not the entire payment merited by my industry, and other messages were added worthy of so courteous a lady. Lucagnolo, who was burning to compare his packet with mine, burst into the shop, then in the presence of twelve journeymen and some neighbors, eager to behold the result of this competition, he seized his packetd, scornfully exclaiming "Ou! Ou!" three or four times, while he poured his money on the counter with a great noise. They were twenty-five crowns in giulios; and he fancied that mine would be four or five crowns di moneta. I for my part, stunned and stifled by his cries, and by the looks and smiles of the bystanders, first peeped into my packet; then, after seeing that it contained nothing but gold, I retired to one end of the counter, and keeping my eyes lowered and making no noise at all, I lifted it with both hands suddenly above my head, and emptied it like a mill hopper. My coin was twice as much as his; which caused the onlookers, who had fixed their eyes on me with some derision, to turn round suddenly to him and say: "Lucagnolo, Benvenuto's pieces, being all of gold and twice as many as yours, make a far finer effect." I thought for certain that, what with jealousy and what with shame, Lucagnolo would have fallen dead upon the spot; and though he took the third part of my gain, since I was a journeymen (for such is the custom of the trade, two-thirds fall to the workman and one-third to the masters of the shop), yet inconsiderate envy had more power in him than avarice: it ought indeed to have worked quite the other way; he being a peasant's son from Iesi. He cursed his art and those who taught it to him, vowing that thenceforth he would never work at large plate, but give his whole attention to those whoreson gewgaws, since they were so well paid. Equally engaged on my side, I answered that every bird sang its own note; that he talked after the fashion of the hovels he came from; but that I dared swear that I should succeed with ease in making his lubberly lumber, while he would never be successful in my whoreson gewgaws. Thus I flung off in a passion, telling him that I would soon show him that I spoke truth. The bystanders openly declared against him, holding him for a lout, as indeed he was, and me for a man, as I had proved myself.

• • •

XXIII

While I was pushing forward Salamanca's vase, I had only one little boy as help, whom I had taken at the entreaty of friends, and half against my own will, to be my workman. He was about fourteen years of age, bore the name of Paulino, and was son to a Roman burgess, who lived upon the income of his property. Paulino was the best-mannered, the most honest, and the most beautiful boy I ever saw in my whole life. His modest ways and actions, together with his superlative beauty and his devotion to myself, bred in me as great an affection for him as a man's breast can hold. This passionate love led me often-times to delight the lad with music; for I observed that his marvellous features, which by complexion wore a tone of modest melancholy, brightened up, and when I took my cornet, broke into a smile so lovely and sweet, that I do not marvel at the silly stories which the Greeks have written about the deities of heaven. Indeed, if my boy had lived in those times, he would probably have turned their heads still more. He had a sister, named Faustina, more beautiful, I verily believe, than that Faustina about whom the old books gossip so. Sometimes he took me to their vineyard, and, so far as I could judge, it struck me that Paulino's good father would have welcomed me as a son-in-law. This affair led me to play more than I was used to do.

It happened at that time that one Giangiacomo of Cesena, a musician in the Pope's band, and a very excellent performer, sent word through Lorenzo, the trumpeter of Lucca, who is now in our Duke's service, to inquire whether I was inclined to help them at the Pope's Ferragosto, playing soprano with my cornet in some motets of great beauty selected by them for that occasion. Although I had the greatest desire to finish the vase I had begun, yet, since music has a wondrous charm of its own, and also because I wished to please my old father, I consented to join them. During eight days before the festival we practised two hours a day together; then on the first of August we went to the Belvedere, and while Pope Clemente was at table, we played those carefully studied motets so well that his Holiness protested he had never heard music more sweetly executed or with better harmony of parts. He sent for Giangiacomo, and asked him where and how he had procured so excellent a cornet for soprano, and inquired particularly who I was. Giangiacomo told him my name in full. Whereupon the Pope said: "So, then, he is the son of Maestro Giovanni?" On being assured I was, the Pope expressed his wish to have me in his service with the other bandsmen. Giangiacomo replied: "Most blessed Father, I cannot pretend for certain that you will get him, for his profession, to which he devotes himself assiduously, is that of a goldsmith, and he works in it miraculously well, and earns by it far more than he could do by playing." To this the Pope added: "I am the better inclined to him now that I find him possessor of a talent more than I expected. See that he obtains the same salary as the rest of you; and tell him from me to join my service, and that I will find work enough by the day for him to do at his other trade." Then stretching out his hand, he gave him a hundred golden crowns of the Camera in a handkerchief, and said: "Divide these so that he may take his share."

Questions:

1. What examples and sources are used to support various claims by this author?
2. What relation does this author have to the ancient authors of Rome and Greece?
3. What attitudes and aptitudes seem to describe the Renaissance man? How is Cellini a Renaissance man?

10.6 Marriage: A Serious Business

Marriage relations in Medieval and Renaissance Europe were not just about love—or rather they were not at all about love. Particularly among the elites of long-standing, blood and family ties were valued more than almost anything else. In the following excerpt, we see some of the honor, prestige, and property that were at stake in marriage negotiations in fourteenth-century Italy.

> **Source:** "Letters from Alessandra Strozzi in Florence to her son Filippo in Naples" Alessandra Macinghi Strozzi, *Lettere di una gentildonna florentina*, ed. C. Guasti, (Florence, 1877), pp. 394–95, 458–59, 463–65, 475–76, cited in *The Society of Renaissance Florence: A Documentary Study*, ed. Gene Brucker, (New York: Harper and Row, Inc., 1972), pp. 37–40.

MARRIAGE NEGOTIATIONS: THE STROZZI, 1464–65

[April 20, 1464]... Concerning the matter of a wife [for Filippo], it appears to me that if Francesco di Messer Guglielmino Tanagli wishes to give his daughter, that it would be a fine marriage.... Now I will speak with Marco [Parenti, Alessandra's son-in-law], to see if there are other prospects that would be better, and if there are none, then we will learn if he wishes to give her [in marriage].... Francesco Tanagli has a good reputation, and he has held office, not the highest, but still he has been in office. You may ask: "Why should he give her to someone in exile?" There are three reasons. First, there aren't many young men of good family who have both virtue and property. Secondly, she has only a small dowry, 1,000 florins, which is the dowry of an artisan.... Third, I believe that he will give her away, because he has a large family and he will need help to settle them....

[July 26, 1465]... Marco Parenti came to me and told me that for some time, he has been considering how to find a wife for you.... There is the daughter of Francesco di Messer Guglielmino Tanagli, and until now there hasn't been anyone who is better suited for you than this girl. It is true that we haven't discussed this at length, for a reason which you understand. However, we have made secret inquiries, and the only people who are willing to make a marriage agreement with exiles have some flaw, either a lack of money or something else. Now money is the least serious drawback, if the other factors are positive.... Francesco is a good friend of Marco and he trusts him. On S. Jacopo's day, he spoke to him discreetly and persuasively, saying that for several months he had heard that we were interested in the girl and... that when we had made up our minds, she will come to us willingly. [He said that] you were a worthy man, and that his family had always made good marriages, but that he had only a small dowry to give her, and so he would prefer to send her outside of Florence to someone of worth, rather than to give her to someone here, from among those who were available, with little money.... He invited Marco to his house and he called the girl down.... Marco said that she was attractive and that she appeared to be suitable. We have information that she is affable and competent. She is responsible for a large family (there are twelve children, six boys and six girls), and the mother is always pregnant and isn't very competent....

[August 17, 1465]... Sunday morning I went to the first mass at S. Reparata... to see the Adimari girl, who customarily goes to that mass, and I found the Tanagli girl there. Not knowing who she was, I stood beside her.... She is very attractive, well proportioned, as large or larger than Caterina [Alessandra's daughter].... She has a long face, and her features are not very delicate, but they aren't like a peasant's. From her demeanor, she does not appear to me to be indolent.... I walked behind her as we left the church, and thus I realized that she was one of the Tanagli. So I am somewhat enlightened about her....

[August 31, 1465]... I have recently received some very favorable information [about the Tanagli girl] from two individuals.... They are in agreement that whoever gets her will be content.... Concerning her beauty, they told me what I had already seen, that she is attractive and well-proportioned. Her face is long, but I couldn't look directly into her face, since she appeared to be aware that I was examining her... and so she turned away from me like the wind.... She reads quite well... and she can dance and sing.... Her father is one of the most respected young men of Florence, very civilized in his manners. He is fond of this girl, and it appears that he has brought her up well.

So yesterday I sent for Marco and told him what I had learned. And we talked about the matter for a while, and decided that he should say something to the father and give him a little hope, but not so much that we couldn't withdraw, and find out from him the amount of the dowry.... Marco and Francesco [Tanagli] had a discussion, about this yesterday (I haven't seen him since), and Marco should inform you about it one of these days, and you will then understand more clearly what should follow. May God help us to choose what will contribute to our tranquillity and to the consolation of us all....

[September 13, 1465]... Marco came to me and said that he had met with Francesco Tanagli, who had spoken very coldly, so that I understand that he had changed his mind. They say that he wants to discuss the matter with his brother-in-law, Messer Antonio Ridolfi.... And he [Francesco] says that it would be a serious matter to send his daughter so far away [to Naples], and to a house that might be described as a hotel. And he spoke in such a way that it is clear that he has changed his mind. I believe that this is the result of the long delay in our replying to him, both yours and Marco's. Two weeks ago, he could have given him a little hope. Now this delay has angered him, and he has at hand some prospect that is more attractive.... I am very annoyed by this business; I can't recall when I have been so troubled. For I felt that this marriage would have satisfied our needs better than any other we could have found....

[Filippo Strozzi eventually married Fiametta di Donato Adimari, in 1466.]

Questions:

These questions refer to this document and the following document 10.7 On Wifely Duties.

1. What comparisons can be made between the lives and responsibilities of men and women based on these Renaissance documents?
2. Historian Joan Kelly, in an article published in *Becoming Visible: Women in European History* in 1977, asked "did women have a Renaissance?" How would you answer this question based on the documents provided? Be sure to define what you mean by Renaissance.

10.7 *On Wifely Duties*

Francesco Barbaro wrote On Wifely Duties to his friend and fellow aristocrat, Lorenzo de Medici, on the occasion of the latter's marriage in 1416. He hoped to teach the youth of Florence through de Medici's example and the circulation of his treatise under Medici's auspices. He also wanted to stress the importance of marriage to the maintenance of the aristocratic ruling families of his native Venice in particular and to the Italian city-states more generally.

Source: Francesco Barbaro, On Wifely Duties, trans. Benjamin G. Kohl, cited in *The Earthly Republic: Italian Humanists on Government and Society,* ed. Benjamin G. Kohl and Ronald G. Witt, (University of Pennsylvania Press, 1981, © 1978), pp. 189–230, passim.

CHAPTER 1. ON THE FACULTY OF OBEDIENCE

This is now the remaining part to be done here, in which if wives follow me, either of their own free will or by the commands of their husbands, no one will be so unfair as to think that I have not so established the duties of the wife that youth can enjoy peace and quiet the whole life long. Therefore, there are three things that, if they are diligently observed by a wife, will make a marriage praiseworthy and admirable: love for her husband, modesty of life, and diligent and complete care in domestic matters. We shall discuss the first of these, but before this I want to say something about the faculty of obedience, which is her master and companion, because nothing more important, nothing greater can be demanded of a wife than this.

. . .

If a husband, excited to anger, should scold you more than your ears are accustomed to hear, tolerate his wrath silently. But if he has been struck silent by a fit of depression, you should address him with sweet and suitable words, encourage, console, amuse, and humor him. Those who work with elephants do not wear white clothes, and those who work with wild bulls are right not to wear red; for those beasts are made ever more ferocious by those colors. Many authors report that tigers are angered by drums and made violent by them. Wives ought to observe the same thing; if, indeed, a particular dress is offensive to a husband, then we advise them not to wear it, so that they do not give affront to their husbands, with whom they ought to live peacefully and pleasantly.

. . .

The wife who is angry with her husband because of jealousy and is considering a separation should ask herself this question: If I put myself in a workhouse because I hate a whore, what could make her far happier and more fortunate than this? She would see me almost shipwrecked, while at the same time she was sailing with favorable winds and securely casting her anchor into my marriage bed?

. . .

It was considered very good for domestic peace and harmony if a wife kept her husband's love with total diligence. At the olympic games that were dedicated to the great god Jupiter and attended by all of Greece, Gorgias used his eloquence to urge a union of all the Greeks. Melanthus said: Our patron attempts to persuade us that we should all join together in a league, but he cannot bring himself and his wife and her maid—who are only three people—to a mutual agreement (for the wife was very jealous because Gorgias was wildly enamoured of her maid). Likewise, Philip was for a long time displeased with the queen Olympias and Alexander. And when Demaratus of Corinth returned from Greece, Philip eagerly and closely questioned him about the union of the Greeks. Demaratus said to him: "Philip, I consider it a very bad thing that you are spending all your energy in bringing peace and concord to all of Greece when you are not yet reconciled with your own wife and son." Therefore, if any woman wants to govern her children and servants, she should make sure that she is, first of all, at peace with her husband. Otherwise, it will seem that she wants to imitate the very things that she is trying to correct in them. In order that a wife does her duty and brings peace and harmony to her household, she must agree to the first principle that she does not disagree with her husband on any point. But of this enough has been said.

CHAPTER 2. ON LOVE

In the first place, let wives strive so that their husbands will clearly perceive that they are pensive or joyful according to the differing states of their husbands' fortunes. Surely congratulations are proper in times of good fortune, just as consolations are appropriate in times of adversity. Let them openly discuss whatever is bothering them, provided it is worthy of prudent people, and let them feign nothing, dissemble nothing, and conceal nothing. Very often sorrow and trouble of mind are relieved by means of discussion and counsel that ought to be carried out in a friendly fashion with the husband. If a husband shares all the pressures of her anxieties he will lighten them by participating in them and make their burden lighter; but if her troubles are very great or deeply rooted, they will be relieved as long as she is able to sigh in the embrace of her husband. I would like wives to live with their husbands in such a way that they can always be in agreement, and if this can be done, then, as Pythagoras defines friendship, the two are united in one.

· · ·

I therefore would like wives to evidence modesty at all times and in all places. They can do this if they will preserve an evenness and restraint in the movements of the eyes, in their walking, and in the movement of their bodies; for the wandering of the eyes, a hasty gait, and excessive movement of the hands and other parts of the body cannot be done without loss of dignity, and such actions are always joined to vanity and are signs of frivolity.

· · ·

Moreover, I earnestly beg that wives observe the precept of avoiding immoderate laughter. This is a habit that is indecent in all persons, but it is especially hateful in a woman. On the other hand, women should not be censured if they laugh a little at a good joke and thus lapse somewhat from their serious demeanor. Demosthenes used to rehearse his legal speeches at home in front of a mirror so that with his own eyes he could judge what he should do and what he should avoid in delivering his speeches at court. We may well apply this practice to wifely behavior.

I wish that wives would daily think and consider what the dignity, the status of being a wife requires, so that they will not be lacking in dignified comportment.

· · · ·

We who follow a middle way should establish some rather liberal rules for our wives. They should not be shut up in their bedrooms as in a prison but should be permitted to go out, and this privilege should be taken as evidence of their virtue and propriety. Still, wives should not act with their husbands as the moon does with the sun; for when the moon is near the sun it is never visible, but when it is distant it stands resplendent by itself. Therefore, I would have wives be seen in public with their husbands, but when their husbands are away wives should stay at home. By maintaining an honest gaze in their eyes, they can communicate most significantly as in painting, which is called silent poetry. They also should maintain dignity in the motion of their heads and the other movements of their bodies. Now that I have spoken about demeanor and behavior, I shall now speak of speech.

CHAPTER 4. ON SPEECH AND SILENCE

Isocrates warns men to speak on those matters that they know well and about which they cannot, on account of their dignity, remain silent. We commend women to concede the former as the property of men, but they should consider the latter to be appropriate to themselves as well as to men. Loquacity cannot be sufficiently reproached in women, as many very learned and wise men have stated, nor can silence be sufficiently applauded. For this reason women were prohibited by the laws of the Romans from pleading either criminal or civil law cases.

CHAPTER 8. ON DOMESTIC MATTERS AND THE MANAGEMENT OF HOUSEHOLDS AND SERVANTS

We are interested in the care of our property and the diligence proper to our servants and staff because it is necessary to have both property and servants, without whose help family life itself cannot exist. Surely it is in these two things that the management of domestic matters primarily is involved, for unless a wife imposes her own judgment and precepts on these matters, the operation of the household will have no order and will be in great disarray. Men are naturally endowed with strength of mind and body; both for these and other reasons, they provision their homes by their labor, industry, and willingness to undergo hardships. Conversely, I think we may infer that since women are by nature weak they should diligently care for things concerning the household. For weakness can never be separated from cares nor cares from vigilance. What is the use of bringing home great wealth unless the wife will work at preserving, maintaining, and utilizing it?

• • •

They ought to attend, therefore, to governing their households just as Pericles daily attended to the affairs of Athens.[79] And they ought always to consider how well they are doing so that they will never be deficient in their care, interest, and diligence in household matters. They will surely be successful in this matter if they do what they should do, that is, if they are accustomed to stay at home and oversee everything there.

• • •

So that a wife's duty might be commended to posterity, there were affixed to the bronze statue of Gaia Caecilia, the daughter of Tarquinius, an ordinary shoe and a distaff and spindle, so that those objects might in some way signify that her diligent work at home ought to be imitated by future generations.[81] What neglectful landowner can hope to have hard-working peasants? What slothful general can make his soldiers vigilant for the state? Therefore, if a wife would like to have her maids working hard at home, she should not merely instruct them with words but she ought also by her actions to demonstrate, indicate, and show what they should be doing. Indeed, there is surely nothing more excellent in household affairs than that everything be put in its place, because there is nothing more beautiful, more useful than order, which is always of the greatest importance. We consider that an army or chorus can be called anything but an army or chorus unless its organization is well preserved.[82] I would have wives imitate the leaders of bees, who supervise, receive, and preserve whatever comes into their hives, to the end that, unless necessity dictates otherwise, they remain in their honeycombs where they develop and mature beautifully. Wives may send their maids and manservants abroad if they think this would be useful to them. But if, indeed, these servants are required at home, they should urge, order, and require their presence. Wives should also consider it their duties to see to it that no harm comes to their husbands' winecellars, pantries, and oil cellars.

• • •

It is now proper to speak, as we have promised, about servants, who, provided they are not neglected, can add great luster to our houses and be useful and pleasant. So they will be if wives will instruct them carefully and if they will not get angry with them before, having warned them, they discover that they have made the same mistakes. I should like that wives, in these matters as in others, follow the example of the leaders of the bees, who allow no one under their control to be lazy or negligent.[88]

• • •

Thrifty wives constantly ought to seek out and appoint sober stewards for the provisions and address them courteously and be generous of them, so that by the great interest of the mistress the industry of the steward daily increases. They should feed their servants so that they will satisfy both their human needs and reward their constant labor. Wives should clothe their servants comfortably as befits the season, climate, and place. Moreover, as Hesiod advises, they should always be careful that servants are not separated from their children and families,[90] for servants will always find a way to stay together with their own family, even secretly. Furthermore, servants will be very grateful if especially good medical care is provided when a member of their family is taken sick. For these acts of humanity, this solicitiousness will make servants very conscientious and hardworking for the household.

• • •

After their offspring have passed their infancy, mothers should use all their skill, care, and effort to ensure that their children are endowed with excellent qualities of mind and body. First they should instruct them in their duty toward Immortal God, their country, and their parents, so that they will be instilled from their earliest years with those qualities that are the foundation of all other virtues. Only those children who fear God, obey the laws, honor their parents, respect their superiors, are pleasant with their equals and courteous to their inferiors, will exhibit much hope for themselves. Children should meet all people with a civil demeanor, pleasant countenance, and friendly words. But they should be on the most familiar terms with only the best people. Thus they will learn moderation in food and drink so that they may lay, as it were, the foundation of temperance for their future lives. They should be taught to avoid these pleasures that are dishonorable, and

---

[79] Cf. *Xenophon Oeconomicus* 7.3.5.
[81] Cf. Plutarch *Quaestiones Romanae* 30; *Moralia* 271E.
[82] Cf. Xenophon *Oeconomicus* 1.3.
[88] Cf. Xenophon *Oeconomicus* 7.33.
[90] Probably an allusion to Hesiod *Opera et Dies* 373.

they should apply their efforts and thoughts to those matters that are the most becoming and will be useful and pleasant when they become older. If mothers are able to instruct their children in these matters, their offspring will much more easily and better receive the benefit of education.

• • •

Mothers should often warn their children to abstain from excessive laughter and to avoid words that denote a rash character. That is the mark of stupidity, the evidence of passion. Moreover, children should be warned not ever to speak on those matters that are base in the act. Therefore, mothers should restrain them from vulgar or cutting words. If their children should say anything that is obscene or licentious, mothers should not greet it with a laugh or a kiss, but with a whip.

Moreover, they should teach their children not to criticize anyone because of his poverty or the low birth of his lineage or other misfortunes, for they are sure to make bitter enemies from such actions or develop an attitude of arrogance. Mothers should teach their children sports in which they so willingly learn to exert themselves that, if the occasion arises, they can easily bear even more difficult hardships. I would have mothers sharply criticized for displays of anger, greed, or sexual desire in the presence of their offspring, for these vices weaken virtue. If mothers act appropriately, their children will learn from infancy to condemn, avoid, and hate these most filthy mistresses and they will take care to revere the names of God and will be afraid to take them in vain. For whoever has been taught at an early age to despise the Divinity, will they not as adults surely curse Him? Therefore, it is of great importance to train children from infancy so that they never swear. Indeed, those who swear readily because of some misfortune are not deserving of trust, and those who readily swear very often unwittingly betray themselves. Mothers ought to teach their children to speak the truth.

• • •

Therefore, my Lorenzo, your compatriots ought to be stirred by your example and follow you with great enthusiasm, for in Ginevra you have taken a wife who is a virgin well endowed with virtue charm, a noble lineage, and great wealth. What more outstanding, more worthy model could I propose than yours? What more shining, more worthy example than yours, since in this outstanding city of Florence you are most eminently connected through your father, grandfather, and ancestors? You have taken a wife whose great wealth the entire world indeed admires but whose chastity, constancy, and prudence all men of goodwill esteem highly. They consider that you are blessed and happy to have her as a wife, and she is to have you as a husband. Since you have contracted such an outstanding and fine marriage, these same men ask God Immortal that you will have the best children who will become very honored citizens in your state. These matters might perhaps seem negligible since I am treating them, but indeed they are, in their own fashion, borne out in your marriage. Thus, surely young men who follow your example will profit more than only by following my precepts; just as laws are much more likely to be observed in a city when they are obeyed by its ruler, so, since your own choice of a wife is consistent with my teachings, we may hope that these precepts will be followed by the youth.

Questions:
1. *What elements are considered important for a wife in contracting and in maintaining a marriage?*
2. *What is the role of marriage in Renaissance society? What does marriage have to do with larger concerns? Consider, for instance, the ruling of the state, the extended family, politics, economics, etc.*

PART 11
The Reformation

11.1 Erasmus: A Diatribe Against the Pope

Desidenus Erasmus (ca. 1467–1536), the most renowned of all Northern Renaissance humanists, was Dutch by birth and educated in a school of the Brethern of the Common Life. He was a Biblical scholar, a popular author, and an astute critic of his society and the church, although he ultimately rejected the Protestant Reform. Published anonymously, the following diatribe is directed against Pope Julius II (r. 1503–13), who was known as the Warrior Pope.

Source: Wallace E. Adams, Richard B. Barlow, Gerald R. Kleinfeld, Ronald D. Smith, William W, Wootton, eds. *The Western World To 1700,* (New York: Dodd, Mead & Co., 1969), pp. 372–74.

DIALOGUE: JULIUS LOCKED OUT OF HEAVEN

Persons Of The Dialogue: Pope Julius II, His Genius Or Guardian Angel, and St. Peter

Scene: Before the Gates of Heaven

JULIUS: What's the trouble here? Won't the gates open? I believe the lock as been changed, or else it's jammed.

GENIUS: Better check to see if you've brought the right key. The one for the treasury won't open this door, you know. But why didn't you bring both keys? This is the key of power, not of knowledge.

JULIUS: Why, Hell, this is the only one I've ever used! I've never seen what good the other one was when I've had this one.

GENIUS: Me neither, certainly, except that meanwhile we're locked out.

JULIUS: I'm losing my temper. I'm going to beat on the gate. Hey there! Somebody open this door instantly! What's the matter, nobody here? What's holding up the doorman? Asleep, I suppose; probably drunk.

GENIUS: [*Aside*] This fellow judges everyone by himself.

PETER: It's a good thing we've got a steel door. Otherwise, whoever this is would break down the gates. It must be some giant, or satrap, some sacker of cities. Immortal God! What sewage is this I smell! Well, I certainly won't open the door. I'll just peek out this little barred window and see what kind of monster this is. What do you want? Who are you?

JULIUS: If you knew your business, you would greet me with all the heavenly choirs.

PETER: Rather demanding, isn't he? But first tell me who you are.

JULIUS: As if you couldn't see who I am.

PETER: See? I certainly see a new and never-before-seen spectacle, not to say a monster.

JULIUS: If you are not completely blind, then, I suppose you know this key, even if you don't recognize the golden oak on my coat of arms. And you see the triple crown of the Papacy, besides my cloak, glittering all over with jewels and gold.

PETER: Well, I recognize the silver key, all right, though to be sure there is only one, and it is much different from the keys that Christ, the true Pastor of the Church, once put into my keeping. But how should I recognize that crown, so proud that no barbarian tyrant would ever dare wear it, much less someone wishing to be admitted here? As for that cloak, it does nothing for me. I always kick jewels and gold out of the way, and spurn them like trash. But what's this? Here and there on the key and the crown and the cloak I see the marks of some wretched saloon keeper and impostor, a fellow with my name but not my ways: Simon [Magus], whom I once threw out from the following of Christ for simony.

147

JULIUS: Well, let these trifles go, if you're wise to them. Now I am, if you don't know, Julius the Ligurian, and if I'm not mistaken you recognize these two letters: P.M. You have learned to read, I presume?

PETER: I guess they stand for *Pestis Maxima,* the Universal Calamity.

GENIUS: Ha ha ha! This riddle-guesser hit the nail on the head.

JULIUS: No, no! Pontifex Maxi us, the Pope's title.

PETER: If you were three times maxi us and greater even than thrice-great Hermes, you wouldn't be allowed in here unless you were the best of all; that is, a saint.

JULIUS: Well, if it is so necessary to be called a saint, you're being pretty arrogant to delay opening the gate for me, when you after all these centuries are only called *sanctus—saint* or holy—but nobody ever calls me anything but *sanctissimus*—most sainted, most holy. There are six-thousand bulls....

GENIUS: Real bull!

JULIUS: ... in which I am called not only most holy, but by the very name of holiness itself, whenever it pleased me.

GENIUS: By the name of drunkard, too.

JULIUS: I would make 'em call me the Holiest of the Most Holy Lord Julius.

PETER: Well then, go demand heaven from those flatterers who made you "most holy." Let the same followers who gave you your holiness save you. Though I suppose you still think there is no difference between being called holy and being holy.

JULIUS: I'm getting angry! If only I could live again, I'd show you about this business of not being holy and not being saved!

PETER: Oh, there's an indication of a most holy mind! Although I have been watching you narrowly for a long time now, I've seen no sign of sanctity in you—nothing but impiety. Why have you led here this new, un-papal army? Here you have brought with you some twenty-thousand men, and I can't catch sight of a single one who has even a face that is Christian! I see a horrible flood of soldiers with you, smelling of nothing but brothels, drunkenness, and gun. powder. I guess they are some kind of bandits, or rather fiends broken out of Hell to storm Heaven. As for you, the more I look the less trace of an apostle do I see about you. First of all, what monstrous thing is this, that you wear the garment of a priest and under it you bristle and rattle with bloody armor? And why such belligerent eyes, such a fierce mouth, such a menacing forehead, such proud and arrogant brows? It is shameful to say and painful to see that no part of your body is not spattered with the stains of prodigious and abominable pleasures. Not to mention that even now you are belching and smelling of hangover and drunkenness, and I just saw you [vomit]! The appearance of your whole person suggests that it is not with age and disease but through dissipation that you seem old, withered, and broken.

GENIUS: How vividly he paints him in his true colors!...

Questions:
1. *How does Pope Julius' conduct in office as described in the dialogue compare with Machiavelli's Renaissance prince?*
2. *On what grounds did St. Peter exclude Pope Julius from heaven?*
3. *How do these criticisms of Pope Julius compare to John Hus's condemnation of the papacy?*

11.2 Luther's *Ninety-Five Theses*

The Ninety-Five Theses is the popular term for the Disputation on the Power and the Efficacy of Indulgences. Luther posted these on the Castle church door at Wittenberg on October 31, 1517. When John Tetzel arrived selling indulgences in Luther's parish, chanting slogans that offered years off penance in purgatory for a cash payment, Luther protested against them and took the first steps of the Protestant Reformation. A selection of the Theses below reveals Luther's early position.

Source: *Martin Luther: Selections from His Writings,* ed. and trans. John Dillenberger, (New York: Doubleday & Company, 1961), pp. 489–500. Reprinted with permission from *The Reformation Writings of Martin Luther,* Vol. 1, *The Basis of the Protestant Reformation,* trans. and ed. Bertram Lee Woolf (London: Lutterworth Press, 1953), pp. 32–42, passim.

Out of love and concern for the truth, and with the object of eliciting it, the following heads will be the subject of a public discussion at Wittenberg under the presidency of the reverend father, Martin Luther, Augustinian, Master of Arts and Sacred Theology, and duly appointed Lecturer on these subjects in that place. He requests that whoever cannot be present personally to debate the matter orally will do so in absence in writing.

1. When our Lord and Master, Jesus Christ, said "Repent", He called for the entire life of believers to be one of penitence.

5. The pope has neither the will nor the power to remit any penalties beyond those imposed either at his own discretion or by canon law.

6. The pope himself cannot remit guilt, but only declare and confirm that it has been remitted by God; or, at most, he can remit it in cases reserved to his discretion. Except for these cases, the guilt remains untouched.

20. Therefore the pope, in speaking of the plenary remission of all penalties, does not mean "all" in the strict sense, but only those imposed by himself.

21. Hence those who preach indulgences are in error when they say that a man is absolved and saved from every penalty by the pope's indulgences;

27. There is no divine authority for preaching that the soul flies out of purgatory immediately the money chinks in the bottom of the chest.

28. It is certainly possible that when the money chinks in the bottom of the chest avarice and greed increase; but when the church offers intercession, all depends on the will of God.

32. All those who believe themselves certain of their own salvation by means of letters of indulgence, will be eternally damned, together with their teachers.

35. It is not in accordance with Christian doctrine to preach and teach that those who buy off souls, or purchase confessional licenses, have no need to repent of their own sins.

36. Any Christian whatsoever, who is truly repentant, enjoys plenary remission from penalty and guilt, and this is given him without letters of indulgence.

37. Any true Christian whatsoever, living or dead, participates in all the benefits of Christ and the Church; and this participation is granted to him by God without letters of indulgence.

43. Christians should be taught that one who gives to the poor, or lends to the needy, does a better action than if he purchases indulgences.

45. Christians should be taught that he who sees a needy person, but passes him by although he gives money for indulgences, gains no benefit from the pope's pardon, but only incurs the wrath of God.

50. Christians should be taught that, if the pope knew the exactions of the indulgence preacher he would rather the church of St. Peter were reduced to ashes than be built with the skin, flesh, and bones of his sheep.

62. The true treasure of the church is the Holy Gospel of the glory and the grace of God.

75. It is foolish to think that papal indulgences have so much power that they can absolve a man even if he has done the impossible and violated the mother of God.

76. We assert the contrary, and say that the pope's pardons are not able to remove the least venial of sins as far as their guilt is concerned.

81. This unbridled preaching of indulgences makes it difficult for learned men to guard the respect due to the pope against false accusations, or at least from the keen criticisms of the laity;

82. They ask, e.g.: Why does not the pope liberate everyone from purgatory for the sake of love (a most holy thing) and because of the supreme necessity of their souls? This would be morally the best of all reasons. Meanwhile he redeems innumerable souls for money, a most perishable thing, with which to build St. Peter's church, a very minor purpose.

86. Again: Since the pope's income to-day is larger than that of the wealthiest of wealthy men, why does he not build this one church of St. Peter with his own money, rather than with the money of indigent believers?

90. These questions are serious matters of conscience to the laity. To suppress them by force alone, and not to refute them by giving reasons, is to expose the church and the pope to the ridicule of their enemies, and to make Christian people unhappy.

91. If, therefore, indulgences were preached in accordance with the spirit and mind of the pope, all these difficulties would be easily overcome, and, indeed, cease to exist.

94. Christians should be exhorted to be zealous to follow Christ, their Head, through penalties, deaths, and hells;

95. And let them thus be more confident of entering heaven through many tribulations rather than through a false assurance of peace.

Questions:
1. Why is Luther upset about the sale of indulgences?
2. According to these statements, what is more important in Christian teaching than indulgences?

11.3 The Act of Supremacy: The Church of England

Thwarted by the pope's reluctance from getting an annulment of his marriage, Henry VIII (r. 1509–1547) invoked the principle "the king in Parliament can do anything" to validate by legislation his new position as head of the Church of England. The new Archbishop of Canterbury, Thomas Cranmer, granted the king his annulment and Henry married Anne Boleyn.

> **Source:** *Select Documents of English Constitutional History,* ed. George B. Adams and H. Morse Stephens, (New York: Macmillan, 1918), pp. 239–40, reprinted from *Statutes of the Realm* (London, 1810–28) III, 436–39.

ALBEIT the king's majesty justly and rightfully is and ought to be the supreme head of the Church of England, and so is recognized by the clergy of this realm in their Convocations, yet nevertheless for corroboration and confirmation thereof, and for increase of virtue in Christ's religion within this realm of England, and to repress and extirp all errors, heresies, and other enormities and abuses heretofore used in the same: be it enacted by authority of this present Parliament, that the king our sovereign lord, his heirs and successors, kings of this realm, shall be taken, accepted, and reputed the only supreme head in earth of the Church of England, called *Anglicana Ecclesia;* and shall have and enjoy, annexed and united to the imperial crown of this realm, as well the title and style thereof, as all honours, dignities, preeminences, jurisdictions, privileges, authorities, immunities, profits, and commodities to the said dignity of supreme head of the same Church belonging and appertaining; and that our said sovereign lord, his heirs and successors, kings of this realm, shall have full power and authority from time to time to visit, repress, redress, reform, order, correct, restrain, and amend all such errors, heresies, abuses, offences, contempts, and enormities, whatsoever they be, which by any manner spiritual authority or jurisdiction ought or may lawfully be reformed, repressed, ordered, redressed, corrected, restrained, or amended, most to the pleasure of Almighty God, the increase of virtue in Christ's religion, and for the conservation of the peace, unity, and tranquillity of this realm; any usage, custom, foreign law, foreign authority, prescription, or any other thing or things to the contrary hereof notwithstanding.

Questions:
1. On what grounds did Henry claim the right to exercise authority as "Supreme Head of the Church of England?"
2. How does this law change the relationship between church and state government? between England and other European states?

11.4 A Protestant Woman Argues for Tolerance

In the initial zeal of the Protestant Reformation, women frequently played important roles. Catherine, a cabinetmaker's daughter of Strasbourg (Ca. 1497–1562), married Matthew Zell, an ex-priest turned Lutheran minister. The following selection is from a series of letters she wrote to an angry young Lutheran minister named Ludwig Rabus, whose loathing for the radical protestant movement turned him against the Zells. Now a widow and seeking to vindicate herself, Catherine published the correspondence, consisting chiefly of her own letters.

> **Source:** *Not in God's Image,* ed. Julia O'Faolain and Lauro Martines, (New York: Harper and Row, Inc., 1973), pp. 203–6.

I, Catherine Zell, wife of the late lamented Mathew Zell, who served in Strasbourg, where I was born and reared and still live, wish you peace and enhancement in God's grace.

From my earliest years I turned to the Lord, who taught and guided me, and I have at all times, in accordance with my understanding and His grace, embraced the interests of His church and earnestly sought Jesus. Even in youth this brought me the regard and affection of clergymen and others much concerned with the church, which is why the pious Mathew Zell wanted me as a companion in marriage; and I, in turn, to serve the glory of Christ, gave devotion and help to my husband, both in his ministry and in keeping his house....

Ever since I was ten years old I have been a student and a sort of church mother, much given to attending sermons. I have loved and frequented the company of learned men, and I conversed much with them, not about dancing, masquerades, and worldly pleasures but about the kingdom of God.

Yet I resisted and struggled against that kingdom. Then, as no learned man could find a way of consoling me in my sins, prayers and physical suffering, and as none could make me sure of God's love and grace, I fell gravely ill in body and spirit. I became like that poor woman of the Gospel who, having spent all she had on doctors to no avail, heard speak of Christ, went to Him, and was healed. As I foundered, devoured by care and anxiety, vainly searching for serenity in the practices of the church, God took pity on me. From among our people He drew out and sent forth Martin Luther. This man so persuaded me of the ineffable goodness of our Lord Jesus Christ that I felt myself snatched from the depths of hell and transported to the kingdom of heaven. I remembered the Lord's words to Peter: 'Follow me and I shall make you a fisher of men'. Then did I labor day and night to cleave to the path of divine truth....

While other women decorated their houses and ornamented themselves, going to dances, wedding parties, and giving themselves to pleasure, I went into the houses of poor and rich alike, in all love, faith, and compassion, to care for the sick and the confined and to bury the dead. Was that to plant anxiety and turmoil in the church of Strasbourg?...

Consider the poor Anabaptists, who are so furiously and ferociously persecuted. Must the authorities everywhere be incited against them, as the hunter drives his dog against wild animals? Against those who acknowledge Christ the Lord in very much the same way we do and over which we broke with the papacy? Just because they cannot agree with us on lesser things, is this any reason to persecute them and in them Christ, in whom they fervently believe and have often professed in misery, in prison, and under the torments of fire and water?

Governments may punish criminals, but they should not force and govern belief which is a matter for the heart and conscience not for temporal authorities.

[Urges Rabus to consult the leading reformers on this question and provides him, ironically, with a list.]

... When the authorities pursue one, they soon bring forth tears, and towns and villages are emptied...

Strasbourg does not offer the example of an evil town but rather the contrary-charity, compassion, and hospitality for the wretched and poor. Within its walls, God be thanked, there remains more than one poor Christian whom certain people would have liked to see cast out. Old Mathew Zell would not have approved of that: he would have gathered the sheep, not destroyed them....

Whether they were Lutherans, Zwinglians, Schwenkfeldians, or poor Anabaptist brethren, rich or poor, wise or foolish, according to the word of St. Paul, all came to us [to the Zells in Strasbourg]. We were not compelled to hold the same views and beliefs that they did, but we did owe to all a proof of love, service, and generosity: our teacher Christ has taught us that....

Questions:
1. What activities did Catherine and her husband engage in?
2. Why did Rabus criticize her and how did she defend herself?

11.5   The Edict of Nantes

At the end of decades of religious strife, Henry IV of France (r. 1589–1610) decreed the Edict of Nantes, granting religious toleration to the French Protestants, known as Huguenots. This is the first time in European history that a Christian ruler permitted civil liberty as well as freedom of worship to a religious minority.

Source: Sidney Z. Ehler and John B. Morrall, eds. and trans., *Church and State Through the Centuries: A Collection of Historic Documents* (London: Burns and Gates, 1954), pp. 185–88.

Firstly, that the memory of everything done on both sides from the beginning of the month of March 1585, until our accession to the Crown and during the other previous troubles, and at the outbreak of them, shall remain extinct and suppressed, as if it were something which had never occurred. And it shall not be lawful or permissible to our Procurators-General or to any other persons, public or private, at any time or on any pretext whatsoever, to institute a case, lawsuit or action in any Court or judicial tribunals whatever [concerning those things].

We forbid all our subjects, of whatever rank and quality they may be, to renew the memory of these matters, to attack, be hostile to, injure or provoke each other in revenge for the past, whatever may be the reason and pretext; or to dispute, argue or quarrel about it, or to do violence, or to give offence in deed or word, but let them restrain themselves and live peaceably together as brothers, friends and fellow-citizens, on pain of being liable to punishment as disturbers of the peace and troublers of public quiet.

We ordain that the Catholic, Apostolic and Roman religion shall be restored and re-established in all places and districts of this our kingdom and the countries under our rule, where its practice has been interrupted, so that it can be peacefully and freely practiced there, without any disturbance or hindrance. We forbid very expressly all persons of whatever rank, quality or condition they may be, under the aforesaid penalties, to disturb, molest or cause annoyance to clerics in the celebration of the Divine worship, the enjoyment and receipt of tithes, fruits and revenues of their benefices, and all other rights and duties which belong to them; and we ordain that all those who during the disorders have come into possession of churches, houses, goods and revenues belonging to the said clerics, and who retain and occupy them, shall give back the entire possession and enjoyment of them, with such rights, liberties and safeguards as they had before they were seized. We also forbid very expressly those of the so-called Reformed religion to hold prayer meetings or any devotions of the aforesaid religion in churches, houses and dwellings of the above-said clerics....

And in order not to leave any cause for discords and disputes between our subjects, we have permitted and we permit those of the so-called Reformed religion to live and dwell in all the towns and districts of this our kingdom and the countries under one rule, without being annoyed, disturbed, molested or constrained to do anything against their conscience, or for this cause to be sought out in their houses and districts where they wish to live, provided that they conduct themselves in other respects according to the provisions of our present Edict....

We also permit those of the aforesaid religion to carry out and continue its practice in the towns and districts under our rule, where it was established and carried out publicly several distinct times in the year 1597, until the end of the month of March, notwithstanding all decrees and judgments to the contrary....

We forbid very expressly all those of the aforesaid religion to practice it in so far as ministration, regulation, discipline or public instruction of children and others is concerned, in this our kingdom and the countries under our rule, in matters concerning religion, outside the places permitted and conceded by the present Edict....

Books dealing with the matters of the aforesaid so-called Reformed religion shall not be printed and sold publicly, except in the towns and districts where the public exercise of the said religion is allowed. And with regard to other books which shall be printed in other towns, they shall be seen and inspected by our officials and theologians as laid down by our ordinances. We forbid very specifically the printing, publication and sale of all defamatory books, tracts and writings, under the penalties contained in our ordinances, instructing all our judges and officials to carry out this ruling strictly.

We ordain that there shall be no difference or distinction, because of the aforesaid religion, in the reception of students to be instructed in Universities, Colleges and schools, or of the sick and poor into hospitals, infirmaries and public charitable institutions....

In order to reunite more effectively the wills of our subjects, as is our intention, and to remove all future complaints, we declare that all those who profess or shall profess the aforesaid so-called Reformed religion are capable of holding and exercising all public positions, honours, offices and duties whatsoever, Royal, seigneurial, or offices in the towns of our kingdom, countries, lands and lordships subject to us, notwithstanding all contrary oaths, and of being admitted and received into them without distinction; it shall be sufficient for our courts of Parliament and other judges to ascertain and inquire concerning the life, morals, religion and honest behaviour of those who are or shall be appointed to offices, whether of one religion or the other, without enacting from them any oath other than that of well and faithfully serving the King in the exercise of their functions and keeping the ordinances, as has been perpetually the custom. During vacancies in the aforesaid positions, functions and offices, we shall make—in respect of those which shall be in our disposition—appointments without bias or discrimination of capable persons, as the unity of our subjects requires it. We declare also that members of the aforesaid so-called Reformed religion can be admitted and received into all Councils, conferences, assemblies and gatherings which are connected with the offices in question; they can not be rejected or prevented from enjoying these rights on grounds of the said religion....

And for greater security of the behaviour and conduct which we expect with regard to it [the Edict], we will, command and desire that all the Governors and Lieutenants-General of our provinces, Bailiffs, Seneschals asnd other ordinary judges in towns in our aforesaid kingdom, immediately after the reception of this Edict, swear to cause it to be kept and observed, each one in his own district; likewise the mayors, sheriffs, captains, consuls and magistrates of the towns, annual and perpetual. We also enjoin our said bailiffs, seneschals or their lieutenants and other judges, to cause the principal inhabitants from both religions in the above-mentioned towns to swear to respect the present Edict immediately after its publication. We place all those of the said towns in our protection and safe keeping, each religion being placed in the safe keeping of the other; and we wish them to be instructed respectively and by public acts to answer by due legal process any contraventions of our present Edict which shall be made in the said towns by their inhabitants, or to make known the said contraventions and put them into the hand of justice.

We command our beloved and loyal people who hold our Courts of Parliament, "Chambres des Comptes" and courts of aids that immediately after the present Edict has been received, they are bound, all business being suspended and under penalty of nullity for any acts which they shall make otherwise, to take an oath similar to the above and to make this our Edict to be published and registered in our above-mentioned Courts according to its proper form and meaning, purely and simply, without using any modifications, rectifications, declarations or secret registering and without waiting for further order or commandment from us; and we order our Procurators-General to demand and ensure immediately and without delay the aforesaid publication....

For such is our pleasure. As witness thereof we have signed the present enactment with our own hand, and in order that it may be sure and stable permanently, we have placed and affixed our Seal to it.

Given at Nantes in the month of April, in the year of grace 1598, the ninth year of our reign.

[Signed,]
Henry

Questions:
1. *What specific rights did this edict allow the Huguenots?*
2. *To what extent were they still treated differently from the Catholic majority?*
3. *How might they become a threat someday to royal authority?*

11.6   The Catholic Response: The Council of Trent

The response of the Catholic Church to the Protestant Reformation began, surprisingly, after the election of Pope Paul III (1534–1549), a humanist who immediately appointed his unqualified teenaged grandsons to the college of cardinals. Not only did this action reveal his immoral life, but also his willingness to use his office to increase the wealth and power of his family. Nevertheless, Paul III also appointed able and reform-minded men to offices of authority and called a Church council to deal with the many problems facing the Church. The Council of Trent met intermittently from 1545–1563. Some of its canons and decrees are recorded in the following document.

Source: *Heritage of Western Civilization,* Seventh Edition, ed. John L. Beatty and Oliver A. Johnson, (Prentice Hall, 1991), pp. 452–60.

DECREE TOUCHING THE OPENING OF THE COUNCIL

Doth it please you-unto the praise and glory of the holy and undivided Trinity, Father, and Son, and Holy Ghost; for the increase and exaltation of the Christian faith and religion; for the extirpation of heresies; for the peace and union of the Church; for the reformation of the Clergy and Christian people; for the depression and extinction of the enemies of the Christian name-to decree and declare that the sacred and general council of Trent do begin, and hath begun?

They answered: It pleaseth us.

DECREE CONCERNING ORIGINAL SIN

That our Catholic faith, *without which it is impossible to please God,* may, errors being purged away, continue in its own perfect and spotless integrity, and that the Christian people may not *be carried about with every wind of doctrine;* whereas that old serpent, the perpetual enemy of mankind, amongst the very many evils with which the Church of God is in these our times troubled, has also stirred up not only new, but even old, dissensions touching original sin, and the remedy thereof; the sacred and holy, oecumenical and general Synod of Trent,—lawfully assembled in the Holy See presiding therein,—wishing now to come to the reclaiming of the erring, and the confirming of the wavering—following the testimonies of the sacred Scriptures, of the holy Fathers, or the most approved councils, and the judgement and consent of the Church itself, ordains, confesses, and declares these things touching the said original sin:

1. If any one does not confess that the first man, Adam, when he had transgressed the commandment of God in Paradise, immediately lost the holiness and justice wherein he had been constituted; and that he incurred, through the offense of that prevarication, the wrath and indignation of God, and consequently death, with which God had previously threatened him, and, together with death, captivity under his power who thenceforth *had the empire of death, that is to say, the devil,* and that the entire Adam, through that offence of prevarication, was changed, in body and soul, for the worse; let him be anathema.

3. If any one asserts, that this sin of Adam—which in its origin is one, and being transfused into all by propagation, not by imitation, is in each one as his own—is taken away either by the powers of human nature, or by any other remedy than the merit of the *one mediator our Lord Jesus Christ, who hath reconciled us to God in his own blood, made unto us justice, sanctification, and redemption;* or if he denies that the said merit of Jesus Christ is applied, both to adults and to infants, by the sacrament of baptism rightly administered in the form of the Church; let him be anathema....

ON THE SACRAMENTS IN GENERAL

Canon I. If any one saith, that the sacraments of the New Law were not all instituted by Jesus Christ, our Lord; or, that they are more, or less, than seven, to wit, Baptism, Confirmation, the Eucharist, Penance, Extreme Unction, Order, and Matrimony; or even that any one of these seven is not truly and properly a sacrament; let him be anathema.

Canon IV. If any one saith, that the sacraments of the New Law are not necessary unto salvation, but superfluous; and that, without them, or without the desire thereof, men obtain of God, through faith alone, the grace of justification;-though all (the sacraments) are not indeed necessary for every individual; let him be anathema.

Canon VI. If any one saith, that the sacraments of the New Law do not contain the grace which they signify; or, that they do not confer that grace on those who do not place an obstacle thereunto; as though they were merely outward signs of grace or justice received through faith, and certain marks of the Christian profession, whereby believers are distinguished amongst men from unbelievers; let him be anathema.

Canon X. If any one saith, that all Christians have power to administer the word, and all the sacraments; let him be anathema.

ON THE MOST HOLY SACRAMENT OF THE EUCHARIST

Canon I. If any one deny, that, in the sacrament of the most holy Eucharist, are contained truly, really, and substantially, the body and blood together with the soul and divinity of our Lord Jesus Christ. and consequently the whole Christ: but saith that He is only therein as in a sign, or in figure, or virtue: let him be anathema.

Canon II. If anyone saith that in the sacred and holy sacrament of the Eucharist, the substance of the bread and wine remains conjointly with the body and blood of our Lord .Jesus Christ, and denieth that wonderful and singular conversion of the whole substance of the bread into the Body, and of the whole substance of the wine into the Blood—the species only of the bread and wine remaining—which conversion indeed the Catholic Church most aptly calls transubstantiation; let him be anathema.

ON THE ECCLESIASTICAL HIERARCHY, AND ON ORDINATION

... If any one affirm, that all Christians indiscriminately are priests of the New Testament. or that they are all mutually endowed with an equal spiritual power, he clearly does nothing but confound the ecclesiastical hierarchy; which is *as an army set in array....*

.... It decree, that all those who, being only called and instituted by the people, or by the civil power and magistrate, ascend to the exercise of these ministrations, and those who of their own rashness assume them to themselves, are not ministers of the Church, but are to be looked upon as *thieves and robbers, who have not entered by the door.* These are the things which it hath seemed good to the sacred Synod to teach the faithful of Christ. in general terms, touching the sacrament of Order.

ON THE SACRAMENT OF MATRIMONY

Canon IX. If anyone saith, that clerics constituted in sacred orders or Regulars, who have solemnly professed chastity, are able to contract marriage, and that being contracted it is valid. notwithstanding the ecclesiastical law, or vow: and that the contrary is nothing else than to condemn marriage: and, that all who do not feel that they have the gift of chastity; even though they have made a vow thereof, may contract marriage: let him be anathema: seeing that God refuses not that gift to those who ask for it rightly; neither does *He suffer us to be tempted above that which we are able.*

Canon X. If anyone saith. that the marriage state is to be placed above the state of virginity and of celibacy, and that it is not better and more blessed to remain in virginity, or in celibacy, than to be united in matrimony; let him be anathema.

ON THE INVOCATION, VENERATION, AND RELICS, OF SAINTS, AND ON SACRED IMAGES

The holy Synod enjoins on all bishops and others who sustain the office and charge of teaching, that, agreeably to the usage of the Catholic and Apostolic Church, received from the primitive times of the Christian religion, and agreeably to the consent of the holy Fathers, and to the decrees of sacred Councils, they especially instruct the faithful diligently concerning the intercession and invocation of saints; the honour (paid) to relics; and the legitimate use of images; teaching them that the saints who reign together with Christ, offer up their own prayers to God for men, that it is good and useful supplicantly to invoke them, and to have recourse to their prayers, aid, (and) help for obtaining benefits from God, through His Son, Jesus Christ, our lord, who is alone Redeemer and Saviour; but that they think impiously, who denies that the saints, who enjoy eternal happiness in heaven, are to be invocated or who assert either that they do not pray for men; or, that the invocation of them to pray for each of us even in particular is idolatry or that it is repugnant to the word ogf God; and is opposed to the honour of the *one mediator between God and me, Christ Jesus;* or that it is foolish to supplicate, vocally or mentally, those who reign in heaven. Also, that the holy bodies of holy martyrs, and of others now living with Christ.... They who affirm that veneration and honour are not due to the relics of saints; or, that these, and other sacred monuments, are uselessly honoured by the faithful; and that the places dedicated to the memories of the saints are in vain visited with the view of obtaining their aid; are wholly to be condemned, as the Church has already long since condemned, and now also condemns.

CARDINALS AND ALL PRELATES OF THE CHURCHES SHALL BE CONTENT WITH MODEST FURNITURE AND A FRUGAL TABLE: THEY SHALL NOT ENRICH THEIR RELATIVES OR DOMESTICS OUT OF THE PROPERTY OF THE CHURCH

... Wherefore, after the example of our fathers in the Council of Carthage, it not only orders that bishops be content with modest furniture, and a frugal table and diet, but that they also give heed that in the rest of their manner of living, and in their whole house, there be nothing seen that is alien from this holy institution, and which does not manifest simplicity, zeal toward God, and a contempt of vanities. Also, it wholly forbids them to enrich their own kindred or domestics out of the revenues of the church.... It would seem to be a shame, if they did not at the same time shine so pre-eminent in virtue and in the discipline of their lives, as deservedly to draw upon themselves the eyes of all men.

DECREE CONCERNING INDULGENCES

Whereas the power of conferring Indulgences was granted by Christ to the Church; and she has, even in the most ancient times, used the said power, delivered unto her of God; the sacred holy Synod teaches, and enjoins, that the use of Indulgences for the Christian people most salutary, and approved of by the authority of sacred Councils, is to be retained in the Chruch; and It condemns with anathema those who either assert, that they are useless; or who deny that there is in the Church the power of granting them. In granting them, however, it desires that, in accordance with the ancient and approved custom in the Church, moderation be observed; lest by excessive facility. Ecclesiastical discipline be enervated. And being desirous that the abuses which have crept therein, and by occasion of which this honourable name of Indulgences is blasphemed by heretics, be amended and corrected....

Questions:
1. For what purposes did the pope call the Council of Trent?
2. How well did it achieve them?
3. What concessions did the Council make to the doctrinal criticisms of the Protestants?

11.7   The Execution of Archbishop Cranmer, 21 March 1556 Related by a Bystander

Thomas Cranmer (1489–1556), archbishop of Canterbury under Henry VIII and Edward VI, was a forceful proponent of the annulment of the marriage between Henry VIII and Catherine of Aragon. During the reign of Henry's son Edward, he played a key role in shaping Anglican doctrine. When Mary I, a Catholic, came to throne, Cranmer was convicted of heresy and treason and subsequently executed.

Source: *Eyewitness to History,* by John Casey (New York: Avon Books, 1997), pp. 96–99.

But that I know for our great friendships, and long continued love, you look even of duty that I should signify to you of the truth of such things as here chanceth among us; I would not at this time have written to you the unfortunate end, and doubtful tragedy, of Thomas Cranmer late bishop of Canterbury: because I little pleasure take in beholding of such heavy sights. And, when they are once overpassed, I like not to rehearse them again; being but a renewing of my woe, and doubling my grief. For although his former life, and wretched end, deserves a greater misery, (if any greater might have chanced than chanced unto him), yet, setting aside his offences to God and his country, and beholding the man without his faults, I think there was none that pitied not his case, and bewailed not his fortune, and feared not his own chance, to see so noble a prelate, so grave a counsellor, of so long continued honour, after so many dignities, in his old years to be deprived of his estate, adjudged to die, and in so painful a death to end his life. I have no delight to increase it. Alas, it is too much of itself, that ever so heavy a case should betide to man, and man to deserve it.

But to come to the matter: on Saturday last, being 21 of March, was his day appointed to die. And because the morning was much rainy, the sermon appointed by Mr Dr Cole to be made at the stake, was made in St Mary's church: whither Dr Cranmer was brought by the mayor and aldermen, and my lord Williams: with whom came divers gentlemen of the shire, sit T. A. Bridges, sit John Browne, and others. Where was prepared, over against the pulpit, an high place for him, that all the people might see him. And, when he had ascended it, he kneeled him down and prayed, weeping tenderly: which moved a great number to tears, that had conceived an assured hope of his conversion and repentance . . .

When praying was done, he stood up, and, having leave to speak, said, 'Good people, I had intended indeed to desire you to pray for me; which because Mr Doctor hath desired, and you have done already, I thank you most heartily for it. And now will I pray for myself, as I could best devise for mine own comfort, and say the prayer, word for word, as I have here written it.' And he read it standing: and after kneeled down, and said the Lord's Prayer; and all the people on their knees devoutly praying with him . . .

And then rising, he said, 'Every man desireth, good people, at the time of their deaths, to give some good exhortation, that other may remember after their deaths, and be the better thereby. So I beseech God grant me grace, that I may speak something, at this my departing, whereby God may be glorified, and you edified . . .

'And now I come to the great thing that troubleth my conscience more than any other thing that ever I said or did in my life: and that is, the setting abroad of writings contrary to the truth. Which here now I renounce and refuse, as things written with my hand, contrary to the truth which I thought in my heart, and written for fear of death, and to save my life, if it might be: and that is, all such bills, which I have written or signed with mine own hand since my degradation: wherein I have written many things untrue. And forasmuch as my hand offended in writing contrary to my heart, therefore my hand shall first be punished: for if I may come to the fire, it shall be first burned. And as for the pope, I refuse him, as Christ's enemy and antichrist, with all his false doctrine.'

And here, being admonished of his recantation and dissembling, he said, "Alas, my lord, I have been a man that all my life loved plainness, and never dissembled till now against the truth; which I am most sorry for it.' He added hereunto, that, for the sacrament, he believed as he had taught in his book against the bishop of Winchester. And here he was suffered to speak no more . . .

Then was he carried away; and a great number, that did run to see him go so wickedly to his death, ran after him, exhorting him, while time was, to remember himself. And one Friar John, a godly and well learned man, all the way travelled with him to reduce him. But it would not be. What they said in particular I cannot tell, but the effect appeared in the end: for at the stake he professed, that he died in all such opinions as he had taught, and oft repented him of his recantation.

Coming to the stake with a cheerful countenance and willing mind, he put off his garments with haste, and stood upright in his shirt: and a bachelor of divinity, named Elye, of Brazen-nose college, laboured to convert him to his former recantation, with the two Spanish friars. And when the friars saw his constancy, they said in Latin one to another 'Let us go from him: we ought not to be nigh him: for the devil is with him.' But the bachelor in divinity was more earnest with him: unto whom he answered, that, as concerning his recantation, he repented it right sore, because he knew it was against the truth; with other words more. Whereby the Lord Williams cried, 'Make short, make short.' Then the bishop took certain of his friends by the hand. But the bachelor of divinity refused to take him by the hand, and blamed all others that so did, and said, he was sorry that ever he came in his company. And yet again he required him to agree to his former recantation. And the bishop answered, (shewing his hand), 'This was the hand that wrote it, and therefore shall it suffer first punishment.'

Fire being now put to him, he stretched out his right hand, and thrust it into the flame, and held it there a good space, before the fire came to any other part of his body; where his hand was seen of every man sensibly burning, crying with a loud voice, 'This hand hath offended.' As soon as the fire got up, he was very soon dead, never stirring or crying all the while.

His patience in the torment, his courage in dying, if it had been taken either for the glory of God, the wealth of his country, or the testimony of truth, as it was for a pernicious error, and subversion of true religion, I could worthily have commended the example, and matched it with the fame of any father of ancient time: but, seeing that not the death, but cause and quarrel thereof, commendeth the sufferer, I cannot but much dispraise his obstinate stubbornness and sturdiness in dying, and specially in so evil a cause. Surely his death much grieved every man; but not after one sort. Some pitied to see his body so tormented with the fire raging upon the silly carcass, that counted not of the folly. Other that passed not much of the body, lamented to see him spill his soul, wretchedly, without redemption, to be plagued for ever. His friends sorrowed for love; his enemies for pity: strangers for a common kind of humanity, whereby we are bound one to another. Thus I have enforced myself, for your sake, to discourse this heavy narration, contrary to my mind: and, being more than half weary, I make a short end, wishing you a quieter life, with less honour; and easier death, with more praise.

Question:
1. Does the writer demonstrate any ambivalence about the execution of Cranmer?

11.8   A Right with Roots in the Bible

The Spanish missionary Bartolome de Las Casas (1574–1576) first visited the Americas in 1502. Appalled by what he saw, he devoted his life to improving the lot of the indigenous people of the New World. Central to his mission was a clear conviction that, as human beings, the peoples of the Americas had rights that Europeans had to respect.

Source: *Las Casas: In Search of the Poor of Jesus Christ*, by Gustavo Gutierrez, translation by Robert R. Bass (New York: Orbis Books, 1993), pp. 27–31.

PREACHING THE GOSPEL TRUTH

It had been nineteen years now since the inhabitants of the so-called Indies had begun to suffer foreign occupation, with its attendant abuse, exploitation, and death at the hands of the "discoverers" (from the European viewpoint) of these lands. The natives were treated "as if they had been useless animals," and the colonists "mourned their deaths only for reason of the inconvenience that now they would no longer be able to work the gold mines and plantations for them," since the Europeans only sought "to grow rich on the blood of those wretches." Sorrowfully the friars asked: "How can so very many people that there had been on this island, according to what we have been told, in such a brief time, a space of fifteen or sixteen years, have so cruelly perished?" The allusion is to the horrible decimation of the population of the island, which we have seen.

A consideration of the "sorrowful life and awful captivity suffered by the native people of this island" now led the Dominican religious of Hispaniola to "set the facts of the case over against the principles of justice and right"—*juntar el derecho con el hecho*, as they put it. That is, it moved them to submit their knowledge of the situation to an ethical reflection and to confront the oppression they saw before them with the "law of Christ" (*H.I.*, bk. 3, ch. 3, *O.E.* 2:174a–b). On that law is based the right which Las Casas says "must be proclaimed." After all, he goes on, "Are we not obliged to preach the law of Christ to them, and to labor with all diligence to convert them?" (ibid.).

Nor was this act of *juntar el derecho con el hecho* to be a mere speculative enterprise on the Dominicans' part. It would move them to make a decision, "after commending themselves to God," to "preach in the public pulpits, and to declare, the state in which our sinful compatriots have held and oppressed these people." Thus they would be performing their function as preachers. Las Casas then makes the ironic observation that it was necessary to call the oppressors' attention to the fact that, by dying in this sin, "as the crown of their inhumanities and greed, they were assuring themselves of their reward." Las Casas remarks the role played in this decision by a former conquistador, Juan Garcés. Garcés had repented his crimes and after passing through a number of personal difficulties had became a "lay friar" of the Dominicans. To the wonder and admiration of the religious, he straightforwardly recounted the "execrable cruelties" that he and others had committed against the Indians (*H.I.*, bk. 3, ch. 3, *O.E.* 2:174b–175a).

The Dominicans ("spiritual individuals," Bartolomé calls them, "and very much the friends of God"; ibid., *O.E.* 2:174b), aware of the gravity of the matter, composed, and all signed, the sermon to be delivered by Friar Antón Montesino (as Las Casas writes the name), whom he calls a great preacher and "most severe in the reprehension of vices. They selected the Fourth Sunday of Advent and took as their text John the Baptist's cry, "I am a 'voice in the desert...' " (John 1:23). They invited all of the notables of the island, among them Admiral Diego Colón, to sit and listen (ibid., *O.E.* 2:175). The content of the sermon is known to us only in Las Casas's version, which—even if he has placed, decades later, something of his own there—is basically authentic, as reactions to the sermon, which we know from other sources as well, credibly attest.

The text is familiar enough, but in view of its historical importance, and especially its influence on our friar's thought, it will be worth our while to examine it here. Las Casas reports that, in keeping with the spirit of the gospel reading for that Sunday, the preacher began with an observation on the "sterility of the desert of the consciences" of those present. Montesino then claims to be the voice crying on that bleak and barren plain.

Let us reproduce verbatim what Friar Bartolomé reports:

You are all in mortal sin! You live in it and you die in it! Why? Because of the cruelty and tyranny you use with these innocent people. Tell me, with what right, with what justice, do you hold these Indians in such cruel and horrible servitude? On what authority have you waged such detestable wars on these people, in their mild, peaceful lands, where you have consumed such infinitudes of them, wreaking upon them this death and unheard-of havoc? How is it that you hold them so crushed and exhausted, giving them nothing to eat, nor any treatment for their diseases, which you cause them to be infected with through the surfeit of their toils, so that they "die on you" [as you say]— you mean, you kill them—mining gold for you day after day? And what care do you take that anyone catechize them, so that they may come to know their God and Creator, be baptized, hear Mass, observe Sundays and Holy Days? Are they not human beings? Have they no rational souls? Are you not obligated to love them as you love yourselves? Do you not understand this? Do you not grasp this? How is it that you sleep so soundly, so lethargically? Know for a certainty that in the state in which you are you can no more be saved than Moors or Turks who have not, nor wish to have, the faith of Jesus Christ. (*H.I.*, bk. 3, ch. 4, *O.E.* 2:176)

Many of the burning questions that would be debated over the next half-century and more are present in seed here. The first fact that provokes the friars' indignation is the oppression of the Indian, of which they themselves are direct and daily witnesses. The natives are subjected to a "horrible servitude," and a lethal one, as they toil in the mines "for gold, day after day." The tragic relationship between *greed* and *death* thus makes its appearance in the very first denunciation. Second, this deadly exploitation—this murder—has only been a prolongation of the initial injustice: that of the "detestable wars" that had been waged against the Indians, for no just reason whatever. Third, Montesino ridicules the official pretext for the *encomiendas:* What genuine concern is there, he scoffs, on the part of the oppressors for the Christian life of their native victims?

The friars go even further. To these three denunciations they add, speaking through the mouth of Montesino, a consideration that will become the material of a distinct tractate. After all, the Indians are persons, and consequently have all the rights of persons. "Are they not human beings? Have they no rational souls?" The preacher's premise is destined to be an important one in the great dispute launched by his sermon. But for Montesino, this humanistic proposition is only a stepping stone to an exigency of the gospel: "Are you not then obliged to love them as yourselves?" This radical Christian requirement, which supposes equality ("as yourselves") between Spaniards and Indians before God, goes beyond the duties of justice, which has been so treacherously violated. It transfers the problem to new ground: that of love, which knows no juridical or philosophic limits.

This evangelical perspective, it seems to us, is the key to an understanding of the Dominicans' mighty challenge. The elaborate theology of law being developed at about this same time by Vitoria Domingo de Soto, and others, based on the thought of Thomas Aquinas, has recently occasioned a retrospective interpretation of the missionaries' theological stance in the light of the *jus gentium*, or Law of Nations—if not indeed of natural law and its theological implications. This is what occurs, it seems to us, in the case of V. Carro, author of a classic work on the sixteenth-century theologians of law. Carro builds his exegesis of the sermon on the pertinent questions—"Are they not human beings? Have they no rational souls?"—and asserts that the friars have indicated the route "the theology of law will take, from that point onward, to give life to the best elements of the Laws of the Indies, the route that theologians like Vitoria and de Soto will develop and broaden. . . . These expressions will give rise to the theories that legal theology will posit for the protection of the rights inherent in human personhood. Very precisely, Montesino reflects the correct teaching, one having its roots in the principles of St. Thomas."

But Carro fails to go on to the next question, which recalls human siblingship along such demanding evangelical lines: "Are you not obliged to love them as yourselves?" Shortly before quoting the text of Montesino's sermon, in a reference to the moment at which the friars decided to denounce "the deeds that the Spaniards were perpetrating upon the Indians," Las Casas sets forth some of the concepts that will be contained in that sermon. In the face of the "ugliness and enormity of such unheard-of injustice," he says, surely we shall have to ask: "Are these not humans? Need not the precepts of *charity* and justice be kept in our dealings with them?' " (*H.I.*, bk. 3, ch. 3, *O.E.* 2:174b; emphasis added). And indeed, uppermost in the Dominicans' mind is the ever new commandment of love.

We are not attempting to set up a facile opposition between the theologico-juridical foundations and the exigencies of the gospel. But we do think it important to call attention to the difference in their quality and extension. After all, without the gospel, the foundations of a theology of law lack their proper, vital context. The various questions of Montesino's homily are interconnected, of course. But the one that recalls the Indian's quality as "neighbor" to the Spaniards, which the missioners see as entailing a duty to love, is the furthest-reaching question, and the one that gives meaning to the others.

In a penetrating and frequently cited passage, Chacón y Calvo asserts, apropos of the sermon upon which we are commenting: "At this solemn moment, in the humble residence of a few courageous friars, a new system of law sprang into being, a law with deep theological roots." And a law with deep biblical roots, let us add, since the power of the cry of Hispaniola is truly rooted in the Bible.

Question:
1. What is behind Las Casas' view of the rights of the native population?

PART 12
Society and Politics in Early Modern Europe

12.1   The German Peasant's Revolt: The Twelve Articles

Luther's stand against pope and emperor coincided with the growing anger and resentment of peasants and urban workers against noble authority. The following year the leaders of the peasants in the south-west German area drew up a manifesto of their demands. Sympathetic to their grievances, yet opposed to social revolution and disruption of public order, Luther urged the peasants to refrain from violence and seek a peaceful resolution. When the nobility disdainfully rejected the Articles, however, a bloody and destructive peasant rebellion erupted that was brutally crushed. Luther sternly approved of the retaliation because of the death and destruction that the rebels' violence had caused.

> **Source:** *Sources of the Western Tradition: Volume I: From Ancient Times to the Enlightenment,* ed. Marvin Perry, Joseph R. Peden, and Theodore H. Von Laue, (Boston: Houghton Mifflin Co., 1995), p 329–30. Reprinted with permission from *Translations and Reprints from the Original Sources of European History,* (1895 series) ed. D. C. Munro (Philadelphia: University of Pennsylvania, 1899), Vol.2, pp. 25–30.

Peace to the Christian reader and the grace of God through Christ:

There are many evil writings put forth of late which take occasion, on account of the assembling of the peasants, to cast scorn upon the Gospel, saying: "Is this the fruit of the new teaching, that no one should obey but all should everywhere rise in revolt, and rush together to reform, or perhaps destroy entirely, the authorities, both ecclesiastical and lay?" The articles below shall answer these godless and criminal fault-finders, and serve, in the first place, to remove the reproach from the word of God and, in the second place, to give a Christian excuse for the disobedience or even the revolt of the entire Peasantry....

The Second Article According as the just tithe [a tax paid in grain] is established by the Old Testament and fulfilled in the New, we are ready and willing to pay the fair tithe of grain. The word of God plainly provides that in giving... to God and distributing to his people the services of a pastor are required. We will that for the future our church provost [manager of a feudal estate], whomsoever the community may appoint, shall gather and receive this tithe. From this he shall give to the pastor, elected by the whole community, a decent and sufficient maintenance for him and his, as shall seem right to the whole community.... The small tithes,*whether ecclesiastical or lay, we will not pay at all, for the Lord God created cattle for the free use of man. We will not, therefore, pay farther an unseemly tithe which is of man's invention.

The Third Article It has been the custom hitherto for men to hold us as their own property, which is pitiable enough, considering that Christ has delivered and redeemed us all, without exception, by the shedding of his precious blood, the lowly as well as the great. Accordingly it is consistent with Scripture that we should be free and should wish to be so. Not that we would wish to be absolutely free and under no authority. God does not teach us that we should lead a disorderly life in the lusts of the flesh, but that we should love the Lord our God and our neighbor. We would gladly observe all this as God has commanded us in the celebration of the communion. He has not commanded us not to obey the authorities, but rather that we should be humble, not only towards those in authority, but towards every one. We are thus ready to yield obedience according to God's law to our elected and regular authorities in all proper things becoming to a Christian. We therefore take it for granted that you will release us from serfdom as true Christians, unless it should be shown us from the gospel that we are serfs....

The Tenth Article In the tenth place, we are aggrieved by the appropriation by individuals of meadows and fields which at one time belonged to a community. These we will take again into our own hands. It may, however, happen that the land was rightfully purchased, but when the land has unfortunately been purchased in this way, some brotherly arrangement should be made according to circumstances.

The Eleventh Article In the eleventh place, we will entirely abolish the due called [heriot, a death tax], and will no longer endure it nor allow widows and orphans to be thus shamefully robbed against God's will....

Questions:
1. What influence did Luther's reformation doctrine have on these Articles?
2. What were their social and political demands?

---

* This is, tithes of other products than the staple crops-for example, tithes of pigs or lambs.

12.2 Elizabeth's Act of Uniformity, 1559

When Elizabeth I (1533–1603) came to the throne in 1558, England had endured more than twenty years of religious upheaval. The Act of Uniformity of Common Prayer, and Service in Church, and Administration of the Sacraments (1559) was an effort to reach a religious compromise that the majority of Elizabethans could live with. It was, in large measure, a success.

Source: *Documents of the Christian Church*, ed. Henry Bettenson (New York: Oxford University Press, 1970), pp. 235–239.

Where at the death of our late sovereign lord King Edward VI there remained one uniform order of common service and prayer, and of the administration of sacraments, rites, and ceremonies in the Church of England, which was set forth in one book, intituled: The Book of Common Prayer, and Administration of Sacraments, and other rites and ceremonies in the Church of England; authorized by Act of Parliament holden in the fifth and sixth years of our said late sovereign lord King Edward VI, intituled: An Act for the uniformity of common prayer, and administration of the sacraments; the which was repealed and taken away by Act of Parliament in the first year of the reign of our late sovereign lady Queen Mary, to the great decay of the due honour of God, and discomfort to the professors of the truth of Christ's religion:

Be it therefore enacted by the authority of this present Parliament, that the said statute of repeal, and everything therein contained, only concerning the said book, and the service, administration of sacraments, rites, and ceremonies contained or appointed in or by the said book, shall be void and of none effect, from and after the feast of the Nativity of St John Baptist next coming; and that the said book, with the order of service, and of the administration of sacraments, rites, and ceremonies, with the alterations and additions therein added and appointed by this statute, shall stand and be, from and after the said feast of the Nativity Of St John Baptist, in full force and effect, according to the tenor and effect of this statute; anything in the aforesaid statute of repeal to the contrary notwithstanding.

And further be it enacted by the queen's highness, with the assent of the Lords and Commons in this present Parliament assembled, and by authority of the same, that all and singular ministers in any cathedral or parish church, or other place within this realm of England, Wales, and the marches of the same, or other the queen's dominions, shall from and after the feast of the Nativity of St John Baptist next coming be bounden to say and use the Matins, Evensong, celebration of the Lord's Supper and administration of each of the sacraments, and all their common and open prayer, in such order and form as is mentioned in the said book, so authorized by Parliament in the said fifth and sixth years of the reign of King Edward VI, with one alteration or addition of certain lessons to be used on every Sunday in the year,[1] and the form of the Litany altered and corrected,[2] and two sentences only added in the delivery of the sacrament to the communicants,[3] and none other or otherwise.

And that if any manner of parson, vicar, or other whatsoever minister, that ought or should sing or say common prayer mentioned in the said book, or minister the sacraments, from and after the feast of the Nativity of St John Baptist next coming, refuse to use the said common prayers, or to minister the sacraments in such cathedral or parish church, or other places as he should use to minister the same, in such order and form as they be mentioned and set forth in the said book, or shall, wilfully or obstinately standing in the same, use any other rite, ceremony, order, form, or manner of celebrating of the Lord's Supper, openly or privily, or Matins, Evensong, administration of the sacraments, or other open prayers, than is mentioned and set forth in the said book (open prayer in and throughout this Act, is meant that prayer which is for other to come unto, or hear, either in common churches or private chapels or oratorios, commonly called the service of the Church), or shall preach, declare, or speak anything in the derogation or depraving of the said book, or anything therein contained, or of any part th7ereof, and shall be thereof lawfully convicted, according to the laws of this realm, by verdict of twelve men, or by his own confession, or by the notorious evidence of the fact, shall lose and forfeit to the queen's highness, her heirs and successors, for his first offence, the profit of all his spiritual benefices or promotions coming or arising in the one whole year next after his conviction; and also that the person so convicted shall for the same offence suffer imprisonment by the space of six months, without bail or mainprize.

---

[1] Proper Lessons for Sundays were given in 1st P.B. of Edw. VI (1549), but omitted in the 1552 Book.

[2] The more important changes were: the omission of the deprecation, 'From the tyranny of the bishop of Rome and all his detestable enormities,' which appeared in 1549 and 1552, and the inclusion of the *Prayer of the Queen's Majesty*, and the *Prayer for the Clergy and People*, which have been, since 1662, included in Morning and Evening Prayer.

[3] In the 1549 Book the words of administration were, 'The body (blood) of our Lord Jesus Christ which Was given (shed) for thee, preserve thy body and soul unto everlasting life.' In 1552 there was substituted, 'Take and eat this (Drink this) in remembrance that Christ died (Christ's blood was shed) for thee, and feed on him in thy heart by faith with thanksgiving (and be thankful).' The two forms were combined in 1559 and retained thus in 1662.

And if any such person once convicted of any offence concerning the premises, shall after his first conviction eftsoons offend, and be thereof, in form aforesaid, lawfully convicted, that then the same person shall for his second offence suffer imprisonment by the space of one whole year, and also shall therefor be deprived, *ipso facto*, of all his spiritual promotions; and that it shall be lawful to all patrons or donors of all and singular the same spiritual promotions, or of any of them, to present or collate to the same, as though the person and persons so offending were dead.

And that if any such person or persons, after he shall be twice convicted in form aforesaid, shall offend against any of the premises the third time, and shall be thereof, in form aforesaid, lawfully convicted, that then the person so offending and convicted the third time, shall be deprived, *ipso facto*, of all his spiritual promotions, and also shall suffer imprisonment during his life.

And if the person that shall offend, and be convicted in form aforesaid, concerning any of the premises, shall not be beneficed, nor have any spiritual promotion, that then the same person so offending and convicted shall for the first offence suffer imprisonment during one whole year next after his said conviction, without bail or mainprize. And if any such person, not having any spiritual promotion, after his first conviction shall eftsoons offend in anything concerning the premises, and shall be, in form aforesaid, thereof lawfully convicted, that then the same person shall for his second offence suffer imprisonment during his life.

And it is ordained and enacted by the authority aforesaid, that if any person or persons whatsoever, after the said feast of the Nativity of St John Baptist next coming, shall in any interludes, plays, songs, rhymes, or by other open words, declare or speak anything in the derogation, depraving, or despising of the same book, or anything therein contained, or any part thereof, or shall, by open fact, deed, or by open threatenings, compel or cause, or otherwise procure or maintain, any parson, vicar, or other minister in any cathedral or parish church, or in chapel, or in any other place, to sing or say any common or open prayer, or to minister any sacrament otherwise, or in any other manner and form, than is mentioned in the said book; or that by any of the said means shall unlawfully interrupt or let any parson, vicar, or other minister in any cathedral or parish church, chapel, or any other place, to sing or say common and open prayer, or to minister the sacraments or any of them, in such manner and form as is mentioned in the said book; that then every such person, being thereof lawfully convicted in form abovesaid, shall forfeit to the queen our sovereign lady, her heirs and successors, for the first offence a hundred marks.

And if any person or persons, being once convicted of any such offence, eftsoons offend against any of the last recited offences, and shall, in form aforesaid, be thereof lawfully convicted, that then the same person so offending and convicted shall, for the second offence, forfeit to the queen our sovereign lady, her heirs and successors, four hundred marks.

And if any person, after he, in form aforesaid, shall have been twice convicted of any offence concerning any of the last recited offences, shall offend the third time, and be thereof, in form abovesaid, lawfully convicted, that then every person so offending and convicted shall for his third offence forfeit to our sovereign lady the queen all his goods and chattels, and shall suffer imprisonment during his life.

And if any person or persons, that for his first offence concerning the premises shall be convicted, in form aforesaid, do not pay the sum to be paid by virtue of his conviction, in such manner and form as the same ought to be paid, within six weeks next after his conviction; that then every person so convicted, and so not paying the same, shall for the same first offence, instead of the said sum, suffer imprisonment by the space of six months, without bail or mainprize. And if any person or persons, that for his second offence concerning the premises shall be convicted in form aforesaid, do not pay the said sum to be paid by virtue of his conviction and this statute, in such manner and form as the same ought to be paid, within six weeks next after his said second conviction; that then every person so convicted, and not so paying the same, shall, for the same second offence, in the stead of the said sum, suffer imprisonment during twelve months, without bail or mainprize.

And that from and after the said feast of the Nativity of St John Baptist next coming, all and every person and persons inhabiting within this realm, or any other the queen's majesty's dominions, shall diligently and faithfully, having no lawful or reasonable excuse to be absent, endeavour themselves to resort to their parish church or chapel accustomed, or upon reasonable let thereof, to some usual place where common prayer and such service of God shall be used in such time of let, upon every Sunday and other days ordained and used to be kept as holy days, and then and there to abide orderly and soberly during the time of the common prayer, preachings, or other service of God there to be used and ministered; upon pain of punishment by the censures of the Church, and also upon pain that every person so offending shall forfeit for every such offence twelve pence, to be levied by the churchwardens of the parish where such offence shall be done, to the use of the poor of the same parish, of the goods, lands, and tenements of such offender, by way of distress.

And for due execution hereof, the queen's most excellent majesty, the Lords temporal (*sic*), and all the Commons, in this present Parliament assembled, do in God's name earnestly require and charge all the archbishops, bishops, and other ordinaries, that they shall endeavour themselves to the uttermost of their knowledges, that the due and true execution hereof may be had throughout their dioceses and charges, as they will answer before God, for such evils and plagues wherewith Almighty God may justly punish His people for neglecting this good and wholesome law. . . .

Question:
1. Which side in the struggle would have been the most satisfied with this Act? The least?

12.3 The Arrest of the Catholic Priest Edmund Campion and his Associates 17 July 1581—Report of a Government Agent

The English Jesuit Edmund Campion (c. 1540–1581) was ordained a Catholic priest in Douai, a town in what is now northern France but which, in the sixteenth century, was controlled by the Spanish Hapsburgs. He was sent to England as a missionary in 1580 where he devoted himself to preserving Catholicism in England. In 1581 he was captured by the English government, tortured, and then executed. He was made a saint by the Roman Catholic Church in 1970.

Source: *Eyewitness to History*, by John Casey (New York: Avon Books, 1997), pp. 121–127.

It happened that after the receipt of our Commission, we consulted between ourselves, What way were best to take first? For we were utterly ignorant where, or in what place, certainly to find out the said Campion, or his compeers. And our consultation was shortly determined: for the greatest part of our travail and dealings in this service did lie chiefly upon mine own determination, by reason of mine acquaintance and knowledge of divers of the like sect.

It then presently came to my remembrance of certain acquaintance which I once had with one Thomas Cooper a cook, who, in November [1578] was two years, served Master Thomas Roper of [Orpington in] Kent; where, at that time, I in like manner served: and both of us, about the same month, departed the said Master Roper his service; I into Essex, and the said Cooper to Lyford in Berkshire, to one Master Yate. From whence, within one half year after, I was advertised in Essex, that the said Cook was placed in service; and that the said Master Yate was a very earnest Papist, and one that gave great entertainment to any of that sect.

Which tale, being told me in Essex two years before we entered [on] this journey, by God's great goodness, came to my memory but even the day before we set forth. Hereof I informed the said David Jenkins, being my fellow in Commission, and told him it would be our best way to go thither first: for that it was not meant that we should go to any place but where indeed I either had acquaintance; or by some means possible in our journey, could get acquaintance. And told him we would dispose of our journey in such sort as we might come to the said Master Yate's upon the Sunday about eight of the clock in the morning: 'where,' said I, 'if we find the said Cook, and that there be any Mass to be said there that day, or any massing Priest in the house; the Cook, for old acquaintance and for that he supposeth me to be a Papist, will bring me to the sight thereof.'

And upon this determination, we set from London the 14th day of July last; and came to the said Master Yate's house, the 16th of the same month, being Sunday, about the hour aforesaid.

Where, without the gates of the same house, we espied one of the servants of the house, who most likely seemed, by reason of his lying aloof, to be as it were a Scout Watcher, that they within might accomplish their secret matters more safely.

I called the said servant, and inquired of him for the said Thomas Cooper the Cook.

Who answered, That he could not well tell, whether he were within or not.

I prayed him that he would friend me so much as to see; and told him my name.

The said servant did so, it seemed; for the Cook came forth presently unto us where we sat still upon horseback. And after a few such speeches, as betwixt friend and friend when they have been long asunder, were passed; still sitting upon our horses, I told him That I had longed to see him; and that I was then travelling into Derbyshire to see my friends, and came so far out of my way to see him. And said I, 'Now I have seen you, my mind is well satisfied; and so fare you well!'

'No,' saith he, 'that shall you not do before dinner.'

I made the matter very earnest to be gone; and he, more earnest and importune to stay me. But in truth I was as willing to stay as he to have me.

And so, perforce, there was no remedy but stay we must. And having lighted from horseback; and being by him brought into the house, and so into the buttery, and there caused to drink: presently after, the said Cook came and whispered with me, and asked, Whether my friend (meaning the said Jenkins) were within the Church or not? Therein meaning, Whether he were a Papist or no?

To which I answered, 'He was not; but yet,' said I, 'he is a very honest man, and one that wisheth well that way.'

Then said the Cook to me, 'Will you go up?' By which speech, I knew he would bring me to a Mass.

And I answered him and said, 'Yea, for God's sake, that let me do: for seeing I must needs tarry, let me take something with me that is good.'

And so we left Jenkins in the buttery; and I was brought by the Cook through the hall, the dining parlour, and two or three other odd rooms, and then into a fair large chamber: where there was, at the same instant, one Priest, called Satwell, saying Mass; two other Priests kneeling by, whereof one was Campion, and the other called Peters *alias* Collington; three Nuns, and 37 other people.

When Satwell had finished his Mass; then Campion he invested himself to say Mass, and so he did: and at the end thereof, made holy bread and delivered it to the people there, to every one some, together with holy water; whereof he gave me part also.

And then was there a chair set in the chamber something beneath the altar, wherein the said Campion did sit down; and there made a sermon very nigh an hour long: the effect of his text being, as I remember, 'That Christ wept over Jerusalem, &c.' And so applied the same to this our country of England for that the Pope his authority and doctrine did not so flourish here as the same Campion desired.

At the end of which sermon, I gat down unto the said Jenkins so soon as I could. For during the time that the Masses and the sermon were made, Jenkins remained still beneath in the buttery or hall; not knowing of any such matter until I gave him some intelligence what I had seen.

And so we departed, with as convenient expedition as we might, and came to one Master Fettiplace, a Justice of the Peace in the said country: whom we made privy of our doings therein; and required him that, according to the tenour of our Commission, he would take sufficient Power, and with us thither.

Whereupon the said Justice of Peace, within one quarter of an hour, put himself in a readiness, with forty or fifty men very well weaponed: who went, in great haste, together with the said Master Fettiplace and us, to the said Master Yate his house.

Where, at our coming upon the sudden, being about one of the clock in the afternoon of the same day, before we knocked at the gates which were then (as before they were continually accustomed to be) fast shut (the house being moated round about; within which moat was great store of fruit trees and other trees, with thick hedgerows: so that the danger for fear of losing of the said Campion and his associates was the more doubted); we beset the house with our men round about the moat in the best sort we could devise: and then knocked at the gates, and were presently heard and espied; but kept out by the space of half an hour.

In which time, as it seemeth, they had hidden Campion and the other two Priests in a very secret place within the said house; and had made reasonable purveyance for him as hereafter is mentioned: and then they let us into the house.

Where came presently to our sight, Mrs Yate, the good wife of the house; five Gentlemen, one Gentlewoman, and three Nuns: the Nuns being then disguised in Gentlewomen's apparel, not like unto that they heard Mass in. All which I well remembered to have seen, the same morning, at the Masses and Sermon aforesaid: yet every one of them a great while denied it. And especially the said Mistress Yate; who could not be content only to make a plain denial of the said Masses and the Priests: but, with great and horrible oaths, forsware the same, betaking herself to the Devil if any such there were; in such sort as, if I had not seen them with mine own eyes, I should have believed her.

But knowing certainly that these were but bare excuses, and that we should find the said Campion and his compeers if we made narrow search; I eftsoons put Master Fettiplace in remembrance of our Commission: and so he, myself, and the said Jenkins Her Majesty's Messenger, went to searching the house; where we found many secret corners.

Continuing the search, although with no small toil, in the orchards, hedges, and ditches, within the moat and divers other places; at the last found out Master Edward Yate, brother to the good man of the house, and two countrymen called Weblin and Mansfield, fast locked together in a pigeon house: but we could not find, at that time, Campion and the other two Priests whom we specially sought for.

It drew then something towards evening, and doubting lest we were not strong enough; we sent our Commission to one Master Foster, High Sheriff of Berkshire; and to one Master Wiseman, a justice of Peace within the same County; for some further aid at their hands.

The said Master Wiseman came with very good speed unto us the same evening, with ten or twelve of his own men, very able men and well appointed: but the said Master Foster could not be found, as the messenger that went for him returned us answer.

And so the said house was beset the same night with at the least three score men well weaponed; who watched the same very diligently.

And the next day, being Monday, in the morning very early, came one Master Christopher Lydcot, a Justice of Peace of the same shire, with a great sort of his own men, all very well appointed: who, together with his men, shewed such earnest loyal and forward service in those affairs as was no small comfort and encouragement to all those which were present, and did bear true hearts and good wills to Her Majesty.

The same morning, began a fresh search for the said Priests; which continued with very great labour until about ten of the clock in the forenoon of the same day: but the said Priests could not be found, and every man almost persuaded that they were not there.

Yet still searching, although in effect clean void of any hope for finding of them, the said David Jenkins, by God's great goodness, espied a certain secret place, which he quickly found to be hollow; and with a pin of iron which he had in his hand much like unto a harrow tine, he forthwith did break a hole into the said place: where then presently he perceived the said Priests lying all close together upon a bed, of purpose there laid for them; where they had bread, meat, and drink sufficient to have relieved them three or four days together.

The said Jenkins then called very loudly, and said, 'I have found the traitors!'; and presently company enough was with him: who there saw the said Priests, when there was no remedy for them but *nolens volens*, courteously yielded themselves.

Shortly after came one Master Reade, another justice of the Peace of the said shire, to be assistant in these affairs.

Of all which matters, news was immediately carried in great haste to the Lords of the Privy Council: who gave further Commission that the said Priests and certain others their associates should be brought to the Court under the conduction of myself and the said Jenkins; with commandment to the Sheriff to deliver us sufficient aid forth of his shire, for the safe bringing up of the said people.

After the rumour and noise for the finding out of the said Campion, Satwell, and Peters *alias* Collington, was in the said house something assuaged; and that the sight of them was to the people there no great novelty: then was the said High Sheriff sent for once again; who all that while had not been seen in this service. But then came, and received into his charge the said Priests and certain others from that day until Thursday following.

The fourth Priest which was by us brought up to the Tower, whose name is William Filbie, was not taken with the said Campion and the rest in the said house: but was apprehended and taken in our watch by chance, in coming to the said house to speak with the said Peters, as he said; and thereupon delivered likewise in charge to the Sheriff, with the rest.

Upon Thursday, the 20th day of July last, we set forwards from the said Master Yate his house towards the Court, with our said charge; being assisted by the said Master Lydcot and Master Wiseman, and a great sort of their men; who never left us until we came to the Tower of London. There were besides, that guarded us thither, 50 or 60 Horsemen; very able men and well appointed: which we received by the said Sheriff his appointment.

We went that day to Henley upon Thames, where we lodged that night.

And about midnight we were put into great fear by reason of a very great cry and noise that the said Filbie made in his sleep; which wakened the most that were that night in the house, and that in such sort that every man almost thought that some of the prisoners had been broken from us and escaped; although there was in and about the same house a very strong watch appointed and charged for the same. The aforesaid Master Lydcot was the first that came unto them: and when the matter was examined, it was found no more but that the said Filbie was in a dream; and, as he said, he verily thought one to be a ripping down his body and taking out his bowels.

Question:
1. What is revealed about the qualities and character of the people trying to capture the priest?

12.4 The Peace of Westphalia, 1648

The Peace of Westphalia (1648) brought the Thirty Years War to a close. The treaty brought some measure of religious toleration to Europe, contributed to France's emergence as the dominant power on the continent, and dealt a mortal blow to France's chief rival, the Holy Roman Empire.

Source: *Documents of the Christian Church*, ed. Henry Bettenson (New York: Oxford University Press, 1970), pp. 216–217.

V. Religious Grievances

I. Confirmation of the Convention of Passau and the Peace of Augsburg.

15. The Ecclesiastical Reservation. Catholics or Lutherans holding an ecclesiastical dignity to vacate it and its income if they change their religion.

21. The investiture of Protestant Prelates to take place when they have taken the due oaths.

34. Toleration given to those who, in 1624, had not the right to exercise their religion, being subjects of a lord of the other faith.

35. Subjects whose religion differs from that of their prince are to have equal rights with his other subjects.

36. Those emigrating for religious reasons retain the administration of their property.

43. The religious position in provinces where the lordship is contested.

50. Disputes about the religious peace of Augsburg and the peace of Westphalia to be carried before the diet. All doctrines contrary of these treaties are forbidden.

VI. The independence of the Swiss is acknowledged.

VII. 1. The Reformed [Calvinists] are to have equal rights in religion and other matters with the other states and subjects.

2. . . . but, besides the religions named [Catholic, Lutheran, Calvinist] above, no other shall be accepted or tolerated in the Holy Roman Empire.

Question:
1. What is the great importance of the Peace of Westphalia?

12.5   Putting the Poor to Work

In response to a perceived increase in the numbers of the poor, as well as to the disorder attributed to them, the Elizabethan parliament passed a series of poor laws in 1601. The laws defined central and local governmental responsibilities with respect to the poor, limited internal migration, and established poorhouses.

> **Source:** *Select Statutes and other Constitutional Documents Illustrative of the Reigns of Elizabeth and James I*, ed. G. W. Prothero, 4th edition, (New York: Oxford at the Clarendon Press, 1934, original 4th edition 1913, I" edition 1894), pp. 72–75, 96–103.

AN ACT FOR THE RELIEF OF THE POOR.

I. Be it enacted, That the churchwardens of every parish and four substantial householders there being subsidy men, or (for want of subsidy men) four other substantial householders of the said parish, who shall be nominated yearly in Easter week under the hand and seal of two or more justices of the peace in the same county, whereof one to be of the quorum, dwelling in or near the same parish, shall be called overseers of the poor of the same parish; and they . . . shall take order from time to time with the consent of two or more such justices of peace for setting to work of the children of all such [*sic*] whose parents shall not by the said persons be thought able to keep and maintain their children, and also all such persons, married or unmarried, as, having no means to maintain them, use no ordinary and daily trade of life to get their living by; and also to raise . . . by taxation of every inhabitant and every occupier of lands in the said parish . . . a convenient stock of flax, hemp, wool, thread, iron and other stuff to set the poor on work, and also competent sums of money for the necessary relief of the lame, impotent, old, blind and such other among them being poor and not able to work, and also for the putting out of such children to be apprentices . . . and to do all other things . . . concerning the premises as to them shall seem convenient:

· · · ·

II. And be it also enacted, That if the said justices of peace do perceive that the inhabitants of any parish are not able to levy among themselves sufficient sums of money for the purposes aforesaid, that then the said justices shall tax . . . any other of other parishes . . . within the hundred where the said parish is, to pay such sums of money . . . as the said justices shall think fit, according to the intent of this law; and if the said hundred shall not be thought to the said justices able to relieve the said several parishes . . . then the justices of peace at their general quarter sessions shall rate and assess as aforesaid any other of other parishes . . . within the said county for the purposes aforesaid as in their discretion shall seem fit.

III. And that it shall be lawful for the said churchwardens and overseers or any of them by warrant from any such two justices of peace to levy as well the said sums of money of every one that shall refuse to contribute . . . by distress and sale of the offender's goods, as the sums of money or stock which shall be behind upon any account to be made as aforesaid . . .; and in defect of such distress it shall be lawful for any such two justices of the peace to commit him to prison, there to remain . . . till payment of the said sum or stock; and the said justices of peace or any one of them to send to the house of correction such as shall not employ themselves to work being appointed thereunto as aforesaid; and also any two such justices of peace to commit to prison every one of the said churchwardens and overseers which shall refuse to account, there to remain . . . till he have made a true account and paid so much as upon the said account shall be remaining in his hands.

IV. And be it further enacted, That it shall be lawful for the said churchwardens and overseers by the assent of any two justices of the peace to bind any such children as aforesaid to be apprentices when they shall see convenient, till such man-child shall come to the age of 24 years and such woman-child to the ahe of 21 years . . .

. . . .

X. And be it further enacted, That . . . no person shall go wandering abroad and beg in any place whatsoever, by licence or without, upon pain to be taken and punished as a rogue: provided always that this present Act shall not extend to any poor people which shall ask relief of victuals only in the same parish where such poor people do dwell, so the same be . . . according to such order as shall be made by the churchwardens and overseers of the poor of the same parish . . .

XI. And be it further enacted, That all penalties and forfeitures before mentioned in this Act shall be employed to the use of the poor of the same parish, and towards a stock and habitation for them and other necessary uses and relief . . .

. . . .

XIII. And be it also enacted, That the said justices of the peace at their general quarter sessions . . . shall set down what competent sum of money shall be sent quarterly out of every county or place corporate for the relief of the poor prisoners of the King's Bench and Marshalsea, and also of such hospitals and almshouses as shall be in the said county . . . so as there be sent out of every county yearly 20*s*. at the least to the prisoners of the King's Bench and Marshalsea;

. . . .

XIV. And be it further enacted, That all the surplusage of money which shall be remaining in the said stock of any county shall by . . . the justices of peace in their quarter sessions be ordered and bestowed for the relief of the poor hospitals of that county, and of those that shall sustain losses by fire . . . or other casualties, and to such other charitable purposes . . . as to the said justices of peace shall seem convenient.

. . . .

AN ACT FOR PUNISHMENT OF ROGUES, VAGABONDS AND STURDY BEGGARS

II. Be it further enacted, That all persons calling themselves scholars going about begging, all seafaring men pretending losses [&c.] shall be deemed rogues, vagabonds and sturdy beggars, and shall sustain such punishment as by this Act is in that behalf appointed.

III. And be it enacted, That every person which is by this present Act declared to be a rogue, vagabond or sturdy beggar, which shall be . . . taken begging, vagrant or misordering themselves . . . shall upon their apprehension . . . be stripped naked from the middle upwards and shall be openly whipped until his or her body be bloody, and shall be forthwith sent from parish to parish . . . the next straight way to the parish where he was born, if the same may be known . . . ., and if the same be not known, then to the parish where be last dwelt . . . one whole year, there to put himself to labour as a true subject ought to do; or not being known where he was born or last dwelt, then to the parish through which he last passed without punishment; . . . and the party so whipped and not known where he was born or last dwelt by the space of a year, shall by the officers of the said village where he so last passed through without punishment be conveyed to the house of correction . . . or to the common gaol of that county or place, there to remain and be employed in work until he shall be placed in some service, and so to continue by the space of one whole year, or not being able of body, . . . to remain in some almshouse in the same county or place.

IV. Provided, That if any of the said rogues shall appear to be dangerous . . . or such as will not be reformed . . . it shall be lawful to the said justices . . . or any two of them . . . to commit that rogue to the house of correction or to the gaol of that county, there to remain until their next quarter sessions . . . ; and then such of the same rogues so committed, as by the justices of the peace . . . shall be thought fit not to be delivered, shall . . . be banished out of this realm . . . and at the charge of that county shall be conveyed unto such parts beyond the seas as shall be at any time hereafter for that purpose assigned by the privy council . . . or by any six or niore of them, whereof the Lord Chancellor or Lord Keeper of the Great Seal or the Lord Treasurer to be one, or be judged perpetually to the galleys of this realm, as by the same justices shall be thought fit; and if any such rogue so banished as aforesaid shall return again into any part of this realm or dominion of Wales without lawful licence . . . such offence shall be felony, and the party offending therein suffer death as in case of felony . . .

XIV. Provided, That every seafaring man suffering shipwreck, not having wherewith to relieve himself in his travels homewards, but having a testimonial under the hand of some one justice of the peace of the place where he landed, . . . may without incurring the penalty of this Act . . . ask to receive such 1 relief as shall be necessary for his passage.

AN ACT FOR ERECTING OF HOSPITALS OR ABIDING AND WORKING HOUSES FOR THE POOR.

I. Whereas at the last session of parliament provision was made as well as for maimed soldiers, by collection in every parish, as for other poor, that it should be lawful for every person, during twenty years next after the said parliament . . . , to give and bequeath in fee-simple, as well to the use of the poor as for the provision or maintenance of any house of correction or abiding-houses, or of any stocks or stores, all or any part of his lands [&c.]; her most excellent Majesty understanding that the said good law hath not taken such effect as was intended, by reason that no person can erect or incorporate any hospital [&c.] but her Majesty or by her Highness' special licence . . . , is of her princely care . . . for the relief of maimed soldiers, mariners and other poor and impotent people pleased that it be enacted . . . and be it enacted, That all persons seised of an estate in fee-simple, their heirs, executors or assigns . . . shall have full power, . . . at any time during the space of twenty yeals next ensuing, by deed enrolled in the High Court of Chancery, to found and establish one or more hospitals, maisons de dieu, abiding-places or houses of correction . . . to have continuance for ever, and from time to time to place therein such head and members and such number of poor as to him [&c.] shall seem convenient . . .

V. Provided, That no such hospital [&c.] shall be erected, founded or incorporated by force of this Act, unless upon the foundation or erection thereof the same be endowed for ever with lands, tenements or hereditaments of the clear yearly value of £10.

AN ACT FOR THE SETTING OF THE POOR ON WORK, AND FOR THE AVOIDING OF IDLENESS

IV. . . . That in every city and town corporate within this realm a competent store and stock of wool, hemp, flax, iron or other stuff by order of the mayor . . . or other head officers . . . shall be provided; and that likewise in every other market-town or other place where (to the justices of peace in their general sessions yearly next after Easter shall be thought most meet) a like competent store and stock of wool [&c.] or other stuff as the country is most meet for . . . shall be provided, the said stores and stocks in such cities and towns corporate to be committed to the custody of such persons as shall by the mayor or other head officers in every such city or town corporate be appointed, and in other towns and places to such persons as by the said justices of peace in their said general sessions . . . shall be by them appointed; which said persons . . . shall from henceforth be called the collectors and governors of the poor, to the intent every such poor and needy person . . . able to do any work . . . shall not for want of work go abroad either begging or committing pilferings or other misdemeanours . . . ; which collectors from time to time (as cause requireth) shall, of the same stock and store, deliver to such poor and needy person a competent portion to be wrought into yarn or other matter . . . , for which they shall make payment to them which work the same according to the desert of the work . . . ; which hemp [&c.] or other stuff, wrought from time to time, shall be sold by the said collectors . . . and with the money coming of the sale to buy more stuff . . . ; and if hereafter any such person able to do any such work shall refuse to work . . . or taking such work shall spoil or embezzle the same . . . he, she or they shall be received into such house of correction, there to be straightly kept, as well in diet as in work, and also punished from time to time . . .

V. And moreover be it enacted, That within every county of this realm one, two or more abiding houses or places convenient in some market-town or corporate town or other place, by . . . order of the justices of peace in their said general sessions . . . shall be provided, and called houses of correction, and also stock and store and implements be provided for setting on work and punishing not only of those which by the collectors and governors of the poor for causes aforesaid to the said houses of correction shall be brought, but also of such as be inhabiting in no parish, or be taken as rogues . . . or for any other cause ought to be abiding and kept within the same county . . .

VI. And be it also further enacted, That the said justices of peace, in their said general sessions, shall appoint from time to time overseers of every such house of correction, which said persons shall be called the censors and wardens of the houses of correction . . . ; and shall also appoint others for the gathering of such money as shall he taxed upon any persons within their several jurisdictions towards the maintenance of the said houses of correction, which shall be called the collectors for the houses of correction; and if any person refuse to be collector and governor of the poor or censor and warden or collector for any the houses of correction, that every person so refusing shall forfeit the sum of £5 . . .

Questions:

1. What concerns are expressed in the laws?
2. Who are the poor? Who is to be responsible for them?
3. What restrictions are put on them?
4. Can these concerns and responses be related in any way to present-day concerns?

12.6   The *Ecclesiastical Ordinances* of Geneva

John Calvin (1509–1564), influenced by both Luther's theology and Erasmus' humanism, experienced a sudden conversion in 1533 and became the great leader of a new generation of reformers. In 1541 his Ecclesiastical Ordinances were approved by the citizens of Geneva, allowing him to put his understanding of the church into practice. Reprinted here is part of the central section of the Ordinances.

Source: *The Protestant Reformation,* ed. Hans J Hillerbrand, (New York: Harper Torchbooks, 1968), pp. 173–78.

Of the Frequency, Place and Time of Preaching

Each Sunday, at daybreak, there shall be a sermon in St. Peter's and St. Gervaise's, also at the customary hour at St. Peter, Magdalene and St. Gervaise. At three o'clock, as well, in all three parishes, the second sermon....

On work days, besides the two sermons mentioned, there shall be preaching three times each week, on Monday, Wednesday, and Friday. These sermons shall be announced for an early hour so that they may be finished before the day's work begins. On special days of prayer the Sunday order is to be observed.

To carry out these provisions and the other responsibilities pertaining to the ministry, five ministers and three coadjutors will be needed. The latter will also be ministers and help and reinforce the others as the occasion arises.

Concerning the Second Order, Called Teachers

The proper duty of teachers is to instruct the faithful in sound doctrine so that the purity of the gospel is not corrupted by ignorance or evil opinions. We include here the aids and instructions necessary to preserve the doctrines and to keep the church from becoming desolate for lack of pastors and ministers. To use a more familiar expression, we shall call it the order of the schools.

The order nearest to the ministry and most closely associated with the government of the church is that of lecturer in theology who teaches the Old and the New Testament. Since it is impossible to profit by such instruction without first knowing languages and the humanities, and also since it is necessary to prepare for the future in order that the church may not be neglected by the young, it will be necessary to establish a school to instruct the youth, to prepare them not only for the ministry but for government.

First of all, a proper place for teaching purposes must be designated, fit to accommodate children and others who wish to profit by such instruction; to secure someone who is both learned in subject matter and capable of looking after the building, who can also read. This person is to be employed and placed under contract on condition that he provide under his charge readers in the languages and in dialectics, if it be possible. Also to secure men with bachelor degrees to teach the children. This we hope to do to further the work of God.

These teachers shall be subject to the same ecclesiastical discipline as the ministers. There shall be no other school in the city for small children; the girls shall have their school apart, as before.

No one shall be appointed unless he is approved by the ministers, who will make their selection known to the authorities, after which he shall be presented to the council with their recommendation. In any case, when he is examined, two members of the Little Council shall be present.

The Third Order is That of Elders, Those Commissioned or Appointed to the Consistory By the Authorities

Their office is to keep watch over the lives of everyone, to admonish in love those whom they see in error and leading disorderly lives. Whenever necessary they shall make a report concerning these to the ministers who will be designated to make brotherly corrections and join with the others in making such corrections.

If the church deems it wise, it will be well to choose two from the Little Council, four from the Council of Two Hundred, honest men of good demeanor, without reproach and free from all suspicion, above all fearing God and possessed of good and spiritual judgment. It will be well to elect them from every part of the city so as to be able to maintain supervision over all. This we desire to be instituted.

This shall be the manner of their selection, inasmuch as the Little Council advises that the best men be nominated, and to call the minister so as to confer with them, after which those whom they suggest may be presented to the Council of Two Hundred for their approval. If they are found worthy, after being approved, they shall take an oath similar to that required of the ministers. At the end of the year, after the election of the council, they shall present themselves to the authorities in order that it may be decided if they are to remain in office or be replaced. It will not be expedient to replace them often without cause, or so long as they faithfully perform their duties.

The Fourth Order or the Deacons

There were two orders of deacons in the ancient church, the one concerned with receiving, distributing and guarding the goods of the poor, their possessions, income and pensions as well as the quarterly offerings; the other, to take heed to and care for the sick and administer the pittance for the poor. This custom we have preserved to the present. In order to avoid confusion, for we have both stewards and managers, one of the four stewards of the hospital is to act as receiver of all its goods and is to receive adequate remuneration in order that he may better exercise his office.

The number of four stewards shall remain as it is, of which number one shall be charged with the common funds, as directed, not only that there may be greater efficiency, but also that those who wish to make special gifts may be better assured that these will be distributed only as they desire. If the income which the officials assign is not sufficient, or if some emergency should arise, the authorities shall instruct him to make adjustments according to the need.

The election of the managers, as well as of the stewards, is to be conducted as that of the elders; in their election the rule is to be followed which was delivered by St. Paul respecting deacons.

Concerning the office and authority of stewards, we confirm the articles which have already been proposed, on condition that, in urgent matters, especially when the issue is no great matter and the expenditure involved is small, they not be required to assemble for every action taken, but that one or two of them may be permitted to act in the absence of the others, in a reasonable way.

It will be his task to take diligent care that the public hospital is well administered and that it is open not only to the sick but also to aged persons who are unable to work, to widows, orphans and other needy persons. Those who are sick are to be kept in a separate lodging, away from those who cannot work, old persons, widows, orphans and other needy persons.

Also the care of the poor who are scattered throughout the city is to be conducted as the stewards may order.

Also, that another hospital is established for the transients who should be helped. Separate provision is to be made for any who are worthy of special charity. To accomplish this, a room is to be set aside for those who shall be recommended by the stewards, and it is to be used for no other purpose.

Above all, the families of the managers are to be well managed in an efficient and godly fashion, since they are to manage the houses dedicated to God.

The ministers and the commissioners or elders, with one of the syndics, for their part, are carefully to watch for any fault or negligence of any sort, in order to beg and admonish the authorities to set it in order. Every three months they are to cause certain of their company, with the stewards, to visit the hospital to ascertain if everything is in order.

It will be necessary, also, for the benefit of the poor in the hospital and for the poor of the city who cannot help themselves, that a doctor and a competent surgeon be secured from among those who practice in the city to have the care of the hospital and to visit the poor.

The hospital, for the pestilence in any case, is to be set apart; especially should it happen that the city is visited by this rod from God.

Moreover, to prevent begging, which is contrary to good order, it will be necessary that the authorities delegate certain officers. They are to be stationed at the doors of the churches to drive away any who try to resist and, if they act impudently or answer insolently, to take them to one of the syndics. In like manner, the heads of the precincts should always watch that the law against begging is well observed.

The Persons Whom the Elders Should Admonish, and Proper Procedure in This Regard

If there shall be anyone who lays down opinions contrary to received doctrine, he is to be summoned. If he recants, he is to be dismissed without prejudice. If he is stubborn, he is to be admonished from time to time until it shall be evident that he deserves greater severity. Then, he is to be excommunicated and this action reported to the magistrate.

If anyone is negligent in attending worship so that a noticeable offense is evident for the communion of the faithful, or if anyone shows himself contemptuous of ecclesiastical discipline, he is to be admonished. If he becomes obedient, he is to be dismissed in love. If he persists, passing from bad to worse, after having been admonished three times, he is to be excommunicated and the matter reported to the authorities.

For the correction of faults, it is necessary to proceed after the ordinance of our Lord. That is, vices are to be dealt with secretly and no one is to be brought before the church for accusation if the fault is neither public nor scandalous, unless he has been found rebellious in the matter.

For the rest, those who scorn private admonitions are to be admonished again by the church. If they will not come to reason nor recognize their error, they are to be ordered to abstain from communion until they improve.

As for obvious and public evil, which the church cannot overlook: if the faults merit nothing more than admonition, the duty of the elders shall be to summon those concerned, deal with them in love in order that they may be reformed and, if they correct the fault, to dismiss the matter. If they persevere, they are to be admonished again. If, in the end, such procedure proves unsuccessful, they are to be denounced as contemptuous of God, and ordered to abstain from communion until it is evident that they have changed their way of life.

As for crimes that merit not only admonition but punitive correction: if any fall into such error, according to the requirements of the case, it will be necessary to command them to abstain from communion so that they humble themselves before God and repent of their error.

If anyone by being contumacious or rebellious attempts that which is forbidden, the duty of the ministers shall be to reject him, since it is not proper that he receive the sacrament.

Nevertheless, let all these measures be moderate; let there not be such a degree of rigor that anyone should be cast down, for all corrections are but medicinal, to bring back sinners to the Lord.

And let all be done in such a manner as to keep from the ministers any civil jurisdiction whatever, so that they use only the spiritual sword of the word of God as St. Paul ordered them. Thus the consistory may in no wise take from the authority of the officers or of civil justice. On the contrary, the civil power is to be kept intact. Likewise, when it shall be necessary to exercise punishment or restraint against any party, the ministers and the consistory are to hear the party concerned, deal with them and admonish them as it may seem good, reporting all to the council which, for its part, shall deliberate and then pass judgment according to the merits of the case.

Questions:
1. Besides setting up the preaching ministry, what else did these Ordinances establish?
2. What was John Calvin's position on the separation of church and secular government?

12.7   Mercantilism: Financing Absolutism

Jean Baptiste Colbert (1619–83), a merchant's son who had served as a financial secretary under Cardinal Mazarin, became Controller General of Finances shortly after Louis XIV took personal charge of the government in 1661. He inaugurated extensive fiscal reforms, but was unable to create a new tax base which could provide a stable income for the crown and a solid foundation for the French budgetary apparatus. Forced to adopt emergency policies to cope with Louis XIV's extravagance at court and in warfare, the economy remained buried in mercantilist regulations and red tape that contributed to the French Revolution of 1789.

> **Source:** *The Western World: Volume I to 1700*, ed. Wallace E. Adams, et al., (New York: Dodd, Mead &Co., 1968), pp. 545–50.

DISSERTATION ON ALLIANCES, 1669

Every nation engages in two types of trading activity: domestic trade, which is carried on within the boundaries of the nation's home territories, and foreign trade, which, with the aid of shipping, is carried on outside the boundaries of the home territories. With respect to domestic trade, almost all nations foster it in the form of goods circulating within the country by means of internal transportation systems. With respect to foreign trade, which is a matter of capital importance, we must understand its structure if we are to have all the information we need for settling the question of alliances.

There are five principal categories of ocean-borne trading:

(1) The movement of goods and wares from one port to another, or from one province to another, for consumption within the kingdom.

(2) The importation from neighboring countries of goods and wares to be sold on the domestic market either as basic living commodities or. as luxury items.

(3) The exportation of European wares necessary to the development of the Orient and the importation from the Orient of goods necessary throughout Europe for domestic consumption or for manufacturing processes. Our trade with the Orient is the source of most of our commercial prosperity. It is conducted along two principal sea routes: the first proceeds through the Mediterranean to the Levantine ports of the Turkish Empire; the second extends across the ocean, by way of the Cape of Good Hope, to India.

(4) Trade with the West Indies, of which there are two main streams. The first supplies the Spanish with the products which they need throughout the breadth of their vast empire, stretching from the straits of Magellan to the tip of California Island in the South Sea. These are delivered either to the port of Cadiz, where they are loaded into vessels and delivered to the Spanish colonies where no foreigner is allowed entry, or they are delivered directly to the West Indies, which is a difficult task. In exchange for the merchandise, the same vessels bring back silver from the West Indies and deliver it to the harbor at Cadiz where it is distributed among all the nations which have invested in the enterprise. The other stream is that which delivers similar products and wares to those islands which are held by other European nations and which bring back the sugar, tobacco and indigo that grow there.

(5) Exportation to Northern Europe of all the manufactured wares and agricultural products which are processed in Middle and Southern Europe after having been imported from either the East or the West Indies, and importation from

the North of all the market products which grow there: in particular, wood, hemp, ship masts, copper, iron and other shipping materials. It is an established fact that through this exchange, Northern Europe makes all the other exchanges possible, which makes it the most important of all the trade regions.

These different types of trade have always existed in Europe, but when they have been carried out by a single nation, demand has fallen and prices have risen. Thus, trade relations have always drawn more money away from the other parties and have always prospered those who initiate them. Trade with the Near East, which used to include trade with the Far East until the Portuguese sailed around the Cape of Good Hope, was long in the hands of the Venetians. The French and the English enjoyed but a minimal portion of that trade. Subsequently, through exploration and military victories on the coast of Africa, through their business ventures and military successes throughout Asia, not excluding China, the Portuguese have won the biggest part of this trade away from the Venetians and have increased the supply of imported goods. Consequently, consumption is greater and prices have been reduced. Following the example of the Portuguese, the Spaniards have discovered the West Indies which have such an abundance of wealth that there is room for all investors to profit from it.

During the period when these nations dominated foreign trade in the South, the French and the English had a small share of the trade in the North. But for the French this share supplied only an insignificant fraction of their material needs. As for the English, this share provided them with virtually all their needs and in addition met part of the needs of the other northern nations, for the English have always had good trade relations with the North. At first, Bruges was the principal exchange mart for this trading activity. Then the inhabitants of Antwerp took advantage of their port, facilities and attracted trade there. After the wars between the Spanish and the Dutch, the self-discipline, the moderation and the zeal of the Dutch attracted world trade to Amsterdam and to the other cities of Holland. But they were not satisfied with being the central exchange mart for all Europe and especially for the North. They decided to gain control of foreign trade at its very source. To this end they ruined the Portuguese in the East Indies. They inhibited or disturbed in every possible way the business ventures which the English had established there. They employed and are still employing every means, are exerting every effort, are applying their full resources to assume full control of world trade and to keep it out of the hands of all other nations. Their whole government is based upon this single principle. They know that as long as they maintain their commercial superiority, their power on both land and sea will keep on increasing and will make them so powerful that they will become the arbiters of peace and war in Europe. They can set whatever limits they please upon the law and the design of kings.

As to whether they have the will power and the physical power to become the masters of all trade, there is no doubt at all in the first respect. With regard to their physical power, if we consider their powers in the Near East, in the East Indies, in the neighboring kingdoms and in the North, we can only conclude that they currently occupy first position and need only to maintain that status. In proof of my point, we have been keeping a check on their sea vessels for 4 or 5 years, and we estimate that they possess the incredible number of 15,000 to 16,000.

On the basis of this information, and after a very careful analysis, we can assert definitively that European trade is supported by some 20,000 vessels of all sizes. It is easy to see that this number cannot be increased, inasmuch as the population remains constant in all the nations and that consumer activity remains constant. Of this total of 20,000 ships, the Dutch have 15,000 to 16,000, the English 3,000 to 4,000 and the French 500 to 600.

This, then, has been and remains at present the state of European trade. But before proceeding further, we must note that the naval power of a nation plays an important role in the development of its trading program. In a sense, naval power follows on the heels of trading power because of the vast numbers of sailors and seamen involved, the experience which the captains and other officers accumulate, and the enormous number of ships to which it gives rise. But there is this difference. However superior the Dutch may be to the English in the total number of ships and seamen, they can never excel the English in naval power. The English may have lesser numbers, but they are superior in their experience and their knowledge of sea war and they infinitely excel the Dutch in genuine courage.

As for the French, their naval power and its use are still in the nascent stage. Certainly, therefore, it would be folly for France to try to attain in a few years a power to which the two other nations attained in the one case a century ago and in the other case several centuries ago. One need only consider the limited number of vessels in her merchant fleet to perceive clearly that she can give support to her naval strength only in proportion to that number. This issues from the general axiom that merchant shipping contributes to the strength and substance of all sea power and that no nation can have sea power without having shipping.

With all these factors clearly in mind, we must now return to our original consideration: in the alliance under examination, England is seeking principally to strengthen its trade. This strengthening process can be effected only if England uses more of the vessels belonging to her private citizens and if she increases their number. Such an increase can occur only if England discovers some hitherto unknown trading arenas or by reducing the number of vessels of one of the other nations.

The discovery of a new trading arena is highly unlikely. There is no point even in considering such a tenuous possibility. To be quite frank, such a circumstance could not possibly develop. Even if it should develop, it would not produce a new consumers' market for the products necessary to life and creature comforts. Rather it would offer to one nation and deny to another the means of drawing on those already in use and belonging to a pattern of international consumption that is common to all Europe.

It must be, then, through the reduction in number of the ships of one of the other nations. But that other nation cannot be the French, because there is nothing to be gained from them. In all their ports, both on the Atlantic and on the Mediterranean, they have only 500 or 600 ships which carry a small portion of their wares and goods from port to port, without any trade in the North or elsewhere. We are obliged to conclude, therefore, that England cannot use any more of her subjects' vessels nor can she increase the number without reducing the number of Dutch vessels. Consequently, it is difficult to establish a close alliance when its principal aim would be to increase one's power at the expense of the ally.

The political philosophies of great rulers have always taught that it is not to a weak ruler's advantage to ally himself willingly with a ruler more powerful than he, lest that superior power overwhelm and destroy him. That has happened on numerous occasions. The same political philosophies insist that the weak ruler always work to maintain a balance of power by allying himself to the nearest force in order to hold in check the growth of a third nation.

Applying the same philosophy to the present instance, we see that the Dutch have the most powerful trading system which exists or which has ever existed in the world. The English have a less flourishing system and the French the least flourishing of all. Therefore, reason declares that neither of these two nations may ally itself to the Dutch, for fear that, in the attempt to strengthen their trading power, they would be overwhelmed and completely destroyed. The same reasoning insists that the two nations pool their interests and apply their full might to undertaking a secret war against Dutch trade. They would profit from all the advantages that their location and their power give them to cut the Dutch off from what rightfully belongs to them. We shall outline hereafter several means for accomplishing this.

We should add that trade problems give rise to a continuing battle both in peace and in war among the nations of Europe to see who will win the upper hand. The Dutch, the English and the French are the contestants in this match. Through their zeal the Dutch have amassed sufficient power to fight with 16,000 ships. The English bring 3,000 to 4,000 vessels to the fray, the French bring 500 to 600. It is easy to see who will be victorious. And if the 3,000 to 4,000 align themselves with the 16,000, it is child's play to predict that the 16,000 can lose nothing and that the 3,000 to 4,000 run the risk of keeping on losing and even of being totally destroyed. We should add to these arguments the fact that, in spite of the superior numbers of ships which the Dutch possess in their trade war with the English, the Dutch are a thriftier, more economical people than the English. The former are more industrious, more profit-conscious than the latter. Their government draws its primary financial strength from its trade relations. Since both of these governments shape all their policies in terms of this commercial structure, the English cannot fail to come out second best in such an alliance. These reasons are, of course, quite persuasive in themselves, but there are yet others which must be considered.

It is generally agreed that the English have always demonstrated an instinctive aversion for the French. It is further agreed that this aversion was intensified by the recent war with all its attendant misfortunes. Despite this aversion, however, these kingdoms and their monarchs have remained at complete peace with each other for more than 100 years. This peace was interrupted by the war of La Rochelle which lasted but a few months and once again, subsequently, by the Dutch war. In view of this lengthy period of harmony one may conclude that the two nations can without difficulty live in a mutually comfortable relationship.

It is possible that the citizens of London show a greater hostility to the French now than in the past. But we can assume with a considerable certainty of being right that this hostility is fanned by Spanish and Dutch sympathizers who are in turn abetted by those who favored the recent disorders because they did not want to see the legitimate English government strengthened by such a powerful alliance as one with France. But we may rest assured that this distemper will cool. England has the means to prevent its persisting. What is more, when the alliance is made, the citizens will begin to enjoy its fruits. Thus, the close understanding which has always joined the two nations will be reaffirmed. This is particularly true because in joining forces, the two nations will enjoy real and substantial benefits in the exercise of their trading activities.

We must readily allow that psychologically and temperamentally the English are more akin to the Dutch than to the French. But it is plain to see that if they relish peace and tranquility and if they would not betray their political interests, they can draw no real advantages from an alliance with a people who are ruled by a government of merchants, whose political principles and power function only as an adjunct to their trade relations. Their prosperity will all too easily make the English see what differences separate a republic and a monarchy with respect to their commercial interests, which are the only interests to hold the attention of said republicans. But the alliance and union with the French produces an entirely different effect.

As for any jealousy which the English might feel over French naval power, it could not be a logical jealousy. Control of the earth's land masses lies in the hands of the rulers of those states which are abundantly populated by a naturally courageous and warrior-like people. Control of the seas, however, does not depend on population counts. Control of the sea goes to those who have enjoyed a long and intimate association with the sea. It goes to that nation whose maritime trade relations are elaborate enough to provide a sufficiently large reservoir of sailors from whose numbers a sea force may be formed. It is an established fact that the size of a nation's navy is proportional to that of its merchant marine. But if we are absolutely bound to attribute any jealousy to the English, it would be more logical to suspect that they feel it with respect to the Dutch. Only the Dutch presume to equal England's power in the recent war. Indeed, in view of their continually expanding trade relations, their sea power cannot fail to increase proportionally. As for the mutual aid which nations can bring to each other in their trade relations, the English will destroy themselves if they ally with the Dutch. Everything we have said points to it. An infinite number of examples prove it.

Now that we have given careful consideration to our main point—the advantages to be reaped by the peoples of the two nations—let us consider the interests and the reputations of the rulers of the two nations.

In this connection, there are endless reasons why an alliance with France should be preferable to an alliance with Holland: the blood kinship of the two monarchs; the similarity of their intellects and their personalities; the geographical location of their domains; the similarity of their type of government; the striking dissimilarities of the English monarchy and the Dutch republic; the domestic tranquility which they can bring to their respective nations by a union of interests; their willingness to consider candidly all the advantages and glories which will accrue to them.

To realize this great dream: [1] the monarchs need only join in a close alliance which no subject or no occasion can trouble or interrupt; [2] they need only establish a policy of equal and reciprocal relations between the two nations throughout the breadth of their kingdoms; [3] to this end they need only establish two advisory councils in the two capital cities which will act in common accord, cooperating in every way possible to enhance the quality and extend the scope of the trade relations of the two nations.... It would profit the two kingdoms enormously.

Questions:
1. What European nation most impressed Colbert and why?
2. By what steps did he propose that France win commercial supremacy?
3. How does this treatise illustrate Colbert's mercantilist policies?

PART 13
Thought and Culture in Early Modern Europe

13.1 Francis Bacon: from *First Book of Aphorisms*

The English philosopher Francis Bacon (1561–1626) lived an active and varied life. In his time, he was a leading statesman, philosopher, scholar, and scientist. He died in 1626 as the result of an illness he contracted while carrying out an experiment on the use of cold to preserve chicken.

Source: *The Age of Reason; The Seventeenth Century Philosophers, Selected, with Introduction and Interpretive Commentary*, ed. Stuart Hampshire (New York: Books for Libraries, 1970), pp. 24–30.

III

Human knowledge and human power meet in one; for where the cause is not known the effect cannot be produced. Nature to be commanded must be obeyed; and that which in contemplation is as the cause is in operation as the rule.

IV

Towards the effecting of works, all that man can do is to put together or put asunder natural bodies. The rest is done by nature working within.

VII

The productions of the mind and hand seem very numerous in books and manufactures. But all this variety lies in an exquisite subtlety and derivations from a few things already known; not in the number of axioms.

VIII

Moreover the works already known are due to chance and experiment rather than to science; for the sciences we now possess are merely systems for the nice ordering and setting forth of things already invented; not methods of invention or directions for new works.

XI

As the sciences which we now have do not help us in finding out new works, so neither does the logic which we now have help us in finding out new sciences.

XII

The logic now in use serves rather to fix and give stability to the errors which have their foundation in commonly received notions than to help the search after truth. So it does more harm than good.

XIV

The syllogism consists of propositions, propositions consists of words, words are symbols of notions. Therefore if the notions themselves (which is the root of the matter) are confused and over-hastily abstracted from the facts, there can be no firmness in the superstructure. Our only hope therefore lies in a true induction.

XIX

There are and can be only two ways of searching into and discovering truth. The one flies from the senses and particulars to the most general axioms, and from these principles, the truth of which it takes for settled and immovable, proceeds to judgment and to the discovery of middle axioms. And this way is now in fashion. The other derives axioms from the senses and particulars, rising by a gradual and unbroken ascent, so that it arrives at the most general axioms last of all. This is the true way, but as yet untried.

XXII

Both ways set out from the senses and particulars, and rest in the highest generalities; but the difference between them is infinite. For the one just glances at experiment and particulars in passing, the other dwells duly and orderly among them. The one, again, begins at once by establishing certain abstract and useless generalities, the other rises by gradual steps to that which is prior and better known in the order of nature.

XXIV

It cannot be that axioms established by argumentation should avail for the discovery of new works; since the subtlety of nature is greater many times over than the subtlety of argument. But axioms duly and orderly formed from particulars easily discover the way to new particulars, and thus render sciences active.

XXV

The axioms now in use, having been suggested by a scanty and manipular experience and a few particulars of most general occurrence, are made for the most part just large enough to fit and take these in: and therefore it is no wonder if they do not lead to new particulars. And if some opposite instance, not observed or not known before, chance to come in the way, the axiom is rescued and preserved by some frivolous distinction; whereas the truer course would be to correct the axiom itself.

XXXI

It is idle to expect any great advancement in science from the superinducing and engraving of new things upon old. We must begin anew from the very foundations, unless we would revolve for ever in a circle with mean and contemptible progress.

XXXVI

One method of delivery alone remains to us; which is simply this: We must lead men to the particulars themselves, and their series and order; while men on their side must force themselves for awhile to lay their notions by and begin to familiarise themselves with facts.

XLVI

The human understanding when it has once adopted an opinion (either as being the received opinion or as being agreeable to itself) draws all things else to support and agree with it. And though there be a greater number and weight of instances to be found on the other side, yet these it either neglects and despises, or else by some distinction sets aside and rejects; in order that by this great and pernicious predetermination the authority of its former conclusions may remain inviolate. And therefore it was a good answer that was made by one who when they showed him hanging in a temple a picture of those who had paid their vows as having escaped shipwreck, and would have him say whether he did not now acknowledge the power of the gods,—"Aye," asked he again, "but where are they painted that were drowned, after their vows?" And such is the way of all superstition, whether in astrology, dreams, omens, divine judgments, or the like; wherein men, having a delight in such vanities, mark the events where they are fulfilled, but where they fail, though this happen much oftener, neglect and pass them by. But with far more subtlety does this mischief insinuate itself into philosophy and the sciences; in which the first conclusion colours and brings into conformity with itself all that come after, though far sounder and better. Besides, independently of that delight and vanity which I have described, it is the peculiar and perpetual error of human intellect to be more moved and excited by affirmatives than by negatives; whereas it ought properly to hold itself indifferently disposed towards both alike. Indeed in the establishment of any true axiom, the negative instance is the more forcible of the two.

C

But not only is a greater abundance of experiments to be sought for and procured, and that too of a different kind from those hitherto tried; an entirely different method, order, and process for carrying on and advancing experience must also be introduced. For experience, when it wanders in its own track, is, as I have already remarked, mere groping in the dark, and confounds men rather than instructs them. But when it shall proceed in accordance with a fixed law, in regular order, and without interruption, then may better things be hoped of knowledge.

CIV

The understanding must not however be allowed to jump and fly from particulars to remote axioms and of almost the highest generality (such as the first principles, as they are called, of arts and things), and taking stand upon them as truths that cannot be shaken, proceed to prove and frame the middle axioms by reference to them; which has been the practice hitherto; the understanding being not only carried that way by a natural impulse, but also by the use of syllogistic demonstration trained and inured to it. But then, and then only, may we hope well of the sciences, when in a just scale of ascent, and by successive steps not interrupted or broken, we rise from particulars to lesser axioms; and then to middle axioms, one above the other; and last of all to the most general. For the lowest axioms differ but slightly from bare experience, while the highest and most general (which we now have) are notional and abstract and without solidity. But the middle are the true and solid and living axioms, on which depend the affairs and fortunes of men; and above them again, last of all, those which are indeed the most general; such I mean as are not abstract, but of which those intermediate axioms are really limitations.

The understanding must not therefore be supplied with wings, but rather hung with weights, to keep it from leaping and flying. Now this has never been done; when it is done, we may entertain better hopes of the sciences.

CV

In establishing axioms, another form of induction must be devised than has hitherto been employed; and it must be used for proving and discovering not first principles (as they are called) only, but also the lesser axioms, and the middle, and indeed all. For the induction which proceeds by simple enumeration is childish; its conclusions are precarious, and exposed to peril from a contradictory instance; and it generally decides on too small a number of facts, and on those only which are at hand. But the induction which is to be available for the discovery and demonstration of sciences and arts, must analyse nature by proper rejections and exclusions; and then, after a sufficient number of negatives, come to a conclusion on the affirmative instances; which has not yet been done or even attempted, save only by Plato, who does indeed employ this form of induction to a certain extent for the purpose of discussing definitions and ideas. But in order to furnish this induction or demonstration well and duly for its work, very many things are to be provided which no mortal has yet thought of: insomuch that greater labour will have to be spent in it than has hitherto been spent on the syllogism. And this induction must be used not only to discover axioms, but also in the formation of notions. And it is in this induction that our chief hope lies.

CVI

But in establishing axioms by this kind of induction, we must also examine and try whether the axiom so established be framed to the measure of those particulars only from which it is derived, or whether it be larger and wider. And if it be larger and wider, we must observe whether by indicating to us new particulars it confirm that wideness and largeness as by a collateral security; that we may not either stick fast in things already known, or loosely grasp at shadows and abstract forms; not at things solid and realised in matter. And when the process shall have come into use, then at last shall we see the dawn of a solid hope.]

The following is Aphorism X from the *Second Book of Aphorisms*.

[Now my directions for the interpretation of nature embrace two generic divisions; the one how to educe and form axioms from experience; the other how to deduce and derive new experiments from axioms. The former again is divided into three ministrations; a ministration to the sense, a mainstration to the memory, and a ministration to the mind or reason.

For first of all we must prepare a *Natural and Experimental History*, sufficient and good; and this is the foundation of all; for we are not to imagine or suppose, but to discover, what nature does or may be made to do.

But natural and experimental history is so various and diffuse, that it confounds and distracts the understanding, unless it be ranged and Presented to view in a suitable order. We must therefore form *Tables and Arrangements of Instances*, in such a method and order that the understanding may be able to deal with them.

And even when this is done, still the understanding, if left to itself and its own spontaneous movements, is incompetent and unfit to form axioms, unless it be directed and guarded. Therefore in the third place we must use Induction, true and legitimate induction, which is the very key of interpretation.

Question:
1. *How does Bacon propose to find truth? What are the strengths and weaknesses of his inductive method?*

13.2 Miguel de Cervantes: Chapter I from *Don Quixote*

Miguel Cervantes (1547–1616) is often credited with authoring the first European novel. Don Quixote (1605), Cervantes' satire of chivalric ideals, was a huge success and established his reputation as a writer. In the selection included here, Cervantes sketches the circumstances and character of his hero, Don Quixote de la Mancha.

Source: *The Adventures of Don Quixote* by Miguel del Cervantes. Penguin Classics, translation by J. M. Cohen (New York: Penguin Books, 1988), pp. 31–35.

In a certain village in La Mancha, which I do not wish to name, there lived not long ago a gentleman—one of those who have always a lance in the rack, an ancient shield, a lean hack and a grey-hound for coursing. His habitual diet consisted of a stew, more beef than mutton, of hash most nights, boiled bones on Saturdays, lentils on Fridays, and a young pigeon as a Sunday treat; and on this he spent three-quarters of his income. The rest of it went on a fine cloth doublet, velvet breeches and slippers for holidays, and a homespun suit of the best in which he decked himself on weekdays. His household consisted of a housekeeper of rather more than forty, a niece not yet twenty, and a lad for the field and market, who saddled his horse and wielded the pruning-hook.

Our gentleman was verging on fifty, of tough constitution, lean-bodied, thin-faced, a great early riser and a lover of hunting. They say that his surname was Quixada or Quesada—for there is some difference of opinion amongst authors on this point. However, by very reasonable conjecture we may take it that he was called Quexana. But this does not much concern our story; enough that we do not depart by so much as an inch from the truth in the telling of it.

The reader must know, then, that this gentleman, in the times when he had nothing to do—as was the case for most of the year—gave himself up to the reading of books of knight errantry; which he loved and enjoyed so much that he almost entirely forgot his hunting, and even the care of his estate. So odd and foolish, indeed, did he grow on this subject that he sold many acres of cornland to buy these books of chivalry to read, and in this way brought home every one he could get. And of them all he considered none so good as the works of the famous Feliciano de Silva. For his brilliant style and those complicated sentences seemed to him very pearls, especially when he came upon those love-passages and challenges frequently written in the manner of: 'The reason for the unreason with which you treat my reason, so weakens my reason that with reason I complain of your beauty'; and also when he read: 'The high heavens that with their stars divinely fortify you in your divinity and make you deserving of the desert that your greatness deserves.'

These writings drove the poor knight out of his wits; and he passed sleepless nights trying to understand them and disentangle their meaning, though Aristotle himself would never have unravelled or understood them, even if he had been resurrected for that sole purpose. He did not much like the wounds that Sir Belianis gave and received, for he imagined that his face and his whole body must have been covered with scars and marks, however skilful the surgeons who tended him. But, for all that, he admired the author for ending his book with the promise to continue with that interminable adventure, and often the desire seized him to take up the pen himself, and write the promised sequel for him No doubt he would have done so, and perhaps successfully, if other greater and more persistent preoccupations had not prevented him.

Often he had arguments with the priest of his village, who was a scholar and a graduate of Siguenza, as to which was the better knight—Paimerin of England or Amadis of Gaul. But Master Nicholas, the barber of that village, said that no one could compare with the Knight of the Sun. Though if anyone could, it was Sir Galaor, brother of Amadis of Gaul. For he had a very accommodating nature, and was not so affected nor such a sniveller as his brother, though he was not a bit behind him in the matter of bravery.

In short, he so buried himself in his books that he spent the nights reading from twilight till daybreak and the days from dawn till dark; and so from little sleep and much reading, his brain dried up and he lost his wits. He filled his mind with all that he read in them, with enchantments, quarrels, battles, challenges, wounds, wooings, loves, torments and other impossible nonsense; and so deeply did he steep his imagination in the belief that all the fanciful stuff he read was true, that to his mind no history in the world was more authentic. He used to say that the Cid Ruy Diaz must have been a very good knight, but that he could not be compared to the Knight of the Burning Sword, who with a single backstroke had cleft a pair of fierce and monstrous giants in two. And he had an even better opinion of Bernardo del Carpio for slaying the enchanted Roland at Roncesvalles, by making use of Hercules' trick when he throttled the Titan Antaeus in his arms.

He spoke very well of the giant Morgante; for, though one of that giant brood who are all proud and insolent, he alone was affable and well-mannered. But he admired most of all Reynald of Montalban, particularly when he saw him sally forth from his castle and rob everyone he met, and when in heathen lands overseas he stole that idol of Mahomet, which history says was of pure gold. But he would have given his housekeeper and his niece into the bargain, to deal the traitor Galaon a good kicking.

In fact, now that he had utterly wrecked his reason he fell into the strangest fancy that ever a madman had in the whole world. He thought it fit and proper, both in order to increase his renown and to serve the state, to turn knight errant and travel through the world with horse and armour in search of adventures, following in every way the practice of the knights errant he had read of, redressing all manner of wrongs, and exposing himself to chances and dangers, by the overcoming of which he might win eternal honour and renown. Already the poor man fancied himself crowned by the valour of his arm, at least with the empire of Trebizond; and so, carried away by the strange pleasure he derived from these agreeable thoughts, he hastened to translate his desires into action.

The first thing that he did was to clean some armour which had belonged to his ancestors, and had lain for ages forgotten in a corner, eaten with rust and covered with mould. But when he had cleaned and repaired it as best he could, he found that there was one great defect: the helmet was a simple head-piece without a visor. So he ingeniously made good this deficiency by fashioning out of pieces of pasteboard a kind of half-visor which, fitted to the helmet, gave the appearance of a complete headpiece. However, to see if it was strong enough to stand up to the risk of a sword-cut, he took out his sword and gave it two strokes, the first of which demolished in a moment what had taken him a week to make. He was not too pleased at the ease with which he had destroyed it, and to safeguard himself against this danger, reconstructed the visor, putting some strips of iron inside, in such a way as to satisfy himself of his protection; and, not caring to make another trial of it, he accepted it as a fine jointed headpiece and put it into commission.

Next he went to inspect his hack, but though, through leanness, he had more quarters than there are pence in a groat, and more blemishes than Gonelia's horse, which was nothing but skin and bone, he appeared to our knight more than the equal of Alexander's Bucephalus and the Cid's Babieca. He spent four days pondering what name to give him; for, he reflected, it would be wrong for the horse of so famous a knight, a horse so good in himself, to be without a famous name. Therefore he tried to fit him with one that would signify what he had been before his master turned knight errant, and what he now was; for it was only right that as his master changed his profession, the horse should change his name for a sublime and high-sounding one, befitting the new order and the new calling he professed. So, after many names invented, struck out and rejected, amended, cancelled and remade in his fanciful mind, he finally decided to call him Rocinante, a name which seemed to him grand and sonorous, and to express the common horse he had been before arriving at his present state: the first and foremost of all hacks in the world.

Having found so pleasing a name for his horse, he next decided to do the same for himself, and spent another eight days thinking about it. Finally he resolved to call himself Don Quixote. And that is no doubt why the authors of this true history, as we have said, assumed that his name must have been Quixada and not Quesada, as other authorities would have it. Yet he remembered that the valorous Amadis had not been content with his bare name, but had added the name of his kingdom and native country in order to make it famous, and styled himself Amadis of Gaul. So, like a good knight, he decided to add the name of his country to his own and call himself Don Quixote de la Mancha. Thus, he thought, he very clearly proclaimed his parentage and native land and honoured it by taking his surname from it.

Now that his armour was clean, his helmet made into a complete head-piece, a name found for his horse, and he confirmed in his new title, it struck him that there was only one more thing to do: to find a lady to be enamoured of. For a knight errant without a lady is like a tree without leaves or fruit and a body without a soul. He said to himself again and again: If I for my sins or by good luck were to meet with some giant hereabouts, as generally happens to knights errant, and if I were to overthrow him in the encounter, or cut him down the middle or, in short, conquer him and make him surrender, would it not be well to have someone to whom I could send him as a present, so that he could enter and kneel down before my sweet lady and say in tones of humble submission: "Lady, I am the giant Caracutiambro, lord of the island of Malindrania, whom the never-sufficiently-to-be-praised knight, Don Quixote de la Mancha, conquered in single combat and ordered to appear before your Grace, so that your Highness might dispose of me according to your will"?' Oh, how pleased our knight was when he had made up this speech, and even gladder when he found someone whom he could call his lady. It happened, it is believed, in this way: in a village near his there was a very good-looking farm girl, whom he had been taken with at one time, although she is supposed not to have known it or had proof of it. Her name was Aidonza Lorenzo, and she it was he thought fit to call the lady of his fancies; and, casting around for a name which should not be too far away from her own, yet suggest and imply a princess and great lady, he resolved to call her Dulcinea del Toboso—for she was a native of El Toboso—, a name which seemed to him as musical, strange and significant as those others that he had devised for himself and his possessions.

Question:
1. What does the author think of his hero?

13.3 John Bunyan: from *Pilgrim's Progress*

A tinker throughout most of his life, John Bunyan (1628–1688) preached and published his understanding of Christianity in vivid, accessible English. In and out of trouble with the government, Bunyan wrote much of his body of work while in prison. In this excerpt from Pilgrim's Progress, Bunyan explained his reason for publishing and defended his approach to writing.

Source: *The Pilgrim's Progress*, by John Bunyan, Penguin Classics, ed. Roger Sharrock (New York: Penguin Books, 1987) pp. 43–49.

THE AUTHOR'S APOLOGY FOR HIS BOOK

When at the first I took my pen in hand,
Thus for to write, I did not understand
That I at all should make a little book
In such a mode; nay, I had undertook
To make another, which when almost done,
Before I was aware, I this begun.

And thus it was: I writing of the way
And race of saints in this our Gospel-day,
Fell suddenly into an allegory
About their journey, and the way to glory,
In more than twenty things, which I set down;
This done, I twenty more had in my crown,
And they again began to multiply, Like sparks that from
the coals of fire do fly.
Nay then, thought I, if that you breed so fast,
I'll put you by yourselves, lest you at last
Should prove *ad infinitum*, and eat out
The book that I already am about.

Well, so I did; but yet I did not think
To show to all the world my pen and ink
In such a mode; I only thought to make
I knew not what, nor did I undertake
Thereby to please my neighbour; no, not I,
I did it mine own self to gratify.
Neither did I but vacant seasons spend
in this my scribble, nor did I intend

But to divert myself in doing this,
From worser thoughts which make me do amiss.

Thus I set pen to paper with delight,
And quickly had my thoughts in black and white.
For having now my method by the end,
Still as I pulled it came, and so I penned
It down, until it came at last to be
For length and breadth the bigness which you see.

Well, when I had thus put mine ends together,
I show'd them others that I might see whether
They would condemn them, or them justify:
And some said, 'let them live'; some, 'let them die':
Some said, 'John, print it'; others said, 'not so':
Some said, 'It might do good'; others said, 'no'.

Now was I in a strait, and did not see
Which was the best thing to be done by me:
At last I thought, since you are thus divided,
I print it will, and so the case decided.

For, thought I, some I see would have it done,
Though others in that channel do not run.
To prove then who advised for the best,
Thus I thought fit to put it to the test.

I further thought, if now I did deny
Those that would have it thus, to gratify,
I did not know, but hinder them I might,
Of that which would to them be great delight.

For those that were not for its coming forth,
I said to them, offend you I am loth;
Yet since your brethren pleased with it be,
Forbear to judge, to you do further see.

If that thou wilt not read, let it alone;
Some love the meat, some love to pick the bone:
Yea, that I might them better palliate,
I did too with them thus expostulate.

May I not write in such a style as this?
In such a method too, and yet not miss
Mine end, thy good? why may it not be done?
Dark clouds bring waters, when the bright bring none;
Yea, dark, or bright, if they their silver drops
Cause to descend, the earth by yielding crops
Gives praise to both, and carpeth not at either,
But treasures up the fruit they yield together:
Yea, so commixes both, that in her fruit
None can distinguish this from that, they suit
Her well when hungry, but if she be full
She spews out both, and makes their blessings null.

You see the ways the fisherman doth take
To catch the fish, what engines doth he make?

Behold! how he engageth all his wits
Also his snares, lines, angles, hooks and nets.
Yet fish there be, that neither hook, nor line,
Nor snare, nor net, nor engine can make thine;
They must be groped for, and be tickled too,
Or they will not be catched, what e'er you do.

181

How doth the fowler seek to catch his game?
By divers means, all which one cannot name.
His gun, his nets, his lime-twigs, fight and bell:
He creeps, he goes, he stands; yea, who can tell
Of all his postures? Yet there's none of these
Will make him master of what fowls he please.
Yea, he must pipe, and whistle to catch this,
Yet if he does so, that bird he will miss.

If that a pearl may in a toad's head dwell,
And may be found too in an oyster-shell;
If things that promise nothing, do contain
What better is than gold, who will disdain
(That have an inkling of it) there to look,
That they may find it? Now my little book
(Though void of all those paintings that may make
It with this or the other man to take)
Is not without those things that do excel,
What do in brave but empty notions dwell.

'Well, yet I am not fully satisfied,
That this your book will stand, when soundly tried.

Why, what's the matter? 'It is dark', What tho'?
'But it is feigned', What of that I trow?
Some men by feigning words as dark as mine,
Make truth to spangle, and its ray to shine.

'But they want solidness.' Speak man thy mind.
'They drowned the weak; metaphors make us blind.'
Solidity, indeed becomes the pen
Of him that writeth things divine to men:
But must I needs want solidness, because
By metaphors I speak; was not God's laws,
His Gospel-laws in olden time held forth
By types, shadows and metaphors? Yet loth
Will any sober man be to find fault
With them, lest he be found for to assault
The highest wisdom. No, he rather stoops,
And seeks to find out what by pins and loops,
By calves, and sheep, by heifers, and by rams,
By birds and herbs, and by the blood of lambs
God speaketh to him: and happy is he
That finds the light, and grace that in them be.

Be not too forward therefore to conclude
That I want solidness, that I am rude:
All things solid in show not solid be;
All things in parables despise not we
Lest things most hurtful lightly we receive;
And things that good are, of our souls bereave.

My dark and cloudy words they do but hold
The truth, as cabinets enclose the gold.

The prophets used much by metaphors
To set forth truth; yea, who so considers
Christ, his Apostles too, shall plainly see,
That truths to this day in such mantles be.

Am I afraid to say that Holy Writ,
Which for its style and phrase puts down all wit,
Is everywhere so full of all these things,
(Dark figures, allegories), yet there springs
From that same book that lustre and those rays
Of light that turns our darkest nights to days.

Come, let my carper to his life now look,
And find there darker lines than in my book
He findeth any. Yea, and let him know
That in his best things there are worse lines too.

May we but stand before impartial men,
To his poor one, I durst adventure ten
That they will take my meaning in these lines
Far better than his lies in silver shrines.
Come, truth, although in swaddling-clouts, I find
Informs the judgement, rectifies the mind,
Pleases the understanding, makes the will
Submit; the memory too it doth fill
With what doth our imagination please,
Likewise, it tends our troubles to appease.

Sound words I know Timothy is to use,
And old wives' fables he is to refuse,
But yet grave Paul him nowhere doth forbid
The use of parables; in which lay hid
That gold, those pearls, and precious stones that were
Worth digging for, and that with greatest care.

Let me add one word more, O man of God!
Art thou offended? Dost thou wish I had
Put forth my matter in another dress,
Or that I had in things been more express?
Three things let me propound, then I submit
To those that are my betters (as is fit).

1. I find not that I am denied the use
Of this my method, so I no abuse
Put on the words, things, readers, or be rude
In handling figure, or similitude,
In application; but all that I may
Seek the advance of Truth this or that way.
Denied did I say? Nay, I have leave
(Example too, and that from them that have

God better please by their words or ways
Than any man that breatheth nowadays),
Thus to express my mind, thus to declare
Things unto thee that excellentest are.

2. I find that men (as high as trees) will write
Dialogue-wise;[6] yet no man doth them slight
For writing so: indeed if they abuse
Truth, cursed be they, and the craft they use
To that intent: but yet let truth be free
To make her sallies upon thee, and me,
Which way it pleases God. For who knows how,
Better than he that taught us first to plough,
To guide our mind and pens for his design?
And he makes base things usher in divine.

3. I find that Holy Writ in many places
Hath semblance with this method, where the cases
Doth call for one thing to set forth another:
Use it I may then, and yet nothing smother
Truth's golden beams, nay, by this method may
Make it cast forth its rays as light as day.

And now, before I do put up my pen,
I'll show the profit of my book, and then
Commit both thee, and it unto that hand
That pulls the strong down, and makes weak ones stand.

This book it chalketh out before thine eyes
The man that seeks the everlasting prize:
It shows you whence he comes, whither he goes,
What he leaves undone, also what he does:
It also shows you how he runs, and runs,
Till he unto the Gate of Glory comes.

It shows too who sets out for life amain,
As if the lasting crown they would attain:
Here also you may see the reason why
They lose their labour, and like fools do die.

This book will make a traveller of thee,
If by its counsel thou wilt ruled be;
It will direct thee to die Holy Land,
If thou wilt its directions understand:
Yea, it will make the slothful active be,
The blind also delightful things to see.

Art thou for something rare, and profitable?
Would'st thou see a truth within a fable?
Art thou forgetful? Wouldest thou remember
From New Year's Day to the last of December?
Then read my fancies, they will stick like burrs,
And may be to the helpless, comforters.

This book is writ in such a dialect
As may the minds of listless men affect:

It seems a novelty, and yet contains
Nothing but sound and honest gospel-strains.

Would'st thou divert thyself from melancholy?
Would'st thou be pleasant, yet be far from folly?
Would'st thou read riddles and their explanation,
Or else be drownded in they contemplation?
Dost thou love picking-meat?[7] Or would'st thou see
A man i' the clouds, and hear him speak to thee?
Would'st thou be in a dream, and yet not sleep?
Or would'st thou in a moment laugh and weep?
Wouldest thou lose thyself, and catch no harm
And find thyself again without a charm?
Would'st read thyself, and read thou know'st not what
And yet know whether thou art blest or not,
By reading the same lines? O then come hither,
And lay may book, thy head and heart together.

JOHN BUNYAN

Question:
1. What does the author see as his purpose for the book?

13.4 Thomas Hobbes: Chapter XIII from *Leviathan*

The English philosopher Thomas Hobbes (1588–1679) applied a mechanistic world view to his political philosophy. In his opinion, kings ruled with absolute power, but not by divine right. Rather, power had been given to them by their subjects in exchange for protection and an end to the violence and chaos that characterized the state of nature.

> **Source:** *The Leviathan* by Thomas Hobbes, Cambridge Texts in the History of Political Thought, ed. RIchard Tuck (New York: Cambridge University Press, 1996), pp. 86–90.

MEN BY NATURE EQUALL

Nature hath made men so equall, in the faculties of body, and mind; as that though there bee found one man sometimes manifestly stronger in body, or of quicker mind then another; yet when all is reckoned together, the difference between man, and man, is not so considerable, as that one man can thereupon claim to himselfe any benefit, to which another may not pretend, as well as he. For as to the strength of body, the weakest has strength enough to kill the strongest, either by secret machination, or by confederacy with others, that are in the same danger with himselfe.

And as to the faculties of the mind, (setting aside the arts grounded upon words, and especially that skill of proceeding upon generall, and infallible rules, called Science; which very few have, and but in few things; as being not a native faculty, born with us; nor attained, (as Prudence,) while we look after somewhat els,) I find yet a greater equality amongst men, than that of strength. For Prudence, is but Experience; which equall time, equally bestowes on all men, in those things they equally apply themselves unto. That which may perhaps make such equality incredible, is but a vain conceipt of ones owne wisdome, which almost all men think they have in a greater degree, than the Vulgar; that is, than all men but themselves, and a few others, whom by Fame, or for concurring with themselves, they approve. For such is the nature of men, that howsoever they may acknowledge many others to be more witty, or more eloquent, or more learned; Yet they will hardly believe there be many so wise as themselves: For they see their own wit at hand, and other mens at a distance. But this proveth rather that men are in that point equall, than unequall. For there is not ordinarily a greater signe of the equall distribution of any thing, than that every man is contented with his share.

FROM EQUALITY PROCEEDS DIFFIDENCE

From this equality of ability, ariseth equality of hope in the attaining of our Ends. And therefore if any two men desire the same thing, which neverthelesse they cannot both enjoy, they become enemies; and in the way to their End, (which is principally their owne conservation, and sometimes their delectation only,) endeavour to destroy, or subdue one an other. And from hence it comes to passe, that where an Invader hath no more to feare, than an other mans single power; if one plant, sow, build, or possesse a convenient Seat, others may probably be expected to come prepared with forces united, to dispossesse, and deprive him, not only of the fruit of his labour, but also of his life, or liberty. And the Invader again is in the like danger of another.

FROM DIFFIDENCE WARRE

And from this diffidence of one another, there is no way for any man to secure himselfe, so reasonable, as Anticipation; that is, by force, or wiles, to master the persons of all men he can, so long, till he see no other power great enough to endanger him: And this is no more than his own conservation requireth, and is generally allowed. Also because there be some, that taking pleasure in contemplating their own power in the acts of conquest, which they pursue farther than their security requires; if others, that otherwise would be glad to be at ease within modest bounds, should not by invasion increase their power, they would not be able, long time, by standing only on their defence, to subsist. And by consequence, such augmentation of dominion over men, being necessary to a mans conservation, it ought to be allowed him.

Againe, men have no pleasure, (but on the contrary a great deale of griefe) in keeping company, where there is no power able to over-awe them all. For every man looketh that his companion should value him, at the same rate he sets upon himselfe: And upon all signes of contempt, or undervaluing, naturally endeavours, as far as he dares (which amongst them that have no common power to keep them in quiet, is far enough to make them destroy each other,) to extort a greater value from his contemners, by dommage; and from others, by the example.

So that in the nature of man, we find three principall causes of quarrell. First, Competition; Secondly, Diffidence; Thirdly, Glory.

The first, maketh men invade for Gain; the second, for Safety; and the third, for Reputation. The first use Violence, to make themselves Masters of other mens persons, wives, children, and cattell; the second, to defend them; the third, for trifles, as a word, a smile, a different opinion, and any other signe of undervalue, either direct in their Persons, or by reflexion in their Kindred, their Friends, their Nation, their Profession, or their Name.

OUT OF CIVIL STATES, THERE IS ALWAYS WARRE OF EVERYONE AGAINST EVERY ONE

Hereby it is manifest, that during the time men live without a common Power to keep them all in awe, they are in that condition which is called Warre; and such a warre, as is of every man, against every man. For WARRE, consisteth not in Battell onely, or the act of fighting; but in a tract of time, wherein the Will to contend by Battell is sufficiently known: and therefore the notion of *Time*, is to be considered in the nature of WARRE; as it is in the nature of Weather. For as the nature of Foule weather, lyeth not in a showre or two of rain; but in an inclination thereto of many dayes together: So the nature of War, consisteth not in actuall fighting; but in the known disposition thereto, during all the time there is no assurance to the contrary. All other time is PEACE.

THE INCOMMODITIES OF SUCH A WAR

Whatsoever therefore is consequent to a time of Warre, where every man is Enemy to every man; the same is consequent to the time, wherein men live without other security, than what their own strength, and their own invention shall furnish them withall. In such condition, there is no place for Industry; because the fruit thereof is uncertain: and consequently no Culture of the Earth; no Navigation, nor use of the commodities that may be imported by Sea; no commodious Building; no Instruments of moving, and removing such things as require much force; no Knowledge of the face of the Earth; no account of Time; no Arts; no Letters; no Society; and which is worst of all, continuall feare, and danger of violent death; And the life of man, solitary, poore, nasty, brutish, and short.

It may seem strange to some man, that has not well weighed these things; that Nature should thus dissociate, and render men apt to invade, and destroy one another: and he may therefore, not trusting to this Inference, made from the Passions, desire perhaps to have the same confirmed by Experience. Let him therefore consider with himselfe, when taking a journey, he armes himselfe, and seeks to go well accompanied; when going to sleep, he locks his dores; when even in his house he locks his chests; and this when he knowes there bee Lawes, and publike Officers, armed, to revenge all injuries shall bee done him; what opinion he has of his fellow subjects, when he rides armed; of his fellow Citizens, when he locks his dores; and of his children, and servants, when he locks his chests. Does he not there as much accuse mankind by his actions, as I do by my words? But neither of us accuse mans nature in it. The Desires, and other Passions of man, are in themselves no Sin. No more are the Actions, that proceed from those Passions, till they know a Law that forbids them: which till Lawes be made they cannot know: nor can any Law be made, till they have agreed upon the Person that shall make it.

It may peradventure be thought, there was never such a time, nor condition of warre as this; and I believe it was never generally so, over all the world: but there are many places, where they live so now. For the savage people in many places of *America*, except the government of small Families, the concord whereof dependeth on naturall lust, have no government at all; and live at this day in that brutish manner, as I said before. Howsoever, it may be perceived what manner of life there would be, where there were no common Power to feare; by the manner of life, which men that have formerly lived under a peacefull government, use to degenerate into, in a civill Warre.

But though there had never been any time, wherein particular men were in a condition of warre one against another; yet in all times, Kings, and Persons of Soveraigne authority, because of their Independency, are in continuall jealousies, and in the state and posture of Gladiators; having their weapons pointing, and their eyes fixed on one another; that is, their Forts, Garrisons, and Guns upon the Frontiers of their Kingdomes; and continuall Spyes upon their neighbours, which is a posture of War. But because they uphold thereby, the Industry of their Subjects; there does not follow from it, that misery, which accompanies the Liberty of particular men.

IN SUCH A WARRE, NOTHING IS UNJUST

To this warre of every man against every man, this also is consequent; that nothing can be Unjust. The notions of Right and Wrong, Justice and Injustice have there no place. Where there is no common Power, there is no Law: where no Law, no Injustice. Force, and Fraud, are in warre the two Cardinall vertues. Justice, and Injustice are none of the Faculties neither of the Body, nor Mind. If they were, they might be in a man that were alone in the world, as well as his Senses, and Passions. They are Qualities, that relate to men in Society, not in Solitude. It is consequent also to the same condition, that there be no Propriety, no Dominion, no *Mine* and *Thine* distinct; but onely that to be every mans, that he can get; and for so long, as he can keep it. And thus much for the ill condition, which man by meer Nature is actually placed in; though with a possibility to come out of it, consisting partly in the Passions, partly in his Reason.

THE PASSIONS THAT INCLINE MEN TO PEACE

The Passions that encline men to Peace, are Feare of Death; Desire of such things as are necessary to commodious living; and a Hope by their Industry to obtain them. And Reason suggesteth convenient Articles of Peace, upon which men may be drawn to agreement. These Articles, are they, which otherwise are called the Lawes of Nature: whereof I shall speak more particularly, in the two following Chapters.

Question:
1. What are the causes of perpetual war that is the state of nature?

13.5   Rejecting Aristotle: Galileo Defends the Heliocentric View

Galileo Galilei (1564–1642) was the foremost mathematician and physicist of his day. With the help of a telescope he helped refine, Galileo made astronomical discoveries that supported Copernicus' heliocentric view of the Universe. In addition, his contributions to terrestrial mechanics paved the way for Newtonian physics.

> **Source:** "Third Letter on Sunspots, from Galileo Galilei to Mark Welser," in *Discoveries and Opinions of Galileo*, trans. Stillman Drake, (Garden City, NY: Doubleday Anchor Books, 1957), pp. 122–44, passim.

THIRD LETTER ON SUNSPOTS, FROM GALILEO GALILEI TO MARK WELSER

In which Venus, the Moon, and the Medicean Planets are also dealt with, and new appearances of Saturn are revealed.

[I]in my opinion we need not entirely give up contemplating things just because they are very remote from us, unless we have indeed determined that it is best to defer every act of reflection in favor of other occupations. For in our speculating we either seek to penetrate the true and internal essence of natural substances, or content ourselves with a knowledge of some of their properties. The former I hold to be as impossible an undertaking with regard to the closest elemental substances as with more remote celestial things. The substances composing the earth and the moon seem to me to be equally unknown, as do those of our elemental clouds and of sunspots. I do not see that in comprehending substances near at hand we have any advantage except copious detail; all the things among which men wander remain equally unknown, and we pass by things both near and far with very little or no real acquisition of knowledge. When I ask what the substance of clouds may be and am told that it is a moist vapor, I shall wish to know in turn what vapor is. Peradventure I shall be told that it is water, which when attenuated by heat is resolved into vapor. Equally curious about what water is, I shall then seek to find that out, ultimately learning that it is this fluid body which runs in our rivers and which we constantly handle. But this final information about water is no more intimate than what I knew about clouds in the first place; it is merely closer at hand and dependent upon more of the senses. In the same way I know no more about the true essences of earth or fire than about those of the moon or sun, for that knowledge is withheld from us, and is not to be understood until we reach the state of blessedness.

But if what we wish to fix in our minds is the apprehension of some properties of things, then it seems to me that we need not despair of our ability to acquire this respecting distant bodies just as well as those close at hand—and perhaps in some cases even more precisely in the former than in the latter. Who does not understand the periods and movements of the planets better than those of the waters of our various oceans? Was not the spherical shape of the moon discovered long before that of the earth, and much more easily? Is it not still argued whether the earth rests motionless or goes wandering, whereas we know positively the movements of many stars? Hence I should infer that although it may be vain to seek to determine the true substance of the sunspots, still it does not follow that we cannot know some properties of them, such as their location, motion, shape, size, opacity, mutability, generation, and dissolution. These in turn may become the means by which we shall be able to philosophize better about other and more controversial qualities of natural substances. And finally by elevating us to the ultimate end of our labors, which is the love of the divine Artificer, this will keep us steadfast in the hope that we shall learn every other truth in Him, the source of all light and verity.

. . . .

Your Excellency remarks that at your first reading of my tract on floating bodies it appeared paradoxical to you, but that in the end the conclusions were seen to be true and clearly demonstrated. You will be pleased to learn that the same has happened here with many persons who have the reputation of good judgment and sound reasoning. There remain in opposition to my work some stern defenders of every minute point of the Peripatetics. So far as I can see, their education consisted in being nourished from infancy on the opinion that philosophizing is and can be nothing but to make a comprehensive survey of the texts of Aristotle, that from divers passages they may quickly collect and throw together a great number of solutions to any proposed problem. They wish never to raise their eyes from those pages—as if this great book of the universe had been written to be read by nobody but Aristotle, and his eyes had been destined to see for all posterity. . . .

. . . .

Now I fail to see any reason for placing the spots with things differing from them in a hundred ways and having but a single property in common, instead of with things that agree with them in every way. I liken the sunspots to clouds or smokes. Surely if anyone wished to imitate them by means of earthly materials, no better model could be found than to put some drops of incombustible bitumen on a red-hot iron plate. From the black spot thus impressed on the iron, there will arise a black smoke that will disperse in strange and changing shapes. And if anyone were to insist that continual food and nourishment would have to be supplied for the refueling of the immense light that our great lamp, the sun, continually diffuses through the universe, then we have countless experiences harmoniously agreeing in showing us the conversion of burning materials first into something black or dark in color. Thus we see wood, straw, paper, candlewicks, and every burning thing to have its flame planted in and rising from neighboring parts of the material that have first become black. It might even be that if we more accurately observed the bright spots on the sun that I have mentioned, we should find them occurring in the very places where large dark spots had been a short time before. But as to this I do not mean to assert anything positively, nor to oblige myself to defend the conjecture, for I do not wish to mix dubious things with those which are definite and certain.

I believe that there are not a few Peripatetics on this side of the Alps who go about philosophizing without any desire to learn the truth and the causes of things, for they deny these new discoveries or jest about them, saying that they are illusions. It is about time for us to jest right back at these men and say that they likewise have become invisible and inaudible. They go about defending the inalterability of the sky, a view which perhaps Aristotle himself would abandon in our age.

Question:
1. What arguments does Galileo refute? How does he defend his own views?

13.6 Rethinking the *Bible*: Galileo Confronts his Critics

Galileo Galilei's (1564–1642) support of the Copernican system brought him into conflict with the church. In defense of his position, he argued that the Bible does not teach us how the heavens go, but rather how to go to Heaven. He was eventually forced to renounce his views and lived out the last years of his life under house arrest.

Source: "Letter to Madame Christina of Lorraine, Grand Duchess of Tuscany, Concerning the Use of Biblical Quotations in Matters of Science," in *Discoveries and Opinions of Galileo*, trans. Stillman Drake, (Garden City, NY: Doubleday Anchor Books, 1957), pp. 172–216; quoted pp. 172–85, passim.

GALILEO GALILEI TO THE MOST SERENE GRAND DUCHESS MOTHER:

Some years ago, as Your Serene Highness well knows, I discovered in the heavens many things that had not been seen before our own age. The novelty of these things, as well as some consequences which followed from them in contradiction to the physical notions commonly held among academic philosophers, stirred up against me no small number of professors—as if I had placed these things in the sky with my own hands in order to upset nature and overturn the sciences. They seemed to forget that the increases of known truths stimulates the investigation, establishment, and growth of the arts; not their diminution or destruction.

Showing a greater fondness for their own opinions than for truth, they sought to deny and disprove the new things which, if they had cared to look for themselves, their own senses would have demonstrated to them. To this end they hurled various charges and published numerous writings filled with vain arguments, and they made the grave mistake of sprinkling these with passages taken from places in the Bible which they had failed to understand properly, and which were ill suited to their purposes.

These men would perhaps not have fallen into such error had they but paid attention to a most useful doctrine of St. Augustine's, relative to our making positive statements about things which are obscure and hard to understand by means of reason alone. Speaking of a certain physical conclusion about the heavenly bodies, he wrote: "Now keeping always our respect for moderation in grave piety, we ought not to believe anything inadvisedly on a dubious point, lest in favor to our error we conceive a prejudice against something that truth hereafter may reveal to be not contrary in any way to the sacred books of either the Old or the New Testament."[1]

. . . .

Persisting in their original resolve to destroy me and everything mine by any means they can think of, these men are aware of my views in astronomy and philosophy. They know that as to the arrangement of the parts of the universe, I hold the sun to be situated motionless in the center of the revolution of the celestial orbs while the earth rotates on its axis and revolves about the sun. They know also that I support this position not only by refuting the arguments of Ptolemy and Aristotle, but by producing many counterarguments; in particular, some which relate to physical effects whose causes can perhaps be assigned in no other way. In addition there are astronomical arguments derived from many things in my new celestial discoveries that plainly confute the Ptolemaic system while admirably agreeing with and confirming the contrary hypothesis. Possibly because they are disturbed by the known truth of other propositions of mine with which they disagree, and therefore mistrusting their defense so long as they confine themselves to the field of philosophy, these men have resolved to fabricate a shield for their fallacies out of the mantle of pretended religion and the authority of the Bible. These they apply, with little judgment, to the refutation of arguments that they do not understand and have not even listened to.

First they have endeavored to spread the opinion that such propositions in general are contrary to the Bible and are consequently damnable and heretical. They know that it is human nature to take up causes whereby a man may oppress his neighbor, no matter how unjustly, rather than those from which a man may receive some just encouragement. Hence they have had no trouble in finding men who would preach the damnability and heresy of the new doctrine and its followers but to all mathematics and mathematicians in general. Next, becoming bolder, and hoping (though vainly) that this seed which first took root in their hypocritical minds would send out branches and ascend to heaven, they began scattering rumors among the people that before long this doctrine would be condemned by the supreme authority. They know, too, that official condemnation would not only suppress the two propositions which I have mentioned, but would render damnable all other astronomical and physical statements and observations that have any necessary relation or connection with these.

In order to facilitate their designs, they seek so far as possible (at least among the common people) to make this opinion seem new and to belong to me alone. They pretend not to know that its author, or rather its restorer and confirmer, was Nicholas Copernicus; and that he was not only a Catholic, but a priest and a canon. He was in fact so esteemed by the

---

[1] *De Genesi ad literam*, end of bk. ii. (Citations of theological works are taken from Galileo's marginal notes, without verification.)

church that when the Lateran Council under Leo X took up the correction of the church calendar, Copernicus was called to Rome from the most remote parts of Germany to undertake its reform. At that time the calendar was defective because the true measures of the year and the lunar month were not exactly known.

. . . .

Since that time not only has the calendar been regulated by his teachings, but tables of all the motions of the planets have been calculated as well.

. . . .

Now as to the false aspersions which they so unjustly seek to cast upon me, I have thought it necessary to justify myself in the eyes of all men, whose judgment in matters of religion and of reputation I must hold in great esteem.

. . . .

To this end they make a shield of their hypocritical zeal for religion. They go about invoking the Bible, which they would have minister to their deceitful purposes. Contrary to the sense of the Bible and the intention of the holy Fathers, if I am not mistaken, they would extend such authorities until even in purely physical matters—where faith is not involved—they would have us altogether abandon reason and the evidence of our senses in favor of some biblical passage, though under the surface meaning of its words this passage may contain a different sense.

I hope to show that I proceed with much greater piety than they do, when I argue not against condemning this book, but against condemning it in the way they suggest—that is, without understanding it, weighing it, or so much as reading it. For Copernicus never discusses matters of religion or faith, nor does he use arguments that depend in any way upon the authority of sacred writings which he might have interpreted erroneously. He stands always upon physical conclusions pertaining to the celestial motions, and deals with them by astronomical and geometrical demonstrations, founded primarily upon sense experiences and very exact observations. He did not ignore the Bible, but he knew very well that if his doctrine were proved, then it could not contradict the Scriptures when they were rightly understood.

. . . .

Therefore I declare (and my sincerity will make itself manifest) not only that I mean to submit myself freely and renounce any errors into which I may fall in this discourse through ignorance of matters pertaining to religion, but that I do not desire in these matters to engage in disputes with anyone, even on points that are disputable. My goal is this alone; that if, among errors that may abound in these considerations of a subject remote from my profession, there is anything that may be serviceable to the holy Church in making a decision concerning the Copernican system, it may be taken and utilized as seems best to the superiors. And if not, let my book be torn and burnt, as I neither intend nor pretend to gain from it any fruit that is not pious and Catholic.

. . . .

I think that in discussions of physical problems we ought to begin not from the authority of scriptural passages, but from sense-experiences and necessary demonstrations; for the holy Bible and the phenomena of nature proceed alike from the divine Word, the former as the dictate of the Holy Ghost and the latter as the observant executrix of God's commands. It is necessary for the Bible, in order to be accommodated to the understanding of every man, to speak many things which appear to differ from the absolute truth so far as the bare meaning of the words is concerned. But Nature, on the other hand, is inexorable and immutable; she never transgresses the laws imposed upon her, or cares a whit whether her abstruse reasons and methods of operation are understandable to men. For that reason it appears that nothing physical which sense-experience sets before our eyes, or which necessary demonstrations prove to us, ought to be called in question (much less condemned) upon the testimony of biblical passages which may have some different meaning beneath their words. For the Bible is not chained in every expression to conditions as strict as those which govern all physical effects; nor is God any less excellently revealed in Nature's actions than in the sacred statements of the Bible.

From this I do not mean to infer that we need not have an extraordinary esteem for the passages of holy Scripture. On the contrary, having arrived at any certainties in physics, we ought to utilize these as, the most appropriate aids in the true exposition of the Bible and in the investigation of those meanings which are necessarily contained therein, for these must be concordant with demonstrated truths. I should judge that the authority of the Bible was designed to persuade men of those articles and propositions which, surpassing all human reasoning, could not be made credible by science, or by any other means than through the very mouth of the Holy Spirit.

Yet even in those propositions which are not matters of faith, this authority ought to be preferred over that of all human writings which are supported only by bare assertions or probable arguments, and not set forth in a demonstrative way. This I hold to be necessary and proper to the same extent that divine wisdom surpasses all human judgment and conjecture.

But I do not feel obliged to believe that that same God who has endowed us with senses, reason, and intellect has intended to forgo their use and by some other means to give us knowledge which we can attain by them. He would not require us to deny sense and reason in physical matters which are set before our eyes and minds by direct experience or necessary demonstrations.

Question:

1. How does Galileo's interpretation of the Bible respond to his critics' use of the Bible to attack his views? How does he embrace scientific principles?

PART 14
European Expansion

14.1 Before Europe: The Zheng He Expeditions

The Muslim eunuch Zheng He (spelled Cheng Ho in the document below) undertook seven expeditions by sea to India and Africa, nearly a century before Columbus sailed the Atlantic. While Columbus sailed with about 100 men, the Chinese crew, all state servants, consisted of thousands of men, ranging from civil officers and soldiers to scribes and cooks. The ships too dwarfed Columbus', with 62 galleons and more than 100 auxiliary vessels. The largest ships each had 9 masts and 12 sails, measured 440¢ ¥ 180¢, and weighed 1500 tons. Columbus' three ships had three masts each, were 150' long, and weighed 415 tons all together. A stone tablet, engraved in 1432, commemorates the expeditions, part of which is excerpted below.

> **Source:** J.J.L. Duyvendak, "The True Dates of the Chinese Maritime Expeditions in the Early Fifteenth Century," *ToungPao 24* (1938), pp. 349–355; reprinted in Richard L. Graves, et al., *Civilizations of the World: The Human Adventure,* 3rd edition, (New York: Longman, Addison-Wesley Educational Publishers Inc., 1997), p. 573.

The Imperial Ming dynasty in unifying seas and continents... even goes beyond the Han and the Tang. The countries beyond the horizon and from the ends of the earth have all become subjects.... Thus the barbarians from beyond the seas... have come to audience bearing precious objects.... The emperor has ordered us, Cheng Ho... to make manifest the transforming power of the Imperial virtue and to treat distant people with kindness.... We have seven times received the commission of ambassadors [and have visited] altogether more than thirty countries large and small. We have traversed immense water spaces and have beheld huge waves like mountains rising sky-high, and we have set eyes on barbarian regions far away hidden in a blue transparency of light vapors, while our sails loftily unfurled like clouds day and night continued their course, traversing those savage waves as if we were treading a public thoroughfare.... We have received the high favor of a gracious commission of our Sacred Lord, to carry to the distant barbarians the benefits of his auspicious example.... Therefore we have recorded the years and months of the voyages. [Here follows a detailed record of places visited and things one on each of the seven voyages.] We have anchored in this port awaiting a north wind to take the sea... and have thus recorded an inscription in stone... erected by the principal envoys, the Grand Eunuchs Cheng Ho and Wang Ching-hung, and the assistant envoys.

Questions:
1. How do the Chinese, in this document, perceive their role in these expeditions?
2. How do the Chinese perceive those they meet in traveling?

14.2 From King to King: Letters from Kongo to Portugal

The Portuguese made contact with the kingdom of Kongo in Africa in the 1480s. By the 1490s, King John I of Kongo and some of his nobles were baptized as Christians. He and his successors and the king of Portugal exchanged letters for the next half century. Excerpts from the Kongo kings' letters appear below.

> **Source:** "Letters from the Kings of the Kongo to the King of Portugal," *MonumentaMissionaria Africana,* ed. Antonio Brasio, (Lisboa: Agencia Geral do Ultramar, 1952), vol. 1: 262–63, 294–95, 335, 404, 470, 488, trans. Linda Wimmer; reprinted in *The Global Experience: Readings in World History,* ed. Stuart B. Schwartz, et al., (New York: Addison Wesley, Longman, Inc., 1997), pp. 240–42.

PORTUGUESE MILITARY AID DURING CIVIL WAR (1512)

And our brother who usurped us, and without justice occupied us, with arms and a great number of people... became empowered in all of our kingdom, and lordships, with which when we saw the only solution for our person we feigned sickness; and it being so with us, by a divine inspiration of our Lord, we raised and strengthened ourself, and called up our 36 men, and with them we appeared, and went with them to the main square of the city, where our Father died, and where people of infinite number were with our said brother, and... for our Lord Jesus Christ, and we began to fight with our adversaries... our 36 men, inspired by grace, and aided by God, our adversaries quickly fled... and chaos ensued, and with them witnessing... there appeared in the air a white Cross, and the blessed Apostle St. James with many men armed and on horseback, and dressed in white battle garments, and killed them, and so great was the chaos, and mortality, that it was a thing of great wonder.

In this defeat our brother was taken prisoner and with justice condemned to die, as he died, for having rebelled against us; and finally we made peace in our kingdoms... as it is today, with the Grace of God... and through the miracle made by our Lord, and we send word to the King Dom Emanuel of Portugal... and we send to him Dom Pedro our brother, who was one of the 36 men with us... and with the letters that the king sent of great works given....

And as the King of Portugal saw the good example... followed... for the greater growth of our Holy Catholic Faith, he sent by our cousin Dom Pedro and by Simao da Sylva noblemen of your house who came with him, the arms pictured in this card, and the shields with insignias... [A]nd as these weapons arrived a cross was seen in the sky, and so the Apostle St. James and all the other Saints fought with us, and with the help of our Lord God we were given victory, and so also as by the King sent us his [men] took part with the said arms....

PROBLEMS IN CONVERSION EFFORTS (1515)

Very High and Powerful Lord,

We the King Dom Alfonso... Lord, much holy grace and praise I give to the Holy God the Father and the Son and the Holy Spirit... all good and holy things are done through the will of God, without which we can do nothing... our faith is still like glass in this kingdom, due to the bad examples of the men who come here to teach it, because through worldly greed for a few riches truth is destroyed, as through greed the Jews crucified the Son of God, my brother, until today he is crucified through bad examples and bad deeds... in our time by us who walk crying in this real valley of misery and tears.

... [I]n teaching the word of Our Lord [these bad priests] become bad examples and so take the key to the Celestial Kingdom that is the Doctrine of our Holy Catholic Faith, to open the hearts of our simple people... and by entering into a life of sin take the key to Hell... due to the greed of this world, do not merely take their own bodies and souls to Hell, but guide those most blind with them through their bad examples. I ask of you, Brother, to aid me in establishing our Holy Catholic Faith, because, Lord my Brother, for us it were better... that the souls of our relatives and brothers and cousins and nephews and grandchildren who are innocent, to see... good examples.

... I ask you to send stonemasons and house carpenters to build a school to teach our relatives and our people, because Lord, although greedy and jealous men still give bad examples... with the Holy Sacred Scripture we may change that, because the world of the Holy Spirit is contrary to the world, the flesh and the devil....

ATTEMPTS TO BUY A CARAVEL (1517)

Very Powerful and Very High Prince and King My Brother

... I have several times written you of the necessity of having a ship, telling you to make me one to buy, and I don't know why Your Highness does not want to consent, because I want nothing more than... to use it in God's service....

EFFECTS OF PORTUGUESE TRADE (1526)

Lord,

... [Y]our factors and officials give to the men and merchants that come to this Kingdom... and spread... so that many vassals owing us obedience... rebel because they have more goods [through trade with Portuguese] than us, who before had been content and subject to our... jurisdiction, which causes great damage....

... And each day these merchants take our citizens, native to the land and children of our nobles and vassals, and our relations, because they are thieves and men of bad conscience, steal them with the desire to have things of this kingdom... take them to sell... our land is all spoiled... which is not to your service.... For this we have no more necessity for other than priests and educators, but [send] no more merchandise... nor merchants....

EXPANSION AND REGULATION OF THE SLAVE TRADE (1526)

[M]any of our subjects, through the desire for merchandise and things of this Kingdoms which you bring... to satisfy their appetite, steal many of our free and exempt subjects. And nobles and their children and our relatives are often stolen to be sold to white men... hidden by night.... And the said white men are so powerful... they embark and... buy them, for which we want justice, restoring them to liberty....

And to avoid this great evil, by law all white men in our kingdom who buy slaves... must make it known to three nobles and officials of our court... to see these slaves....

14.3 "The Chronicle of Peru: The Incas"

The Incas lived in the Andes mountains, on the western coast of South America from about 1100. Much of what we know about the Incas comes from accounts by the Spanish who destroyed the Inca empire in the mid-1500s. Pedro Cieza de Leon, one such nobleman and soldier, wrote The Chronicle of Peru in 1547–1550, immediately after his involvement in the military campaigns against the Incas. Relying on first-hand accounts from the Incas, his "Chronicle" is considered one of the most authoritative accounts available.

> **Source:** Pedro Cieza de Leon, "The Chronicle of Peru: The Incas"; reprinted in *Primary Source Document Workbook to Accompany World Civilizations,* by Philip J. Adier; prepared by Robert Welborn, (New York: West Publishing Company, 1996), pp. 35–36. (Introduction based on Welborn's introduction to the document.)

It should be well understood that great prudence was needed to enable these kings to govern such large provinces, extending over so vast a region, parts of it rugged and covered with forests, parts mountainous, with snowy peaks and ridges, parts consisting of deserts of sand, dry and without trees or water. These regions were inhabited by many different nations, with varying languages, laws, religions, and the kings had to maintain tranquility and to rule so that all should live in peace and in friendship towards their lord. Although the city of Cuzco was the head of the empire,... yet at certain points, as we shall also explain, the king stationed his delegates and governors, who were the most learned, the ablest, and the bravest men that could be found, and none was so youthful that he was not already in the last third part of his age. As they were faithful and none betrayed their trusts,... none of the natives, though they might be more powerful, attempted to rise in rebellion; or if such a thing ever did take place, the town where the revolt broke out was punished, and the ringleaders were sent prisoners to Cuzco....

All men so feared the king, that they did not dare to speak evil even of his shadow. And this was not all. If any of the king's captains or servants went forth to visit a distant part of the empire on some business, the people came out on the road with presents to receive them, not daring, even if one came alone, to omit to comply with all his commands.

So great was the veneration that the people felt for their princes, throughout this vast region, that every district was as well regulated and governed as if the lord was actually present to chastise those who acted contrary to his rules. This fear arose from the known valor of the lords and their strict justice. It was felt to be certain that those who did evil would receive punishment without fail, and that neither prayers nor bribes would avert it. At the same time, the Incas always did good to those who were under their sway, and would not allow them to be ill-treated, nor that too much tribute should be exacted from them. Many who dwelt in a sterile country where they and their ancestors have lived with difficulty, found that through the orders of the Inca their lands were made fertile and abundant, the things being supplied which before were wanting. In other districts, where there was scarcity of clothing, owing to the people having no flocks, orders were given that cloth should be abundantly provided. In short, it will be understood that these lords knew how to enforce service and the payment of tribute, so they provided for the maintenance of the people, and took care that they should want for nothing. Through these good works, and because the lord always gave women and rich gifts to his principal vassals, he gained so much on their affections that he was most fondly loved....

One of the things which I admired most, in contemplating and noting down the affairs of this kingdom, was to think how and in what manner they can have made such grand and admirable roads as we now see, and what a number of men would suffice for their construction, and with what tools and instruments they can have leveled the mountains and broken through the rocks to make them so broad and good as they are. For it seems to me that if the King of Spain should desire to give orders for another royal road to be made, like that which goes from Quito to Cuzco,... with all his power I believe that he could not get it done; nor could any force of men achieve such results unless there was also the perfect order by means of which the commands of the Incas were carried into execution....

Questions:
1. What does the author find to admire about the Incas?
2. What can we learn about Spain from what he says about the Incas?
3. How do you think he could both praise the Incas and participate in their destruction?

14.4   The Jamestown Charter

The colony of Jamestown became the first permanent English settlement in America. Though the colony almost failed, because of disease, hunger, and Indian attacks, it survived with the arrival of new men and more supplies. The following excerpt comes from the letters patent (or First Charter) from the English government in 1606.

> **Source:** "Letters patent to Sir Thomas Gates and others, 10 April 1606," in *The Jamestown Voyages Under the First Charter,* 1606–1609, vol. I, ed. Philip L. Barbour, (Cambridge: Cambridge University Press, 1969), pp. 24–34 passim.

I. 10 April 1606.
Letters patent to Sir Thomas Gates and others.

James by the grace of God &c Whereas our loving and well disposed subiects Sir Thomas Gates and Sir George Somers Knightes Richard Hackluit Clarke *pre*bendarie of West*minster* and Edwarde Maria Winghfeilde Thomas Hannam and Raleighe Gilberde Esquiers William Parker and George Popham Gentlemen and divers others of our loving subiects haue been humble sutors vnto vs that wee woulde vouchsafe vnto them our licence to make habitacion plantaion and to deduce a Colonie of sondrie of our people into that parte of America commonly called Virginia and other parts and territories in America either appertaining vnto vs or which are not nowe actuallie possessed by anie Christian Prince or people scituate lying and being all along the sea Coastes

. . . .

and to that ende and for the more speedy accomplishemente of theire saide intended plantacion and habitacion there are desirous to devide themselues into two severall Colonies and Companies the one consisting of certaine Knightes Gentlemen marchauntes and other Adventurers of our Cittie of London and elsewhere

. . . .

and the other consisting of sondrie Knightes Gentlemen merchauntes and other Adventurers of our Cities of Bristoll and Exeter and of our towne of Plymouthe and of other places which doe ioyne themselues vnto that Colonie

. . . .

wee greatly com*m*ending and graciously accepting of theire desires to the furtherance of soe noble a worke which may be the providence of Almightie God hereafter tende to the glorie of hys divyne maiestie in propagating of Christian religion to suche people as yet live in darkenesse and myserable ignorance of the true knowledge and worshippe of god and may in tyme bring the infidels and salvages lyving in those partes to humane civilitie and to a setled and quiet governmente doe by theise our lettres Patentes graciously accepte of and agree to theire humble and well intended desires

. . . .

And that they shall haue all the landes woodes soyle Groundes havens portes Ryvers Mynes Myneralls Marshes waters Fyshings Com*m*odities and hereditamentes whatsoever from the said first seate of theire plantacion and habytacion by the space of Fyftie miles of Englishe statute measure all alongest the saide Coaste of Virginia and America towardes the Weste and southeweste as the Coaste lyeth with all the Islandes within one hundred myles directlie over againste the same sea Coaste

. . . .

and

   towards the Easte and Northeaste

. . . .

And

   directly into the mayne lande by the space of One hundred like Englishe myles and shall and may inhabyt and remaine there and shall and may alsoe buylde and fortifie within anie the same for theire better safegarde and defence according to theire best discrecions and the direction of the Counsell of that Colonie and that noe other of our subiects shalbe permitted or suffered to plante or inhabyt behinde or on the backside of them towardes the mayne lande without the expresse lycence or consente of the Counsell of that Colonie thereunto in writing firste had or obtained

. . . .

And wee doe alsoe ordaine establishe and agree for vs our heires and successors that eache of the saide Colonies shall haue a Counsell which shall governe and order all matters and Causes which shall arise growe or happen to or within the same severall Colonies according to such lawes ordynaunces and Instructions as shalbe in that behalfe given and signed with our hande or signe manuell and passe vnder the privie seale of our Realme of Englande Eache of which Counsells shall consist of Thirteene parsons [i.e., persons] and to be ordained made and removed from tyme to tyme according as shalbe directed and comprised in the same Instructions and shall haue a severall seale for all matters that shall passe or concerne the same severall Counsells Eache of which seales shall haue the Kinges Armes engraven on the one syde thereof and hys pourtraiture on the other

. . . .

And that alsoe ther shalbe a Counsell established here in Englande which shall in like manner consist of thirteene parsons to be for that purpose appointed by vs our heires and successors which shalbe called our Counsell of Virginia And shall from tyme to tyme haue the superior managing and direction onelie of and for all matters that shall or may concerne the govermente aswell of the said seuerall Colonies as of and for anie other parte or place within the aforesaid preinctes

. . . .

And moreover wee doe graunte and agree for vs our heires and successors that the saide severall Counsells of and for the saide severall Colonies shall and lawfully may by vertue hereof from tyme to tyme without intervpcion of vs our heires or successors giue and take order to digg myne and searche for all manner of Mynes of Goulde Silver and Copper aswell within anie parte of theire saide severall Colonies as of the saide Mayne landes on the backeside of the same Colonies and to haue and enjoy the Goulde Silver and Copper to be gotten thereof to the vse and behoofe of the same Colonies and the plantacions thereof yielding therefore yerelie to vs our heires and successors the Fifte parte onelie of all the same Goulde and Silver and the Fifteenth parte of all the same Copper soe to be gotten or had as ys aforesaide without anie other manner of profytt or Accompte to be given or yeilded to vs our heires or successors for or in respecte of the same

And that they shall or lawfullie may establishe and cawse to be made a coyne to passe currant there betweene the people of those severall Colonies for the more ease of traffique and bargaining betweene and amongst them and the natives there of such mettall and in suche manner and forme as the same severall Counsells there shall lymitt and appointe

. . . .

Moreover wee doe by theise presentes for vs our heires and successors giue and graunte licence vnto the said Sir Thomas Gates Sir George Sumers Richarde Hackluite Edwarde Maria Winghfeilde Thomas Hannam Raleighe Gilberde William Parker and George Popham and to everie of the said Colonies that they and everie of them shall and may from tyme to tyme and at all tymes for ever hereafter for their severall defences incounter or expulse repell and resist as well by sea as by lande by all waies and meanes whatsoever all and everie suche parson and parsons as without especiall licence of the said severall Colonies and plantacions shall attempt to inhabit within the saide seuerall precinctes and lymittes of the saide severall Colonies and plantacions or anie of them or that shall enterprise or attempt at anie tyme hereafter the hurte detrymente or annoyance of the saide severall Colonies or plantacions

Alsoe wee doe vor vs our heires and successor declare by theise presentes that all and everie the parsons being our subiectes which shall dwell and inhabit within everie or anie of the saide severall Colonies and plantacions and everie of theire children which shall happen to be borne within the lymittes and precinctes of the said severall Colonies and plantacyons shall haue and enioy all liberties Franchises and Immunities within anie of our other domynions to all intentes and purposes as yf they had been abyding and borne within this our Realme of Englande or anie other of our saide Domynions

. . . .

Prouided alwaies and our will and pleasure ys and wee doe hereby declare to all Christian Kings Princes and estates that yf anie parson or parsons which shall hereafter be of anie of the said severall Colonies and plantacions or anie other by his theire or anie of theire licence or appointement shall at anie tyme or tymes hereafter robb or spoile by sea or by lande or doe anie Acte of vniust and vnlawfull hostilitie to anie the subiectes of vs our heires or successors or anie of the subiects of anie King Prince Ruler Governor or State being then in league or Amitie with vs our heires or successors and that vpon suche Iniurie or vpon iuste complainte of such Prince Ruler Governor or State or theire subiects wee our heires or successors shall make open proclamacion within anie the portes of our Realme of Englande commodious for that purpose that the saide parson or parsons having committed anie such Robberie or spoyle shall within the tearme to be lymitted by suche Proclamacions make full restitucion or satisfactin of all suche Iniuries done soe as the saide Princes or others soe complained may houlde themselues fully satisfied and contented and that yf the saide parson or parsons having comitted such robberie or spoyle shall not make or cause to be made satisfaction accordingly with[in] such tyme soe to be lymitted

That then yt shalbe lawfull to vs our heires and successors to put the saide parson or parsons having comitted such robberie or spoyle and theire procurers Abbettors or Comfortors out of our allegeaunce and protection and that yt shalbe lawefull and free for all Princes and others to pursue with hostilitie the saide Offenders and everie of them and theire and everie of theire procurors Ayders Abbettors and comforters in that behalfe

Questions:
1. Why did these Englishmen want to form colonies in the new lands?
2. Of what advantage was this to England?

14.5   First Contact: The English Describe Pawatah's People

When the English arrived, they recorded their impressions of the countryside and of the people already living in the area, the Pawatah. The description of the Pawatah follows.

> Source: "21 May-21 June 1607, Description of the People," in *The Jamestown Voyages Under the First Charter, 1606–1609*, vol. I, ed. Philip L. Barbour, (Cambridge: Cambridge University Press, 1969), pp. 102–04.

15. 21 May-21 June 1607.
Descriptin of the People.

A Brief discription of the People.

There is a king in this land called great Pawatah, vnder whose dominions are at least 20th several kingdomes, yet each king potent as a prince in his owne territory. these have their Subiectes at so quick Comaund, as a beck bringes obedience, even to the resticucion of stolne goodes which by their naturall inclinac[i]on they are loth to leave. They goe all naked save their privityes, yet in coole weather they were deare skinns, with the hayre on loose: some have leather stockinges vp to their twisties,[1] & sandalls on their feet, their hayre is black generally, which they weare long on the left side, tyed vp on a knott, about which knott the kinges and best among them have a kind of Coronett of deares hayre coloured redd, some have chaines of long linckt copper about their neckes, and some chaines of pearle, the comon sort stick long fethers in this knott, I found not a grey eye among them all. their skynn is tawny not so borne, but with dying and paynting them selues, in which they delight greatly. The wemen are like the men, onely this difference; their hayre groweth long al over their heades save clipt somewhat short afore, these do all the labour and the men hunt and goe at their plesure. They live commonly by the water side in litle cottages made of canes and reedes, covered with the barke of trees; they dwell as I guesse by families of kindred & allyance some 40 tie or 50 ti in a Hatto[2] or small village; which townes are not past a myle or half a myle asunder in most places. They live vpon sodden wheat beanes & peaze for the most part, also they kill deare take fish in their weares, & kill fowle aboundance, they eate often and that liberally; they are proper lusty streight men very strong runn exceeding swiftly, their feight is alway in the wood with bow & arrowes, & a short wodden sword, the celerity they vse in skirmish is admirable. the king directes the batle & is alwayes in front. Their manner of entertainment is vpon mattes on the ground vnder some tree, where they sitt themselues alone in the midst of the matt, & two mattes on each side, on which they[r] people sitt, then right against him (making a square forme) satt we alwayes. when they came to their matt they have an vsher goes before them, & the rest as he sittes downe give a long showt. The people steale any thing comes neare them, yea are so practized in this art that lookeing in our face they would with their foot betwene their toes convey a chizell knife, percer or any indifferent light thing: which having once conveyed they hold it an iniury to take the same from them; They are naturally given to trechery, howbeit we could not

Questions:
1. How do the English describe the Pawatah?
2. Why might they describe them as they do? How might the description be distorted by their own beliefs, prejudices, and desires?

---

[1] 'The junction of the thighs' (*OED*).

[2] 'Hatto' possibly represents an element cognate with modern Cree *otānow*, 'town', whch appears as the second element in the village name Kecoughtan. It may have been pronounced with a glottal stop or other initial throaty sound which the author recorded with an 'h'.

14.6 The Experiences of an Indentured Servant

While the men named in the letters patent (Document 4) were men of means (merchants and the like), others also signed on to start a new life in America. Those without money often made the passage as indentured servants, where they gave generally seven years of service to those who paid their passage. After seven years, they were again free men. The following excerpt is from a letter of one indentured servant in 1623.

Source: Richard Frethorne, letter to his father and mother, March 20, April 2 and 3, 1623, in Susan Kingsbury, ed. *The Records of the Virginia Company of London,* (Washington, D.C.: Government Printing Office, 1935), 4: 58–62; reprinted on URL: http://jefferson.village.virginia. edu/vcdh/jamestown/frethorne.html.

LOVING AND KIND FATHER AND MOTHER:

My most humble duty remembered to you, hoping in god of your good health, as I myself am at the making hereof. This is to let you understand that I you child am in a most heavy case by reason of the country, [which] is such that it causeth much sic kness, [such] as the sccurvy and the bloody flux and diverse other diseases, which maketh the body very poor and weak. And when we are sick there is nothing to comfort us; for since I came out of the ship I never ate anything but peas, and loblollie (that is, water gruel). As for deer or venison I never saw any since I came into this land. There is indeed some fowl, but we are not allowed to go and get it, but must work hard both early and late for a mess of water gruel and a mouthful of bread and beef. A mouthful of bread for a penny loaf must serve for four men which is most pitiful. [You would be grieved] if you did know as much as I [do], when people cry out day and night—Oh! That they were in England without their limbs—and would not care to lose any limb to be in England again, yea, though they beg from door to door. For we live in fear of the enemy every hour, yet we have had a combat with them... and we took two alive and made slaves of them. But it was by policy, for we are in great danger; for our plantation is very weak by reason of the death and sickness of our company. For we came but twenty for the merchants, and they are half dead just; and we look every hour when two more should go. Yet there came some four other men yet to live with us, of which there is but one alive; and our Lieutenant is dead, and [also] his father and his brother. And there was some five or six of the last year's twenty, of which there is but three left, so that we are fain to get other men to plant with us; and yet we are but 32 to fight against 3000 if they should come. And the nighest help that we have is ten mile of us, and when the rogues overcame this place [the] last [time] they slew 80 persons. How then shall we do, for we lie even in their teeth? They may easily take us, but [for the fact] that God is merciful and can save with few as well as with many, as he showed to Gilead. And like Gilead's soldiers, if they lapped water, we drink water which is but weak.

And I have nothing to comfort me, nor is there nothing to be gotten here but sickness and death, except [in the event] that one had money to lay out in some things for profit. But I have nothing at all—no, not a shirt to my back but two rags (2), nor clothes but one poor suit, nor but one pair of shoes, but one pair of stockings, but one cap, [and] but two bands [collars]. My cloak is stolen by one of my fellows, and to his dying hour [he] sould not tell me what he did with it; but some of my fellows saw him have butter and beef out of a ship, which my cloak, I doubt [not], paid for. So that I have not a penny, nor a penny worth, to help me too either spice or sugar or strong waters, without the which one cannot live here. For as strong beer in England doth fatten and strengthen them, so water here doth wash and weaken these here [and] only keeps [their] life and soul together. But I am not half [of] a quarter so strong as I was in England, and all is for want of victuals; for I do protest unto you that I have eaten more in [one] day at home than I have allowed me here for a week. You have given more than my day's allowance to a beggar at the door; and if Mr. Jackson had not relieved me, I should be in a poor case. But he like a father and she like a loving mother doth still help me.

For when we go to Jamestown (that is 10 miles of us) there lie all the ships that come to land, and there they must deliver their goods. And when we went up to town [we would go], as it may be, on Monday at noon, and come there by night, [and] then load the next day by noon, and go home in the afternoon, and unload, and then away again in the night, and [we would] be up about midnight. Then if it rained or blowed never so hard, we must lie in the boat on the water and have nothing but a little bread. For when we go into the boat we [would] have a loaf allowed to two men, and it is all [we would get] if we stayed there two days, which is hard; and [we] must lie all that while in the boat. But that Goodman Jackson pitied me and made me a cabin to lie in always when I [would] come up, and he would give me some poor jacks [fish] [to take] home with me, which comforted me more than peas or water gruel. Oh, they be very godly folks, and love me very well, and will do anything for me. And he much marvelled that you would send me a servant to the Company; he saith I had been better knocked on the head. And indeed so I find it now, to my great grief and misery; and [I] saith that if you love me you will redeem me suddenly, for which I do entreat and beg. And if you cannot get the merchants to redeem me for some little money, then for God's sake get a gathering or entreat some good folks to lay out some little sum of money in meal and cheese and butter and beef. Any eating meat will yield great profit. Oil and vinegar is very good; but, father, there is great loss in leaking. But for God's sake send beef and cheese and butter, or the more of one sort and none of another. But if you send cheese, it must be very old cheese; and at the cheesemonger's you may buy very food cheese for twopence farthing or halfpenny, that will be liked very well. But if you send cheese, you must have a care how you pack it in barrels; and you must put cooper's chips between every cheese, or else the heat of the hold will rot them. And look whatsoever you send me—be in never so much—look, what[ever] I make of it, I will deal truly with you. I will send it over and beg the profit to redeem me; and if I die before it come, I have entreated Goodman Jackson to send you the worth of it, who hath promised he will. If you send, you must direct your letters to Goodman Jackson, at Jamestown, a gunsmith. (You must set down his freight, because there be more of his name there.) Good father, do not forget me, but have mercy and pity my miserable case. I know if you did but see me, you would weep to see me; for I have but one suit. (But [though] it is a strange one, it is very well guarded.) Wherefore, for God's sake, pity me. I pray you to remember my love to all my friends and kindred. I hope all my brothers and sisters are in good health, and as for my part I have set down my resolution that certainly will be; that is, that the answer of this letter will be life or death to me. Therefore, good father, send as soon as you can; and if you send me any thing let this be the mark.

ROT
RICHARD FRETHORNE,
MARTIN'S HUNDRED

Questions:
1. How does Frethorne describe life in the colony, as it might apply to all inhabitants?
2. How does Frethorne describe specifically the life of an indentured servant?

PART 15
Absolutism

15.1 Richelieu: Controlling the Nobility

Cardinal Richelieu (1585–1642) was a shrewd and dedicated political leader who accelerated the growth of absolutism in France. He demonstrated tremendous energy, tenacity, and imagination in directing public policy as Louis XIII's chief minister.

> **Source:** *The Western World: Volume I to 1700,* ed. Wallace E. Adams, et al., (New York: Dodd, Mead & Co., 1968), pp. 510–16.

ON THE NOBILITY

After having explained what I consider to be absolutely necessary for the re-establishment of your realm's first order [the clergy], I shall proceed to the second order and say that the nobility must be considered as one of the strengths of the state, capable of contributing much to its preservation and to its stability. But for some time the nobility has been so diminished by... the century's misfortunes that it urgently needs to be protected.... They are rich only in the courage that leads them to devote their lives freely to the state.

As it is necessary to protect them against their oppressors; it is also necessary to take special care to restrain them from exploiting their underlings. It is very common fault on the part of those born into the nobility to use violence against the common people to whom God seems to have given arms for earning a living rather than for defending themselves. It is very important to stop such disorders by a constant sternness which will make the weakest of yours, although disarmed, as secure in the shelter of your laws as those who are armed.

The nobility has demonstrated, in the recent war, that it inherited the virtue of its ancestors; it is now necessary to discipline the nobles so that they may preserve their former reputation and usefully serve the state. Men who are injurious to the public are not useful to the state; it is certain that nobility which does not serve in war is not only useless, but a burden to the state, and can be compared to a body which supports a paralyzed arm....

As gentry they merit being well treated when they do well, but it is necessary to be severe with them when they fail to do the things which their birth binds them to do. I have no qualms in saying that those who are degenerate in terms of the virtue of their ancestors, and who fail to serve the crown with their swords and with their lives, as well as with the confidence and the firmness that the laws of the state require, deserve to be deprived of the advantages of their birth and reduced to carry a part of the peoples' burden. Since honor should be dearer to them than life, it would be more of a punishment to deprive them of the former rather than the latter. To take away the lives of these persons, who expose their lives every day for a pure fancy of honor, is much less than taking away their honor and leaving them a life which would be a perpetual anguish for them. All means must be used to maintain the nobility in the true virtue of their fathers, and one must also omit nothing to preserve the advantages they inherited.... Just as it is impossible to find a remedy for every evil, it is also very difficult to put forth a general expedient for the ends that I am proposing....

It is necessary also to distinguish between the nobility which is at court and that which is in the country.... The nobility at court will be notably relieved if the luxury and the unbearable expenditures of court life were reduced. As to the rural nobility, even though it would not receive as much relief by such a decision, because its poverty does not permit it to have such expenditures, it would also feel the effect of this remedy which is so necessary to avoid the ruin of the entire state.... Further, your majesty should control the venal provincial governments and the military expenses for which the nobility pays a large enough price with its blood.

If your majesty practiced better regulation of the expenses of his house, instead of maintaining all sorts of people who are received there through their purse, entrance would be barred in the future to those who will not have the good fortune to be born of noble birth.... Now, unfortunately, gentlemen can elevate themselves to offices and dignities only at the price of their financial.... Further, if your goodness extends itself enough to bestow honors on their children (those who possess the required learning and piety)... the nobility will be bound more closely to you, for in removing the necessity of purchasing honors which weighs them down you will give them the true means of maintaining their houses.... One will be able to do many other things for the relief of the nobility. But I have suppressed my thoughts on that subject, realizing that they would be very easy to write about but perhaps impossible to put into practice.

THE MEANS OF PREVENTING DUELS

There have been many edicts issued to stop duels, all of them fruitless to the present. Results have been hoped for and waited for, but it has been most difficult to find an effective way to curb this rage. The French scorn their lives in such a way, as experience has made clear to us, that the most rigorous punishments have not always been the best method to stop the frenzy.

The nobility have often thought that there is much more glory in violating rather than obeying your edicts, for they believe such actions demonstrate that their honor is more important to them than their life. Nevertheless, they are in dread of losing their worldly possessions and convenience, without which they could not live happily.... The fear of losing their offices, their belongings and their freedom has a greater impact on their minds than the fear of losing their lives.

I have tried not to forget anything which would make it possible for me to suggest some remedy to cure this dangerous evil. I have often tried to determine whether some duels, within the multitude that occur every day, could be reconciled in advance. And I believe there is a marked possibility that by this means we may be able to save France from this madness. In view of the fact that those individuals found justified in engaging in combat could still do so, they should be willing to submit themselves to judges deputized to consider the seriousness of the offense, which would put a stop to the misfortune of duels. There should be few quarrels that could not be settled by compromise beforehand. I believe, along such lines, that one could abolish this barbarism which dictates that every offended man take justice into his own hands and find satisfaction in the blood of his enemies;... Unfortunately, the blindness of the nobility is so great that some would ignore the course I have suggested and continue to demand combat to soothe their vanity and give proof of their courage.

The deceased king [Henri IV] attempted this path in 1609, using all the means at his power to make it effective. He deprived the nobility of their properties, their offices, and even the lives of those who fought without permission-but to no avail. This is what has forced your majesty, after experiencing the same conditions at the beginning of his reign, to search for another remedy in his edict of March, 1626. That remedy has had a much greater effect than punishment, for it concentrates on those who value their lives less than their possessions and their liberty.

The best laws in the world are useless, however, if they are not inviolably observed. And because those who commit this offense most often cover the evidence of their duel, it is almost impossible to substantiate their crime. I have no fear in saying to your majesty that it is not enough to punish the participants in confirmed duels through the strictness of your edicts. Even when there has been only unconfirmed information, without full proof of a duel, it is absolutely necessary to apprehend the delinquents and make them prisoners at their own expense, for a long or short period according to the circumstances of their action. Otherwise the uncertainty and negligence which now marks the information your attorney generals ordinarily provide to you, plus the indulgence of the Parlements and the general corruption of the age, is such that every man esteems it an honor to aid those who have fought and then disguised their crimes, thereby rendering your edicts and your most careful efforts useless. It is in such cases that the only sure way to have your laws and ordinances followed is for your authority to pass above the form of the law in order to maintain the law and order necessary to the very existence of a state.

If your majesty orders that all encounters will be considered as duels, and will be punished as such until those who have committed them surrender themselves voluntarily as prisoners, and will be absolved or sentenced according to the law, you will have done all that can probably be done to stem the course of this rage....

THE USES OF PUNISHMENTS AND REWARDS

Punishments and rewards are two quite necessary elements in the conduct of states. It is an ordinary allegation, but more true, and often repeated by all men, that rewards and punishments are the two most important tools of government available in a realm.

It is certain that even though one can make use of no other principle than that of being inflexible in punishing those who fail to serve the state, and religiously reward those who perform some notable service, one will not govern badly, since all men will perform their duty through fear or hope. One should, however, place punishment before rewards, because if it is necessary to eliminate either of the two, it would be better to dispense with the latter than the former.

In the strictest sense good should be embraced for its own sake, for one's love of honor, and no reward is owed to those who perform it. But because there is no duel which does not violate the sense of honor it is meant to uphold, punishment due to disobedience is always required. This obligation is so strict that on many occasions the offense cannot be left unpunished without committing a new one. I am speaking here of actions which injure the state by premeditation and not of the many others which happen by chance and by misfortune, of which princes can and should be indulgent.

Even though to pardon in such cases is a commendable thing, not to punish an offense is a criminal omission because impunity opens the door to license. Theologians and politicians are in agreement on this subject; all agree that while in certain cases it is well for the prince to grant his pardon, it would be inexcusable for officials with public responsibility to substitute lenience for severe punishment. The lesson of experience, for those who have dealt with people for a long time, is that men easily forget favors, remain ungrateful, and become ambitious for further rewards. It is clear that punishments are a much surer means of holding each man to his duty. Men are less likely to forget things that make an impression on their emotions; it is more forceful than reason which has no power over many minds. To be rigorous with those individuals who take pride in scorning the laws and the orders of the state is to serve the public well. One could not commit a greater crime against the public interest than to be indulgent to those who violate it.

Among the several combinations, factions, and seditions which have occurred in this realm during my life, I have never observed that lenience ever led any mind to naturally correct itself of its evil inclinations. But, on the contrary, it allowed individuals to return to their troublesome ways, and often they were more successful the second time than the first.

The degree of indulgence hitherto practiced in this realm has often put it in very great and deplorable difficulties. Whenever wrongs go unpunished, everyone will completely disregard the laws and take advantage of their position; instead of honorable compliance with the laws, they will consider only what further profit they can obtain for themselves.

If in the past men felt that it was dangerous to live under a prince who rigorously enforced the law, they also were aware that it was even more dangerous to live under a state in which impunity opened the door to every of license. Princes and magistrates who fear they will commit a sin by being too strict can answer to God, but they will only be blamed by wise men if they fail to exercise that authority which is prescribed by the laws. I have often brought this to the attention of your majesty and I urge you again to reconsider this matter carefully, for just as there are princes who need to be turned away from severity in order to avoid unnecessary cruelty, your majesty needs to be diverted from the fault of clemency. This is more dangerous even than cruelty, because such leniency will later require even greater punishments.

The rod, which is the symbol of justice, must not stand idle. I am also convinced that it must not be used so strictly that it is without mercy; but this last quality should not lead to a state of indulgence which authorizes disorders, however small, for those disorders are injurious to the state and may cause its ruin. There are, of course, some men badly enough advised to condemn the necessary severity in this kingdom because it has not been practiced in earlier times. It is only necessary to open their eyes, and make them know that leniency has been too common in the past and has caused the breakdown of law and order, and that the continuation of disorders has demanded recourse to extreme measures. So many of the factions that in the past have ranged themselves against the king have had no other source than excessive royal indulgence. Finally, provided that one knows our history, one can not ignore this truth, for which I can produce testimony straight from the mouths of our enemies....

In crimes against the state, it is necessary to close the door to, pity and scorn the complaints of involved parties, and the cries of an ignorant multitude which sometimes finds fault with everything that is useful and even essential to its well-being. Christians should forget personal offenses, but magistrates are obligated never to forget offenses committed against the public interest. In fact, to let them go unpunished is not to pardon but rather like inviting the individuals to commit the offense again.

There are many people whose ignorance is so immense that they feel it is sufficient to prohibit an evil to remedy it; but they are wrong. I may say in truth that new laws are not as much a remedy for the disorders of states as testimonies to their sickness, and symptoms of the weakness of the government. If the ancient laws had been well executed there would be no need to renovate them or to enact new ones designed to prevent new disorders—which would never have taken place had there existed a strong authority to punish the wrongs committed.

Ordinances and laws are quite useless if they are not followed by vigorous execution. This is so absolutely necessary that while in the course of ordinary affairs justice requires an authentic proof, the same is not true for the state; in such cases, what seems to be conjecture must sometimes be held as sufficiently clear; since the factions and conspiracies which work against the public good are commonly carried on with so much skill and secrecy that there is seldom any proof until after the event, when it is too late to remedy the situation. On such occasions, it is sometimes necessary to begin with direct action and punishment; whereas in all others, as a preliminary to everything else, the facts must be proved by witnesses or irreproachable documents. These maxims seem dangerous, and in fact they are not entirely devoid of peril, but if extreme remedies are not used in the case of wrongs which can be verified only by conjecture, one can only attempt to halt the course of a conspiracy by such innocuous means as the exile or imprisonment of suspected persons.

A man of good conscience and penetrating judicial mind, knowing the course of affairs and the future with almost the same certainty as the present, will protect this practice from abuse. And, if worst comes to worst, the abuses committed are dangerous only to private individuals, which is not too important in comparison to the public interest. However, it is necessary to exercise restraint in order not to open the door to tyranny by these means, which doubtless can be avoided if, as I have said above, one only makes use of mild remedies in doubtful cases.

Punishment is so necessary in regard to the public interest that it is not even proper to compensate a present wrong for a good service performed in the past, that is to say, to allow a crime to go unpunished because the one who committed it had served well on another occasion. This is nevertheless what has been often practiced in this realm in the past. Not only have minor wrongs been ignored in consideration of great services rendered, but great crimes have been ignored for services of no importance, which is completely unacceptable. Good and bad are so different and contrary that they must never be paralleled with one another; they are irreconcilable enemies—if one is worthy of recompense, the other is worthy of punishment, and both must be treated according to their merit. Even when one's conscience could allow a worth-while deed to go without reward, and a notable crime to go unpunished, the needs of the state cannot permit it. Punishment and rewards aim at the future rather than the past;...

THE POWER OF THE PRINCE

The prince must be powerful to be respected by his subjects and by foreigners. Power being one of the most necessary things for the greatness of kings and for the prosperity of their governments, those who conduct the principal business of the state are especially obligated to omit nothing which may contribute to the authority of their master.

As goodness is the object of love, power is the cause of fear, and it is most certain that among all the pressures capable of moving a state, fear, grounded on esteem and reverence, has the power to make everyone perform his duty. If this principle is of great efficiency in respect to domestic affairs, it is not less so with respect to external matters. Subjects and foreigners look with the same eyes upon a redoubtable power, and will avoid offending a prince when they know he is in a position to do them harm if he is so inclined.

I have said that the basis of the power of which I speak must be esteem and respect. If such power is based on any other principle it is very dangerous; instead of creating a reasonable fear, it produces hatred for the prince-and princes are never in a worse condition than when they fall into public aversion.

Like a tree with different branches taking nourishment from the same root, the power which makes princes passionately hated or respected is of different kinds: the prince must be powerful through his reputation; and by maintaining a reasonably sized standing army; and by maintaining sufficient funds in his coffers to meet the unexpected emergencies which often occur when one least expects them. And, finally, the prince's power stems from the possession of the hearts of his subjects, as will be clearly shown.

A good reputation is very necessary, for a prince held in high esteem can do more with his name alone than those princes with large armies but a bad reputation. A prince is obliged to be more concerned with the state of his reputation than with his own life, and must be willing to risk fortune and greatness rather than have his reputation tarnished in any way. It is certain that the first weakening of the reputation of a prince, however small it may be, is a dangerous step which may lead to his ruin.... History teaches that at all times and in all states princes with great reputations are happier than those who, lacking such an esteem, have surpassed them in strength, riches, and other forms of power.

Those who shape their conduct in accordance with the rules and principles contained in this testament, will doubtless acquire a valuable reputation.

Questions:
1. What role did the nobility play in Richelieu's concept of the state?
2. By what means did he control their behavior and activities?
3. How would you compare Richelieu's concepts of government to the ideas expressed by Machiavelli? Henry VIII? James I?

15.2 The Sun King Shines

In the last years of Louis XIV (r. 1643–1715) at the splendid and magnificent palace of Versailles, the duke de Saint-Simon (1675–1755) began to compile notes describing the King and the royal court. Saint-Simon, a proud aristocrat of ancient lineage, was a gossipy and caustic observer.

> **Source:** Lucy Norton, ed. and trans., *Saint-Simon at Versailles* (New York: Harper and Row, 1958), pp. 245–55, 261, 282.

He was a prince in whom no one would deny good and even great qualities but he had many others that were petty or downright bad, and of these it was impossible to determine which were natural and which acquired.... This is not the place to tell of his early childhood. He was king almost from birth, but was deliberately repressed by a mother who loved to govern, and still more so by a wicked and self-interested minister [Cardinal Mazarin], who risked the State a thousand times for his own aggrandizement. So long as that minister lived the King was held down, and that portion of his life should be subtracted from his reign.... After Mazarin's death, he had enough intelligence to realize his deliverance, but not enough vigour to release himself. Indeed, that event was one of the finest moments of his life, for it taught him an unshakable principle namely, to banish all prime ministers and ecclesiastics from his councils. Another ideal, adopted at that time, he could never sustain because in the practice it constantly eluded him. This was to govern alone. It was the quality upon which he most prided himself and for which he received most praise and flattery. In fact, it was what he was least able to do.

Born with an intelligence rather below the average, his mind was very capable of development with training and education, for he could learn easily from others [without imitation]. He profited immensely from having always lived among people of the highest quality with the widest knowledge of life,...

Indeed if I may say so of a King of twenty-three years old, he was fortunate in entering the world surrounded by brilliant people of every kind. His Ministers at home and abroad were the strongest in Europe, his generals the greatest, and all were men whose names have been handed down to posterity by common consent. The disturbances that rocked the very foundations of the State after the death of Louis XIII [the Fronde uprising] produced a Court full of famous men and polished courtiers.... [In the house of Mazarin's niece] all the most distinguished men and women foregathered every day, making [it] the centre of the Court love-affairs, [and] the gallant intrigues and manoeuvres for ambition's sake—schemes in which birth counted for much, for at that time rank was as much prized and respected as it is now despised. Into this brilliant vortex the King was first launched, and there he first acquired that polite, chivalrous manner which he retained all through his life and knew so well how to combine with stateliness and propriety.... Had he been born into private life, he would still have had a genius for entertainments, pleasures, and flirtations, and would have caused innumerable broken hearts.

Let me repeat. The King's intelligence was below the average, but was very capable of improvement. He loved glory; he desired peace and good government. He was born prudent, temperate, secretive, master of his emotions and his tongue—can it be believed?—he was born good and just. God endowed him with all the makings of a good and perhaps even of a fairly great king. All the evil in him came from without. His early training was so dissolute... and he would sometimes speak bitterly of those [youthful] days.... He became very dependent on others, for they had scarcely taught him to read and write and he remained so ignorant that he learned nothing of historical events nor the facts about fortunes, careers, rank, or laws. This lack caused him sometimes, even in public to make many gross blunders.

You might imagine that as king he would have loved the old nobility and would not have cared to see it brought down to the level of other classes. Nothing was further from the truth. His aversion to noble sentiments and his partiality for his Ministers, who, to elevate themselves, hated and disparaged all who were what they themselves were not, nor ever could be, caused him to feel a similar antipathy for noble birth. He feared it as much as he feared intelligence, and if he found these two qualities united in one person, that man was finished.

His ministers, generals, mistresses, and courtiers learned soon after he became their master that glory, to him, was a foible rather than an ambition. They therefore flattered him to the top of his bent, and in so doing, spoiled him. Praise, or better, adulation, pleased him so much that the most fulsome was welcome and the most servile even more delectable. They were the only road to his favour and those whom he liked owed his friendship to choosing their moments well and never ceasing in their ambitions. That is what gave his ministers so much power, for they had endless opportunities of flattering his vanity, especially by suggesting that he was the source of all their ideas and had taught them all that they knew. Falseness, servility, admiring glances, combined with a dependent and cringing attitude, above all, an appearance of being nothing without him, were the only means of pleasing him.

Flattery fed the desire for military glory that sometimes tore him from his loves, which was how Louvois so easily involved him in major wars and persuaded him that he was a better leader and strategist than any of his generals, a theory which those officers fostered in order to please him. All their praise he took with admirable complacency, and truly believed that he was what they said. Hence his liking for reviews,... and his preference for sieges, where he could make cheap displays of courage, be forcibly restrained, and show his ability to endure fatigue and lack of sleep.... He greatly enjoyed the sensation of being admired, as he rode along the lines, for his fine presence and princely bearing, his horsemanship, and other attainments....

Pride and vanity, which tend always to increase, and with which he was fed continually without even his perceiving it, even from preachers in the pulpits in his presence, were the foundations on which his ministers raised themselves above all other ranks. He was cunningly persuaded that their rank was merely an extension of his own, supreme in him, in them capable of increase (since without him they were nothing), and useful to him, because it gave them as his instruments greater dignity and made them more readily obeyed. That is why secretaries of state and ministers gradually left off their cloaks, then their bands, then their black gowns and simple seemly dress, and finally came to clothe themselves like gentlemen of quality. They then began to adopt the manners and later the privileges of the nobility, rising by stages to eat with the King, their wives assuming, as by right, the same prerogatives as their husbands, dining at the royal table, riding in the royal coaches, and in every way appearing equal to ladies of the highest rank.

Personal vanity of another kind led the King to encourage this behaviour. He was well aware that though he might crush a nobleman with the weight of his displeasure, he could not destroy him or his line, whereas a secretary of state or other such minister could be reduced together with his whole family to those depths of nothingness from which he had been elevated. No amount of wealth or possessions would avail him then. That was one reason why he liked to give his ministers authority over the highest in the land, even over the Princes of the Blood and all others who held no office under the crown, and to grant them rank and privileges to match. That is why any man of consequence who possessed anything which the King had no power either to destroy or maintain was carefully kept from the ministry; he would have been a source of danger and a continual anxiety.

Therein lay the reason for the watchful, jealous attitude of his ministers, who made it difficult for the King to hear any but themselves, although he pleased to think that he was easy for any man to approach. Indeed, he considered that it enhanced his majesty and the respect and fear with which he was regarded, and which he used to snub the most noble, that all men should have access to him only as he passed. Thus great lords and underlings alike might speak freely to him as he went from one room to another on his way to or from mass, or stepped into his coach. The more distinguished might wait at the door of his study, but none dared to follow him inside. In fact, approach to him was limited to those moments. Any matters whatsoever had to be explained to him in a few words, very awkwardly, and always within hearing range of his entourage, or, if one knew him well, one might whisper into his wig, which was scarcely more convenient. His almost invariable answer was, "We shall see" *(Je verrai)*, very useful no doubt as a means of gaining time, but often bringing little comfort.

Private audiences in his study were rarely if ever granted, even when the matter concerned State affairs. Never, for example, to envoys returning or going abroad, never to generals, unless in extraordinary circumstances, and private letters written to the King always passed through the hands of some minister, except on one or two most rare and special occasions.

Nevertheless, in spite of the fact that the King had been so spoiled with false notions of majesty and power, that every other thought was stifled in him, there was much to be gained from a private audience, if it might be obtained, and if one knew how to conduct oneself with all the respect due to his dignity and habits. I, indeed, can speak from experience.

Once in his study, however prejudiced he might he, however much displeased, he would listen patiently, good-naturedly, and with a real desire to be informed. You could see that he had a sense of justice and a will to get at the truth, even though he might feel vexed with you, and that quality he retained all through his life. In private audience you could say anything to him, provided, as I have already remarked, that you said it respectfully, with submissiveness and proper deference, for without that you would have been in a worse plight. With the proper manner, however, you could interrupt him when it was your turn to speak, and bluntly deny his accusations, you could even raise your voice above his without vexing him, and he would congratulate himself on the audience and praise the person he interviewed for ridding him of prejudices and the lies he had been told; moreover, he would prove his sincerity by his subsequent attitude.

It is therefore enough to make one weep to think of the wickedness of an education designed solely to suppress the virtue and intelligence of that prince, and the insidious poison of barefaced flattery which made him a kind of god in the very heart of Christendom. His ministers with their cruel politics hemmed him in and made him drunk with power until he was utterly corrupted. If they did not manage entirely to smother such kindness, justice, and love of truth as God had given him, they blunted and obstructed those virtues to the lasting injury of himself and his kingdom.

From such alien and pernicious sources he acquired a pride so colossal that, truly, had not God implanted in his heart the fear of the devil, even in his worst excesses, he would literally have allowed himself to be worshipped. What is more, he would have found worshippers;... From this false pride stemmed all that ruined him.

The Court was yet another device to sustain the King's policy of despotism. Many things combined to remove it from Paris and keep it permanently in the country. The disorders of the minority had been staged mainly in that city and for that reason the King had taken a great aversion to it and had become convinced that it was dangerous to live there.

The awkward situation of his mistresses and the dangers involved in conducting such scandalous affairs in a busy capital, crowded with people of every kind of mentality, played no small part in deciding him to leave, for he was embarrassed by the crowds whenever he went in or out or appeared upon the streets. Other reasons for departure were his love of hunting and the open air, so much more easily indulged in the country than in Paris, which is far from forests and ill-supplied with pleasant walks, and his delight in building, a later and ever-increasing passion, which could not be enjoyed in the town, where he was continually in the public eye. Finally, he conceived the idea that he would be all the more venerated by the multitude if he lived retired and were no longer seen every day.... It was then that he first began to attract society to him with fares and diversions and to let it be known that he wished often to be visited....

The frequent entertainments, the private drives to Versailles, and the royal journeys, provided the King with a means of distinguishing or mortifying his courtiers by naming those who were or were not to accompany him, and thus keeping everyone eager and anxious to please him. He fully realized that the substantial gifts which he had to offer were too few to have any continuous effect, and he substituted imaginary favours that appealed to men's jealous natures, small distinctions which he was able, with extraordinary ingenuity, to grant or withhold every day and almost every hour. The hopes that courtiers built upon such flimsy favours and the importance which they attached to them were really unbelievable, and no one was ever more artful than the King in devising fresh occasions for them.

But there would be no end to describing all the different expedients that followed one after another as the King grew older and the entertainments increased or diminished in number, or to telling of the methods he employed to keep so large a Court always about him.

He not only required the constant attendance of the great, but was also aware of those of lower rank. He would look about him at his *letier* and *coucher,* at meals, and while walking through the state apartments or the Versailles gardens, where none but courtiers might follow him. He saw and noticed every one of them, marked very well the absences of those usually at Court and even of those who attended more rarely, and took care to discover the reason, drawing his own conclusions and losing no opportunity of acting upon them. He took it as an offence if distinguished people did not make the Court their home, or if others came but seldom. And to come never, or scarcely ever, meant certain disgrace.

Louis XIV took enormous pains to be well-informed about all that went on in public places, in private houses, society, family business, or the progress of love-affairs. He had spies and reporters everywhere and of all descriptions. Many of them never realized that their reports reached the King, others wrote directly to him, sending their letters by secret channels of his own devising. Their letters were seen by him alone and he always read them before proceeding to other business. There were even some who spoke privately with him in his study, entering by the back way. Through such secret informants, an immense number of people of all ranks were broken, often most unjustly, and without their ever discovering the reason, for the King, once suspicious, never trusted again, or so rarely that it made no matter....

No other King has ever approached him for the number and quality of his stables and hunting establishments. Who could count his buildings? Who not deplore their ostentation, whimsicality and bad taste?

... He was entirely ruled by [his ministers], even by the youngest and most mediocre, even by those whom he liked and trusted least. Always, he was on guard against influences, and always believed that he had been completely successful in avoiding them.

Questions:
1. *How fairly did Saint-Simon evaluate Louis XIV and the Sun King's court?*
2. *How did Louis's vanity influence royal policy?*
3. *In what ways was Louis XIV isolated from reality?*
4. *How did Louis control the ambitions of the French nobility? How did his methods compare to those of Richelieu?*

15.3   Louis XIV: *Mémoires for the Instruction of the Dauphin*

Louis XIV's (1638–1715) view of kingship was influenced by his experience of the Fronde during his minority. The supporters of the Fronde led armed uprisings as part of their effort to limit royal authority. When the Fronde was defeated and Louis reached his majority, he committed himself to making the absolute power of the monarchy a reality.

> **Source:** Charles Dreyss, ed., *Mémoires de Louis XIV Pour L'Instruction du Dauphin,* Vol. 2 (Paris: Didier, 1860), pp. 95–97, 266–69, 516–17. Translated by Philip F. Riley. (Dauphin is the title of the eldest son of a French King.)

I would not speak to you in this way, my son, if I had seen in you the least tendency toward cruelty, for a bloody and ferocious temper is despicable in a man, and beneath the dignity of a king. On the contrary, I will endeavor to acquaint you with the charm of clemency, the most regal of all virtues since it can only belong to kings; for clemency is one duty for which we can never be repaid. . . .

Whoever pardons too often punishes uselessly the rest of time, for in the terror which restrains men from evil, the hope of pardon lessens the effect of pardon itself. You will not finish the reading of these *Mémoires,* my son, without finding places where I have conquered myself and pardoned offenses that I could justly never forget. But on that occasion when it was a question of state, of the most pernicious examples, and of the most contagious disorder for all my subjects, of a revolt that attacked the very foundations of my authority, I knew that I should overcome my scruples and punish these scoundrels rather than pardoning them. . . .

Whoever is poorly informed cannot avoid poor thinking; and if you search past centuries for all the errors attributed to sovereigns, hardly one can be excused for not knowing something that he should have known, for so it is generally among men that one says "I did not know," or "I did not think."

Frequently after finishing an affair we learn something new and lament that if only we had known this sooner we would have acted differently; in short I believe if a man is fully informed he will always do what he should. Thus it is necessary that a sovereign take the greatest care to be informed of his own times.

But for me, I extended this reflection, for I was convinced that it was not enough to be informed of current affairs but also of ancient times. I consider that a knowledge of these great events, assimilated by a mature mind, can serve to fortify one's reasoning in all important deliberations; for the example of illustrious men and their unique deeds provides very useful perspectives for war and peace, so that a naturally great and generous soul, contemplating these actions, would be inspired by them and ensure that the lessons of history can inspire others as well.

I have heard it said that all the great heroes of the past were conversant with literature and that part of their greatness was due to their literary study. Particularly I found the study of the past to be very useful in becoming wise in the art of war. . . .

But kings must learn not to permit their servants to become too powerful because, if they are promoted too quickly, they are obliged to constantly support them or painfully suffer them; usually only weak or clumsy princes tolerate these monstrous promotions.

I am not saying that we should not for our own interest and grandeur wish that our greatness is shared by those in our good graces, but we must carefully guard against their excess. My advice to guarantee this consists of three principal observations.

The first is that you know your affairs completely, because a king who does not know them is always dependent on those who serve him and cannot defend himself from their wiles.

The second, that you divide your confidence among many, so that each of those you have entrusted will check the elevation of his rival, ensuring that the jealousy of one will bridle the ambition of the other.

And the third, that even though you admit a small number of persons into your secret affairs or into your casual conversations, never permit anyone to imagine that they have the power to speak as they please of their good or bad impressions of the others; but, on the contrary, you must expressly maintain a type of association with all who hold important state posts, and give to everyone the same liberty to propose whatever they believe for your service; so that none of them would believe that they could not turn to you for their needs and they think only of your good graces; and lastly the most distant and the most familiar should be persuaded that they are totally dependent upon you.

But you should know that this independence upon which I insist so strongly raises more than anything the authority of the master, and that it alone shows that he is governing them instead of being governed by them: As to the contrary when it ceases, invariably intrigues, liaisons, and cabals enlarge the power of the court and weaken the reputation of the prince.

Question:
1. Why did Louis XIV believe his son should study history?

15.4   M. de la Colonie: *The Battle of Schellenberg, 2 July 1704—A French Officer's Account*

During the reign of Louis XIV (1638–1715), France was in an almost constant state of war. The cost of these wars contributed to the fiscal problems of the French state and, in turn, were an important cause of the French Revolution. In the document included here, a French officer describes the Battle of Schellenberg, offering the historian insight into the nature and tactics of early eighteenth-century warfare.

   Source: *Eyewitness to History*, by John Casey (New York: Avon Books, 1997), pp. 199–205.

I made a point of impressing upon my men the necessity of attention to orders, and of prompt obedience in carrying out any manoeuvres during the action with courage and in good order. I assured them that herein lay our safety and, perhaps, victory.

I had scarcely finished speaking when the enemy's battery opened fire upon us, and raked us through and through. They concentrated their fire upon us, and with their first discharge carried off Count de la Bastide, the lieutenant of my own company with whom at the moment I was speaking, and twelve grenadiers, who fell side by side in the ranks, so that my coat was covered with brains and blood. So accurate was the fire that each discharge of the cannon stretched some of my men on the ground. I suffered agonies at seeing these brave fellows perish without a chance of defending themselves, but it was absolutely necessary that they should not move from their post.

This cannonade was but the prelude of the attack that the enemy were developing, and I looked upon the moment when they would fling themselves against one point or another in our entrenchments as so instant that I would allow no man even to bow his head before the storm, fearing that the regiment would find itself in disorder when the time came for us to make the rapid movement that would be demanded of us. At last the enemy's army began to move to the assault, and still it was necessary for me to suffer this sacrifice to avoid a still greater misfortune, though I had five officers and eighty grenadiers killed on the spot before we had fired a single shot.

So steep was the slope in front of us that as soon almost as the enemy's column began its advance it was lost in view, and it came into sight only two hundred paces from our entrenchments. I noticed that it kept as far as possible from the glacis of the town and close alongside of the wood, but I could not make out whether a portion might not also be marching within the latter with the purpose of attacking that part of our entrenchments facing it, and the uncertainty caused me to delay movement. There was nothing to lead me to suppose that the enemy had such an intimate knowledge of our defences as to guide them to one point in preference to another for their attack.

Had I been able to guess that the column was being led by that scoundrel of a corporal who had betrayed us, I should not have been in this dilemma, nor should I have thought it necessary to keep so many brave men exposed to the perils of the cannonade, but my doubts came to an end two hours after midday, for I caught sight of the tips of the Imperial standards, and no longer hesitated. I changed front as promptly as possible, in order to bring my grenadiers opposite the part of our position adjoining the wood, towards which I saw that the enemy was directing his advance.

The regiment now left a position awkward in the extreme on account of the cannon, but we soon found ourselves scarcely better off, for hardly had our men lined the little parapet when the enemy broke into the charge, and rushed at full speed, shouting at the top of their voices, to throw themselves into our entrenchments.

The rapidity of their movements, together with their loud yells, were truly alarming, and as soon as I heard them I ordered our drums to beat the 'charge' so as to drown them with their noise, lest they should have a bad effect upon our people. By this means I animated my grenadiers, and prevented them hearing the shouts of the enemy, which before now have produced a heedless panic.

The English infantry led this attack with the greatest intrepidity, right up to our parapet, but there they were opposed with a courage at least equal to their own. Rage, fury, and desperation were manifested by both sides, with the more obstinacy as the assailants and assailed were perhaps the bravest soldiers in the world. The little parapet which separated the two forces became the scene of the bloodiest struggle that could be conceived. Thirteen hundred grenadiers, of whom seven hundred belonged to the Elector's Guards, and six hundred who were left under my command, bore the brunt of the enemy's attack at the forefront of the Bavarian infantry.

It would be impossible to describe in words strong enough the details of the carnage that took place during this first attack, which lasted a good hour or more. We were all fighting hand to hand, hurling them back as they clutched at the parapet; men were slaying, or tearing at the muzzles of guns and the bayonets which pierced their entrails; crushing under their feet their own wounded comrades, and even gouging out their opponents' eyes with their nails, when the grip was so close that neither could make use of their weapons. I verily believe that it would have been quite impossible to find a more terrible representation of Hell itself than was shown in the savagery of both sides on this occasion.

At last the enemy, after losing more than eight thousand men in this first onslaught, were obliged to relax their hold, and they fell back for shelter to the dip in the slope, where we could not harm them. A sudden calm now reigned amongst us, our people were recovering their breath, and seemed more determined even than they were before the conflict. The ground around our parapet was covered with dead and dying, in heaps almost as high as our fascines, but our whole attention was fixed on the enemy and his movements; we noticed that the tops of his standards still showed at about the same place as that from which they had made their charge in the first instance, leaving little doubt but that they were reforming before returning to the assault. As soon as possible we set vigorously to work to render their approach more difficult for them than before, and by means of an increasing fire swept their line of advance with a torrent of bullets, accompanied by numberless grenades, of which we had several wagon loads in rear of our position. These, owing to the slope of the ground, fell right amongst the enemy's ranks, causing them great annoyance and doubtless added not a little to their hesitation in advancing the second time to the attack. They were so disheartened by the first attempt that their generals had the greatest difficulty in bringing them forward again, and indeed would never have succeeded in this, though they tried every other means, had they not dismounted and set an example by placing themselves at the head of the column, and leading them on foot.

Their devotion cost them dear, for General Stirum and many other generals and officers were killed. They once more, then, advanced to the assault, but with nothing like the success of their first effort, for not only did they lack energy in their attack, but after being vigorously repulsed, were pursued by us at the point of the bayonet for more than eighty paces beyond our entrenchments, which we finally re-entered unmolested.

After this second attempt many efforts were made by their generals, but they were never able to bring their men to the assault a third time . . .

But I noticed all at once an extraordinary movement on the part of our infantry, who were rising up and ceasing fire withal. I glanced around on all sides to see what had caused this behaviour, and then became aware of several lines of infantry in greyish white uniforms on our left flank. From lack of movement on their part, their dress and bearing, I verily believed that reinforcements had arrived for us, and anybody else would have believed the same. No information whatever had reached us of the enemy's success, or even that such a thing was the least likely, so in the error I laboured under I shouted to my men that they were Frenchman, and friends, and they at once resumed their former position behind the parapet.

Having, however, made a closer inspection, I discovered bunches of straw and leaves attached to their standards, badges the enemy are in the custom of wearing on the occasion of battle, and at that very moment was struck by a ball in the right lower jaw, which wounded and stupefied me to such an extent that I thought it was smashed. I probed my wound as quickly as possible with the tip of my finger, and finding the jaw itself entire, did not make much fuss about it; but the front of my jacket was so deluged with the blood which poured from it that several of our officers believed that I was dangerously hurt. I reassured them, however, and exhorted them to stand firmly with their men. I pointed out to them that so long as our infantry kept well together the danger was not so great, and that if they behaved in a resolute manner, the enemy, who were only keeping in touch with us without daring to attack us, would allow us to retire without so much as pursuing. In truth, to look at them it would seem that they hoped much more for our retreat than any chance of coming to blows with us. I at once, therefore, shouted as loudly as I could that no one was to quit the ranks, and then formed my men in column along the entrenchments facing the wood, fronting towards the opposite flank, which was the direction in which we should have to retire. Thus, whenever I wished to make a stand, I had but to turn my men about, and at any moment could resume the retirement instantaneously, which we thus carried out in good order. I kept this up until we had crossed the entrenchments on the other flank, and then we found ourselves free from attack. This retreat was not made, however, without loss, for the enemy, although they would not close with us when they saw our column formed for the retirement, fired volleys at close range into us, which did much damage.

My men had no sooner got clear of the entrenchments than they found that the slope was in their favour, and they fairly broke their ranks and took to flight, in order to reach the plain that lay before them before the enemy's cavalry could get upon their track. As each ran his hardest, intending to reform on the further side, they disappeared like a flash of lightning without ever looking back, and I, who was with the rearguard ready to make a stand if necessary against our opponents, had scarcely clambered over the entrenchments when I found myself left entirely alone on the height, prevented from running by my heavy boots.

I looked about on all sides for my drummer, whom I had warned to keep at hand with my horse, but he had evidently thought fit to look after himself, with the result that I found myself left solitary to the mercy of the enemy and my own sad thoughts, without the slightest idea as to my future fate. I cudgelled my brains in vain for some way out of my difficulty, but could think of nothing the least certain; the plain was too wide for me to traverse in my big boots at the necessary speed, and to crown my misfortunes, was covered with cornfields. So far the enemy's cavalry had not appeared on the plain, but there was every reason to believe that they would not long delay their coming; it would have been utter folly on my part to give them the chance of discovering me embarrassed as I was, for as long as I was hampered with my boots, a trooper would always find it an easy affair to catch me.

I noticed, however, that the Danube was not so very far away, and determined to make my way towards it at all risk, with the hope of finding some beaten track or place where there would be some chance of saving my life, as I saw it was now hopeless to think of getting my men together. As a matter of fact, I found a convenient path along the bank of the river, but this was not of much avail to me, for, owing to my efforts and struggles to reach it through several fields of standing corn, I was quite blown and exhausted and could only just crawl along at the slowest possible pace. On my way I met the wife of a Bavarian soldier, so distracted with weeping that she travelled no faster than I did. I made her drag off my boots, which fitted me so tightly about the legs that it was absolutely impossible for me to do this for myself. The poor woman took an immense time to effect this, and it seemed to me at least as if the operation would never come to an end. At last this was effected, and I turned over in my mind the best way to profit by my release, when, raising my head above the corn at the side of the road, I saw a number of the enemy's troopers scattered over the country, searching the fields for any of our people who might be hidden therein, with the intention, doubtless, of killing them for the sake of what plunder might be found upon them. At this cruel prospect all my hopes vanished, and the exultation I felt at my release from the boots died at the moment of its birth. My position was now more perilous than ever; nevertheless, I examined under the cover afforded by the corn the manoeuvres of these cavaliers to see if I could not find some way out of the difficulty. A notion came into my head which, if it could have been carried out, might have had a curious ending. It was that if one trooper only should approach me, and his comrades remained sufficiently distant, I should keep hidden and wait until he got near enough for me to kill him with a shot from my pistol, for I had two on my belt; I would then take his uniform, mount his horse, and make my escape in this disguise, a plan which would be favoured by the approaching darkness. But not seeing any chance of being able to carry out this idea, I thought of another, namely, to get into the river up to my chin in the water under the bushes on the bank, wait for nightfall and the return of the troopers to their camp, and then to escape in the dark. But there were more difficulties to contend with in risking this even than in the other case, and as a last resource it struck me I might save myself by crossing the river, for happily I knew how to swim, although the risk here was very great owing to the breadth and rapidity of the Danube. I hurriedly determined on this plan, as I now saw a number of troopers approaching ever nearer to my hiding place, who were refusing to give quarter to the unhappy wounded they found hidden in the corn, whom they ruthlessly despatched the more easily to despoil them. There was no reason to suppose that they were likely to show any more mercy to me, particularly as I was worth more in the shape of plunder than a private soldier, nor was there time to lose in making up my mind, so I then and there determined to swim the river. Before taking to the water I took the precaution of leaving on the bank my richly embroidered uniform, rather spoiled as it was by the events of the late action. I scattered in a similar manner my hat, wig, pistols, and sword, at one point and another, so that if the troopers came up before I had got well away, they would devote their attention to collecting these articles instead of looking in the water, and it turned out just as I thought. I kept on my stockings, vest, and breeches, simply buttoning the sleeves of the vest and tucking the pockets within my breeches for safety; this done, I threw myself upon the mercy of the stream. I had hardly got any distance when up came the troopers, who, as I had hoped, dismounted as quickly as they could to lay hands on the spoil lying before them; they even set to work to quarrel over it, for I distinctly heard them shouting and swearing in the most delightful manner. Others apparently got no share, and they amused themselves by saluting me with several musket shots, but the current of the river which carried me on my way soon put me out of their range. Finally, after a very long and hard swim, I was lucky enough to reach the other bank, in spite of the strength of the stream.

Question:
1. What does the nature of this conflict tell us about the importance of the fight for both sides?

15.5   G. M. Trevelyan: Chapter I from *History of England*

The historian G. M. Trevelyan (1876–1962) stressed the importance of the historian's use of speculative imagination, the effort to bring the past to life through compelling storytelling based on all available evidence. The excerpt of his work included here comes from his one volume History of England (1926). It deals the development of the British political tradition over the course of the eighteenth century.

Source: *History of England*, by G. M. Trevelyan (London: Longman Group, 1974), pp. 508–512.

The coming over of William of Orange had confirmed the doctrine of the Whigs and confused that of the Tories, but it gave the Whigs no mechanical advantage over their rivals. Throughout the reigns of William and Anne the two parties continued to share power evenly; the Crown and the electorate favored first one side and then the other, according to the circumstances of the hour; the party contest continued to be vigorous, sometimes to fierceness, and in the main fortunate in its outcome for the country's interests. It is only in the reigns of George I and II that we find a state of things that may, with reserves and explanations, be picturesquely described as a 'Whig oligarchy.' Nor would it have come into existence even then, if half the Tory party had not been so gravely compromised with Jacobitism.

Partly for this reason, partly because George I was ignorant of English language and customs, the first two Hanoverians abandoned to the Whig leaders certain prerogatives of the Crown which William III and even Anne would never have let out of their own hands. The formation of Ministries, the dissolution of Parliament, the patronage of the Crown in Church and State, all passed, in effect, from the monarch to the Whig chiefs. In that sense a political oligarchy was indeed established after 1714. But in another aspect the change was a further development of the popular element in our constitution, by the establishment of the omnipotence of Ministries dependent on the vote of the House of Commons, and by the reduction of the power wielded by the hereditary monarch.

1760–1780

Later on, George III attempted in the first twenty years of his reign to take back the patronage of the Crown into the royal hands, in consonance with the undoubted intentions of those who made the Revolution Settlement. But as soon as he had recovered the patronage of the Crown, he used it to corrupt the House of Commons even more systematically than Walpole and the Whig oligarchs had done. Neither the Whig oligarchs nor George III ever tried to stand on the unparliamentary ground of the Stuarts. They never ventured to deny that the executive could only exercise power in agreement with a majority of the House of Commons. But it was possible in the Eighteenth Century to corrupt the members through the distribution of patronage, because the rotten boroughs were becoming less representative of the country with every year that passed.

Under the first two Georges the power of the House of Commons increased, while its connection with the people diminished. The long hibernation of the Tory party and the deadness of all serious political controversy damped public interest in parliamentary affairs, other than the distribution of places and bribes. The Septennial Act, passed in 1716 to secure the House of Hanover against Jacobite reaction, prolonged the normal life of a Parliament; by rendering political tenures more secure, it further deadened political interest in the country and increased the readiness of members to enter the pay of government.

Under George III there was a great revival of public interest in politics, but no increase in democratic control over Parliament. But when, by the Reform Bill of 1832, the middle class recovered more than their old power over the House of Commons, they found in the modern machinery of Parliament and Cabinet a far more effective instrument of government than any which had existed in Stuart times. The Parliamentary aristocracy of the Eighteenth Century had forged and sharpened the future weapons of the democracy. It is doubtful whether nobles and squires would ever have consented to concentrate such powers in the Lower House, if they had thought of it as a strictly popular body. But they thought of it as a house of gentlemen, many of them nominees or relations of the Peerage, as the 'best club in London,' as the 'Roman Senate' to which the highest interests of the country could safely be committed.

Under these conditions, the aristocratic Eighteenth Century made a great contribution of its own to the growth of British political tradition. The aristocrats devised the machinery by which the legislature could control the executive without hampering its efficiency. This machinery is the Cabinet system and the office of Prime Minister. By the Cabinet system we mean in England a group of Ministers dependent on the favour of the House of Commons and all having seats in Parliament, who must agree on a common policy and who are responsible for one another's action and for the government of the country as a whole. Neither Prime Minister nor Cabinet system was contemplated in the Revolution Settlement. They grew up gradually to meet the country's needs in peace and in war. The first approach to a united Cabinet was made by William III merely to fight the war against Louis, but he remained his own Prime Minister and his own Foreign Minister. In Anne's reign Marlborough acted as the head of the State in war time for all military and diplomatic affairs, but he left to his colleagues the management of Parliament. It was Sir Robert Walpole, the Whig peace Minister from 1721 to 1742, who did most to evolve the principle of the common responsibility of the Cabinet, and the supremacy of the Prime Minister as the leading man at once in the Cabinet and in the Commons. It was significant that, unlike his Whig and Tory predecessors in power, Sir Robert remained undazzled by the lure of peerage, and refused to leave the Lower House so long as he aspired to govern the country. When he consented to become Earl of Orford he was retiring for ever from office.

In effecting these changes in the custom of the constitution, Walpole acted not a little from love of personal power, but he did the country a great service. In driving out from his Cabinet all colleagues who did not agree with his policy or would not submit to his leadership as Premier, he set up the machinery by which Britain has since been ruled in peace and war. The Cabinet system is the key by which the English were able to get efficient government by a responsible and united executive, in spite of the fact that the executive was subject to the will of a debating assembly of five or six hundred men. They solved this problem, which many nations have found insoluble, not, as was often contemplated in William III's reign, by excluding the Ministers from the Commons, but on the contrary by insisting that they should sit in and lead the House of Commons, like Sir Robert Walpole. The Cabinet is the link between the executive and legislative, and it is a very close link indeed. It is the essential part of the modern British polity.[1]

It was well for England that the Revolution Settlement did not supply her with a brand-new, water-tight, unalterable, written constitution. A sacrosanct written constitution was necessary to achieve the federal union of the States of North America after they had cut themselves adrift from the old Empire. For England it was not at all necessary, and it would certainly have proved inconvenient. If England had been given a rigid constitution when James II was deposed, the Crown would have had assigned to it, in perpetuity, powers which within thirty years of the coronation of William and Mary it handed over to be exercised by its Parliamentary advisers. It is probable, also, that a rigid constitution, drawn up according to the lights of 1689, would have excluded the King's Ministers from sitting in the House of Commons.

A written constitution, as distinct from the sum of ordinary law and custom, is alien to the English political genius. One of the worst signs of the straits to which Cromwell was driven by his inability to find a basis of national agreement, was the fact that he promulgated written constitutions dividing up by an absolute line—never to be altered—the powers of Protector and Parliament respectively. These expedients were contrary to the real method of English progress. The London fog which decently conceals from view the exact relations of executive and legislative at Westminster, has enabled the constitution to adapt itself unobserved to the requirements of each passing age.

1714–1760

When we speak of the Whig oligarchy under the first two Georges, we mean (so far as we mean anything definite) about

---

[1] The English in those days were better politicians than political theorists. They permitted the French philosopher, Montesquieu, to report to the world in his *Esprit des Lois* (1748) that the secret of British freedom was the separation of executive and legislative, whereas the opposite was much nearer to the truth. Partly on account of Montesquieu's error, confirmed by Blackstone, partly for better local reasons, the Federal Constitution of the United States was drawn up on the idea of separating executive from legislative.

seventy great families, who, in alliance or in rivalry among themselves, exercised the power and patronage of the State, on condition of retaining the constant support of the House of Commons. The heads of the great Whig families mostly sat among the Peers, and their cadets in the Commons. The Peers were able to keep the confidence of the Lower House, partly because they never seriously opposed themselves to its political ideas, and partly because they owned many of the rotten boroughs that returned so many of its members. These great noblemen had therefore no temptation to set up the claims of the more dignified but less powerful chamber in which they themselves sat. The Peers were unofficially but very effectually represented in the House of Commons, and had no objection to the constant increase of its power.

It was not until the Nineteenth Century, during and after the Reform Bill of 1832, that the Peers thought it necessary to assert the direct power of their own chamber. It was only then that they had cause to question the prescriptive right of the House of Commons to legislate at will for the nation. But in the Nineteenth Century such resistance, though by no means wholly ineffectual, came in the main too late. Englishmen had been so long accustomed to be ruled by the House of Commons when it was an aristocratic assembly, that they would not allow its power to be curtailed when it began to be more truly representative of the nation at large.

Question:
1. How does Trevelyan represent Walpole?

15.6 Peter the Great: Correspondence with His Son

Peter the Great (1672–1725) hoped to westernize Russia and make his nation a great power in Europe. To this end, he promulgated a wide variety of reforms and involved Russia in numerous wars. Discontent with his policies led some in Russia to look to his son Alexei for leadership. Alexei was eventually tried and executed for treason.

Source: *The Global Experience*, Vol. 2, by Philip F. Riley, et. al. (Upper Saddle River, NJ: Prentice Hall, 1998), pp. 44–46.

A LETTER TO ALEXEI

October 11, 1715
Declaration to My Son,

You cannot be ignorant of what is known to all the world, to what degree our people groaned under the oppression of the Swedes before the beginning of the present war.

By the usurpation of so many maritime places so necessary to our state. they had cut us off from all commerce with the rest of the world, and we saw with regret that besides they had cast a thick veil before the eyes of the clear-sighted. You know what it has cost us in the beginning of this war (in which God alone has led us, as it were, by the hand. and still guides us) to make ourselves experienced in the art of war, and to put a stop to those advantages which our implacable enemies obtained over us.

We submitted to this with a resignation to the will of God, making no doubt but it was he who put us to that trial, till he might lead us into the right way, and we might render ourselves worthy to experience, that the same enemy who at first made others tremble, now in his turn trembles before us, perhaps in a much greater degree. These are the fruits which, next to the assistance of God, we owe to our own toil and to the labour of our faithful and affectionate children. our Russian subjects.

But at the time that I am viewing the prosperity which God has heaped on our native country, if I cast an eye upon the posterity that is to succeed me, my heart is much more penetrated with grief on account of what is to happen, then I rejoice at those blessings that are past, seeing that you, my son, reject all means of making yourself capable of well-governing after me. I say your incapacity is voluntary. because you cannot excuse yourself with want of natural parts and strength of body, as if God had not given you a sufficient share of either: and though your constitution is none of the strongest, yet it cannot be said that it is altogether weak.

But you even will not so much as hear warlike exercises mentioned; though it is by them that we broke through that obscurity in which we were involved, and that we made ourselves known to nations, whose esteem we share at present.

I do not exhort you to make war without lawful reasons: I only desire you to apply yourself to learn the art of it: for it is impossible well to govern without knowing the rules and discipline of it, was it for no other end than for the defense of the country.

I could place before your eyes many instances of what I am proposing to you. I will only mention to you the Greeks, with whom we are united by the same profession of faith. What occasioned their decay but that they neglected arms? Idleness and repose weakened them, made them submit to tyrants, and brought them to that slavery to which they are now so long since reduced. You mistake, if you think it is enough for a prince to have good generals to act under his order. Everyone looks upon the head; they study his inclinations and conform themselves to them: all the world owns this. My brother during his reign loved magnificence in dress, and great equipages of horses. The nation were not much inclined that way, but the prince's delight soon became that of his subjects. for they are inclined to imitate him in liking a thing as well as disliking it.

If the people so easily break themselves of things which only regard pleasure, will they not forget in time, or will they not more easily give over the practice of arms, the exercise of which is the more painful to them, the less they are kept to it?

You have no inclination to learn war. you do not apply yourself to it, and consequently you will never learn it: And how then can you command others, and judge of the reward which those deserve who do their duty. or punish others who fail of it? You will do nothing, nor judge of anything but by the eyes and help of others. like a young bird that holds up his bill to be fed.

You say that the weak state of your health will not permit you to undergo the fatigues of war: This is an excuse which is no better than the rest. I desire no fatigues, but only inclination, which even sickness itself cannot hinder. Ask those who remember the time of my brother. He was of a constitution weaker by far than yours. He was not able to manage a horse of the least mettle, not could he hardly mount it: Yet he loved horses. hence it came, that there never was, nor perhaps is there actually now in the nation a finer stable than his was.

By this you see that good success does not always depend on pain, but on the will.

If you think there are some, whose affairs do not fail of success, though they do not go to war themselves; it is true: But if they do not go themselves, yet they have an inclination for it, and understand it.

For instance, the late King of France did not always take the field in person; but it is known to what degree he loved war, and what glorious exploits he performed in it, which made his campaigns to be called the theatre and school of the world. His inclinations were not confined solely to military affairs, he also loved mechanics, manufactures and other establishments, which rendered his kingdom more flourishing than any other whatsoever.

After having made to you all those remonstrances, I return to my former subject which regards you.

I am a man and consequently I must die. To whom shall I leave after me to finish what by the grace of God I have begun, and to preserve what I have partly recovered? To a man, who like the slothful servant hides his talent in the earth, that is to say, who neglects making the best of what God has entrusted to him?

Remember your obstinacy and ill-nature, how often I reproached you with it, and even chastised you for it, and for how many years I almost have not spoke to you; but all this has availed nothing, has effected nothing. It was but losing my time: it was striking the air. You do not make the least endeavors. and all your pleasure seems to consist in staying idle and lazy at home; Things of which you ought to be ashamed (forasmuch as they make you miserable) seem to make up your dearest delight, nor do you foresee the dangerous consequences of it for yourself and for the whole state. St. Paul has left us a great truth when he wrote: If a man know not how to rule his own house, how shall he take of the church of God?

After having considered all those great inconveniences and reflected upon them, and seeing I cannot bring you to good by any inducement, I have thought fit to give you in writing this act of my last will, with this resolution however to wait still a little longer before I put it in execution to see if you will mend. If not, I will have you to know that I will deprive you of the succession, as one may cut off a useless member.

Do not fancy, that, because I have no other child but you, I only write this to terrify you. I will certainly put it in execution, if it please God; for whereas I do not spare my own life for my country and the welfare of my people, why should I spare you who do not render yourself worthy of either? I would rather choose to transmit them to a worthy stranger, than to my own unworthy son.

Peter

ALEXEI'S REPLY

Most Clement Lord and Father,

I have read the paper your Majesty gave me on the 27th of October, 1715, after the funeral of my late consort.

I have nothing to reply to it, but, that if your Majesty will deprive me of the succession to the Crown of Russia by reason of my incapacity, your will be done; I even most instantly beg it of you, because I do not think myself fit for the government. My memory is very much weakened, and yet it is necessary in affairs. The strength of my mind and of my body is much decayed by the sicknesses which I have undergone, and which have rendered me incapable of governing so many nations; this requires a more vigorous man than I am.

Therefore I do not aspire after you (whom God preserve many years) to the succession of the Russian Crown, even if I had no brother as I have one at present, whom I pray God preserve. Neither will I pretend for the future to that succession, of which I take God to witness, and swear it upon my soul, in testimony whereof I write and sign this present with my own hand.

I put my children into your hands, and as for myself, I desire nothing of you but a bare maintenance during my life, leaving the whole to your consideration and to your will.

Your most humble servant and son.

Alexei

Question:

1. What does Peter's letter to Alexei reveal about Peter's attitude toward war and his views on Alexei's right of succession?